PETER PARKER

Writers: **BOB GALE** (ISSUES #1-4) **& TOM PEYER** (ISSUE #5)
Pencilers: **PATRICK OLLIFFE** (ISSUES #1-4) **& TODD NAUCK** (ISSUE #5)
Inkers: **PATRICK OLLIFFE** WITH **LIVESAY** (ISSUE #3),
SERGE LAPOINTE (ISSUE #4) **& TODD NAUCK** (ISSUE #5)
Colorists: **ANTONIO FABELA** WITH **ANDREW DALHOUSE** (ISSUE #3)
& JAVIER TARTAGLIA (ISSUE #5)
Letterers: **VC'S JOE CARAMAGNA & JOE SABINO**
Cover Artists: **RAFAEL ALBUQUERQUE, SKOTTIE YOUNG, DOUG BRAITHWAITE
& ANDY TROY, BRANDON MCCARTHY** AND **STEPHANIE HANS**

"APPROACHING STORMS (OR, WHEN PETEY MET JOHNNY)"
Writer & Artist: **FRED HEMBECK**
Colorist: **JAVIER RODRIGUEZ**

Web-Heads: **BOB GALE, MARC GUGGENHEIM, JOE KELLY, DAN SLOTT,
FRED VAN LENTE, MARK WAID & ZEB WELLS**
Editor: **TOM BRENNAN**
Supervising Editor: **STEVE WACKER**
Executive Editor: **TOM BREVOORT**
Digital Production Manager: **TIM SMITH 3**
Digital Coordinator: **HARRY GO**
Vice Presient of Digital Content, MDCU: **JOHN CERILLI**

Collection Editor: **CORY LEVINE**
Editorial Assistants: **JAMES EMMETT & JOE HOCHSTEIN**
Assistant Editors: **ALEX STARBUCK & NELSON RIBEIRO**
Associate Editor: **JOHN DENNING**
Editors, Special Projects: **JENNIFER GRÜNWALD & MARK D. BEAZLEY**
Senior Editor, Special Projects: **JEFF YOUNGQUIST**
Senior Vice President of Sales: **DAVID GABRIEL**

Editor in Chief: **JOE QUESADA**
Publisher: **DAN BUCKLEY**
Executive Producer: **ALAN FINE**

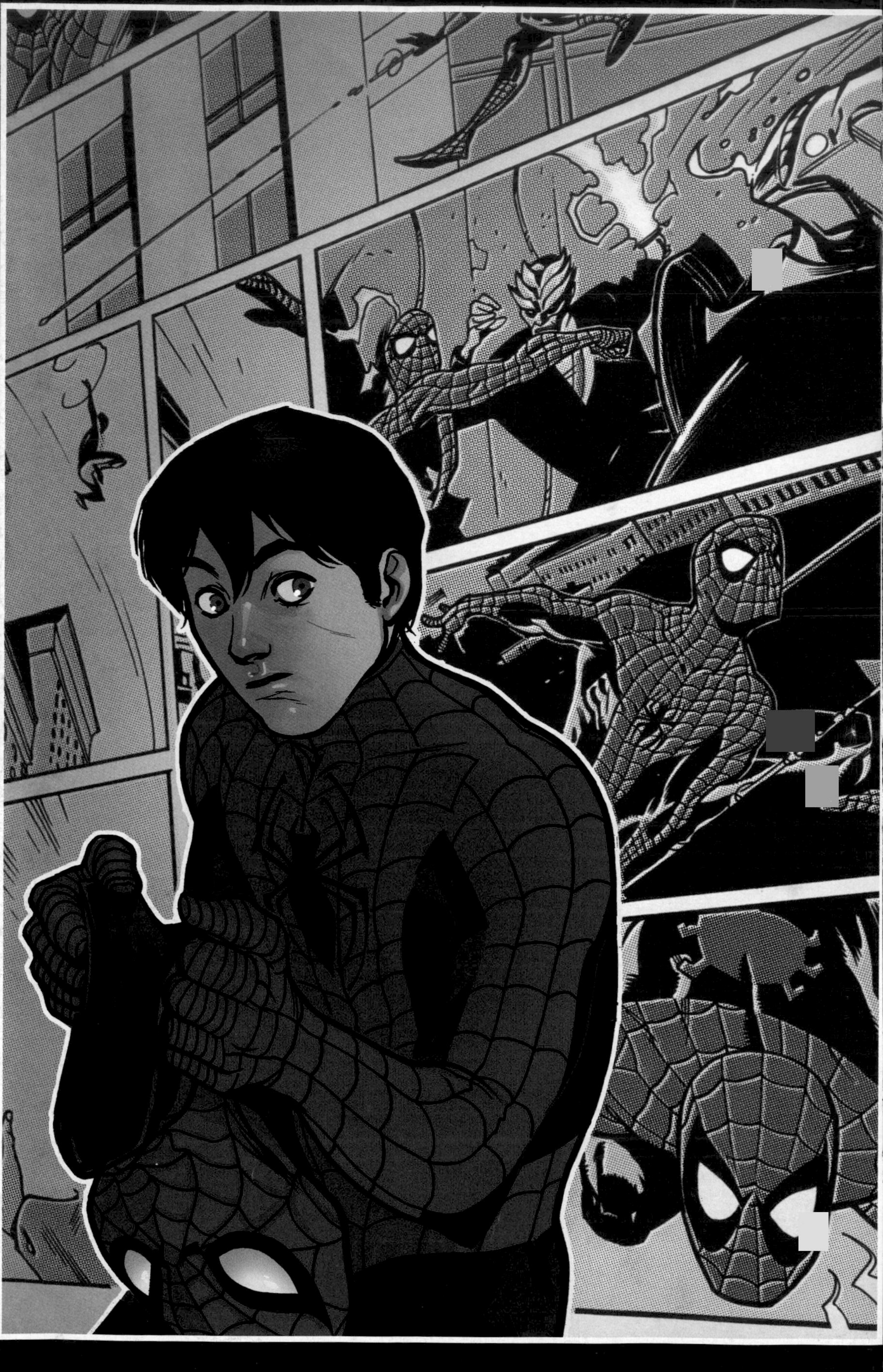

PETER PARKER #1

the AMAZING SPIDER-MAN

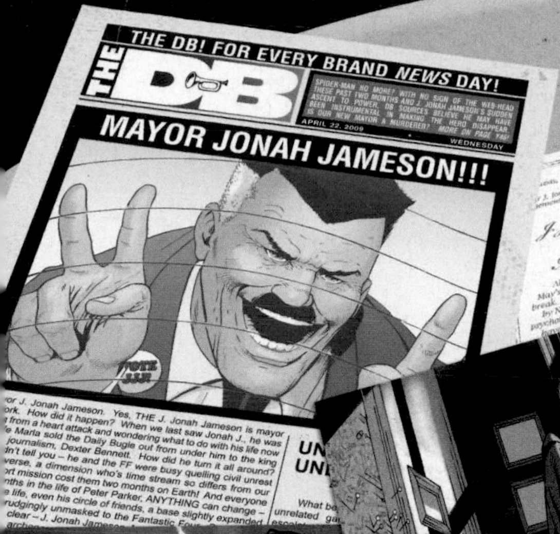
THE DB! FOR EVERY BRAND NEWS DAY!
THE DB
SPIDER-MAN NO MORE? WITH NO SIGN OF THE WEB-HEAD THESE PAST TWO MONTHS AND J. JONAH JAMESON'S SUDDEN ASCENT TO POWER, DB SOURCES BELIEVE HE MAY HAVE BEEN INSTRUMENTAL IN MAKING THE HERO DISAPPEAR. IS OUR NEW MAYOR A MURDERER? MORE ON PAGE 7A!
APRIL 22, 2009
WEDNESDAY
MAYOR JONAH JAMESON!!!

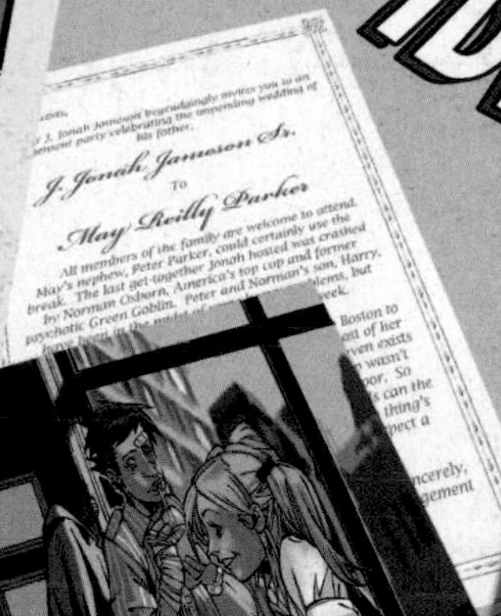
J. Jonah Jameson Sr.
To
May Reilly Parker

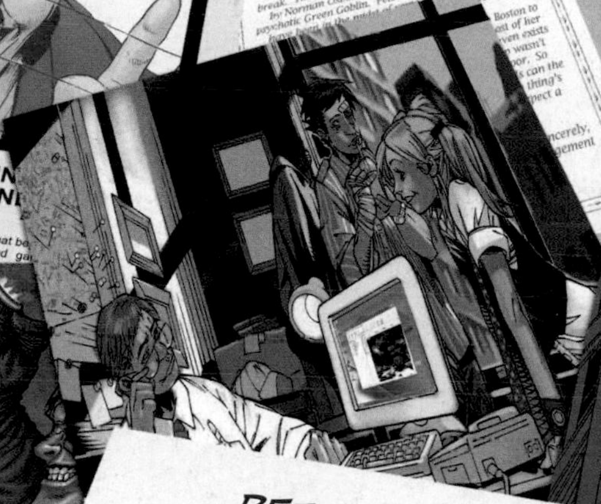

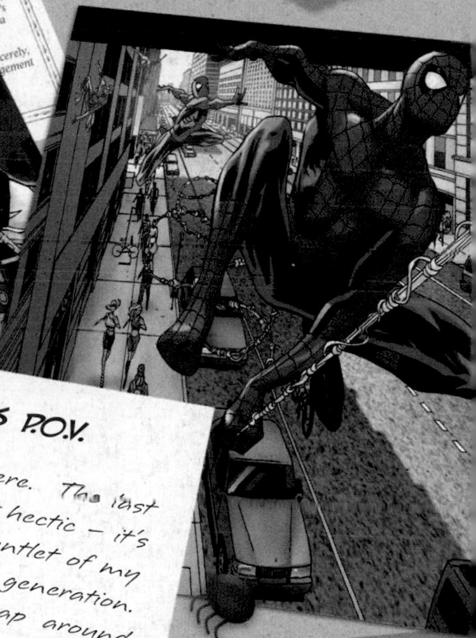

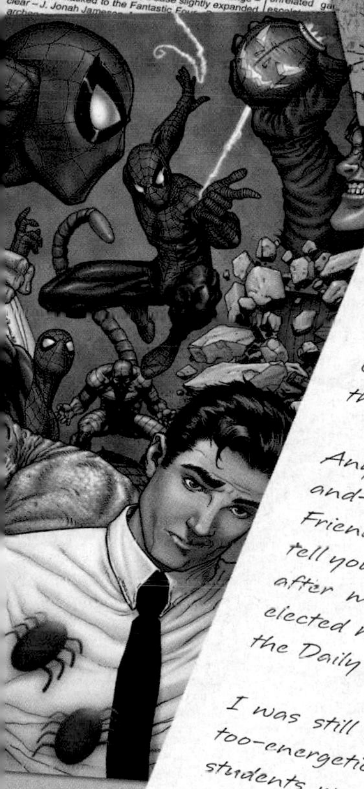

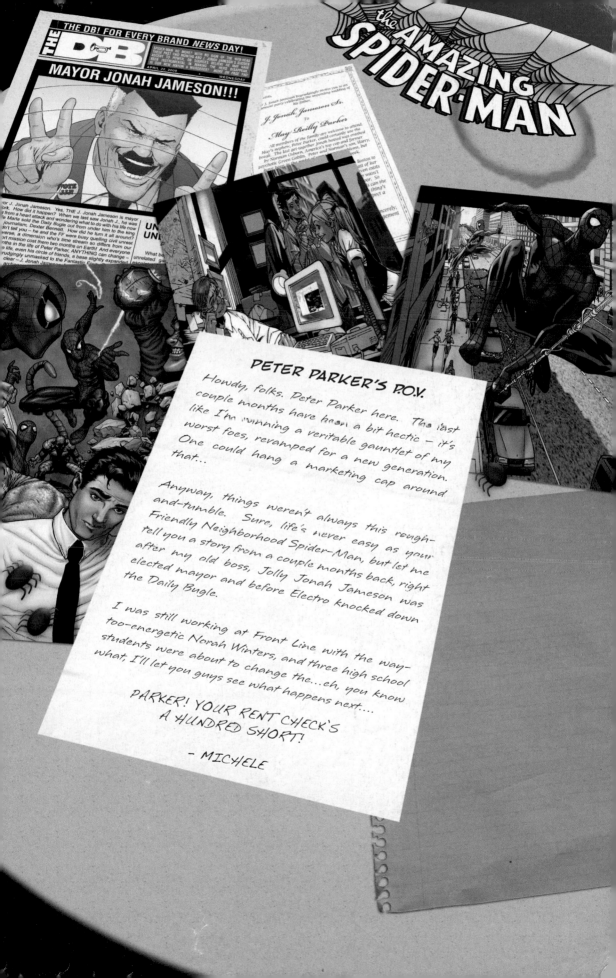

PETER PARKER'S P.O.V.

Howdy, folks. Peter Parker here. The last couple months have been a bit hectic – it's like I'm running a veritable gauntlet of my worst foes, revamped for a new generation. One could hang a marketing cap around that...

Anyway, things weren't always this rough-and-tumble. Sure, life's never easy as your Friendly Neighborhood Spider-Man, but let me tell you a story from a couple months back, right after my old boss, Jolly Jonah Jameson was elected mayor and before Electro knocked down the Daily Bugle.

I was still working at Front Line with the way-too-energetic Norah Winters, and three high school students were about to change the...eh, you know what, I'll let you guys see what happens next....

PARKER! YOUR RENT CHECK'S A HUNDRED SHORT!

– MICHELE

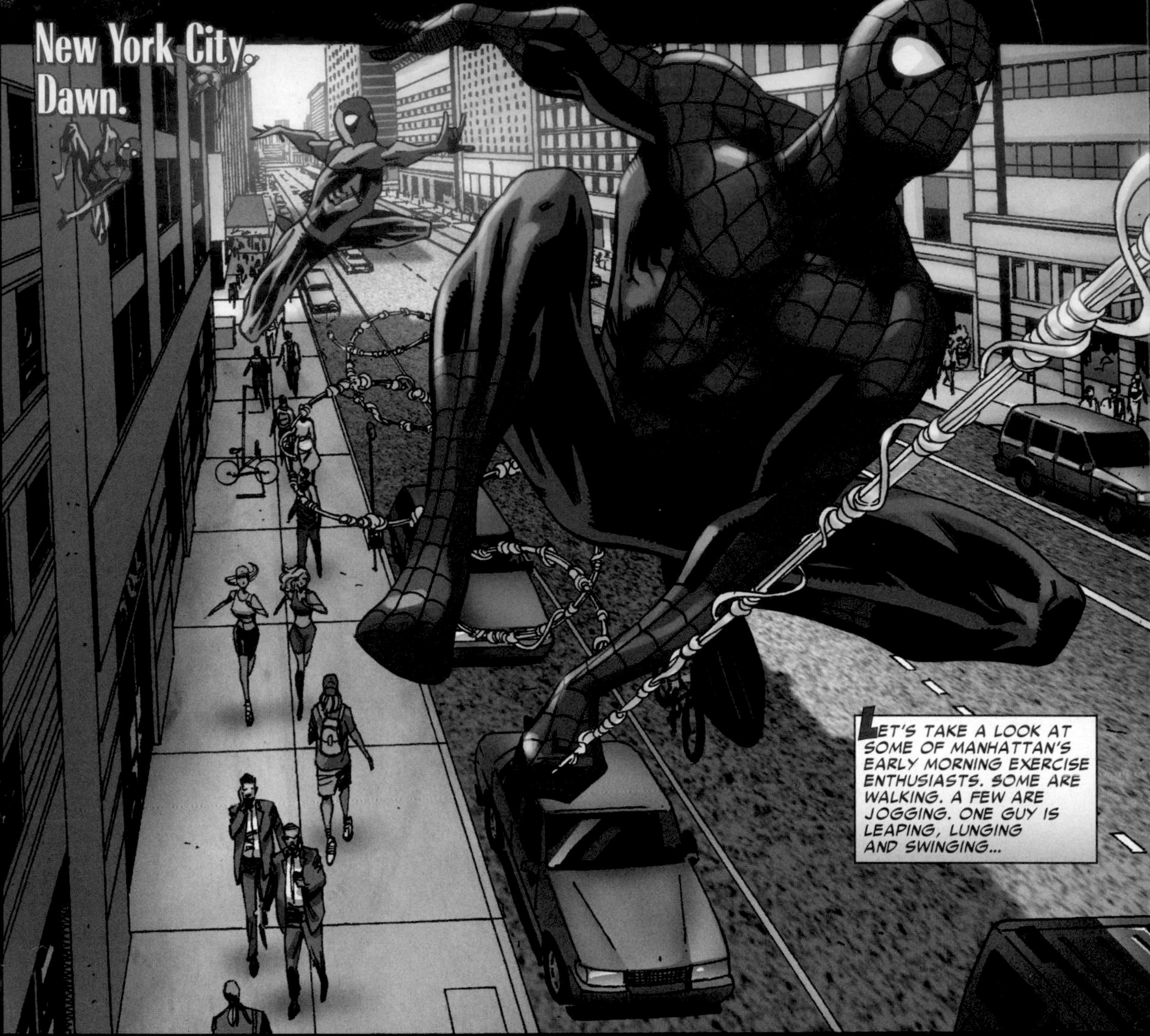
New York City.
Dawn.
LET'S TAKE A LOOK AT SOME OF MANHATTAN'S EARLY MORNING EXERCISE ENTHUSIASTS. SOME ARE WALKING. A FEW ARE JOGGING. ONE GUY IS LEAPING, LUNGING AND SWINGING...
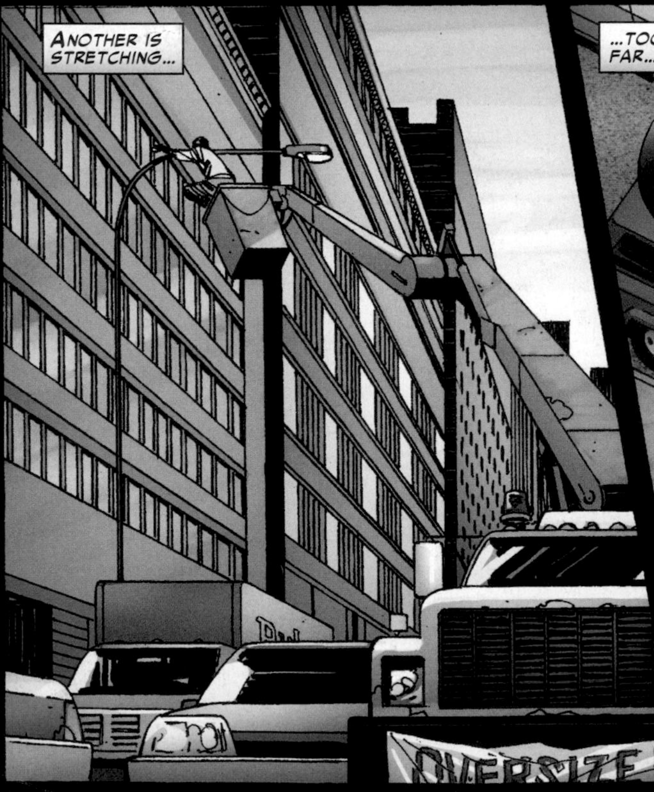
ANOTHER IS STRETCHING...
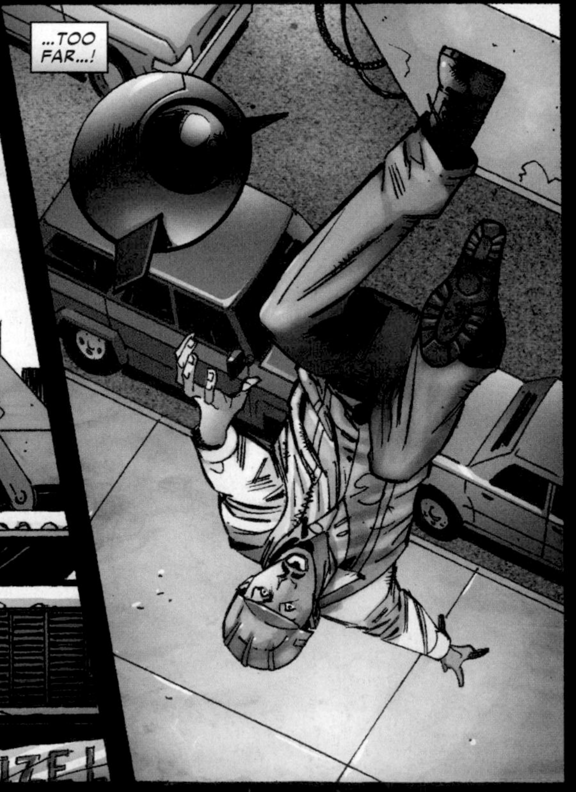
...TOO FAR...!

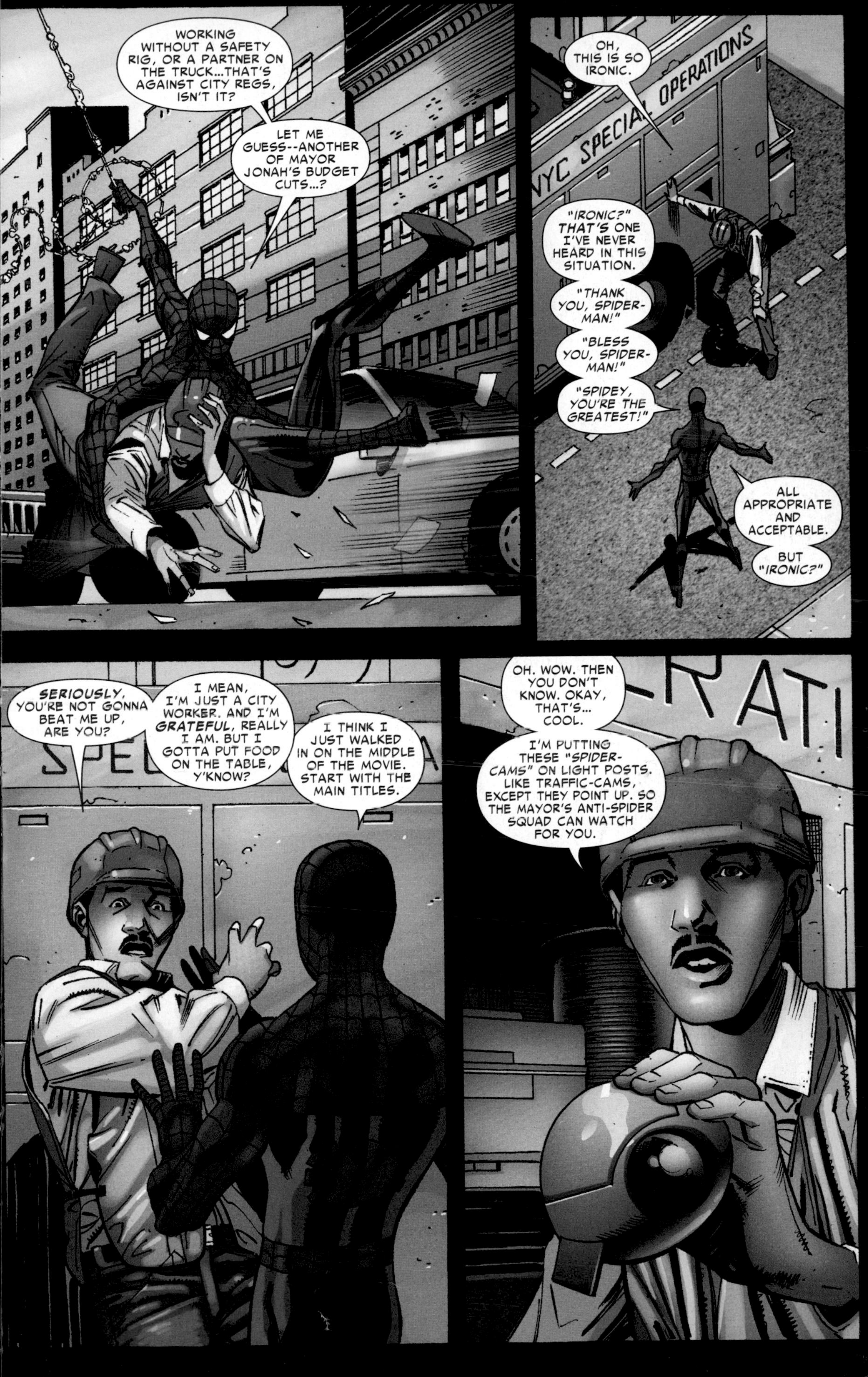

WORKING WITHOUT A SAFETY RIG, OR A PARTNER ON THE TRUCK...THAT'S AGAINST CITY REGS, ISN'T IT?
LET ME GUESS--ANOTHER OF MAYOR JONAH'S BUDGET CUTS...?
OH, THIS IS SO IRONIC.
NYC SPECIAL OPERATIONS
"IRONIC?" THAT'S ONE I'VE NEVER HEARD IN THIS SITUATION.
"THANK YOU, SPIDER-MAN!"
"BLESS YOU, SPIDER-MAN!"
"SPIDEY, YOU'RE THE GREATEST!"
ALL APPROPRIATE AND ACCEPTABLE.
BUT "IRONIC?"
SERIOUSLY, YOU'RE NOT GONNA BEAT ME UP, ARE YOU?
I MEAN, I'M JUST A CITY WORKER. AND I'M GRATEFUL, REALLY I AM. BUT I GOTTA PUT FOOD ON THE TABLE, Y'KNOW?
I THINK I JUST WALKED IN ON THE MIDDLE OF THE MOVIE. START WITH THE MAIN TITLES.
OH. WOW. THEN YOU DON'T KNOW. OKAY, THAT'S... COOL.
I'M PUTTING THESE "SPIDER-CAMS" ON LIGHT POSTS. LIKE TRAFFIC-CAMS, EXCEPT THEY POINT UP. SO THE MAYOR'S ANTI-SPIDER SQUAD CAN WATCH FOR YOU.

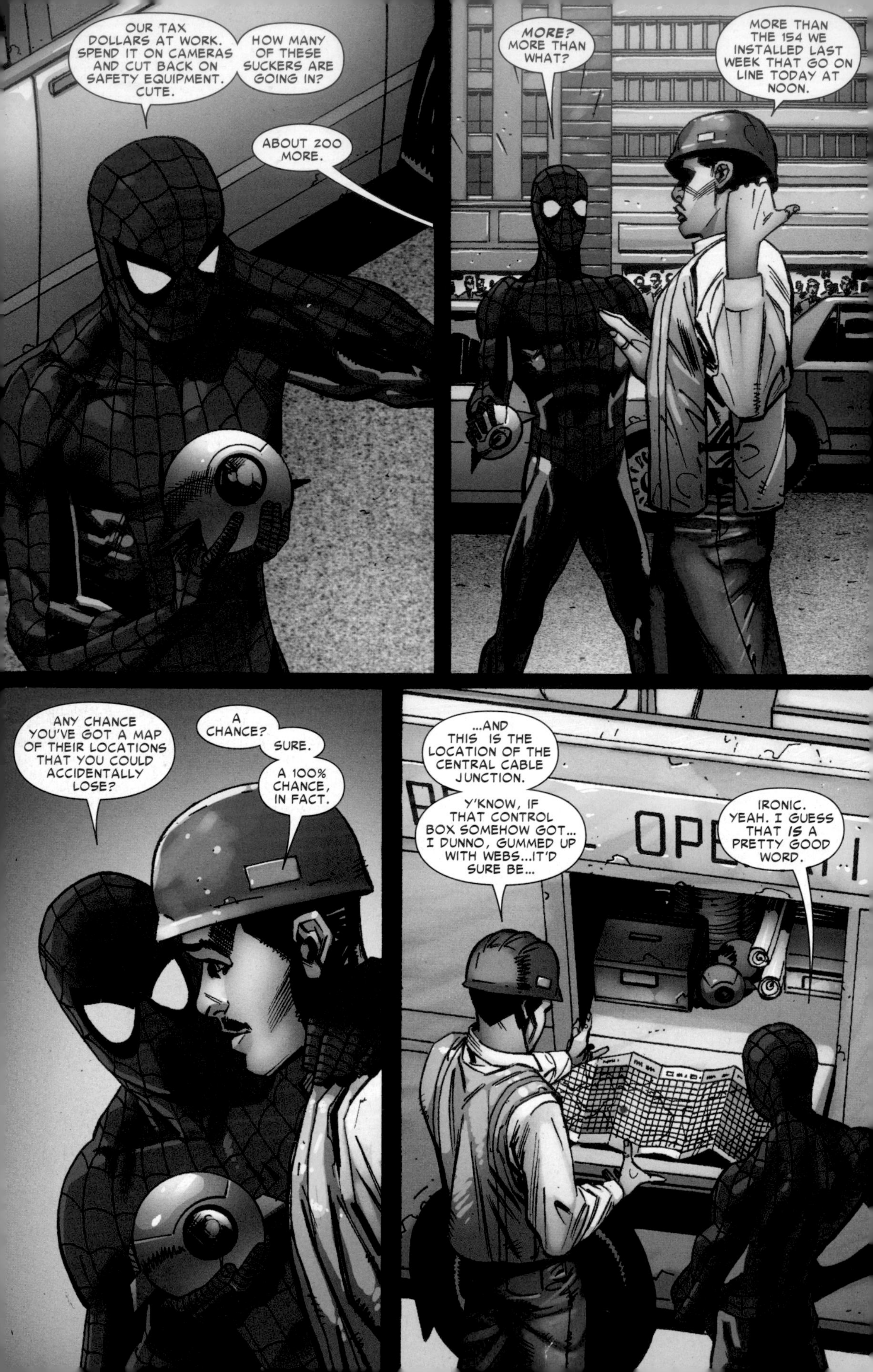
OUR TAX DOLLARS AT WORK. SPEND IT ON CAMERAS AND CUT BACK ON SAFETY EQUIPMENT. CUTE.
HOW MANY OF THESE SUCKERS ARE GOING IN?
ABOUT 200 MORE.
MORE? MORE THAN WHAT?
MORE THAN THE 154 WE INSTALLED LAST WEEK THAT GO ON LINE TODAY AT NOON.
ANY CHANCE YOU'VE GOT A MAP OF THEIR LOCATIONS THAT YOU COULD ACCIDENTALLY LOSE?
A CHANCE?
SURE.
A 100% CHANCE, IN FACT.
...AND THIS IS THE LOCATION OF THE CENTRAL CABLE JUNCTION.
Y'KNOW, IF THAT CONTROL BOX SOMEHOW GOT... I DUNNO, GUMMED UP WITH WEBS...IT'D SURE BE...
IRONIC. YEAH. I GUESS THAT IS A PRETTY GOOD WORD.

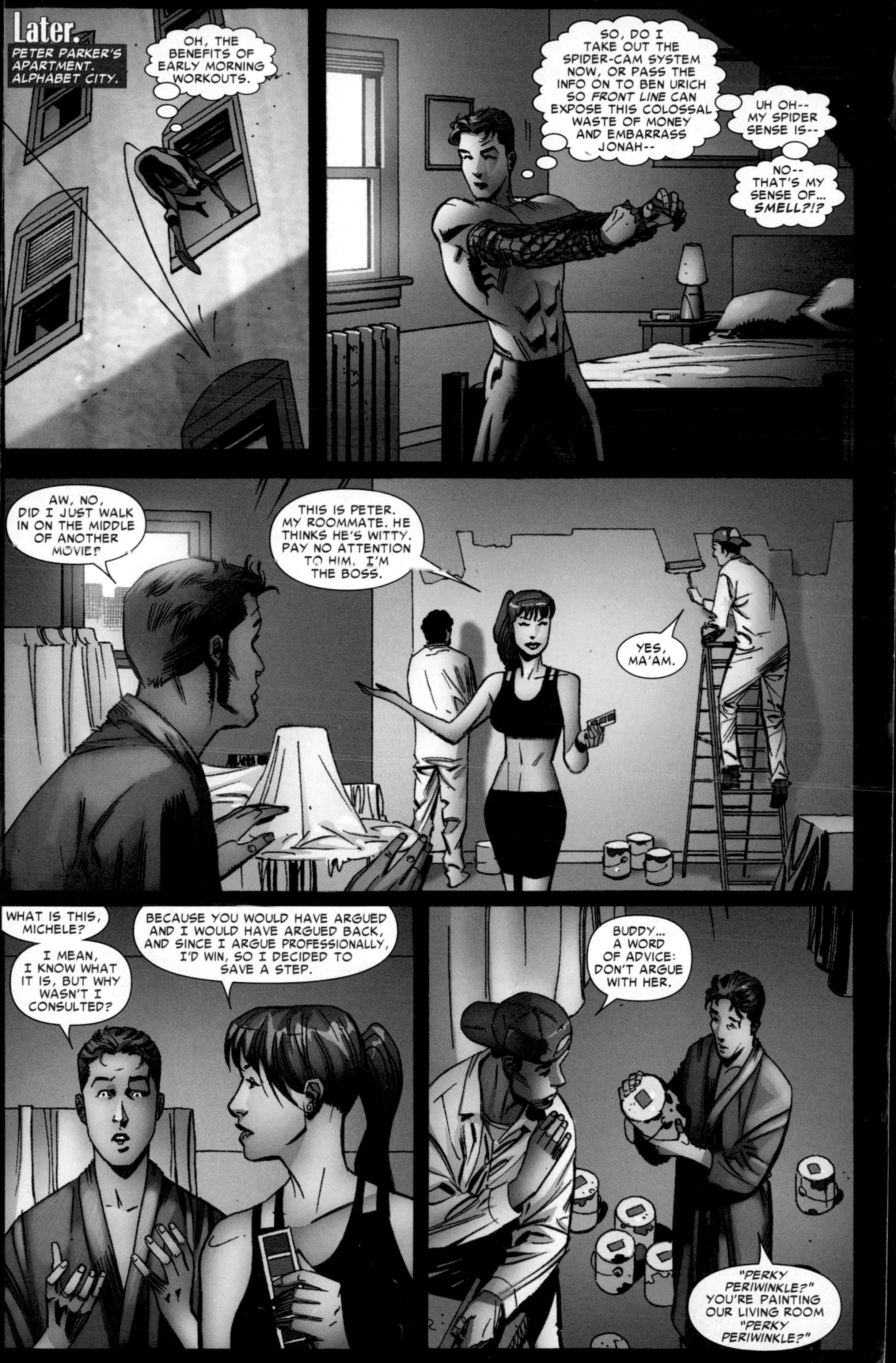
Later.
PETER PARKER'S APARTMENT. ALPHABET CITY.
OH, THE BENEFITS OF EARLY MORNING WORKOUTS.
SO, DO I TAKE OUT THE SPIDER-CAM SYSTEM NOW, OR PASS THE INFO ON TO BEN URICH SO FRONT LINE CAN EXPOSE THIS COLOSSAL WASTE OF MONEY AND EMBARRASS JONAH--
UH OH-- MY SPIDER SENSE IS--
NO-- THAT'S MY SENSE OF... SMELL?!?
AW, NO, DID I JUST WALK IN ON THE MIDDLE OF ANOTHER MOVIE?
THIS IS PETER. MY ROOMMATE. HE THINKS HE'S WITTY. PAY NO ATTENTION TO HIM. I'M THE BOSS.
YES, MA'AM.
WHAT IS THIS, MICHELE?
I MEAN, I KNOW WHAT IT IS, BUT WHY WASN'T I CONSULTED?
BECAUSE YOU WOULD HAVE ARGUED AND I WOULD HAVE ARGUED BACK, AND SINCE I ARGUE PROFESSIONALLY, I'D WIN, SO I DECIDED TO SAVE A STEP.
BUDDY... A WORD OF ADVICE: DON'T ARGUE WITH HER.
"PERKY PERIWINKLE?" YOU'RE PAINTING OUR LIVING ROOM "PERKY PERIWINKLE?"

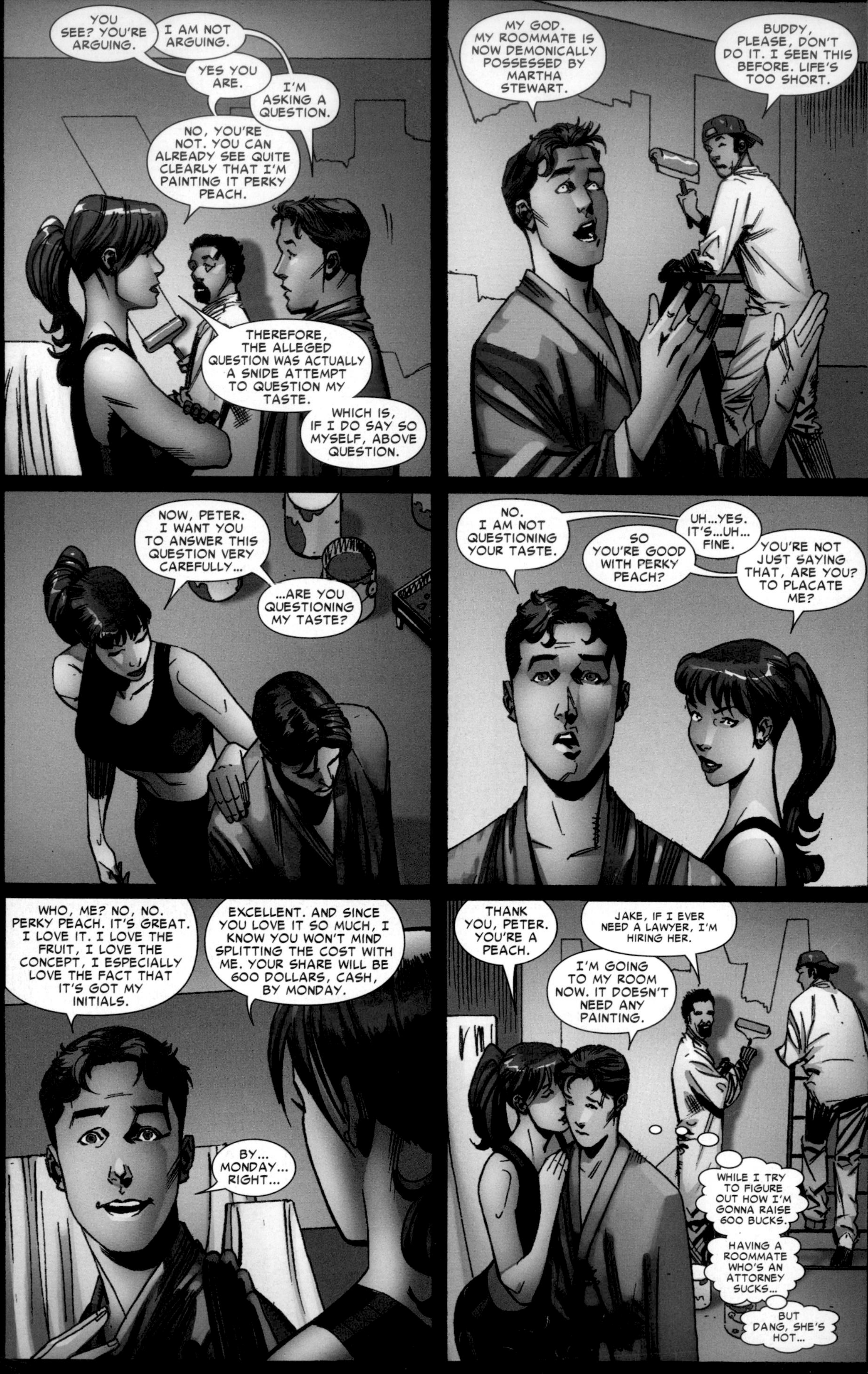
YOU SEE? YOU'RE ARGUING.
I AM NOT ARGUING.
YES YOU ARE.
I'M ASKING A QUESTION.
NO, YOU'RE NOT. YOU CAN ALREADY SEE QUITE CLEARLY THAT I'M PAINTING IT PERKY PEACH.
THEREFORE, THE ALLEGED QUESTION WAS ACTUALLY A SNIDE ATTEMPT TO QUESTION MY TASTE.
WHICH IS, IF I DO SAY SO MYSELF, ABOVE QUESTION.
MY GOD. MY ROOMMATE IS NOW DEMONICALLY POSSESSED BY MARTHA STEWART.
BUDDY, PLEASE, DON'T DO IT. I SEEN THIS BEFORE. LIFE'S TOO SHORT.
NOW, PETER. I WANT YOU TO ANSWER THIS QUESTION VERY CAREFULLY...
...ARE YOU QUESTIONING MY TASTE?
NO. I AM NOT QUESTIONING YOUR TASTE.
SO YOU'RE GOOD WITH PERKY PEACH?
UH...YES. IT'S...UH... FINE.
YOU'RE NOT JUST SAYING THAT, ARE YOU? TO PLACATE ME?
WHO, ME? NO, NO. PERKY PEACH. IT'S GREAT. I LOVE IT. I LOVE THE FRUIT, I LOVE THE CONCEPT, I ESPECIALLY LOVE THE FACT THAT IT'S GOT MY INITIALS.
EXCELLENT. AND SINCE YOU LOVE IT SO MUCH, I KNOW YOU WON'T MIND SPLITTING THE COST WITH ME. YOUR SHARE WILL BE 600 DOLLARS, CASH, BY MONDAY.
BY... MONDAY... RIGHT...
THANK YOU, PETER. YOU'RE A PEACH.
JAKE, IF I EVER NEED A LAWYER, I'M HIRING HER.
I'M GOING TO MY ROOM NOW. IT DOESN'T NEED ANY PAINTING.
WHILE I TRY TO FIGURE OUT HOW I'M GONNA RAISE 600 BUCKS.
HAVING A ROOMMATE WHO'S AN ATTORNEY SUCKS...
BUT DANG, SHE'S HOT...

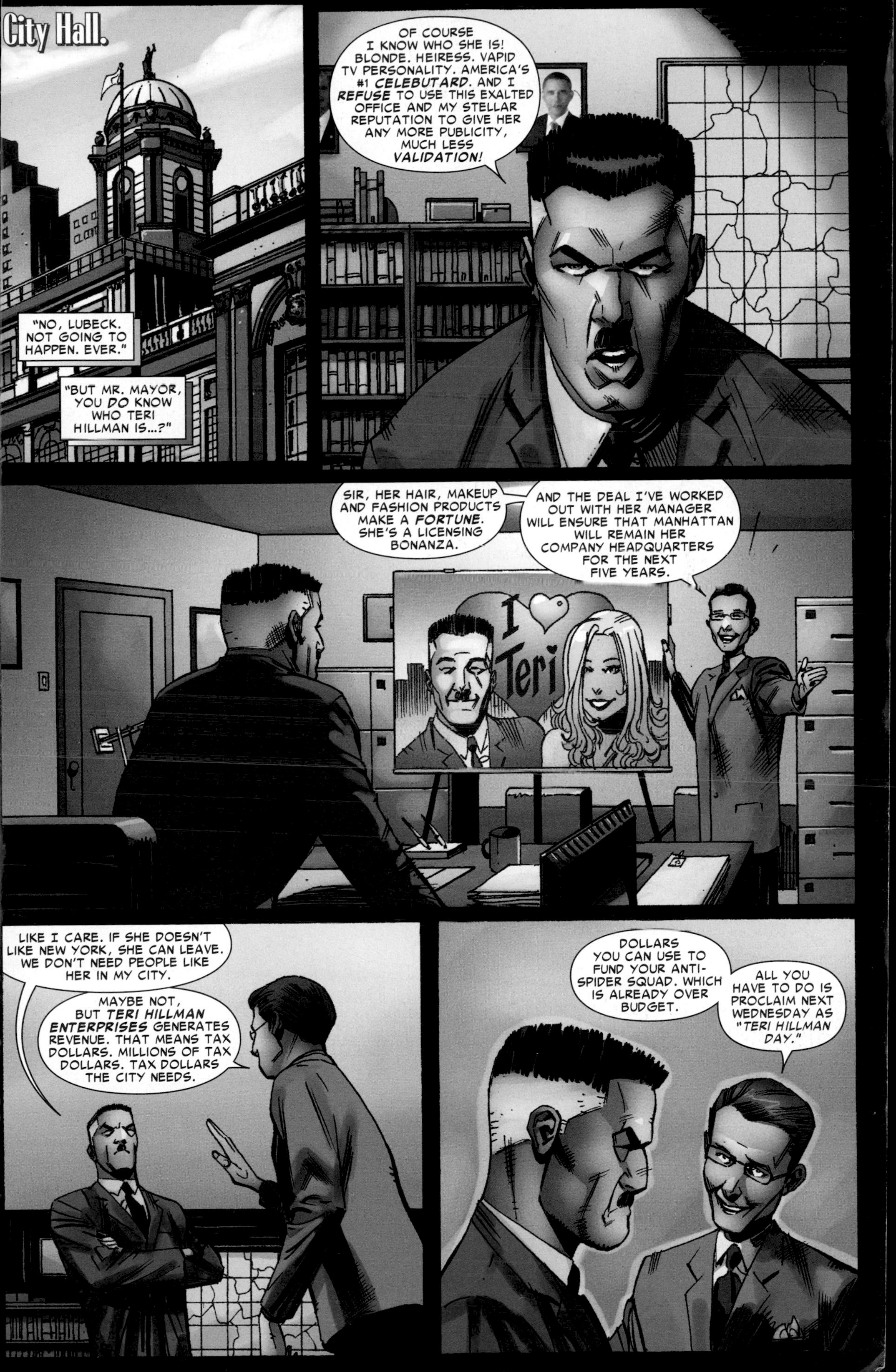
City Hall.
"NO, LUBECK. NOT GOING TO HAPPEN. EVER."
"BUT MR. MAYOR, YOU DO KNOW WHO TERI HILLMAN IS...?"
OF COURSE I KNOW WHO SHE IS! BLONDE. HEIRESS. VAPID TV PERSONALITY. AMERICA'S #1 CELEBUTARD. AND I REFUSE TO USE THIS EXALTED OFFICE AND MY STELLAR REPUTATION TO GIVE HER ANY MORE PUBLICITY, MUCH LESS VALIDATION!
SIR, HER HAIR, MAKEUP AND FASHION PRODUCTS MAKE A FORTUNE. SHE'S A LICENSING BONANZA.
AND THE DEAL I'VE WORKED OUT WITH HER MANAGER WILL ENSURE THAT MANHATTAN WILL REMAIN HER COMPANY HEADQUARTERS FOR THE NEXT FIVE YEARS.
I ♥ Teri
LIKE I CARE. IF SHE DOESN'T LIKE NEW YORK, SHE CAN LEAVE. WE DON'T NEED PEOPLE LIKE HER IN MY CITY.
MAYBE NOT, BUT TERI HILLMAN ENTERPRISES GENERATES REVENUE. THAT MEANS TAX DOLLARS. MILLIONS OF TAX DOLLARS. TAX DOLLARS THE CITY NEEDS.
DOLLARS YOU CAN USE TO FUND YOUR ANTI-SPIDER SQUAD. WHICH IS ALREADY OVER BUDGET.
ALL YOU HAVE TO DO IS PROCLAIM NEXT WEDNESDAY AS "TERI HILLMAN DAY."

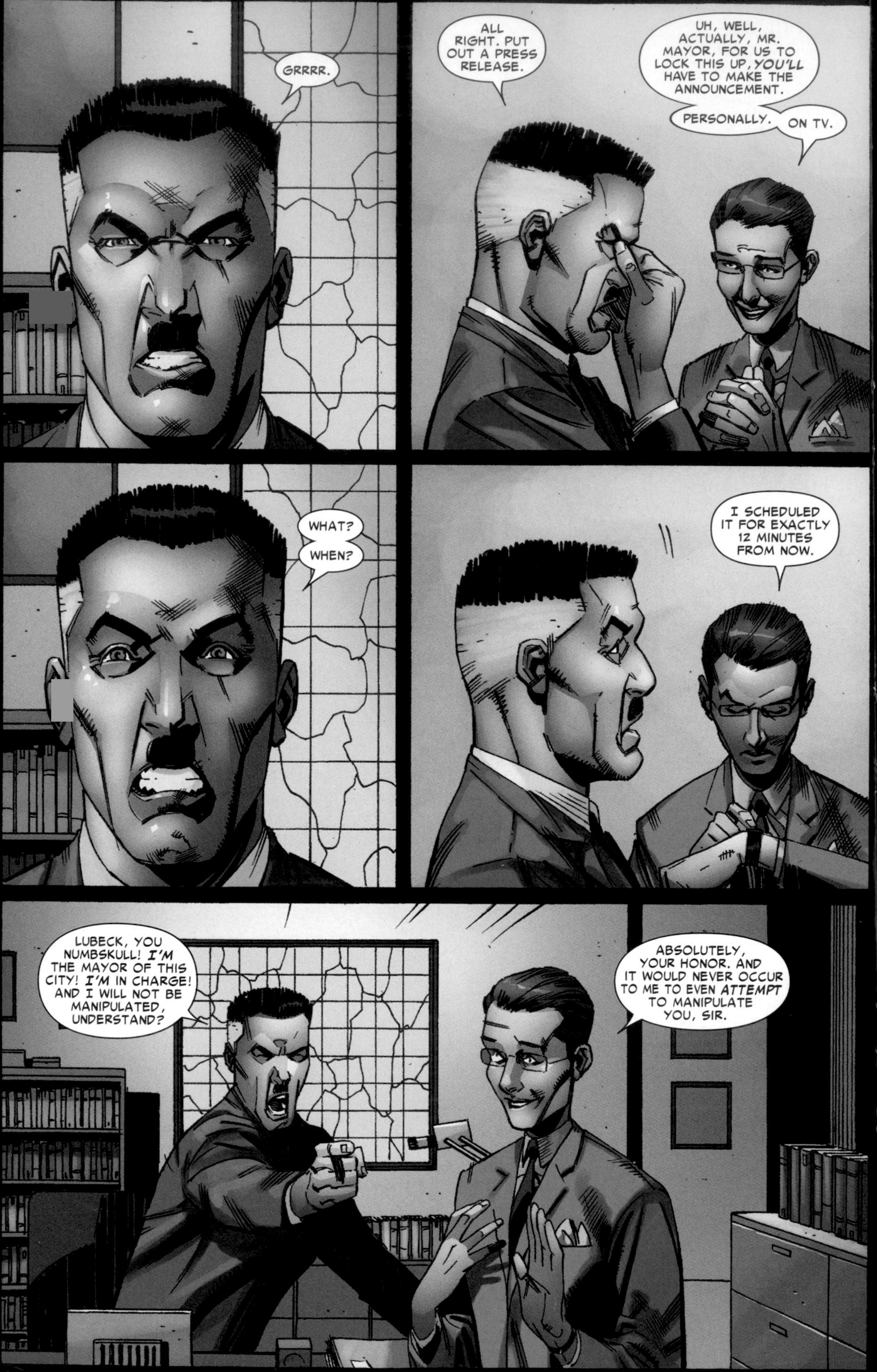
GRRRR.
ALL RIGHT. PUT OUT A PRESS RELEASE.
UH, WELL, ACTUALLY, MR. MAYOR, FOR US TO LOCK THIS UP, YOU'LL HAVE TO MAKE THE ANNOUNCEMENT.
PERSONALLY.
ON TV.
WHAT?
WHEN?
I SCHEDULED IT FOR EXACTLY 12 MINUTES FROM NOW.
LUBECK, YOU NUMBSKULL! I'M THE MAYOR OF THIS CITY! I'M IN CHARGE! AND I WILL NOT BE MANIPULATED, UNDERSTAND?
ABSOLUTELY, YOUR HONOR. AND IT WOULD NEVER OCCUR TO ME TO EVEN ATTEMPT TO MANIPULATE YOU, SIR.

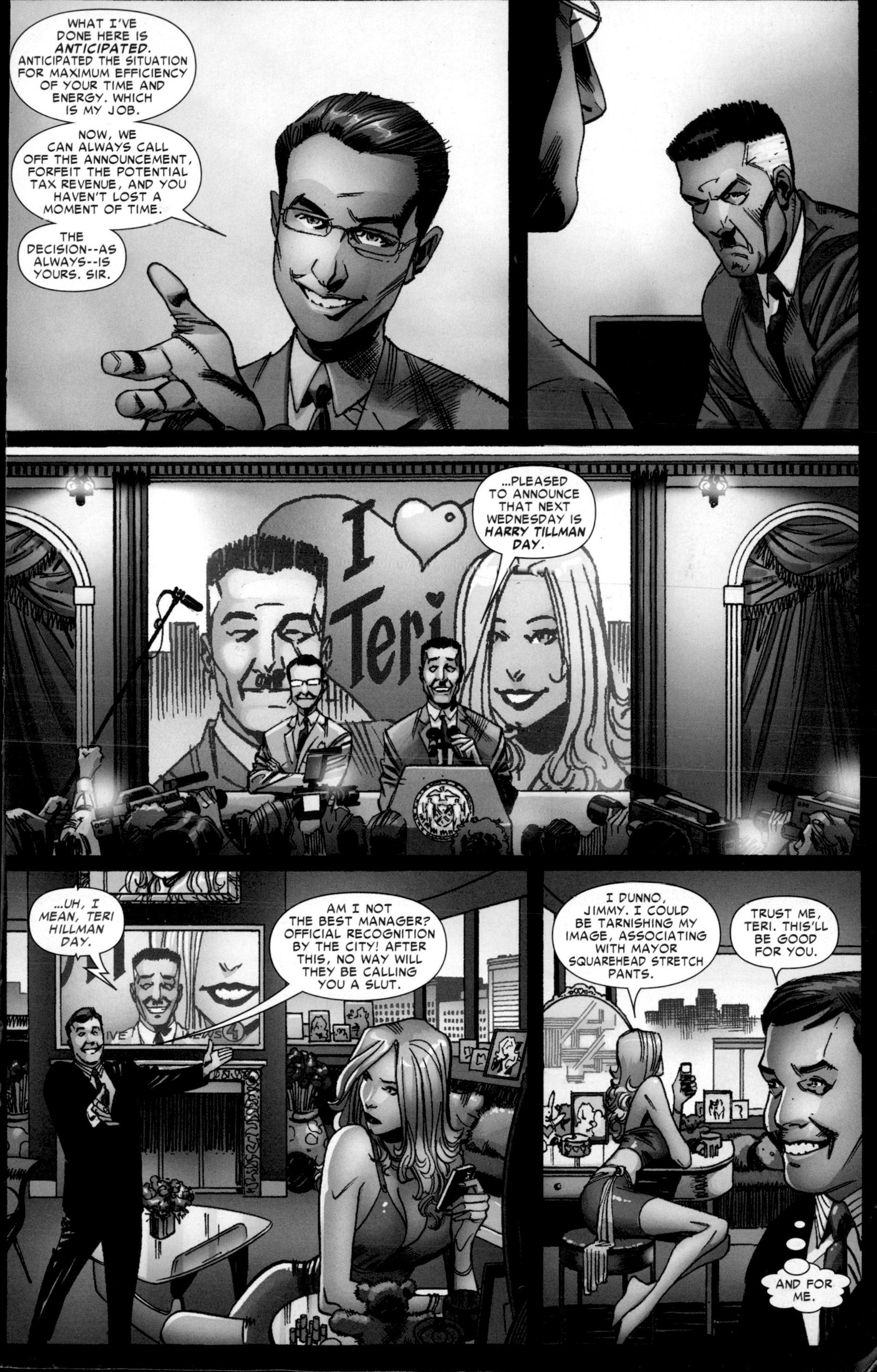
WHAT I'VE DONE HERE IS ANTICIPATED. ANTICIPATED THE SITUATION FOR MAXIMUM EFFICIENCY OF YOUR TIME AND ENERGY. WHICH IS MY JOB.
NOW, WE CAN ALWAYS CALL OFF THE ANNOUNCEMENT, FORFEIT THE POTENTIAL TAX REVENUE, AND YOU HAVEN'T LOST A MOMENT OF TIME.
THE DECISION--AS ALWAYS--IS YOURS. SIR.
...PLEASED TO ANNOUNCE THAT NEXT WEDNESDAY IS HARRY TILLMAN DAY.
I ♥ Teri
...UH, I MEAN, TERI HILLMAN DAY.
AM I NOT THE BEST MANAGER? OFFICIAL RECOGNITION BY THE CITY! AFTER THIS, NO WAY WILL THEY BE CALLING YOU A SLUT.
I DUNNO, JIMMY. I COULD BE TARNISHING MY IMAGE, ASSOCIATING WITH MAYOR SQUAREHEAD STRETCH PANTS.
TRUST ME, TERI. THIS'LL BE GOOD FOR YOU.
AND FOR ME.

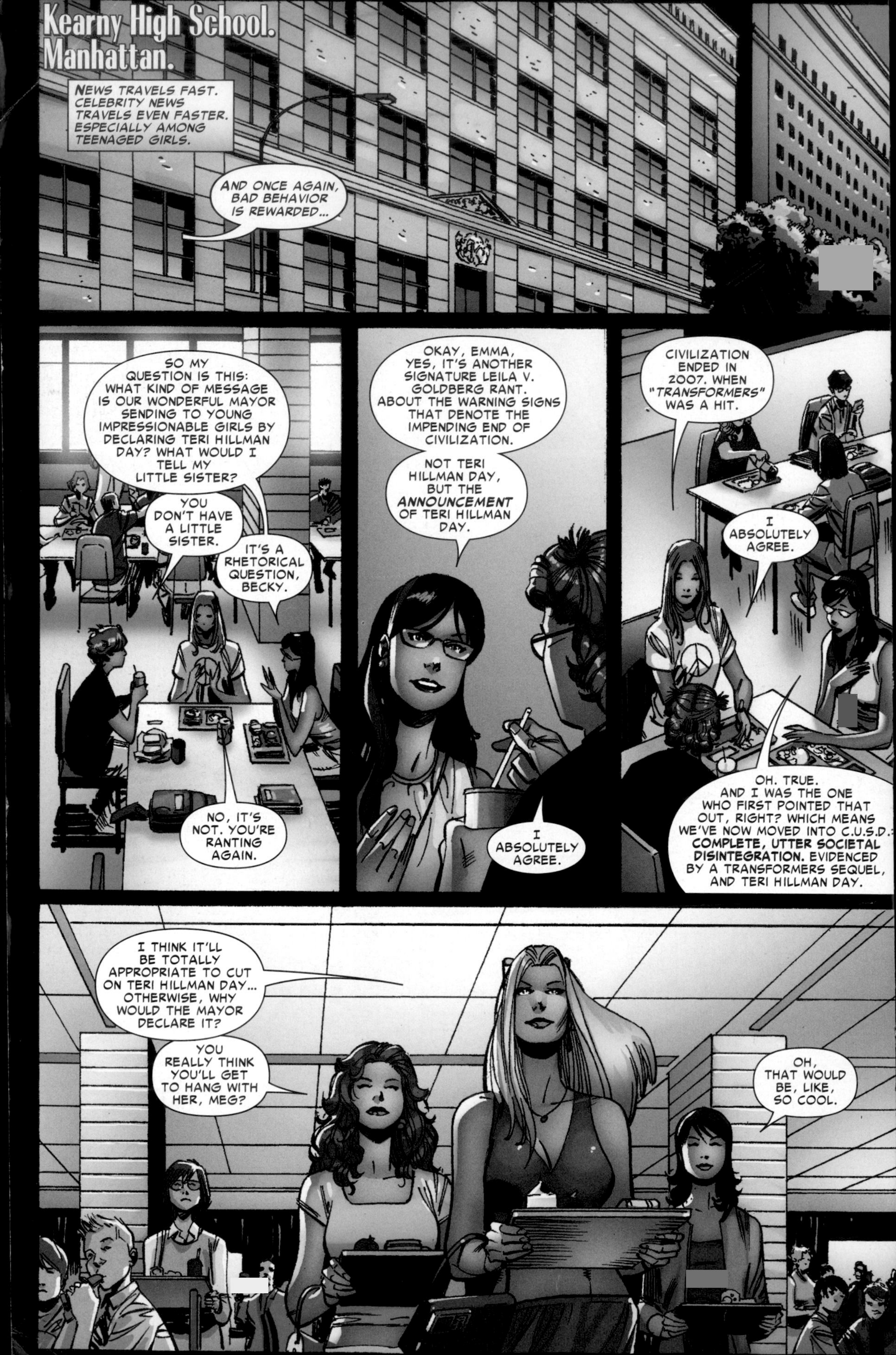

Kearny High School. Manhattan.
NEWS TRAVELS FAST. CELEBRITY NEWS TRAVELS EVEN FASTER. ESPECIALLY AMONG TEENAGED GIRLS.
AND ONCE AGAIN, BAD BEHAVIOR IS REWARDED...
SO MY QUESTION IS THIS: WHAT KIND OF MESSAGE IS OUR WONDERFUL MAYOR SENDING TO YOUNG IMPRESSIONABLE GIRLS BY DECLARING TERI HILLMAN DAY? WHAT WOULD I TELL MY LITTLE SISTER?
YOU DON'T HAVE A LITTLE SISTER.
IT'S A RHETORICAL QUESTION, BECKY.
NO, IT'S NOT. YOU'RE RANTING AGAIN.
OKAY, EMMA, YES, IT'S ANOTHER SIGNATURE LEILA V. GOLDBERG RANT. ABOUT THE WARNING SIGNS THAT DENOTE THE IMPENDING END OF CIVILIZATION.
NOT TERI HILLMAN DAY, BUT THE ANNOUNCEMENT OF TERI HILLMAN DAY.
I ABSOLUTELY AGREE.
CIVILIZATION ENDED IN 2007. WHEN "TRANSFORMERS" WAS A HIT.
I ABSOLUTELY AGREE.
OH. TRUE. AND I WAS THE ONE WHO FIRST POINTED THAT OUT, RIGHT? WHICH MEANS WE'VE NOW MOVED INTO C.U.S.D.: COMPLETE, UTTER SOCIETAL DISINTEGRATION. EVIDENCED BY A TRANSFORMERS SEQUEL, AND TERI HILLMAN DAY.
I THINK IT'LL BE TOTALLY APPROPRIATE TO CUT ON TERI HILLMAN DAY... OTHERWISE, WHY WOULD THE MAYOR DECLARE IT?
YOU REALLY THINK YOU'LL GET TO HANG WITH HER, MEG?
OH, THAT WOULD BE, LIKE, SO COOL.

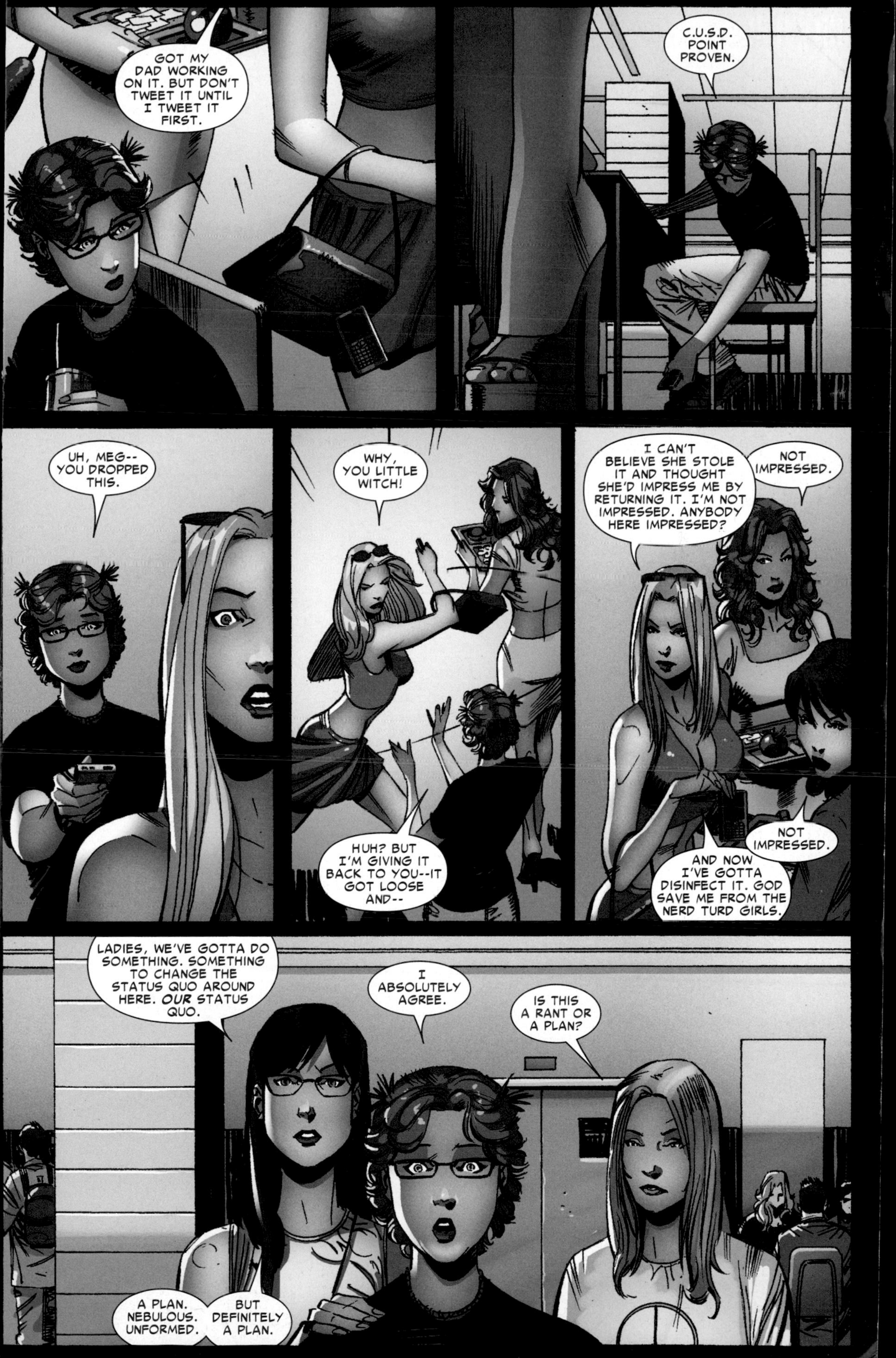
GOT MY DAD WORKING ON IT. BUT DON'T TWEET IT UNTIL I TWEET IT FIRST.
C.U.S.D. POINT PROVEN.
UH, MEG-- YOU DROPPED THIS.
WHY, YOU LITTLE WITCH!
HUH? BUT I'M GIVING IT BACK TO YOU--IT GOT LOOSE AND--
I CAN'T BELIEVE SHE STOLE IT AND THOUGHT SHE'D IMPRESS ME BY RETURNING IT. I'M NOT IMPRESSED. ANYBODY HERE IMPRESSED?
NOT IMPRESSED.
NOT IMPRESSED.
AND NOW I'VE GOTTA DISINFECT IT. GOD SAVE ME FROM THE NERD TURD GIRLS.
LADIES, WE'VE GOTTA DO SOMETHING. SOMETHING TO CHANGE THE STATUS QUO AROUND HERE. ***OUR*** STATUS QUO.
I ABSOLUTELY AGREE.
IS THIS A RANT OR A PLAN?
A PLAN. NEBULOUS. UNFORMED.
BUT DEFINITELY A PLAN.

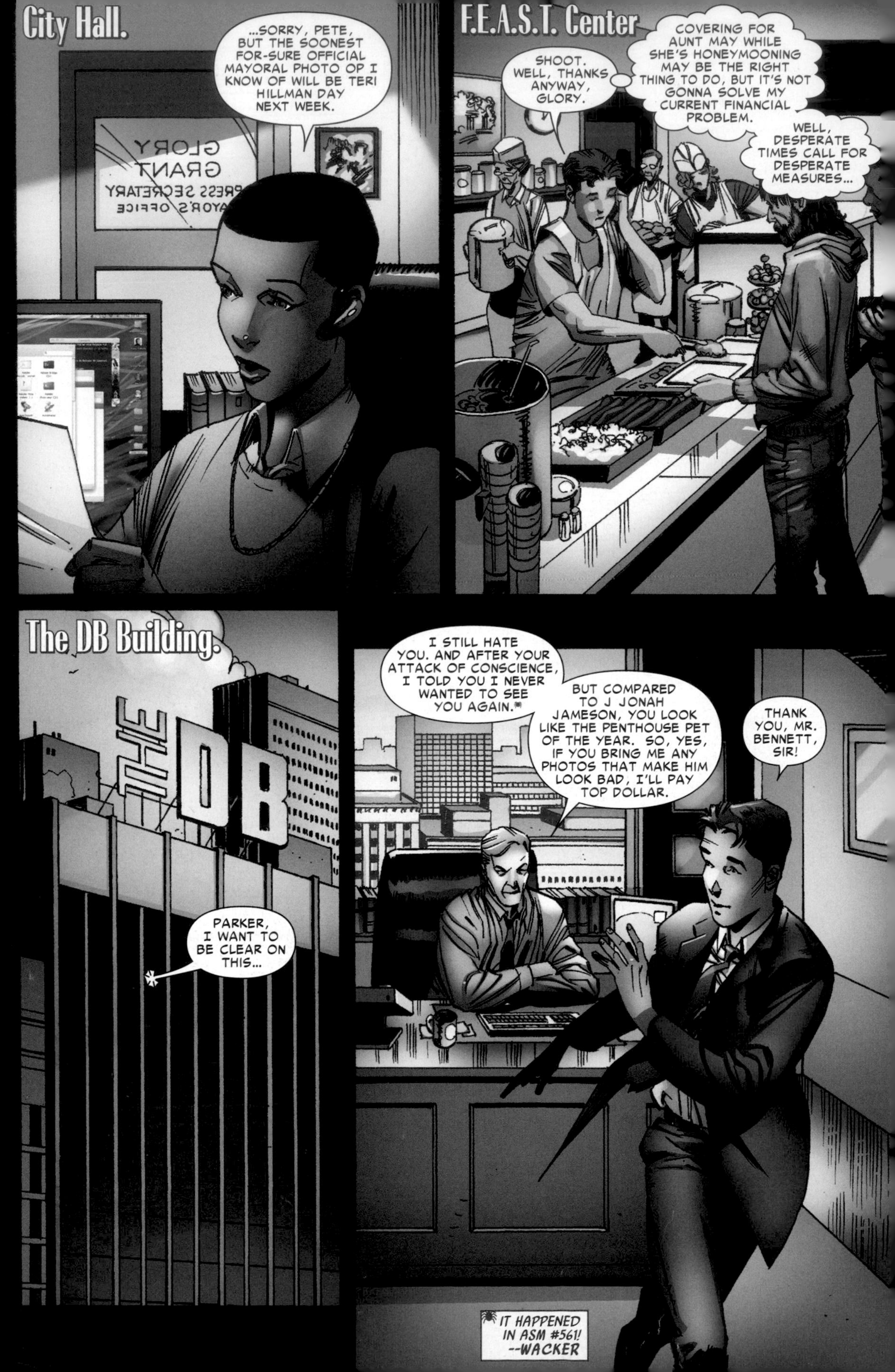
City Hall.
...SORRY, PETE, BUT THE SOONEST FOR-SURE OFFICIAL MAYORAL PHOTO OP I KNOW OF WILL BE TERI HILLMAN DAY NEXT WEEK.
GLORY GRANT PRESS SECRETARY MAYOR'S OFFICE
F.E.A.S.T. Center
SHOOT. WELL, THANKS ANYWAY, GLORY.
COVERING FOR AUNT MAY WHILE SHE'S HONEYMOONING MAY BE THE RIGHT THING TO DO, BUT IT'S NOT GONNA SOLVE MY CURRENT FINANCIAL PROBLEM.
WELL, DESPERATE TIMES CALL FOR DESPERATE MEASURES...
The DB Building.
THE DB
PARKER, I WANT TO BE CLEAR ON THIS...
I STILL HATE YOU. AND AFTER YOUR ATTACK OF CONSCIENCE, I TOLD YOU I NEVER WANTED TO SEE YOU AGAIN.*
BUT COMPARED TO J JONAH JAMESON, YOU LOOK LIKE THE PENTHOUSE PET OF THE YEAR. SO, YES, IF YOU BRING ME ANY PHOTOS THAT MAKE HIM LOOK BAD, I'LL PAY TOP DOLLAR.
THANK YOU, MR. BENNETT, SIR!
*IT HAPPENED IN ASM #561! --WACKER

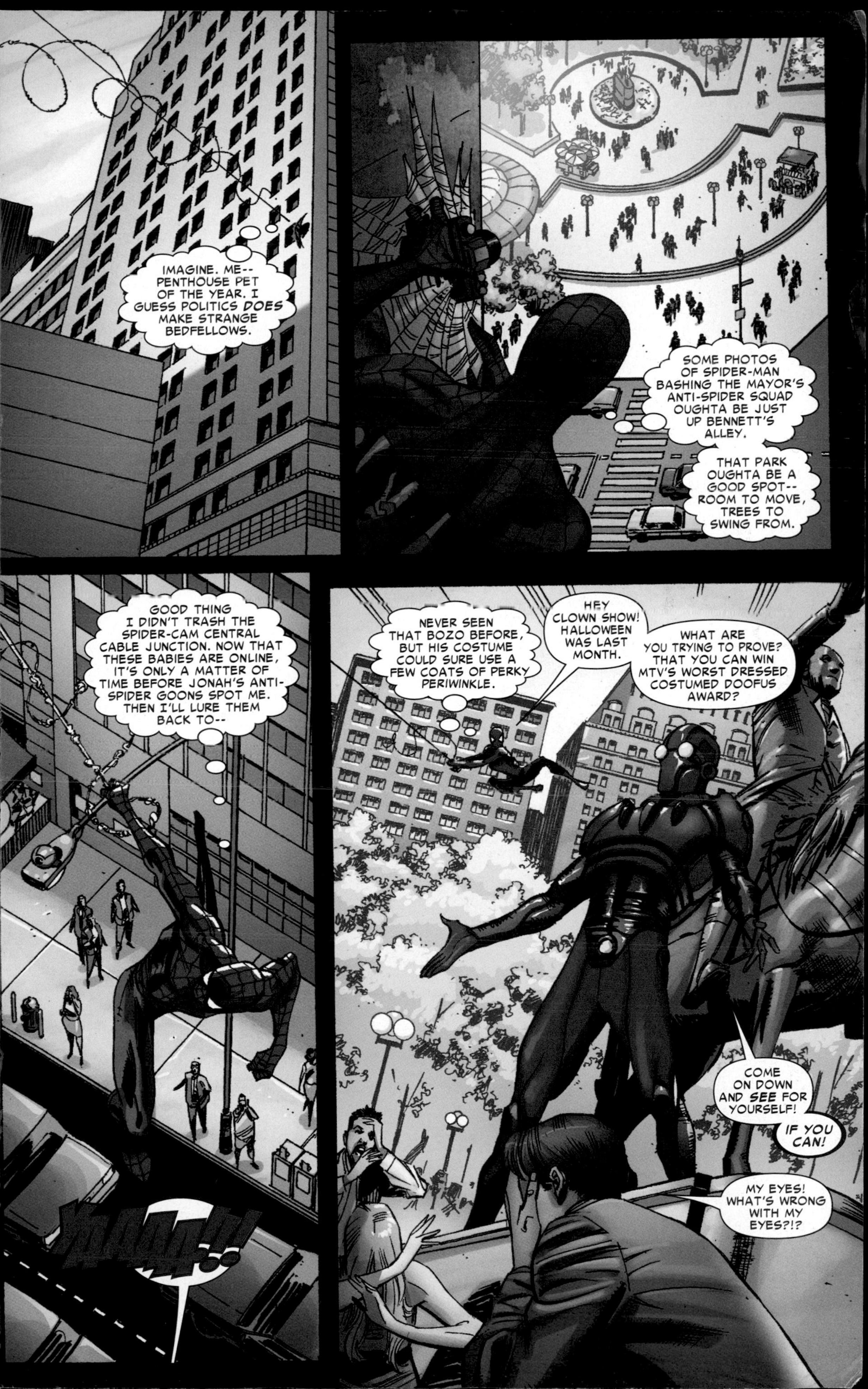
IMAGINE. ME--PENTHOUSE PET OF THE YEAR. I GUESS POLITICS *DOES* MAKE STRANGE BEDFELLOWS.
SOME PHOTOS OF SPIDER-MAN BASHING THE MAYOR'S ANTI-SPIDER SQUAD OUGHTA BE JUST UP BENNETT'S ALLEY.
THAT PARK OUGHTA BE A GOOD SPOT--ROOM TO MOVE, TREES TO SWING FROM.
GOOD THING I DIDN'T TRASH THE SPIDER-CAM CENTRAL CABLE JUNCTION. NOW THAT THESE BABIES ARE ONLINE, IT'S ONLY A MATTER OF TIME BEFORE JONAH'S ANTI-SPIDER GOONS SPOT ME. THEN I'LL LURE THEM BACK TO--
NEVER SEEN THAT BOZO BEFORE, BUT HIS COSTUME COULD SURE USE A FEW COATS OF PERKY PERIWINKLE.
HEY CLOWN SHOW! HALLOWEEN WAS LAST MONTH.
WHAT ARE YOU TRYING TO PROVE? THAT YOU CAN WIN MTV'S WORST DRESSED COSTUMED DOOFUS AWARD?
COME ON DOWN AND *SEE* FOR YOURSELF!
IF YOU CAN!
MY EYES! WHAT'S WRONG WITH MY EYES?!?

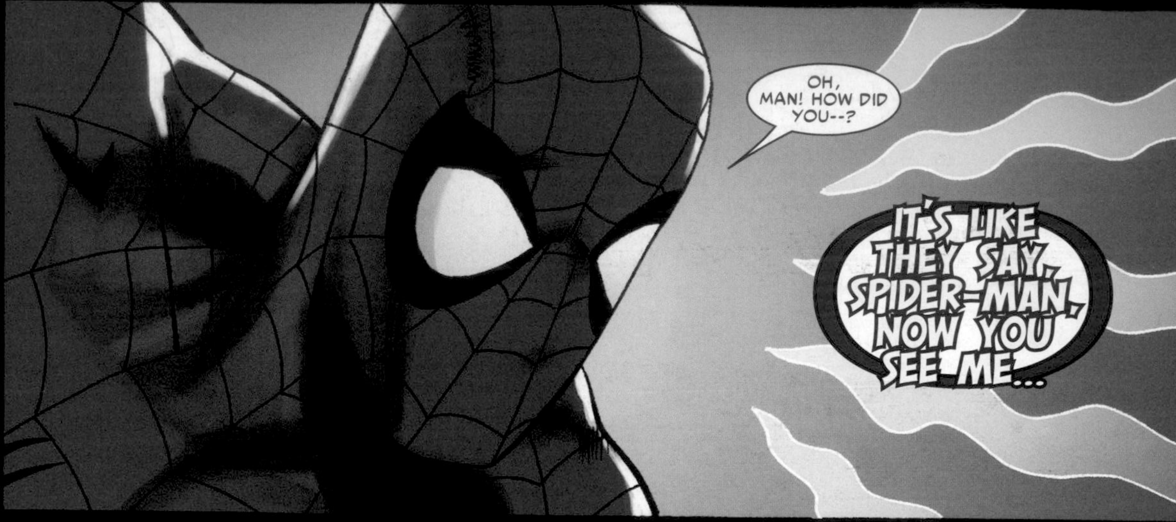
OH, MAN! HOW DID YOU--?
IT'S LIKE THEY SAY, SPIDER-MAN, NOW YOU SEE ME...

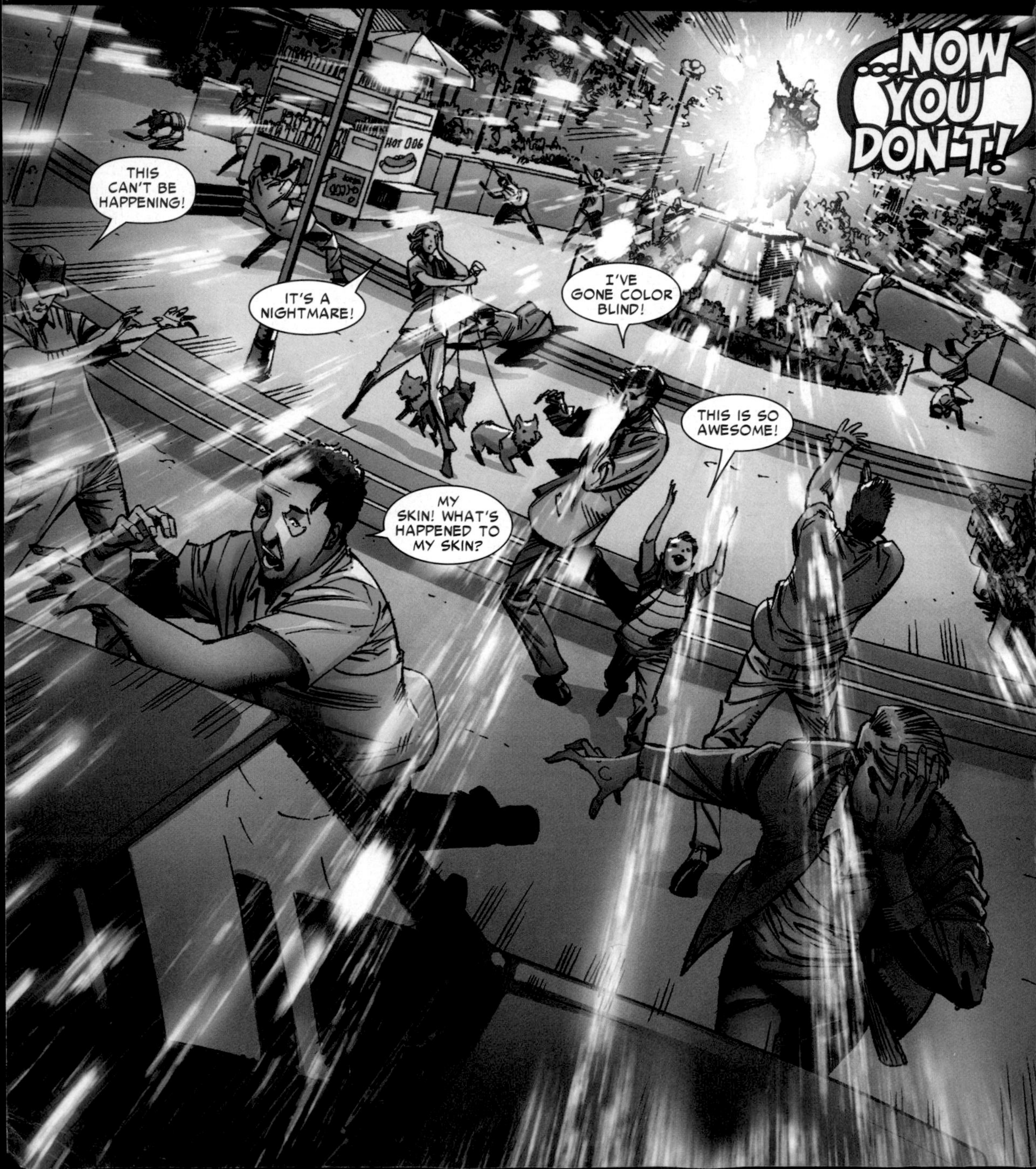
...NOW YOU DON'T!
HOT DOG
THIS CAN'T BE HAPPENING!
IT'S A NIGHTMARE!
I'VE GONE COLOR BLIND!
THIS IS SO AWESOME!
MY SKIN! WHAT'S HAPPENED TO MY SKIN?

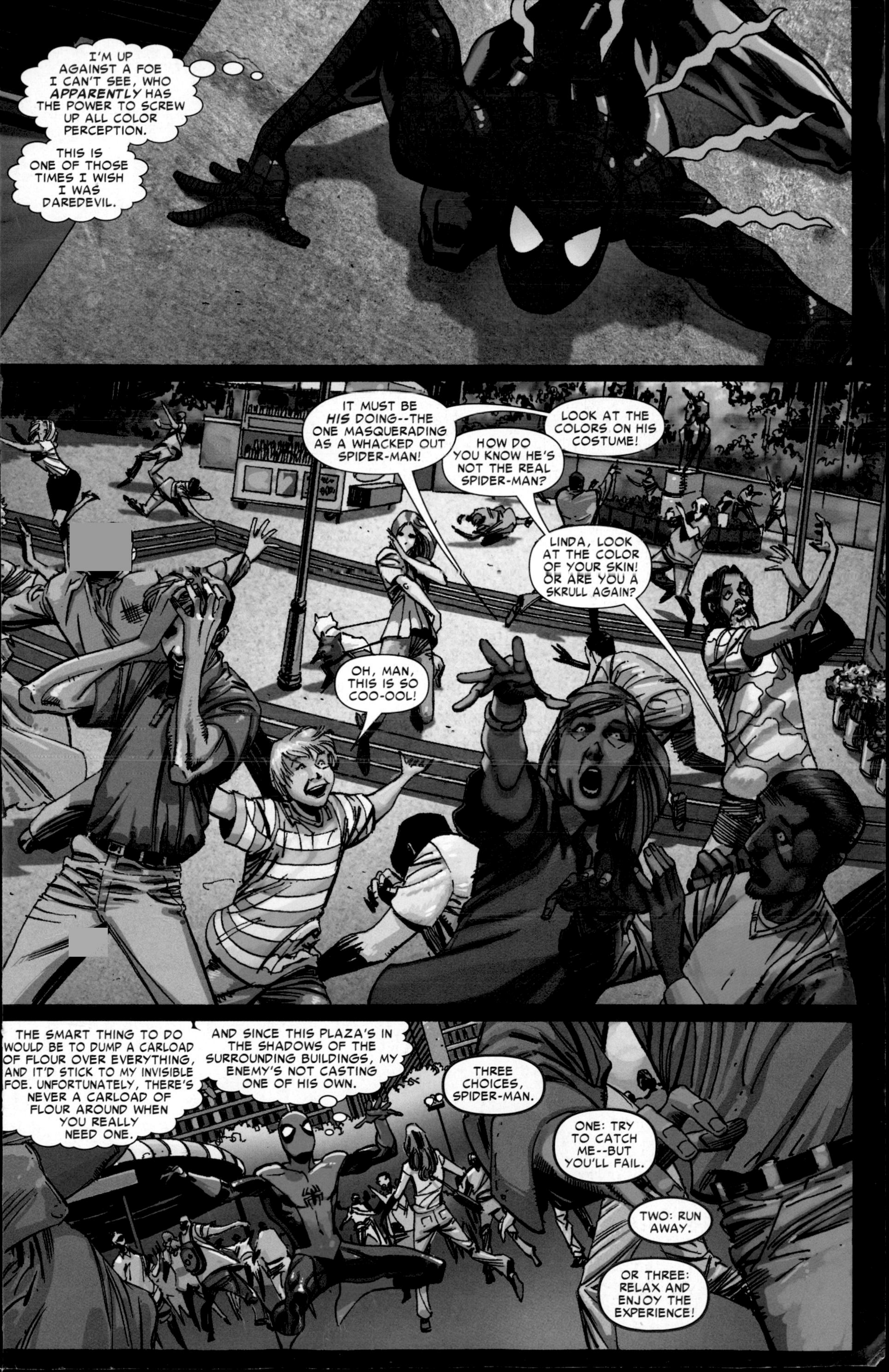
I'M UP AGAINST A FOE I CAN'T SEE, WHO *APPARENTLY* HAS THE POWER TO SCREW UP ALL COLOR PERCEPTION.
THIS IS ONE OF THOSE TIMES I WISH I WAS DAREDEVIL.
IT MUST BE *HIS* DOING--THE ONE MASQUERADING AS A WHACKED OUT SPIDER-MAN!
LOOK AT THE COLORS ON HIS COSTUME!
HOW DO YOU KNOW HE'S NOT THE REAL SPIDER-MAN?
LINDA, LOOK AT THE COLOR OF YOUR SKIN! OR ARE YOU A SKRULL AGAIN?
OH, MAN, THIS IS SO COO-OOL!
THE SMART THING TO DO WOULD BE TO DUMP A CARLOAD OF FLOUR OVER EVERYTHING, AND IT'D STICK TO MY INVISIBLE FOE. UNFORTUNATELY, THERE'S NEVER A CARLOAD OF FLOUR AROUND WHEN YOU REALLY NEED ONE.
AND SINCE THIS PLAZA'S IN THE SHADOWS OF THE SURROUNDING BUILDINGS, MY ENEMY'S NOT CASTING ONE OF HIS OWN.
THREE CHOICES, SPIDER-MAN.
ONE: TRY TO CATCH ME--BUT YOU'LL FAIL.
TWO: RUN AWAY.
OR THREE: RELAX AND ENJOY THE EXPERIENCE!

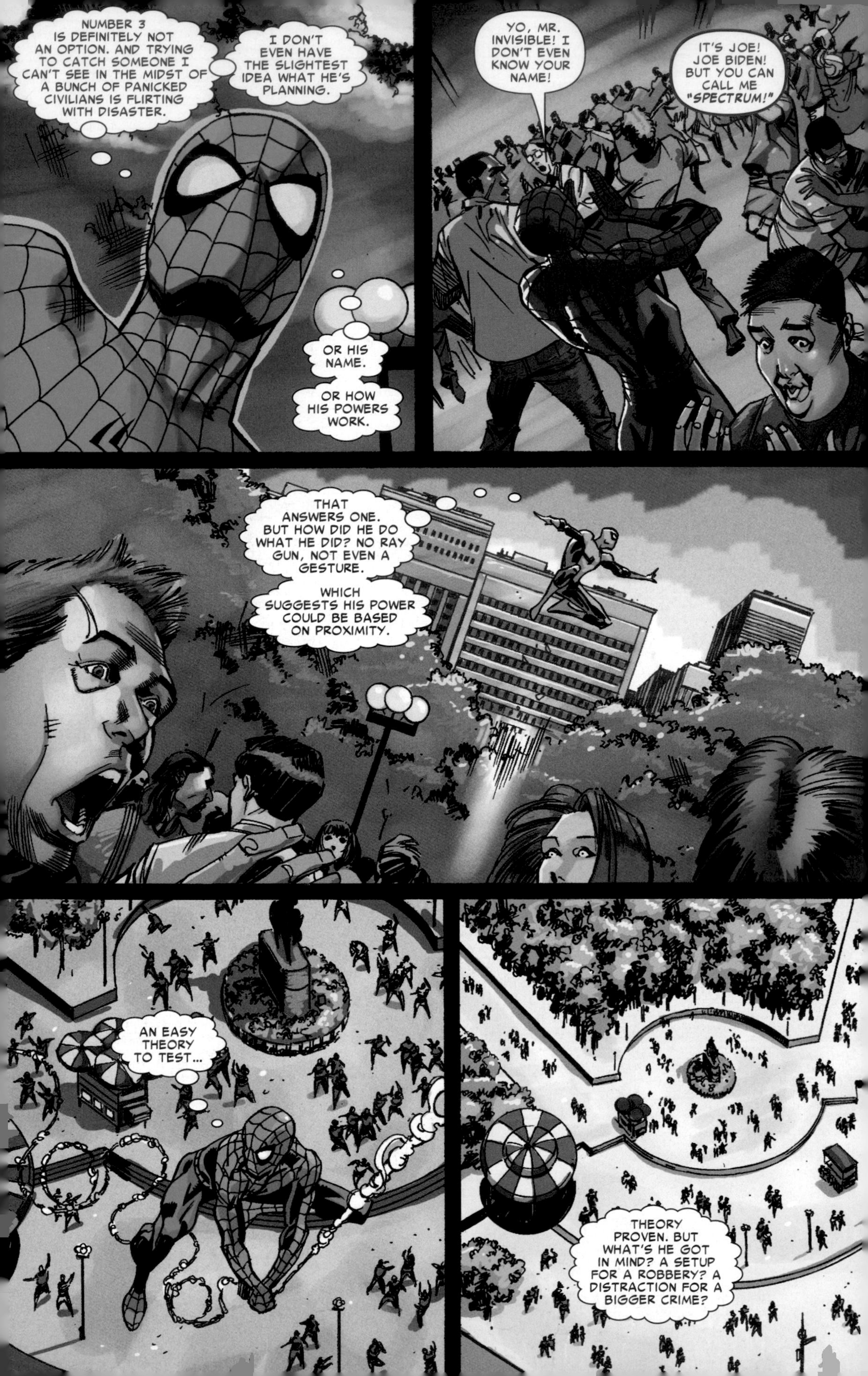
NUMBER 3 IS DEFINITELY NOT AN OPTION. AND TRYING TO CATCH SOMEONE I CAN'T SEE IN THE MIDST OF A BUNCH OF PANICKED CIVILIANS IS FLIRTING WITH DISASTER.
I DON'T EVEN HAVE THE SLIGHTEST IDEA WHAT HE'S PLANNING.
OR HIS NAME.
OR HOW HIS POWERS WORK.
YO, MR. INVISIBLE! I DON'T EVEN KNOW YOUR NAME!
IT'S JOE! JOE BIDEN! BUT YOU CAN CALL ME "*SPECTRUM!*"
THAT ANSWERS ONE. BUT HOW DID HE DO WHAT HE DID? NO RAY GUN, NOT EVEN A GESTURE.
WHICH SUGGESTS HIS POWER COULD BE BASED ON PROXIMITY.
AN EASY THEORY TO TEST...
THEORY PROVEN. BUT WHAT'S HE GOT IN MIND? A SETUP FOR A ROBBERY? A DISTRACTION FOR A BIGGER CRIME?

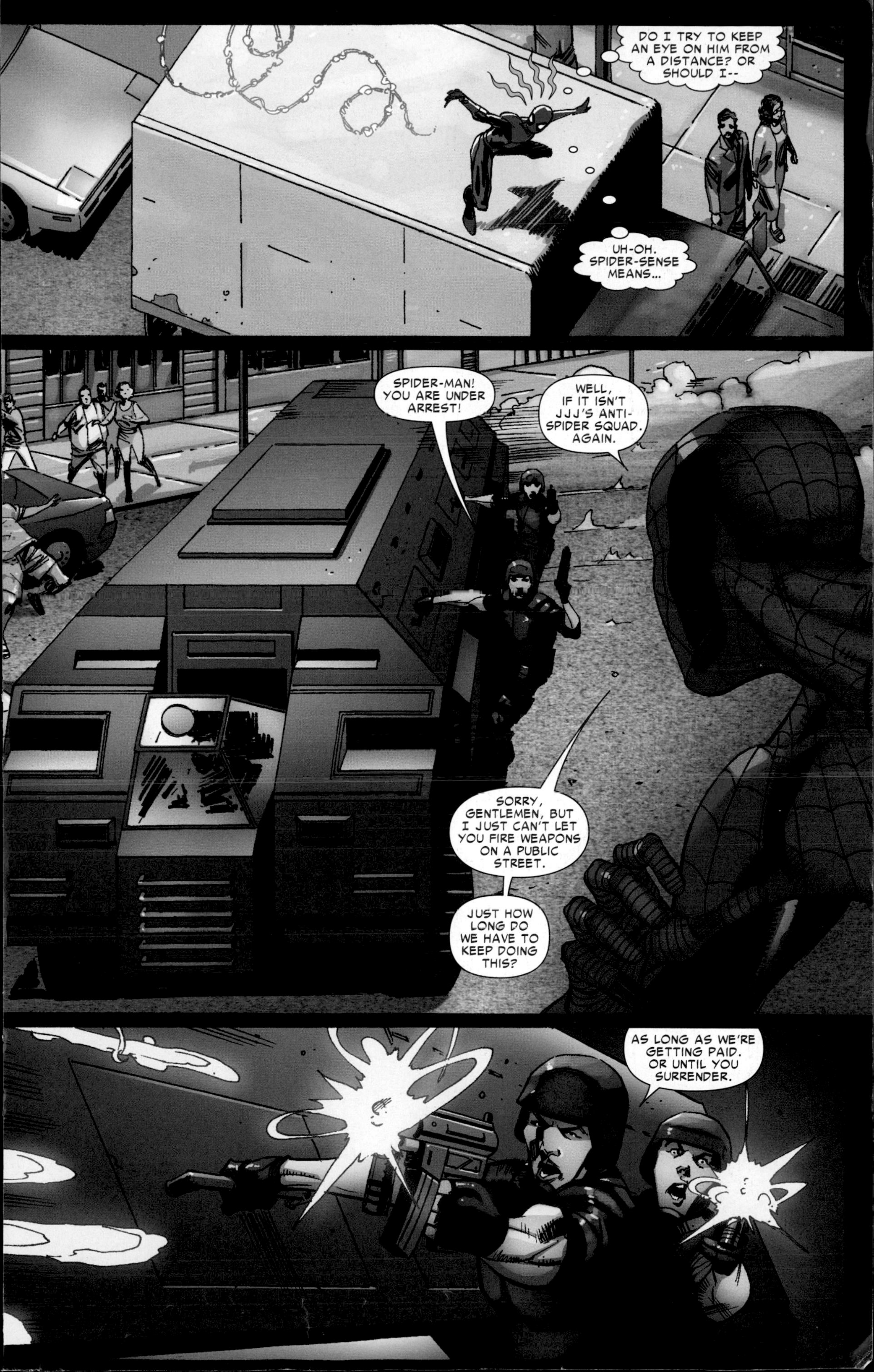
DO I TRY TO KEEP AN EYE ON HIM FROM A DISTANCE? OR SHOULD I--
UH-OH. SPIDER-SENSE MEANS...
SPIDER-MAN! YOU ARE UNDER ARREST!
WELL, IF IT ISN'T JJJ'S ANTI-SPIDER SQUAD. AGAIN.
SORRY, GENTLEMEN, BUT I JUST CAN'T LET YOU FIRE WEAPONS ON A PUBLIC STREET.
JUST HOW LONG DO WE HAVE TO KEEP DOING THIS?
AS LONG AS WE'RE GETTING PAID. OR UNTIL YOU SURRENDER.

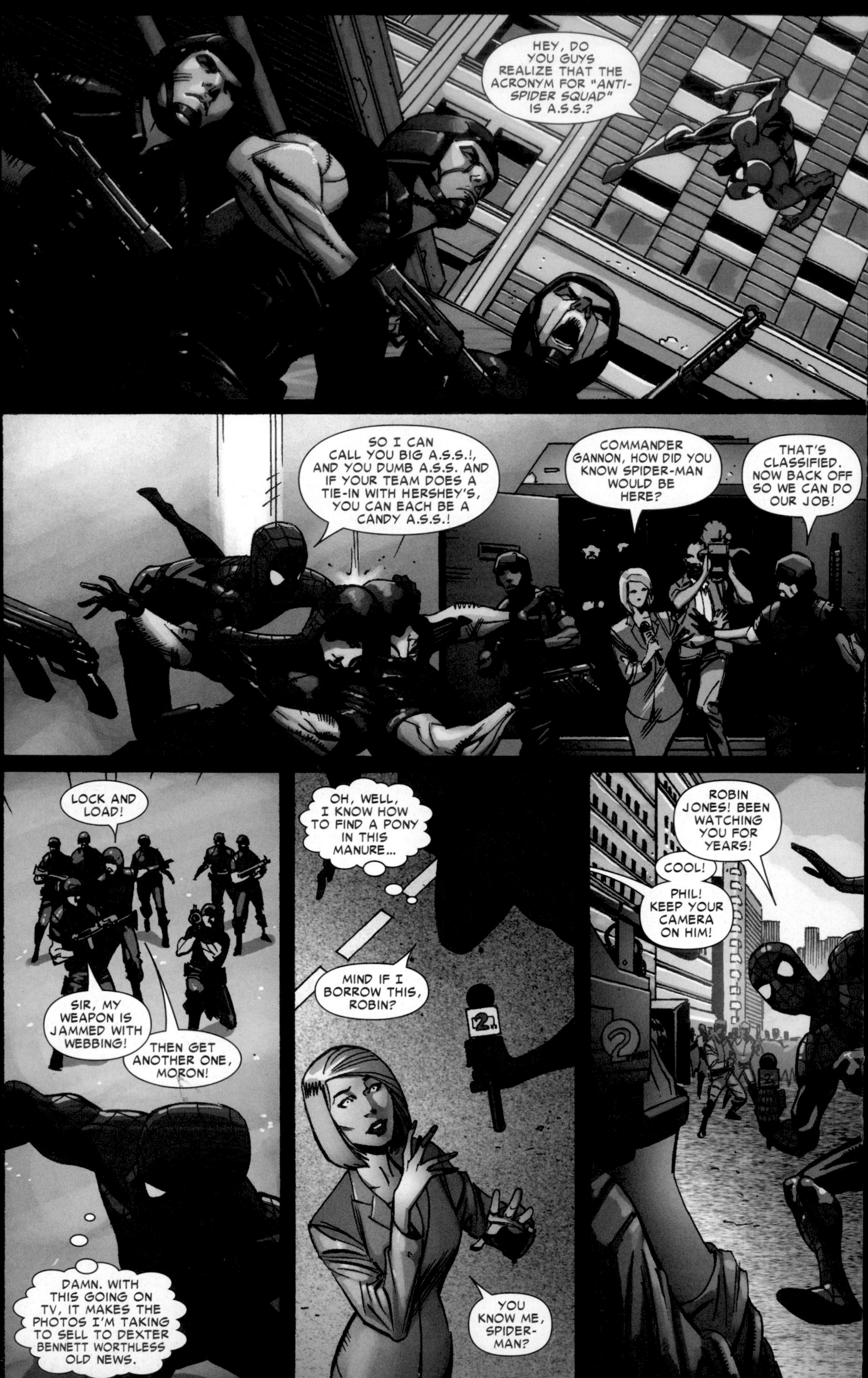
HEY, DO YOU GUYS REALIZE THAT THE ACRONYM FOR "ANTI-SPIDER SQUAD" IS A.S.S.?
SO I CAN CALL YOU BIG A.S.S.!, AND YOU DUMB A.S.S. AND IF YOUR TEAM DOES A TIE-IN WITH HERSHEY'S, YOU CAN EACH BE A CANDY A.S.S.!
COMMANDER GANNON, HOW DID YOU KNOW SPIDER-MAN WOULD BE HERE?
THAT'S CLASSIFIED. NOW BACK OFF SO WE CAN DO OUR JOB!
LOCK AND LOAD!
SIR, MY WEAPON IS JAMMED WITH WEBBING!
THEN GET ANOTHER ONE, MORON!
DAMN. WITH THIS GOING ON TV, IT MAKES THE PHOTOS I'M TAKING TO SELL TO DEXTER BENNETT WORTHLESS OLD NEWS.
OH, WELL, I KNOW HOW TO FIND A PONY IN THIS MANURE...
MIND IF I BORROW THIS, ROBIN?
YOU KNOW ME, SPIDER-MAN?
ROBIN JONES! BEEN WATCHING YOU FOR YEARS!
COOL!
PHIL! KEEP YOUR CAMERA ON HIM!

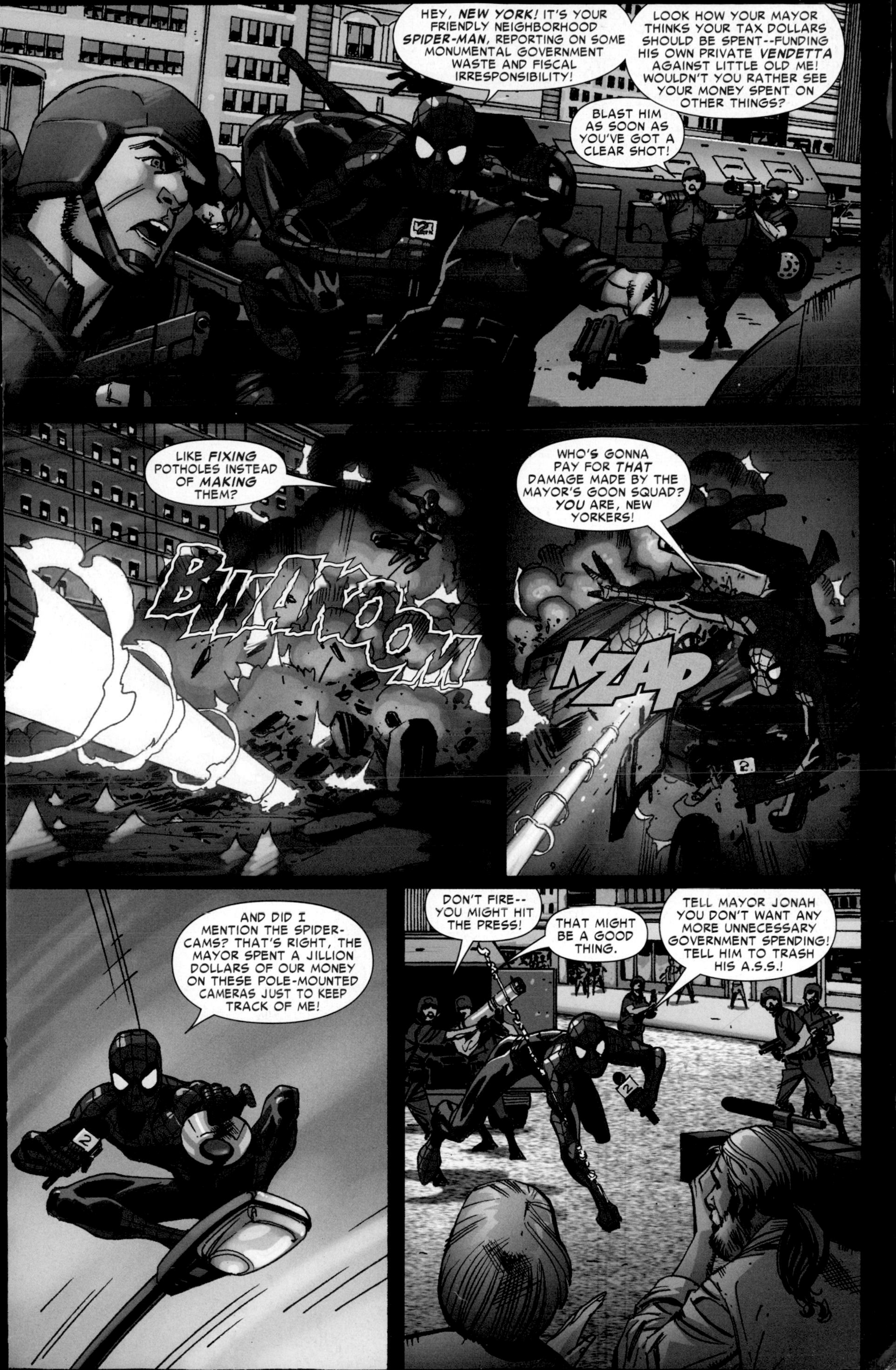
HEY, NEW YORK! IT'S YOUR FRIENDLY NEIGHBORHOOD SPIDER-MAN, REPORTING ON SOME MONUMENTAL GOVERNMENT WASTE AND FISCAL IRRESPONSIBILITY!
LOOK HOW YOUR MAYOR THINKS YOUR TAX DOLLARS SHOULD BE SPENT--FUNDING HIS OWN PRIVATE VENDETTA AGAINST LITTLE OLD ME! WOULDN'T YOU RATHER SEE YOUR MONEY SPENT ON OTHER THINGS?
BLAST HIM AS SOON AS YOU'VE GOT A CLEAR SHOT!
LIKE FIXING POTHOLES INSTEAD OF MAKING THEM?
BWOOOM
WHO'S GONNA PAY FOR THAT DAMAGE MADE BY THE MAYOR'S GOON SQUAD? YOU ARE, NEW YORKERS!
KZAP
AND DID I MENTION THE SPIDER-CAMS? THAT'S RIGHT, THE MAYOR SPENT A JILLION DOLLARS OF OUR MONEY ON THESE POLE-MOUNTED CAMERAS JUST TO KEEP TRACK OF ME!
DON'T FIRE--YOU MIGHT HIT THE PRESS!
THAT MIGHT BE A GOOD THING.
TELL MAYOR JONAH YOU DON'T WANT ANY MORE UNNECESSARY GOVERNMENT SPENDING! TELL HIM TO TRASH HIS A.S.S.!

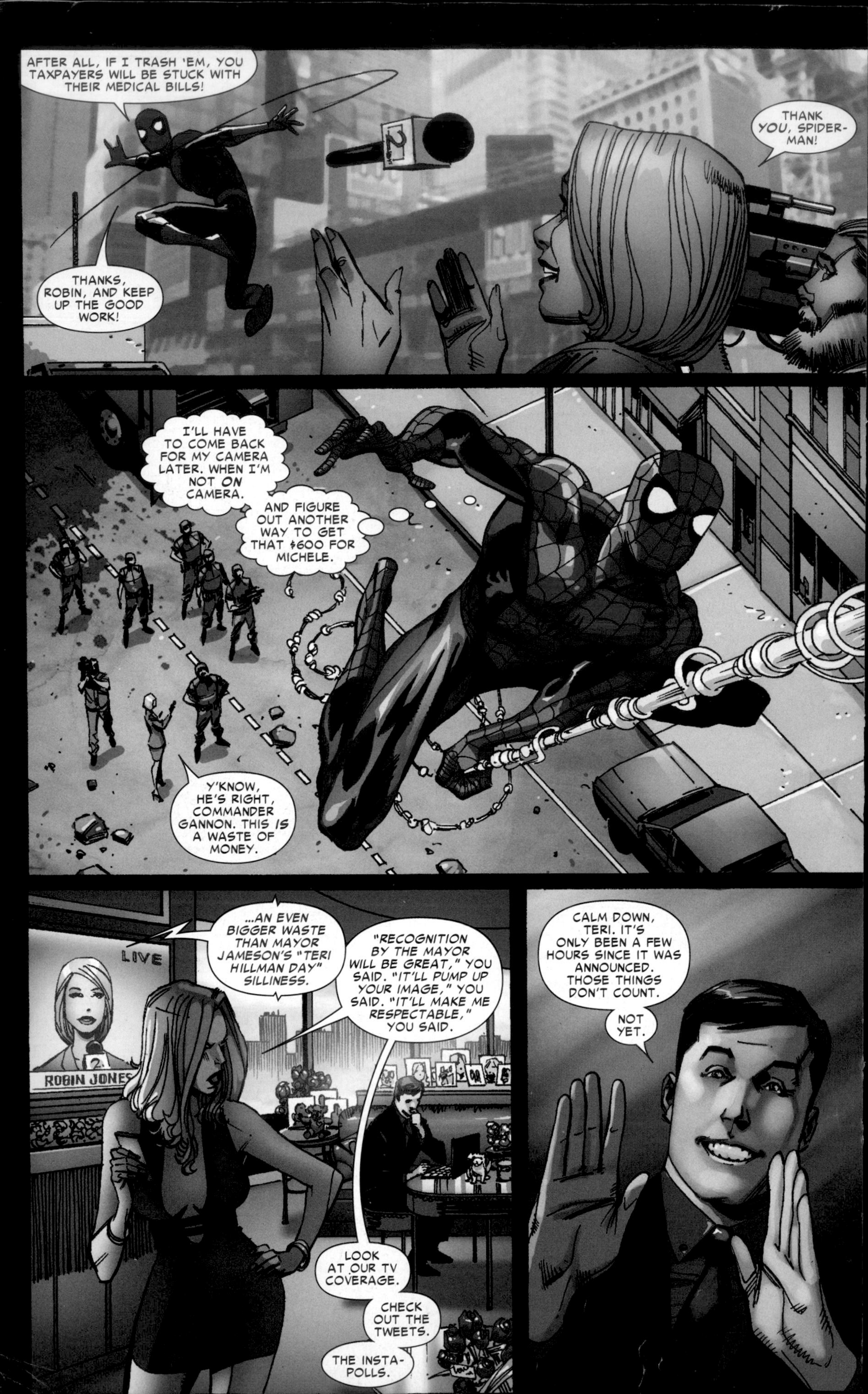
AFTER ALL, IF I TRASH 'EM, YOU TAXPAYERS WILL BE STUCK WITH THEIR MEDICAL BILLS!
THANKS, ROBIN, AND KEEP UP THE GOOD WORK!
THANK YOU, SPIDER-MAN!
I'LL HAVE TO COME BACK FOR MY CAMERA LATER. WHEN I'M NOT ON CAMERA.
AND FIGURE OUT ANOTHER WAY TO GET THAT $600 FOR MICHELE.
Y'KNOW, HE'S RIGHT, COMMANDER GANNON. THIS IS A WASTE OF MONEY.
LIVE
ROBIN JONES
...AN EVEN BIGGER WASTE THAN MAYOR JAMESON'S "TERI HILLMAN DAY" SILLINESS.
"RECOGNITION BY THE MAYOR WILL BE GREAT," YOU SAID. "IT'LL PUMP UP YOUR IMAGE," YOU SAID. "IT'LL MAKE ME RESPECTABLE," YOU SAID.
LOOK AT OUR TV COVERAGE.
CHECK OUT THE TWEETS.
THE INSTA-POLLS.
CALM DOWN, TERI. IT'S ONLY BEEN A FEW HOURS SINCE IT WAS ANNOUNCED. THOSE THINGS DON'T COUNT.
NOT YET.

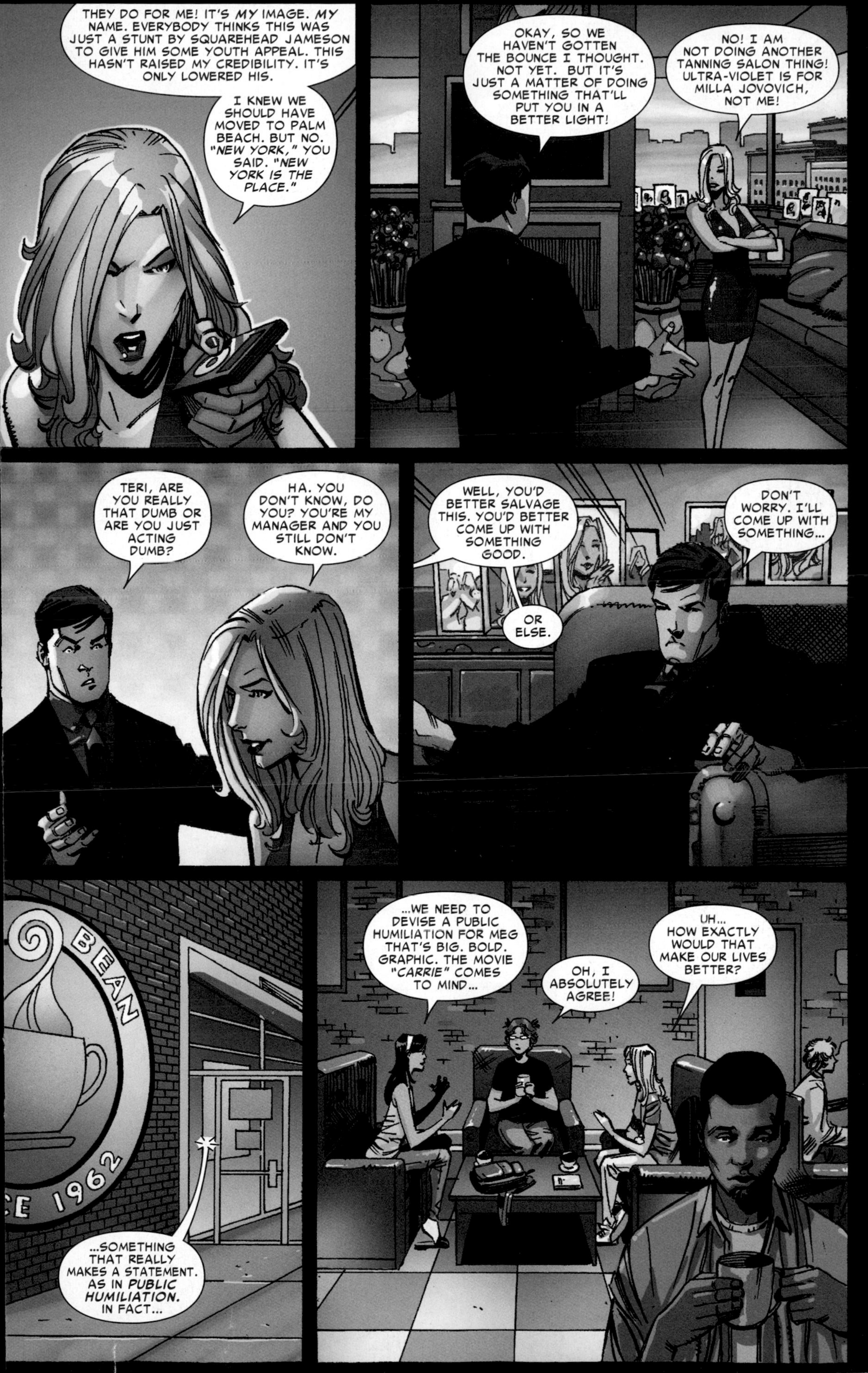
THEY DO FOR ME! IT'S *MY* IMAGE. *MY* NAME. EVERYBODY THINKS THIS WAS JUST A STUNT BY SQUAREHEAD JAMESON TO GIVE HIM SOME YOUTH APPEAL. THIS HASN'T RAISED MY CREDIBILITY. IT'S ONLY LOWERED HIS.
I KNEW WE SHOULD HAVE MOVED TO PALM BEACH. BUT NO. "*NEW YORK,*" YOU SAID. "*NEW YORK IS THE PLACE.*"
OKAY, SO WE HAVEN'T GOTTEN THE BOUNCE I THOUGHT. NOT YET. BUT IT'S JUST A MATTER OF DOING SOMETHING THAT'LL PUT YOU IN A BETTER LIGHT!
NO! I AM NOT DOING ANOTHER TANNING SALON THING! ULTRA-VIOLET IS FOR MILLA JOVOVICH, NOT ME!
TERI, ARE YOU REALLY THAT DUMB OR ARE YOU JUST ACTING DUMB?
HA. YOU DON'T KNOW, DO YOU? YOU'RE MY MANAGER AND YOU STILL DON'T KNOW.
WELL, YOU'D BETTER SALVAGE THIS. YOU'D BETTER COME UP WITH SOMETHING GOOD.
OR ELSE.
DON'T WORRY. I'LL COME UP WITH SOMETHING...
BEAN
CE 1962
...SOMETHING THAT REALLY MAKES A STATEMENT. AS IN *PUBLIC HUMILIATION.* IN FACT...
...WE NEED TO DEVISE A PUBLIC HUMILIATION FOR MEG THAT'S BIG. BOLD. GRAPHIC. THE MOVIE "*CARRIE*" COMES TO MIND...
OH, I ABSOLUTELY AGREE!
UH... HOW EXACTLY WOULD THAT MAKE OUR LIVES BETTER?

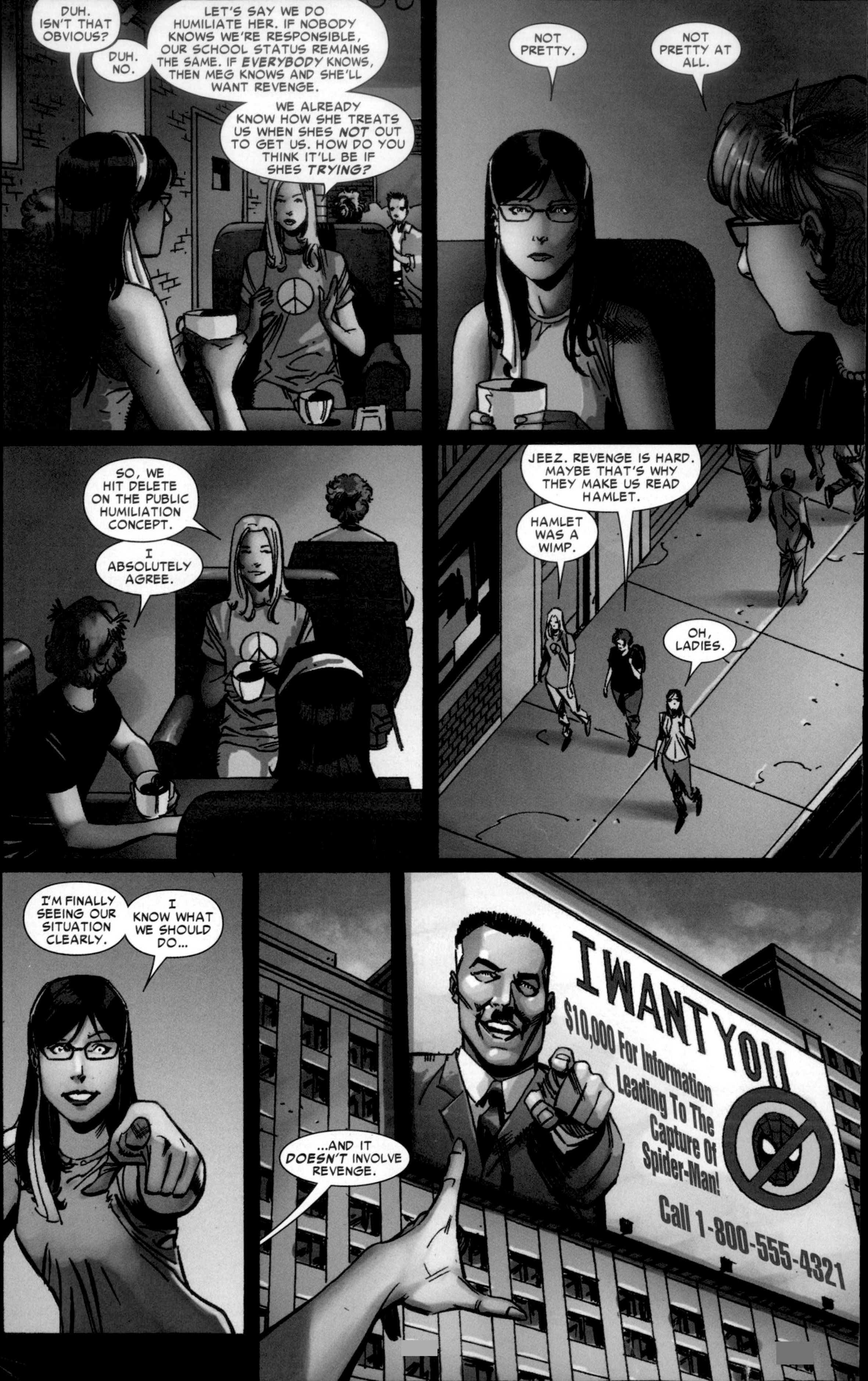

DUH. ISN'T THAT OBVIOUS?
DUH. NO.
LET'S SAY WE DO HUMILIATE HER. IF NOBODY KNOWS WE'RE RESPONSIBLE, OUR SCHOOL STATUS REMAINS THE SAME. IF *EVERYBODY* KNOWS, THEN MEG KNOWS AND SHE'LL WANT REVENGE.
WE ALREADY KNOW HOW SHE TREATS US WHEN SHES *NOT* OUT TO GET US. HOW DO YOU THINK IT'LL BE IF SHES *TRYING?*
NOT PRETTY.
NOT PRETTY AT ALL.
SO, WE HIT DELETE ON THE PUBLIC HUMILIATION CONCEPT.
I ABSOLUTELY AGREE.
JEEZ. REVENGE IS HARD. MAYBE THAT'S WHY THEY MAKE US READ HAMLET.
HAMLET WAS A WIMP.
OH, LADIES.
I'M FINALLY SEEING OUR SITUATION CLEARLY.
I KNOW WHAT WE SHOULD DO...
...AND IT *DOESN'T* INVOLVE REVENGE.
I WANT YOU
$10,000 For Information Leading To The Capture Of Spider-Man!
Call 1-800-555-4321

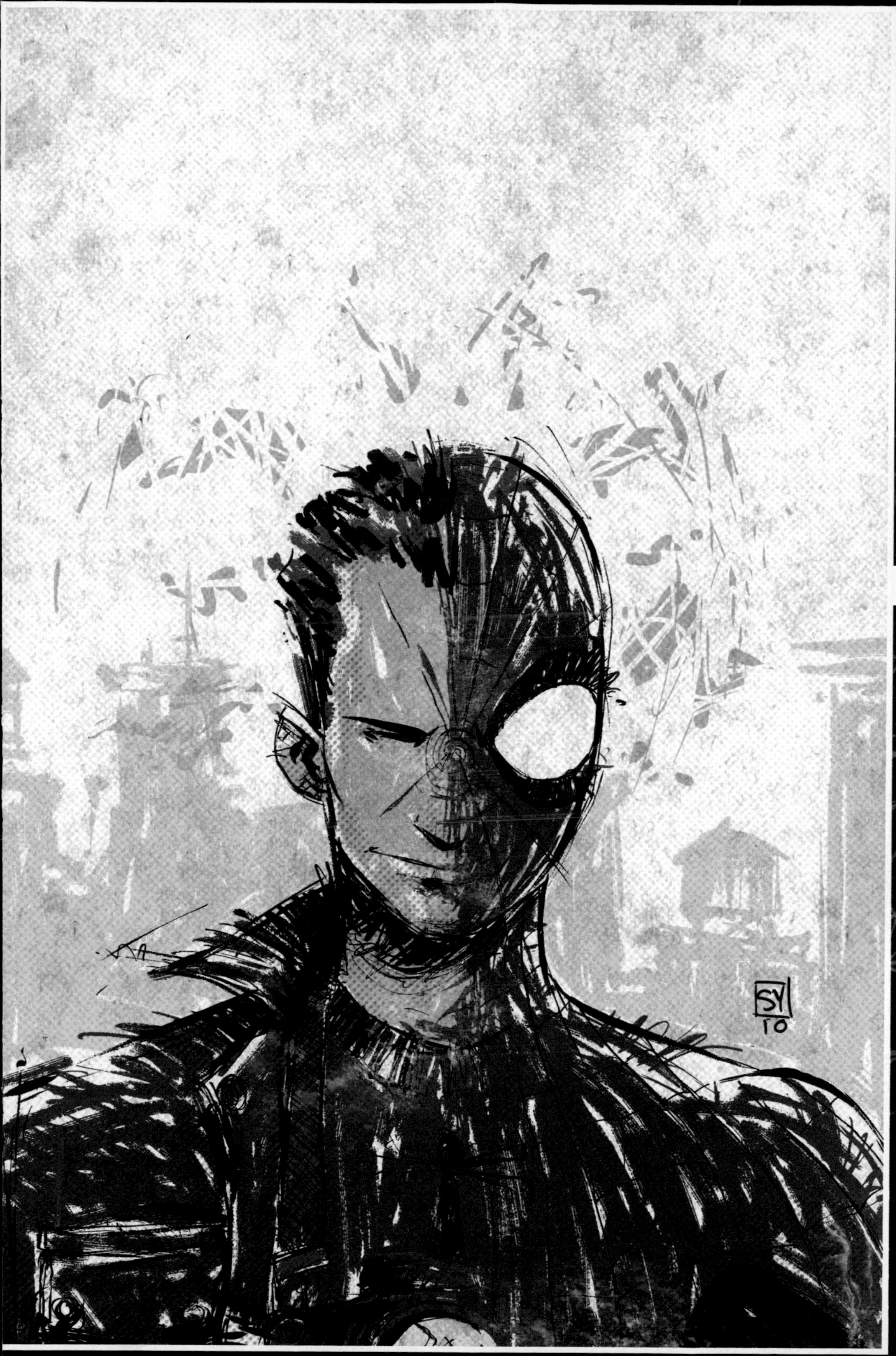
SY
'10

PETER PARKER #2

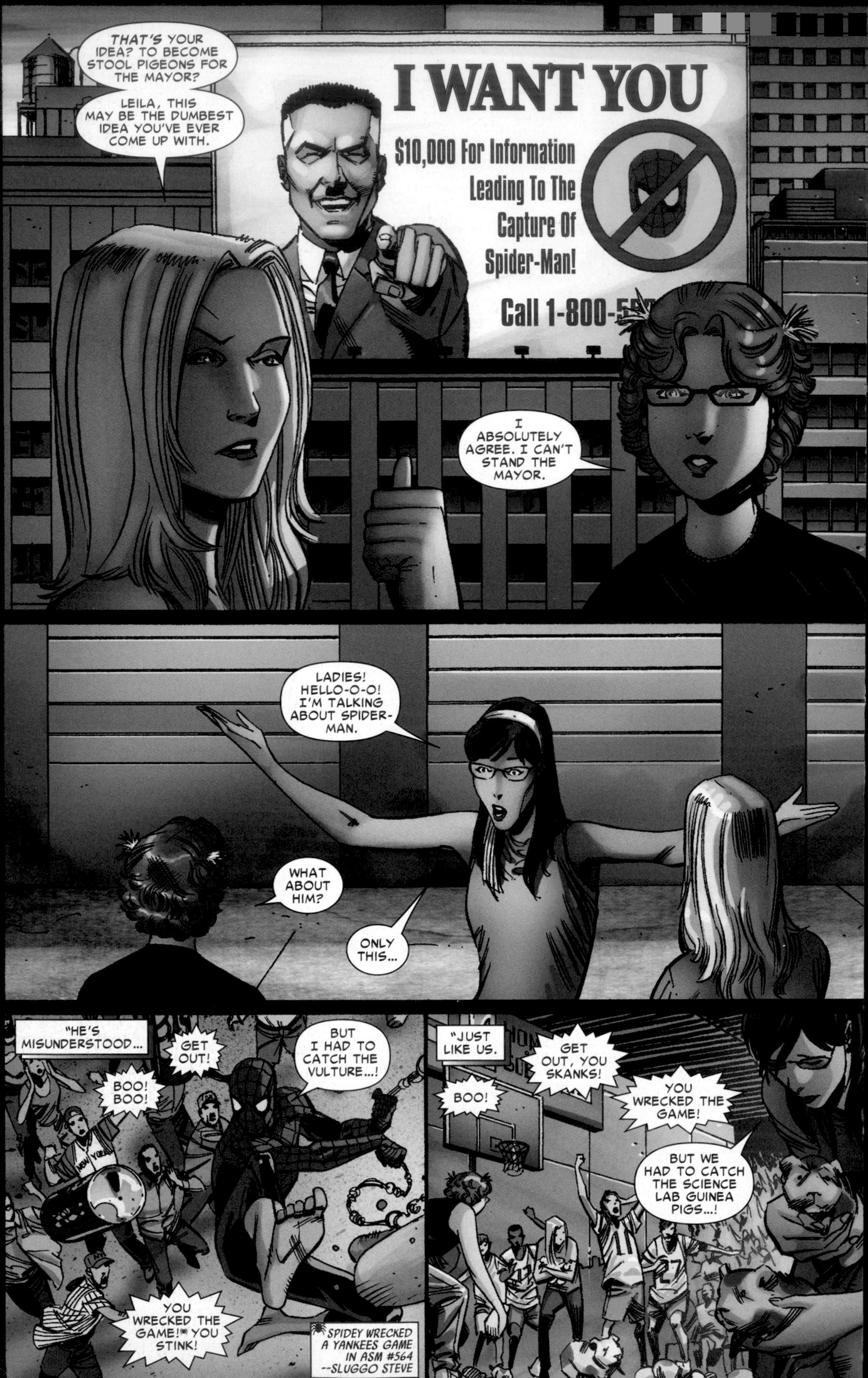
THAT'S YOUR IDEA? TO BECOME STOOL PIGEONS FOR THE MAYOR?
LEILA, THIS MAY BE THE DUMBEST IDEA YOU'VE EVER COME UP WITH.
I WANT YOU
$10,000 For Information Leading To The Capture Of Spider-Man!
Call 1-800-
I ABSOLUTELY AGREE. I CAN'T STAND THE MAYOR.
LADIES! HELLO-O-O! I'M TALKING ABOUT SPIDER-MAN.
WHAT ABOUT HIM?
ONLY THIS...
"HE'S MISUNDERSTOOD...
GET OUT!
BOO! BOO!
BUT I HAD TO CATCH THE VULTURE...!
YOU WRECKED THE GAME!* YOU STINK!
*SPIDEY WRECKED A YANKEES GAME IN ASM #564 --SLUGGO STEVE
"JUST LIKE US.
GET OUT, YOU SKANKS!
BOO!
YOU WRECKED THE GAME!
BUT WE HAD TO CATCH THE SCIENCE LAB GUINEA PIGS...!

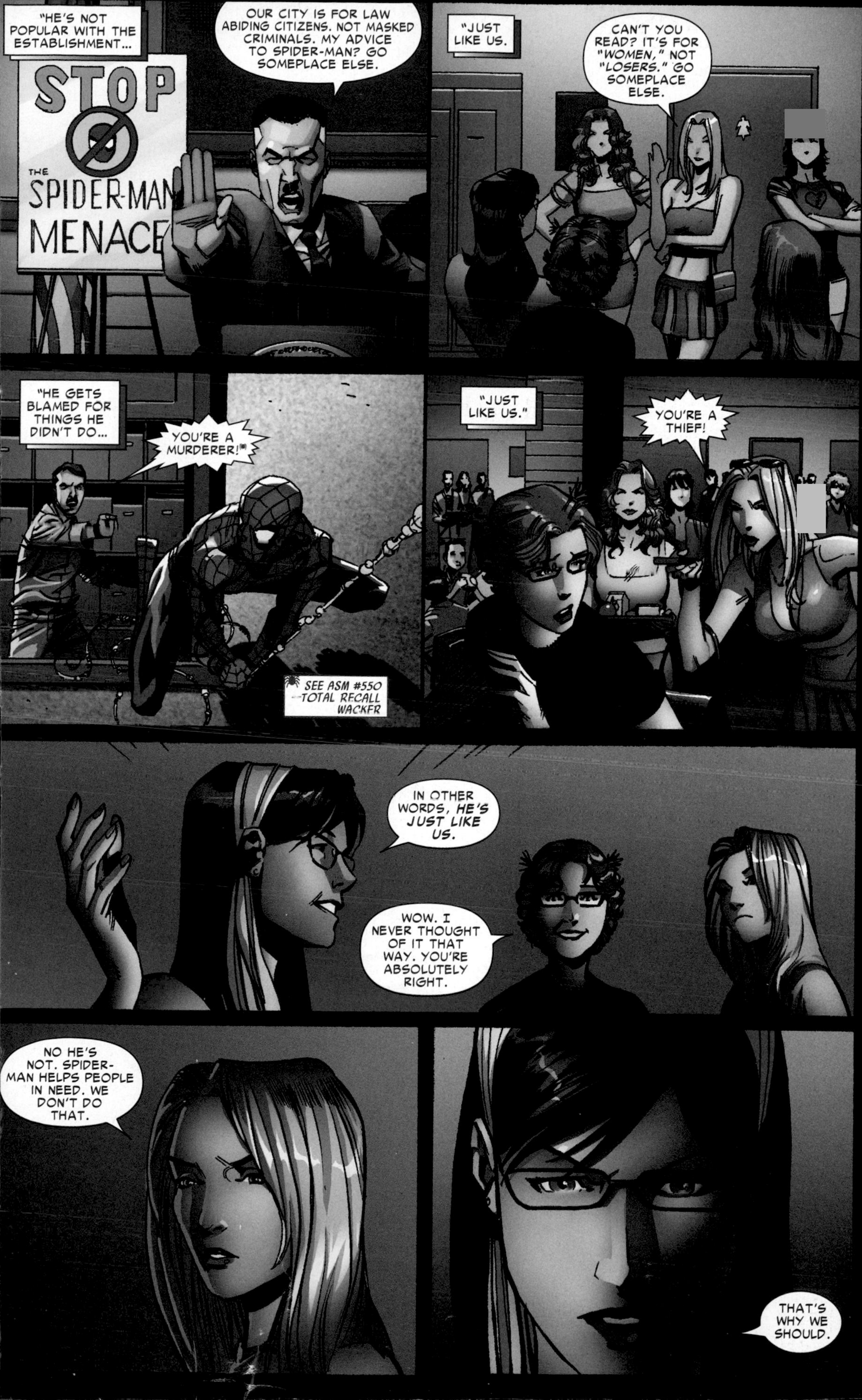
"HE'S NOT POPULAR WITH THE ESTABLISHMENT...
STOP THE SPIDER-MAN MENACE
OUR CITY IS FOR LAW ABIDING CITIZENS. NOT MASKED CRIMINALS. MY ADVICE TO SPIDER-MAN? GO SOMEPLACE ELSE.
"JUST LIKE US.
CAN'T YOU READ? IT'S FOR "*WOMEN*," NOT "*LOSERS*." GO SOMEPLACE ELSE.
"HE GETS BLAMED FOR THINGS HE DIDN'T DO...
YOU'RE A MURDERER!*
*SEE ASM #550 —TOTAL RECALL WACKER
"JUST LIKE US."
YOU'RE A THIEF!
IN OTHER WORDS, ***HE'S JUST LIKE US.***
WOW. I NEVER THOUGHT OF IT THAT WAY. YOU'RE ABSOLUTELY RIGHT.
NO HE'S NOT. SPIDER-MAN HELPS PEOPLE IN NEED. WE DON'T DO THAT.
THAT'S WHY WE SHOULD.

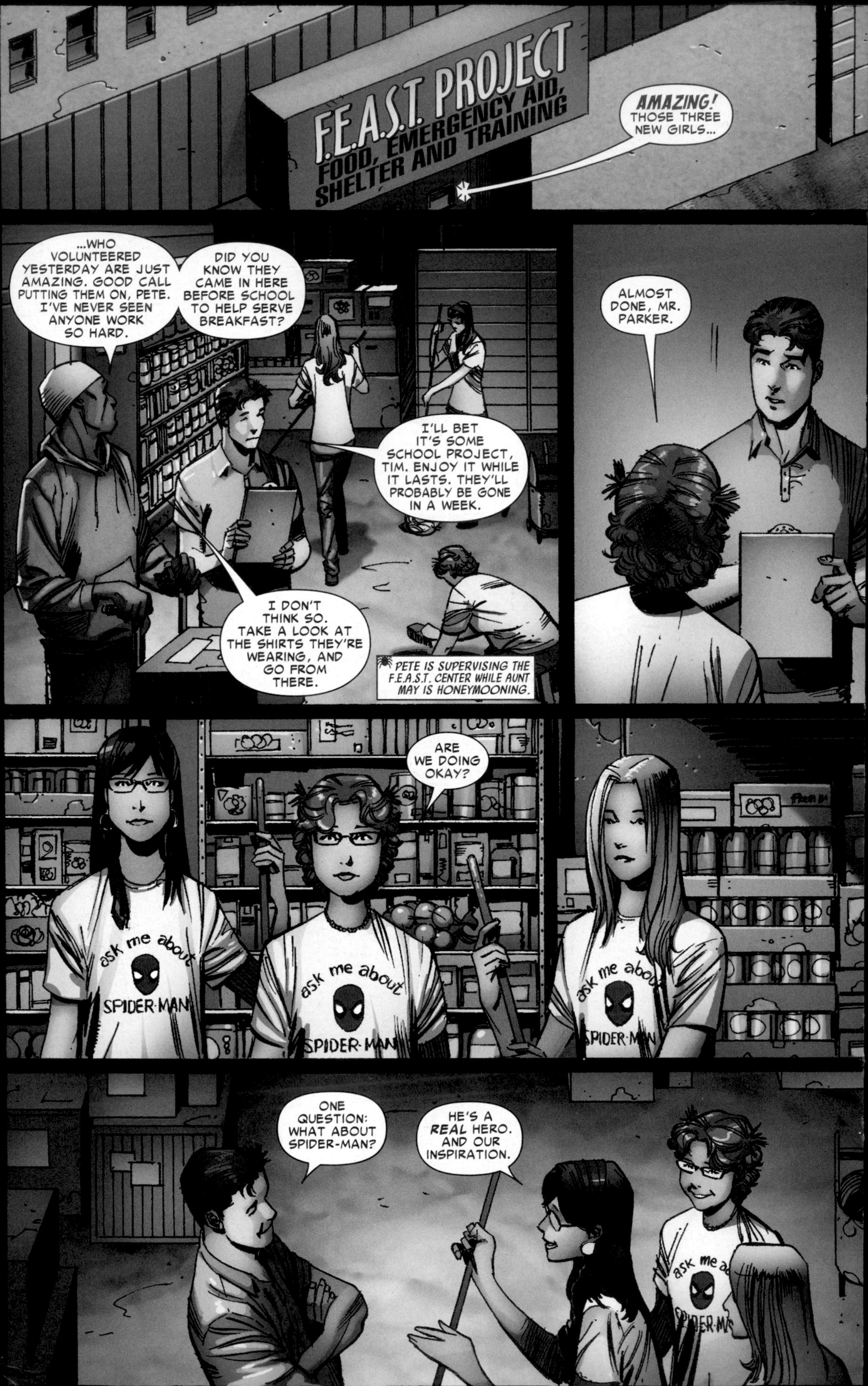
F.E.A.S.T. PROJECT
FOOD, EMERGENCY AID, SHELTER AND TRAINING
AMAZING! THOSE THREE NEW GIRLS...
...WHO VOLUNTEERED YESTERDAY ARE JUST AMAZING. GOOD CALL PUTTING THEM ON, PETE. I'VE NEVER SEEN ANYONE WORK SO HARD.
DID YOU KNOW THEY CAME IN HERE BEFORE SCHOOL TO HELP SERVE BREAKFAST?
I'LL BET IT'S SOME SCHOOL PROJECT, TIM. ENJOY IT WHILE IT LASTS. THEY'LL PROBABLY BE GONE IN A WEEK.
I DON'T THINK SO. TAKE A LOOK AT THE SHIRTS THEY'RE WEARING, AND GO FROM THERE.
PETE IS SUPERVISING THE F.E.A.S.T. CENTER WHILE AUNT MAY IS HONEYMOONING.
ALMOST DONE, MR. PARKER.
ask me about SPIDER-MAN
ARE WE DOING OKAY?
ask me about SPIDER-MAN
ask me about SPIDER-MAN
ONE QUESTION: WHAT ABOUT SPIDER-MAN?
HE'S A REAL HERO. AND OUR INSPIRATION.

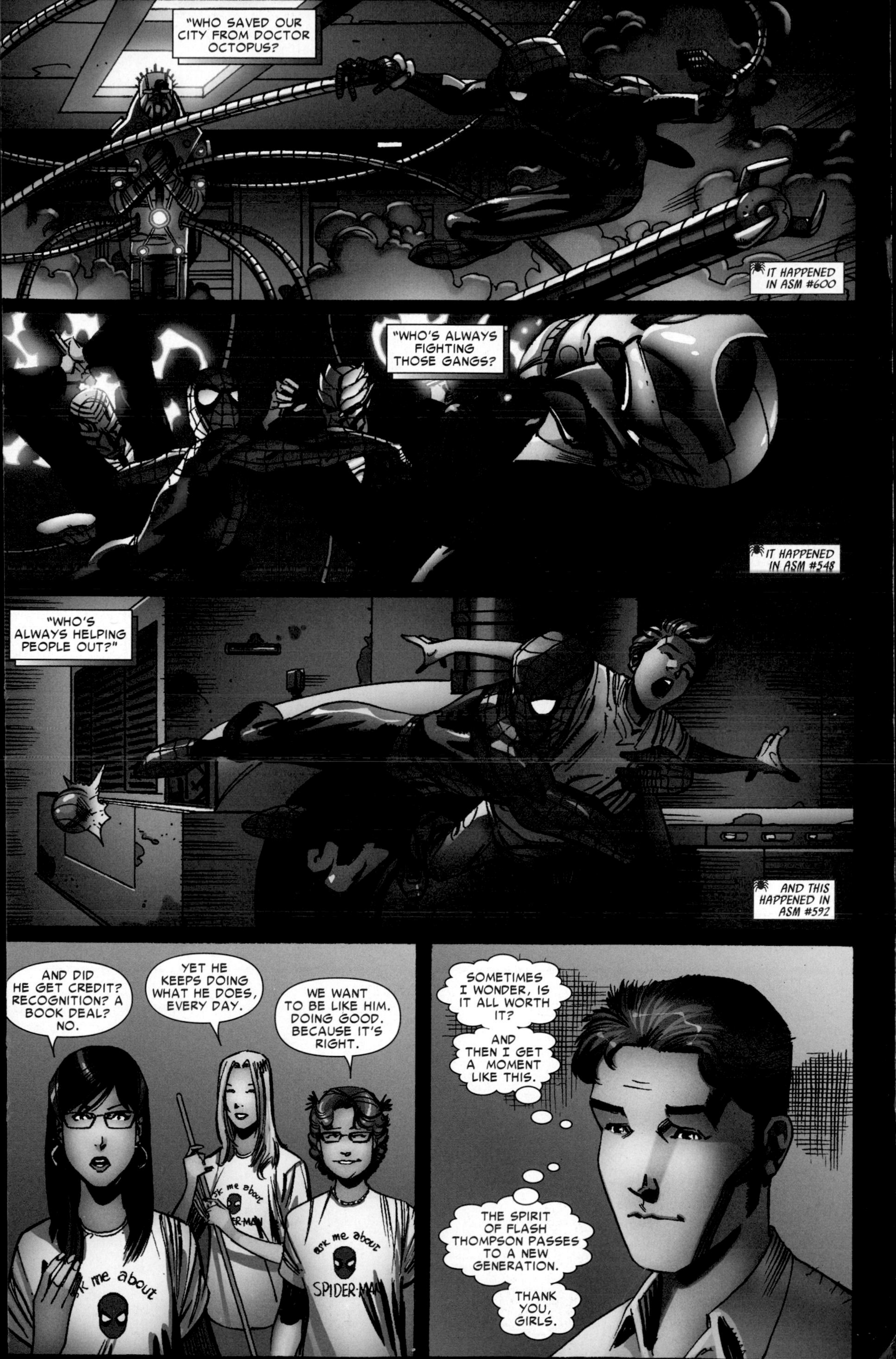
"WHO SAVED OUR CITY FROM DOCTOR OCTOPUS?
IT HAPPENED IN ASM #600
"WHO'S ALWAYS FIGHTING THOSE GANGS?
IT HAPPENED IN ASM #548
"WHO'S ALWAYS HELPING PEOPLE OUT?"
AND THIS HAPPENED IN ASM #592
AND DID HE GET CREDIT? RECOGNITION? A BOOK DEAL? NO.
YET HE KEEPS DOING WHAT HE DOES, EVERY DAY.
WE WANT TO BE LIKE HIM. DOING GOOD. BECAUSE IT'S RIGHT.
ask me about SPIDER-MAN
SOMETIMES I WONDER, IS IT ALL WORTH IT?
AND THEN I GET A MOMENT LIKE THIS.
THE SPIRIT OF FLASH THOMPSON PASSES TO A NEW GENERATION.
THANK YOU, GIRLS.

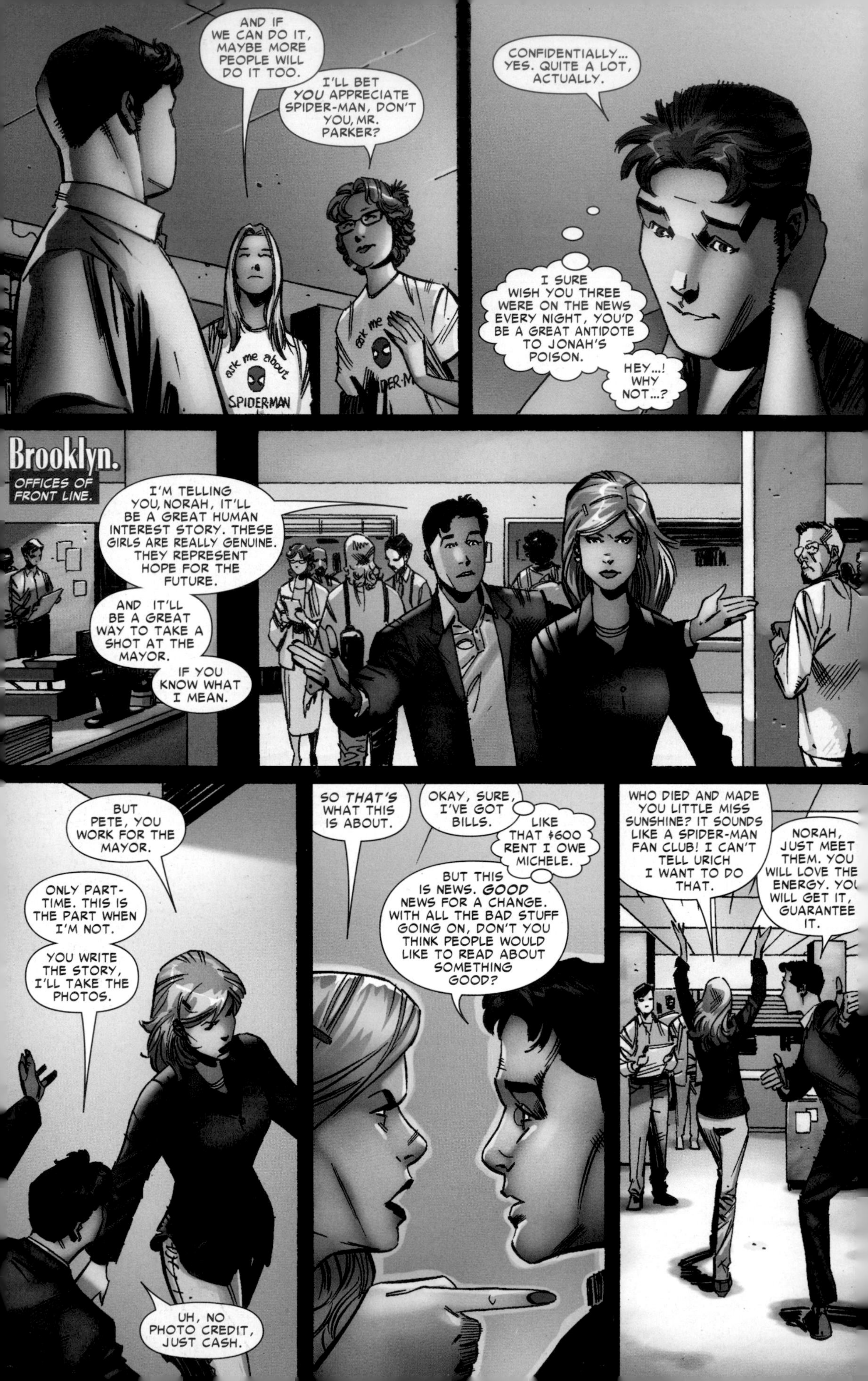
AND IF WE CAN DO IT, MAYBE MORE PEOPLE WILL DO IT TOO.
I'LL BET YOU APPRECIATE SPIDER-MAN, DON'T YOU, MR. PARKER?
ask me about SPIDER-MAN
CONFIDENTIALLY... YES. QUITE A LOT, ACTUALLY.
I SURE WISH YOU THREE WERE ON THE NEWS EVERY NIGHT, YOU'D BE A GREAT ANTIDOTE TO JONAH'S POISON.
HEY...! WHY NOT...?
Brooklyn.
OFFICES OF FRONT LINE.
I'M TELLING YOU, NORAH, IT'LL BE A GREAT HUMAN INTEREST STORY. THESE GIRLS ARE REALLY GENUINE. THEY REPRESENT HOPE FOR THE FUTURE.
AND IT'LL BE A GREAT WAY TO TAKE A SHOT AT THE MAYOR.
IF YOU KNOW WHAT I MEAN.
BUT PETE, YOU WORK FOR THE MAYOR.
ONLY PART-TIME. THIS IS THE PART WHEN I'M NOT.
YOU WRITE THE STORY, I'LL TAKE THE PHOTOS.
UH, NO PHOTO CREDIT, JUST CASH.
SO THAT'S WHAT THIS IS ABOUT.
OKAY, SURE, I'VE GOT BILLS.
LIKE THAT $600 RENT I OWE MICHELE.
BUT THIS IS NEWS. GOOD NEWS FOR A CHANGE. WITH ALL THE BAD STUFF GOING ON, DON'T YOU THINK PEOPLE WOULD LIKE TO READ ABOUT SOMETHING GOOD?
WHO DIED AND MADE YOU LITTLE MISS SUNSHINE? IT SOUNDS LIKE A SPIDER-MAN FAN CLUB! I CAN'T TELL URICH I WANT TO DO THAT.
NORAH, JUST MEET THEM. YOU WILL LOVE THE ENERGY. YOU WILL GET IT, GUARANTEE IT.

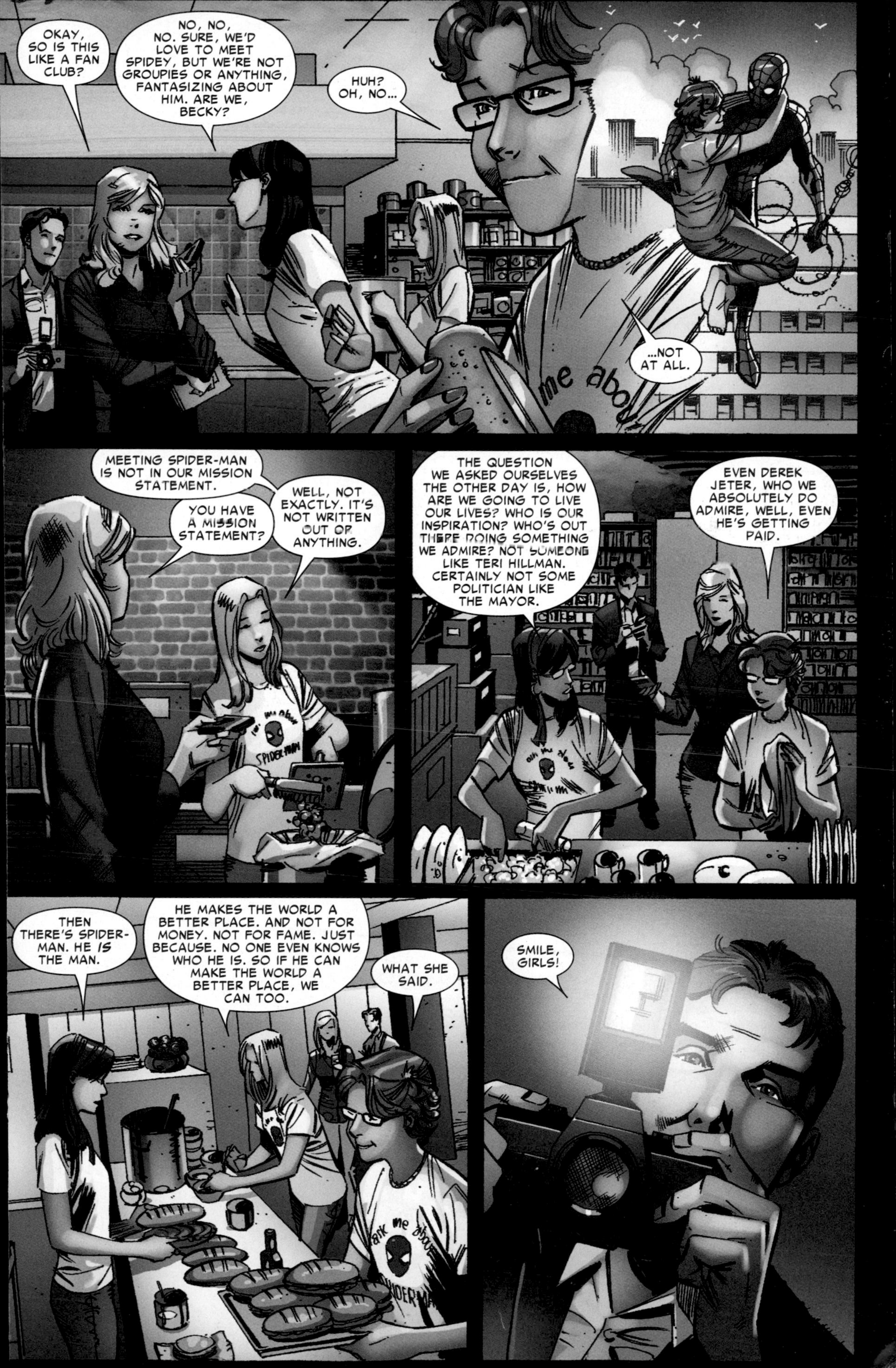
OKAY, SO IS THIS LIKE A FAN CLUB?
NO, NO, NO. SURE, WE'D LOVE TO MEET SPIDEY, BUT WE'RE NOT GROUPIES OR ANYTHING, FANTASIZING ABOUT HIM. ARE WE, BECKY?
HUH? OH, NO...
...NOT AT ALL.
MEETING SPIDER-MAN IS NOT IN OUR MISSION STATEMENT.
YOU HAVE A MISSION STATEMENT?
WELL, NOT EXACTLY. IT'S NOT WRITTEN OUT OR ANYTHING.
THE QUESTION WE ASKED OURSELVES THE OTHER DAY IS, HOW ARE WE GOING TO LIVE OUR LIVES? WHO IS OUR INSPIRATION? WHO'S OUT THERE DOING SOMETHING WE ADMIRE? NOT SOMEONE LIKE TERI HILLMAN. CERTAINLY NOT SOME POLITICIAN LIKE THE MAYOR.
EVEN DEREK JETER, WHO WE ABSOLUTELY DO ADMIRE, WELL, EVEN HE'S GETTING PAID.
THEN THERE'S SPIDER-MAN. HE *IS* THE MAN.
HE MAKES THE WORLD A BETTER PLACE. AND NOT FOR MONEY. NOT FOR FAME. JUST BECAUSE. NO ONE EVEN KNOWS WHO HE IS. SO IF HE CAN MAKE THE WORLD A BETTER PLACE, WE CAN TOO.
WHAT SHE SAID.
SMILE, GIRLS!

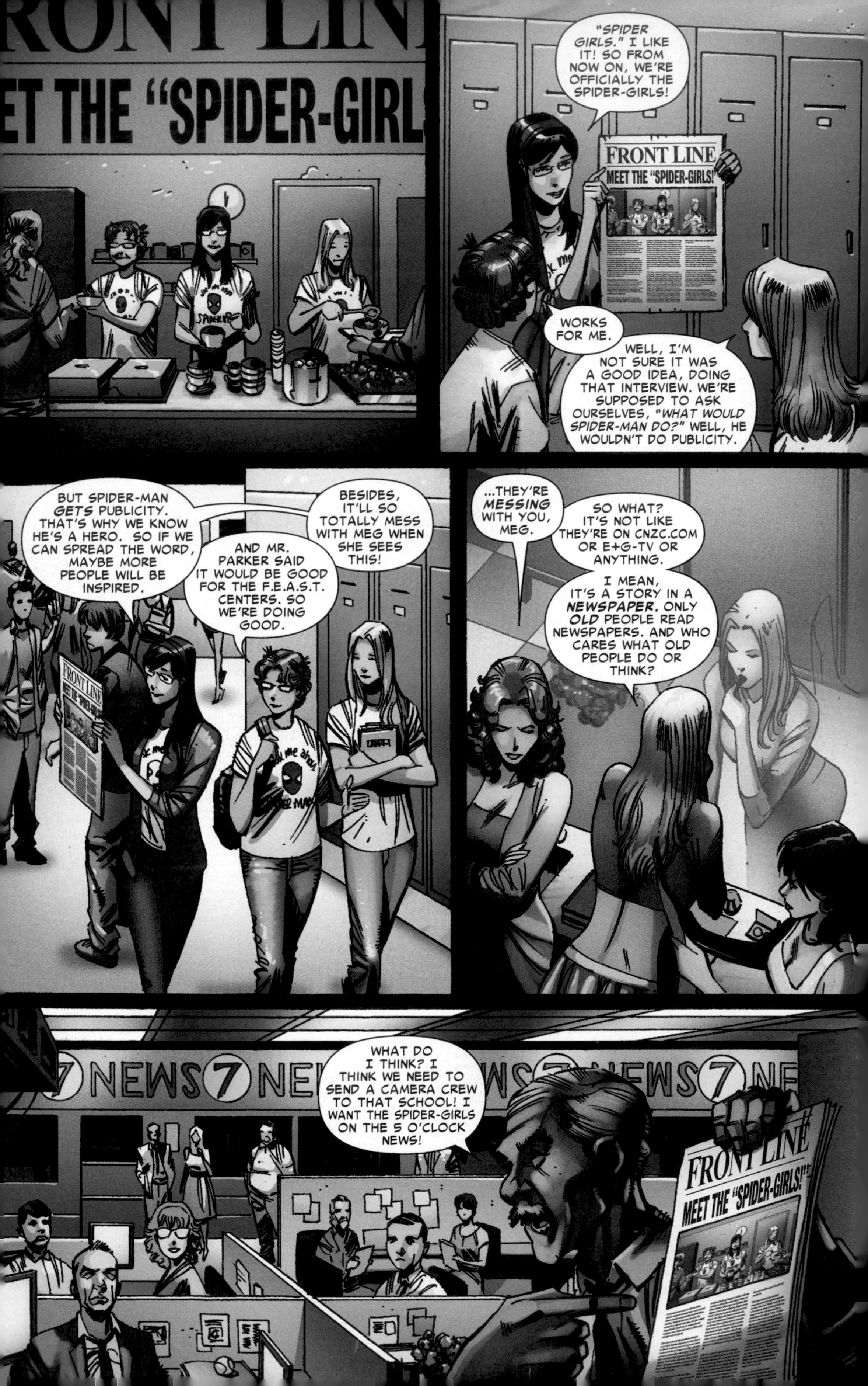
FRONT LINE
ET THE "SPIDER-GIRLS
"SPIDER GIRLS." I LIKE IT! SO FROM NOW ON, WE'RE OFFICIALLY THE SPIDER-GIRLS!
FRONT LINE
MEET THE "SPIDER-GIRLS!"
WORKS FOR ME.
WELL, I'M NOT SURE IT WAS A GOOD IDEA, DOING THAT INTERVIEW. WE'RE SUPPOSED TO ASK OURSELVES, "WHAT WOULD SPIDER-MAN DO?" WELL, HE WOULDN'T DO PUBLICITY.
BUT SPIDER-MAN *GETS* PUBLICITY. THAT'S WHY WE KNOW HE'S A HERO. SO IF WE CAN SPREAD THE WORD, MAYBE MORE PEOPLE WILL BE INSPIRED.
BESIDES, IT'LL SO TOTALLY MESS WITH MEG WHEN SHE SEES THIS!
AND MR. PARKER SAID IT WOULD BE GOOD FOR THE F.E.A.S.T. CENTERS. SO WE'RE DOING GOOD.
FRONT LINE
...THEY'RE *MESSING* WITH YOU, MEG.
SO WHAT? IT'S NOT LIKE THEY'RE ON CNZC.COM OR E+G-TV OR ANYTHING.
I MEAN, IT'S A STORY IN A *NEWSPAPER.* ONLY *OLD* PEOPLE READ NEWSPAPERS. AND WHO CARES WHAT OLD PEOPLE DO OR THINK?
7 NEWS 7 NEWS 7 NEWS 7 NE
WHAT DO I THINK? I THINK WE NEED TO SEND A CAMERA CREW TO THAT SCHOOL! I WANT THE SPIDER-GIRLS ON THE 5 O'CLOCK NEWS!
FRONT LINE
MEET THE "SPIDER-GIRLS!"

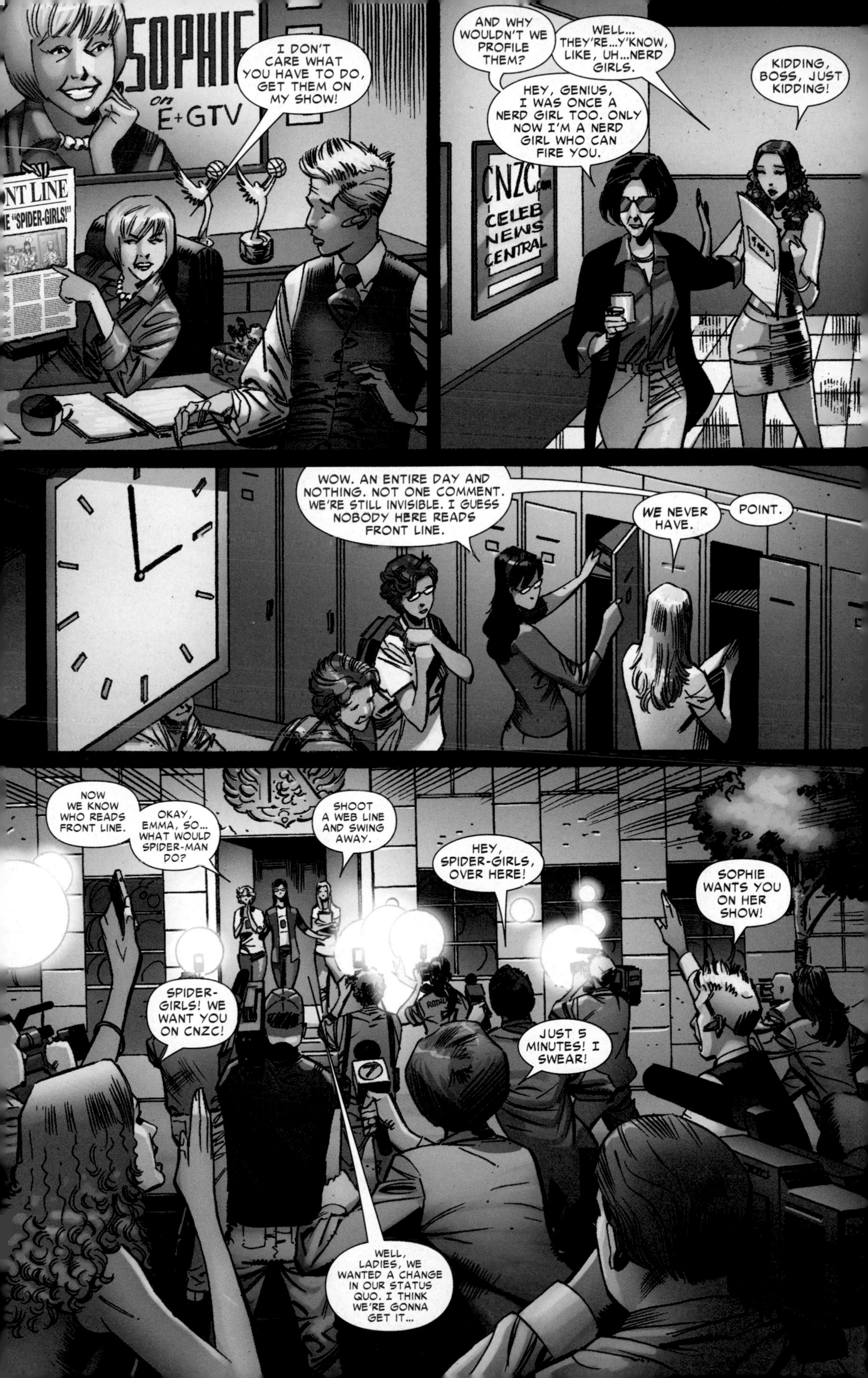
SOPHIE on E+GTV
NT LINE
E "SPIDER-GIRLS!"
I DON'T CARE WHAT YOU HAVE TO DO, GET THEM ON MY SHOW!
AND WHY WOULDN'T WE PROFILE THEM?
WELL... THEY'RE...Y'KNOW, LIKE, UH...NERD GIRLS.
HEY, GENIUS, I WAS ONCE A NERD GIRL TOO. ONLY NOW I'M A NERD GIRL WHO CAN FIRE YOU.
KIDDING, BOSS, JUST KIDDING!
CNZC.com CELEB NEWS CENTRAL
WOW. AN ENTIRE DAY AND NOTHING. NOT ONE COMMENT. WE'RE STILL INVISIBLE. I GUESS NOBODY HERE READS FRONT LINE.
WE NEVER HAVE.
POINT.
NOW WE KNOW WHO READS FRONT LINE.
OKAY, EMMA, SO... WHAT WOULD SPIDER-MAN DO?
SHOOT A WEB LINE AND SWING AWAY.
HEY, SPIDER-GIRLS, OVER HERE!
SOPHIE WANTS YOU ON HER SHOW!
SPIDER-GIRLS! WE WANT YOU ON CNZC!
JUST 5 MINUTES! I SWEAR!
WELL, LADIES, WE WANTED A CHANGE IN OUR STATUS QUO. I THINK WE'RE GONNA GET IT...

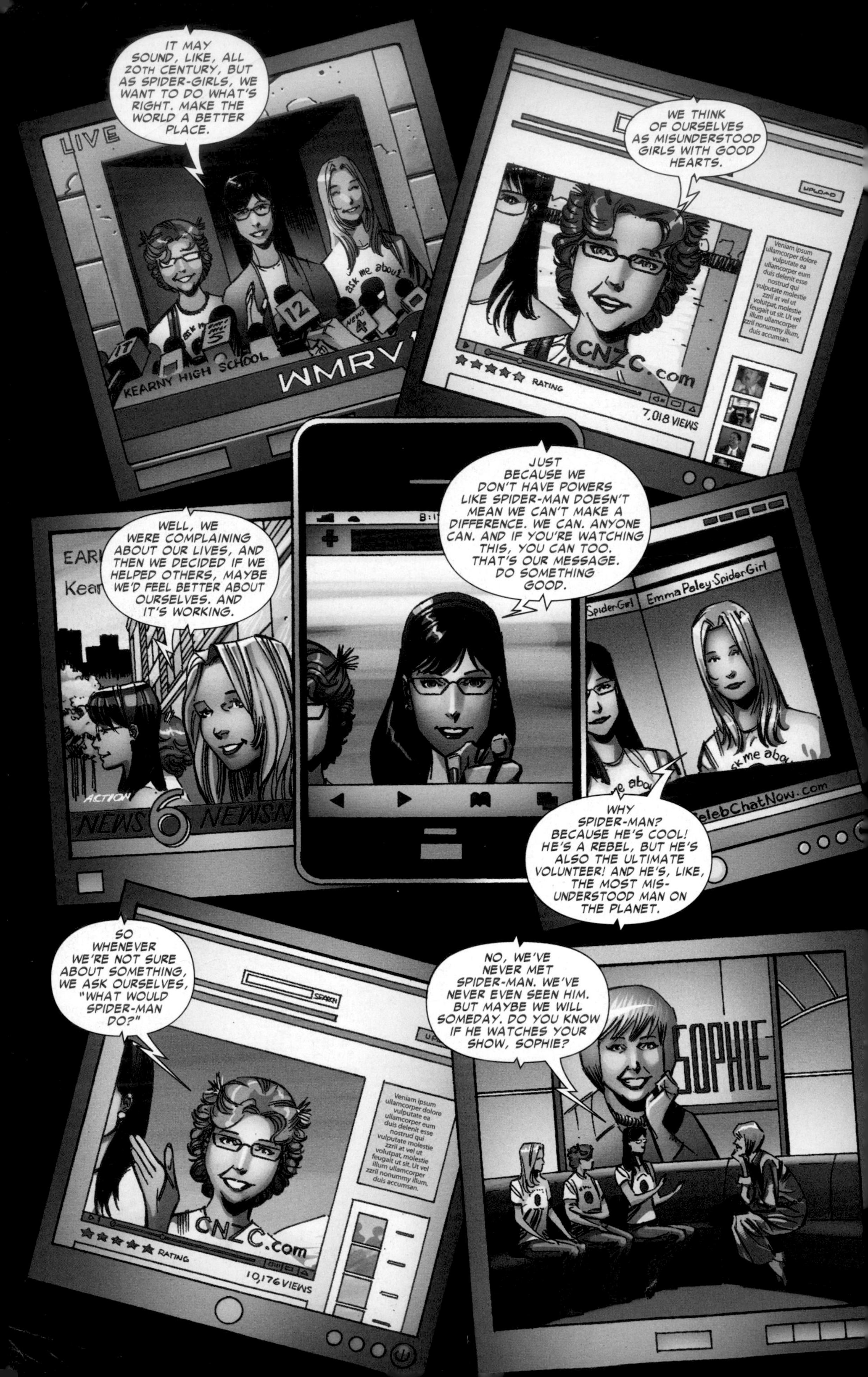
LIVE
IT MAY SOUND, LIKE, ALL 20TH CENTURY, BUT AS SPIDER-GIRLS, WE WANT TO DO WHAT'S RIGHT. MAKE THE WORLD A BETTER PLACE.
KEARNY HIGH SCHOOL
WMRV
WE THINK OF OURSELVES AS MISUNDERSTOOD GIRLS WITH GOOD HEARTS.
UPLOAD
CNZC.com
RATING
7,018 VIEWS
WELL, WE WERE COMPLAINING ABOUT OUR LIVES, AND THEN WE DECIDED IF WE HELPED OTHERS, MAYBE WE'D FEEL BETTER ABOUT OURSELVES. AND IT'S WORKING.
NEWS 6 NEWS
JUST BECAUSE WE DON'T HAVE POWERS LIKE SPIDER-MAN DOESN'T MEAN WE CAN'T MAKE A DIFFERENCE. WE CAN. ANYONE CAN. AND IF YOU'RE WATCHING THIS, YOU CAN TOO. THAT'S OUR MESSAGE. DO SOMETHING GOOD.
Spider-Girl
Emma Paley · Spider-Girl
WHY SPIDER-MAN? BECAUSE HE'S COOL! HE'S A REBEL, BUT HE'S ALSO THE ULTIMATE VOLUNTEER! AND HE'S, LIKE, THE MOST MIS-UNDERSTOOD MAN ON THE PLANET.
SO WHENEVER WE'RE NOT SURE ABOUT SOMETHING, WE ASK OURSELVES, "WHAT WOULD SPIDER-MAN DO?"
SEARCH
CNZC.com
RATING
10,176 VIEWS
NO, WE'VE NEVER MET SPIDER-MAN. WE'VE NEVER EVEN SEEN HIM. BUT MAYBE WE WILL SOMEDAY. DO YOU KNOW IF HE WATCHES YOUR SHOW, SOPHIE?
SOPHIE

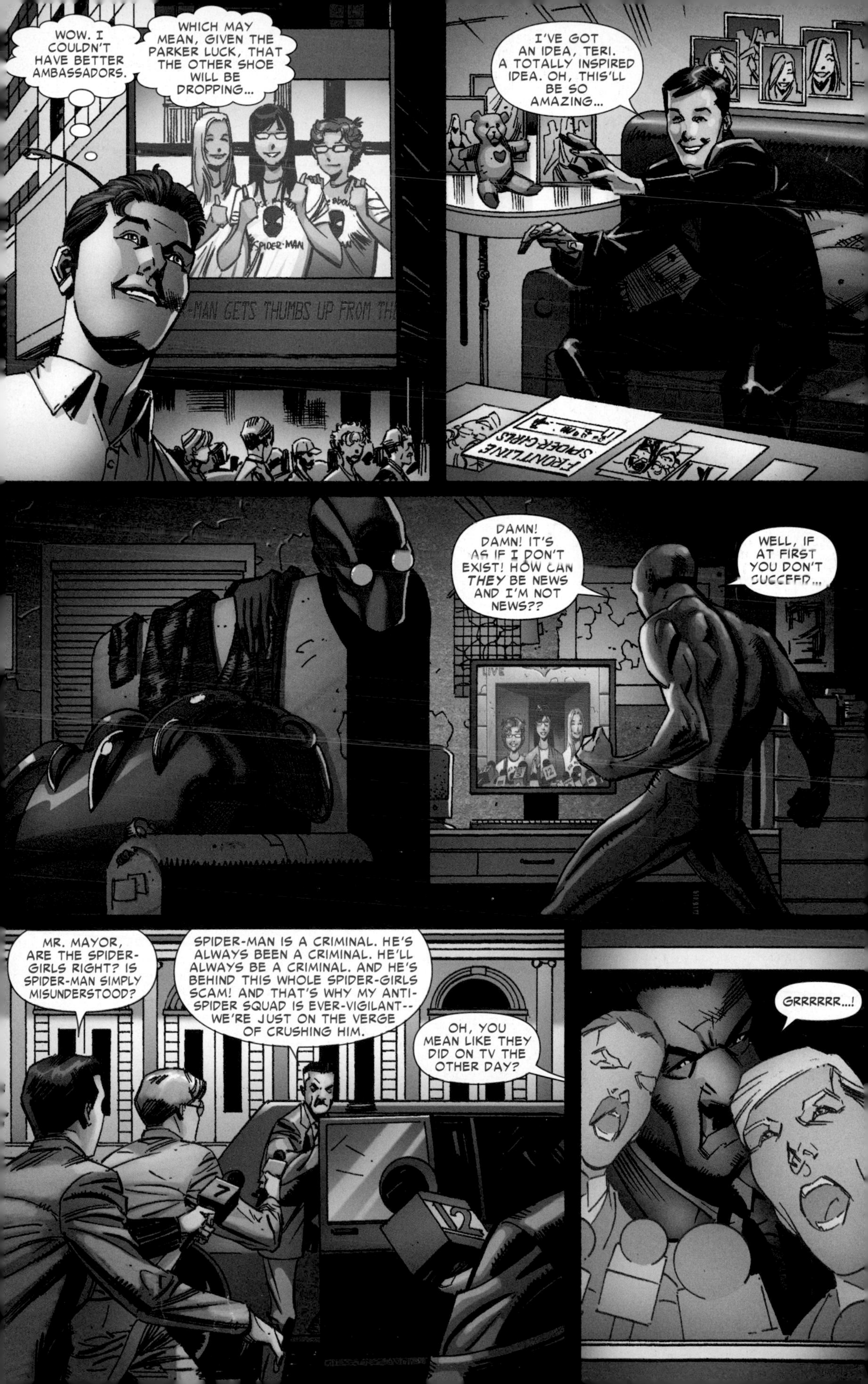
WOW. I COULDN'T HAVE BETTER AMBASSADORS.
WHICH MAY MEAN, GIVEN THE PARKER LUCK, THAT THE OTHER SHOE WILL BE DROPPING...
SPIDER-MAN
-MAN GETS THUMBS UP FROM TH
I'VE GOT AN IDEA, TERI. A TOTALLY INSPIRED IDEA. OH, THIS'LL BE SO AMAZING...
FRONTLINE
SPIDER-GIRLS
DAMN! DAMN! IT'S AS IF I DON'T EXIST! HOW CAN *THEY* BE NEWS AND I'M NOT NEWS??
WELL, IF AT FIRST YOU DON'T SUCCEED...
LIVE
MR. MAYOR, ARE THE SPIDER-GIRLS RIGHT? IS SPIDER-MAN SIMPLY MISUNDERSTOOD?
SPIDER-MAN IS A CRIMINAL. HE'S ALWAYS BEEN A CRIMINAL. HE'LL ALWAYS BE A CRIMINAL. AND HE'S BEHIND THIS WHOLE SPIDER-GIRLS SCAM! AND THAT'S WHY MY ANTI-SPIDER SQUAD IS EVER-VIGILANT--WE'RE JUST ON THE VERGE OF CRUSHING HIM.
OH, YOU MEAN LIKE THEY DID ON TV THE OTHER DAY?
GRRRRRR...!

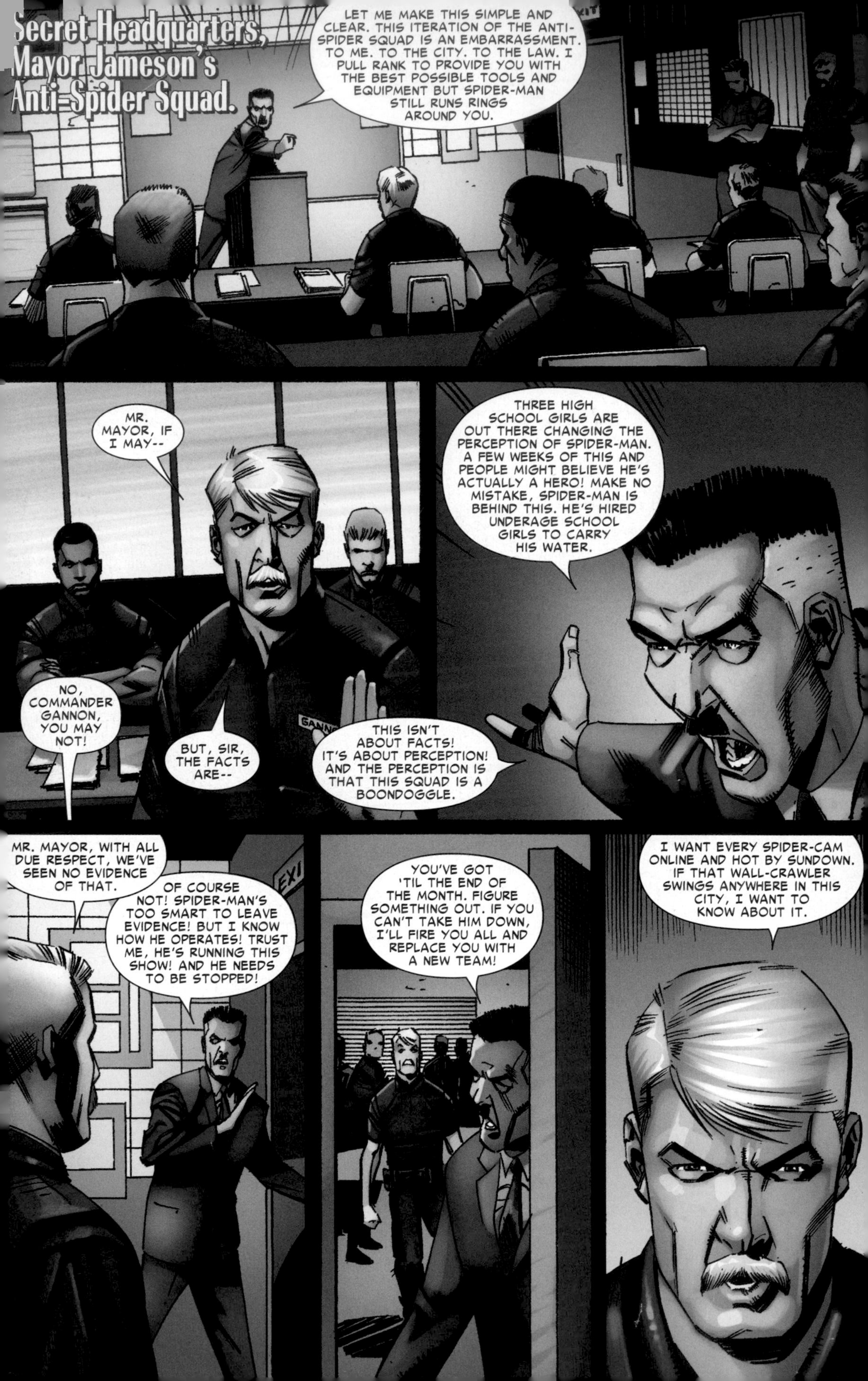
Secret Headquarters, Mayor Jameson's Anti-Spider Squad.
LET ME MAKE THIS SIMPLE AND CLEAR. THIS ITERATION OF THE ANTI-SPIDER SQUAD IS AN EMBARRASSMENT. TO ME. TO THE CITY. TO THE LAW. I PULL RANK TO PROVIDE YOU WITH THE BEST POSSIBLE TOOLS AND EQUIPMENT BUT SPIDER-MAN STILL RUNS RINGS AROUND YOU.
EXIT
MR. MAYOR, IF I MAY--
NO, COMMANDER GANNON, YOU MAY NOT!
BUT, SIR, THE FACTS ARE--
GANNON
THREE HIGH SCHOOL GIRLS ARE OUT THERE CHANGING THE PERCEPTION OF SPIDER-MAN. A FEW WEEKS OF THIS AND PEOPLE MIGHT BELIEVE HE'S ACTUALLY A HERO! MAKE NO MISTAKE, SPIDER-MAN IS BEHIND THIS. HE'S HIRED UNDERAGE SCHOOL GIRLS TO CARRY HIS WATER.
THIS ISN'T ABOUT FACTS! IT'S ABOUT PERCEPTION! AND THE PERCEPTION IS THAT THIS SQUAD IS A BOONDOGGLE.
MR. MAYOR, WITH ALL DUE RESPECT, WE'VE SEEN NO EVIDENCE OF THAT.
OF COURSE NOT! SPIDER-MAN'S TOO SMART TO LEAVE EVIDENCE! BUT I KNOW HOW HE OPERATES! TRUST ME, HE'S RUNNING THIS SHOW! AND HE NEEDS TO BE STOPPED!
YOU'VE GOT 'TIL THE END OF THE MONTH. FIGURE SOMETHING OUT. IF YOU CAN'T TAKE HIM DOWN, I'LL FIRE YOU ALL AND REPLACE YOU WITH A NEW TEAM!
I WANT EVERY SPIDER-CAM ONLINE AND HOT BY SUNDOWN. IF THAT WALL-CRAWLER SWINGS ANYWHERE IN THIS CITY, I WANT TO KNOW ABOUT IT.

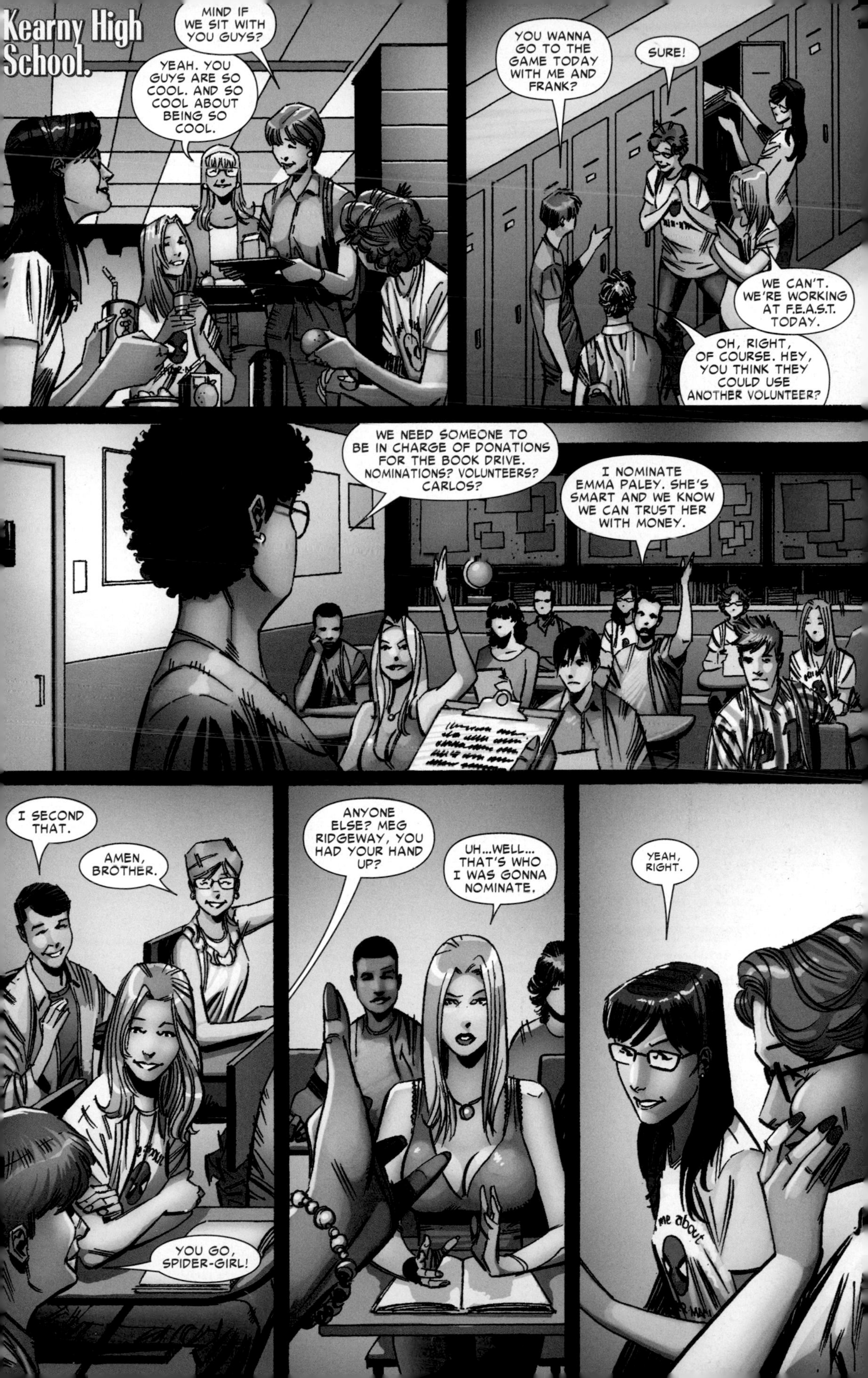
Kearny High School.
MIND IF WE SIT WITH YOU GUYS?
YEAH. YOU GUYS ARE SO COOL. AND SO COOL ABOUT BEING SO COOL.
YOU WANNA GO TO THE GAME TODAY WITH ME AND FRANK?
SURE!
WE CAN'T. WE'RE WORKING AT F.E.A.S.T. TODAY.
OH, RIGHT, OF COURSE. HEY, YOU THINK THEY COULD USE ANOTHER VOLUNTEER?
WE NEED SOMEONE TO BE IN CHARGE OF DONATIONS FOR THE BOOK DRIVE. NOMINATIONS? VOLUNTEERS? CARLOS?
I NOMINATE EMMA PALEY. SHE'S SMART AND WE KNOW WE CAN TRUST HER WITH MONEY.
I SECOND THAT.
AMEN, BROTHER.
YOU GO, SPIDER-GIRL!
ANYONE ELSE? MEG RIDGEWAY, YOU HAD YOUR HAND UP?
UH...WELL... THAT'S WHO I WAS GONNA NOMINATE.
YEAH, RIGHT.

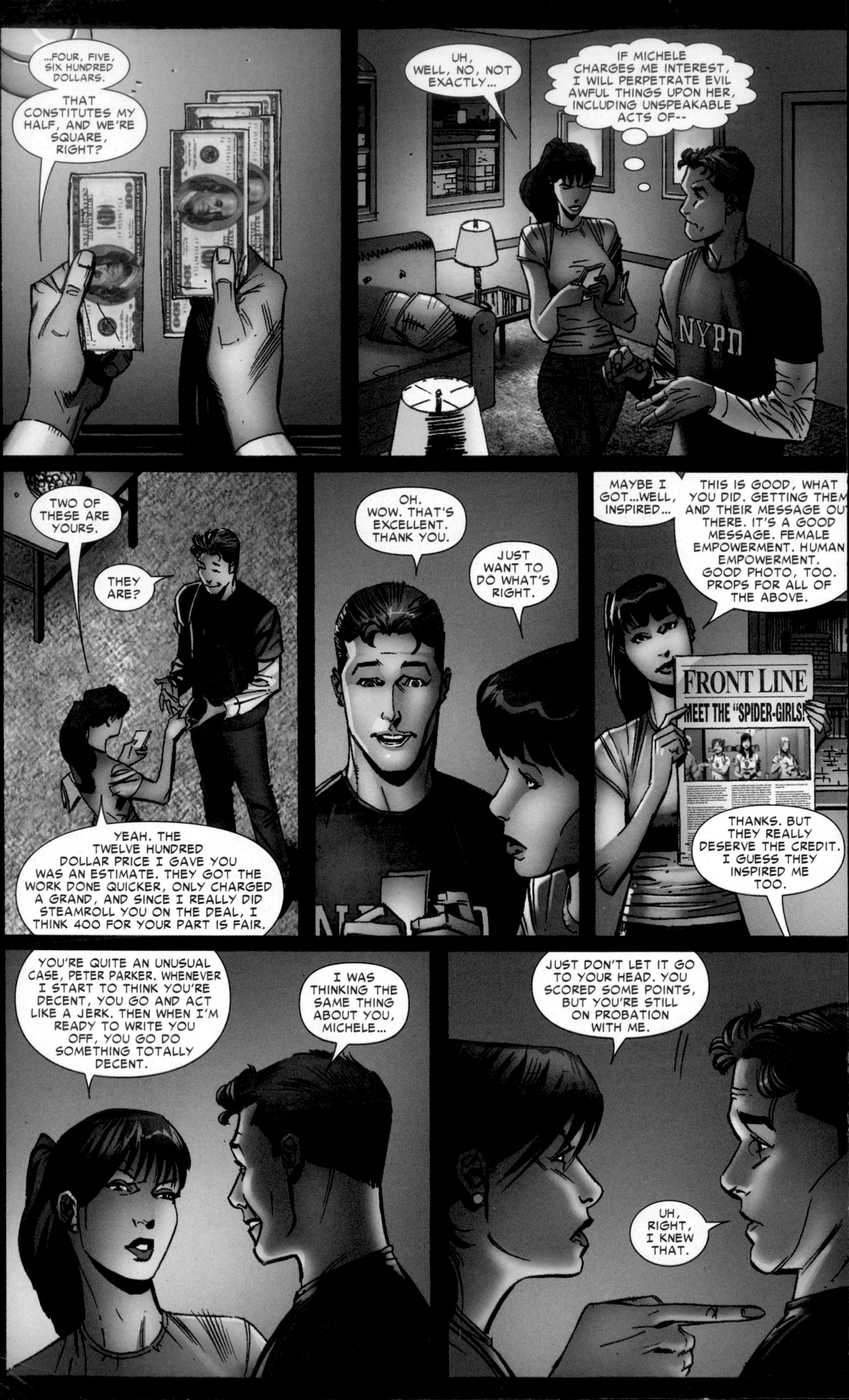
...FOUR, FIVE, SIX HUNDRED DOLLARS.
THAT CONSTITUTES MY HALF, AND WE'RE SQUARE, RIGHT?
UH, WELL, NO, NOT EXACTLY...
IF MICHELE CHARGES ME INTEREST, I WILL PERPETRATE EVIL AWFUL THINGS UPON HER, INCLUDING UNSPEAKABLE ACTS OF--
NYPD
TWO OF THESE ARE YOURS.
THEY ARE?
YEAH. THE TWELVE HUNDRED DOLLAR PRICE I GAVE YOU WAS AN ESTIMATE. THEY GOT THE WORK DONE QUICKER, ONLY CHARGED A GRAND, AND SINCE I REALLY DID STEAMROLL YOU ON THE DEAL, I THINK 400 FOR YOUR PART IS FAIR.
OH. WOW. THAT'S EXCELLENT. THANK YOU.
JUST WANT TO DO WHAT'S RIGHT.
MAYBE I GOT...WELL, INSPIRED...
THIS IS GOOD, WHAT YOU DID. GETTING THEM AND THEIR MESSAGE OUT THERE. IT'S A GOOD MESSAGE. FEMALE EMPOWERMENT. HUMAN EMPOWERMENT. GOOD PHOTO, TOO. PROPS FOR ALL OF THE ABOVE.
FRONT LINE
MEET THE "SPIDER-GIRLS!"
THANKS. BUT THEY REALLY DESERVE THE CREDIT. I GUESS THEY INSPIRED ME TOO.
YOU'RE QUITE AN UNUSUAL CASE, PETER PARKER. WHENEVER I START TO THINK YOU'RE DECENT, YOU GO AND ACT LIKE A JERK. THEN WHEN I'M READY TO WRITE YOU OFF, YOU GO DO SOMETHING TOTALLY DECENT.
I WAS THINKING THE SAME THING ABOUT YOU, MICHELE...
JUST DON'T LET IT GO TO YOUR HEAD. YOU SCORED SOME POINTS, BUT YOU'RE STILL ON PROBATION WITH ME.
UH, RIGHT, I KNEW THAT.

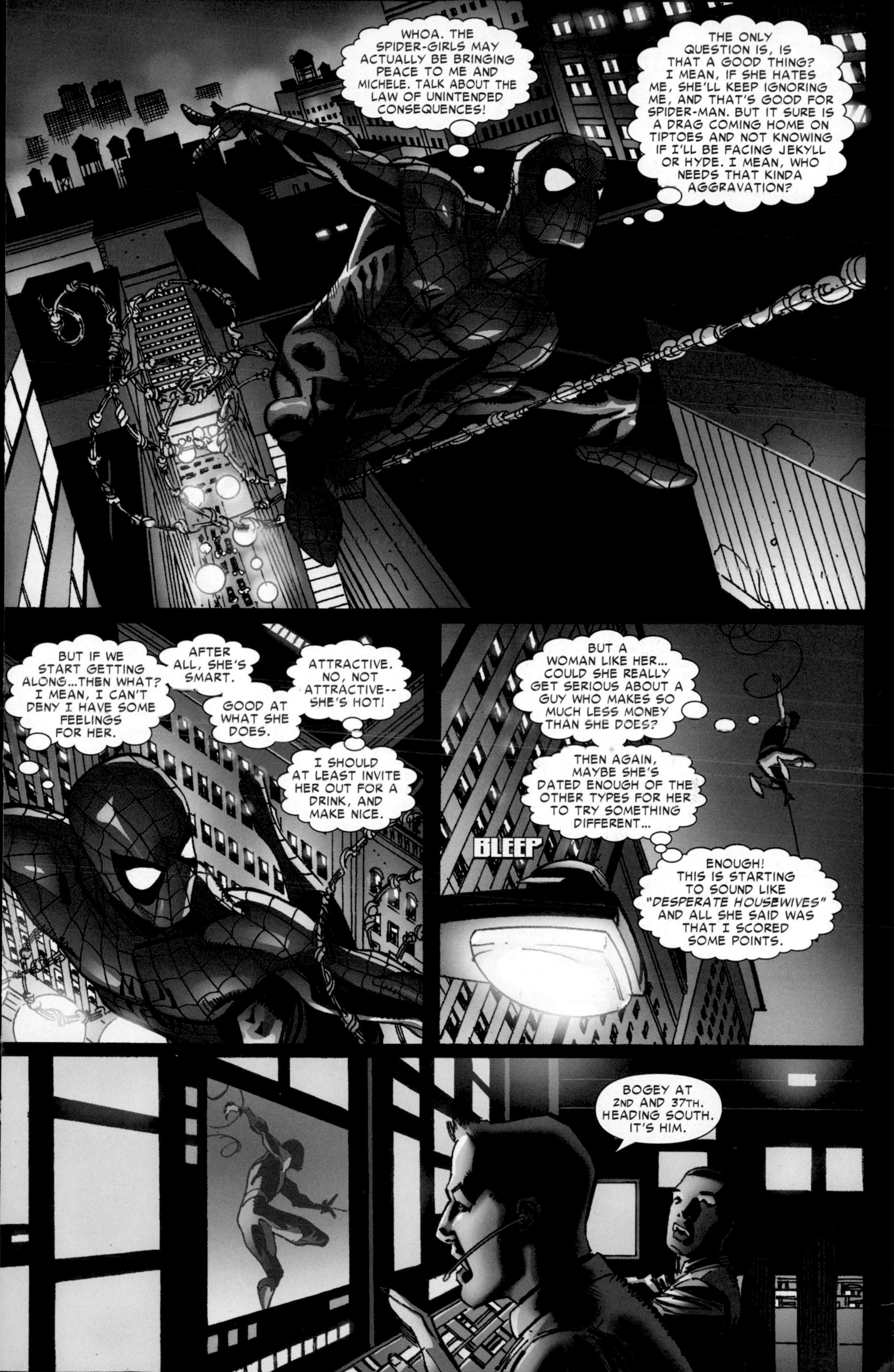

WHOA. THE SPIDER-GIRLS MAY ACTUALLY BE BRINGING PEACE TO ME AND MICHELE. TALK ABOUT THE LAW OF UNINTENDED CONSEQUENCES!
THE ONLY QUESTION IS, IS THAT A GOOD THING? I MEAN, IF SHE HATES ME, SHE'LL KEEP IGNORING ME, AND THAT'S GOOD FOR SPIDER-MAN. BUT IT SURE IS A DRAG COMING HOME ON TIPTOES AND NOT KNOWING IF I'LL BE FACING JEKYLL OR HYDE. I MEAN, WHO NEEDS THAT KINDA AGGRAVATION?
BUT IF WE START GETTING ALONG...THEN WHAT? I MEAN, I CAN'T DENY I HAVE SOME FEELINGS FOR HER.
AFTER ALL, SHE'S SMART.
GOOD AT WHAT SHE DOES.
ATTRACTIVE. NO, NOT ATTRACTIVE--SHE'S HOT!
I SHOULD AT LEAST INVITE HER OUT FOR A DRINK, AND MAKE NICE.
BUT A WOMAN LIKE HER... COULD SHE REALLY GET SERIOUS ABOUT A GUY WHO MAKES SO MUCH LESS MONEY THAN SHE DOES?
THEN AGAIN, MAYBE SHE'S DATED ENOUGH OF THE OTHER TYPES FOR HER TO TRY SOMETHING DIFFERENT...
BLEEP
ENOUGH! THIS IS STARTING TO SOUND LIKE "DESPERATE HOUSEWIVES" AND ALL SHE SAID WAS THAT I SCORED SOME POINTS.
BOGEY AT 2ND AND 37TH. HEADING SOUTH. IT'S HIM.

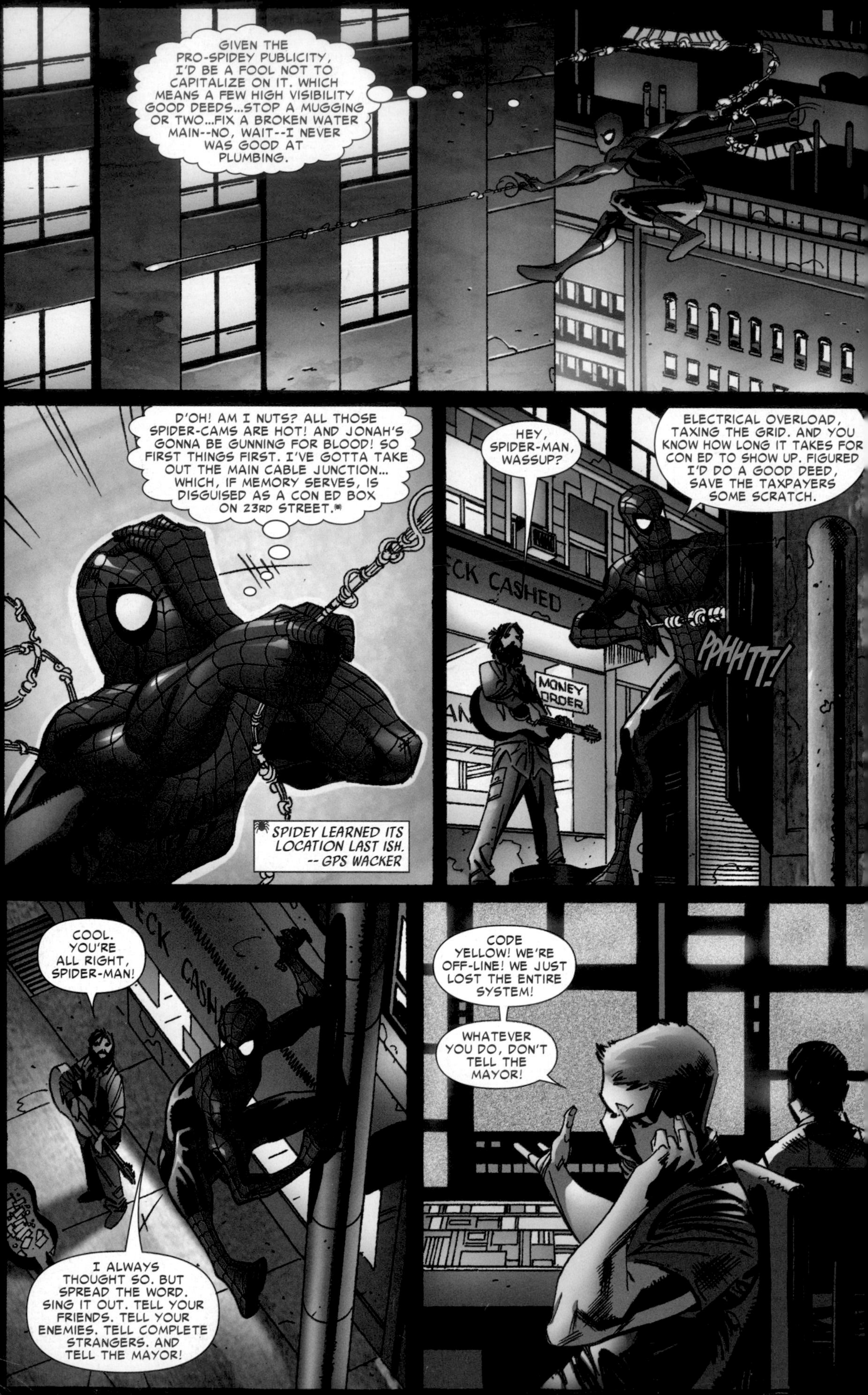
GIVEN THE PRO-SPIDEY PUBLICITY, I'D BE A FOOL NOT TO CAPITALIZE ON IT. WHICH MEANS A FEW HIGH VISIBILITY GOOD DEEDS...STOP A MUGGING OR TWO...FIX A BROKEN WATER MAIN--NO, WAIT--I NEVER WAS GOOD AT PLUMBING.
D'OH! AM I NUTS? ALL THOSE SPIDER-CAMS ARE HOT! AND JONAH'S GONNA BE GUNNING FOR BLOOD! SO FIRST THINGS FIRST. I'VE GOTTA TAKE OUT THE MAIN CABLE JUNCTION... WHICH, IF MEMORY SERVES, IS DISGUISED AS A CON ED BOX ON 23RD STREET.*
*SPIDEY LEARNED ITS LOCATION LAST ISH. -- GPS WACKER
HEY, SPIDER-MAN, WASSUP?
ELECTRICAL OVERLOAD, TAXING THE GRID. AND YOU KNOW HOW LONG IT TAKES FOR CON ED TO SHOW UP. FIGURED I'D DO A GOOD DEED, SAVE THE TAXPAYERS SOME SCRATCH.
CK CASHED
MONEY ORDER
PPHHTT!
COOL. YOU'RE ALL RIGHT, SPIDER-MAN!
I ALWAYS THOUGHT SO. BUT SPREAD THE WORD. SING IT OUT. TELL YOUR FRIENDS. TELL YOUR ENEMIES. TELL COMPLETE STRANGERS. AND TELL THE MAYOR!
CODE YELLOW! WE'RE OFF-LINE! WE JUST LOST THE ENTIRE SYSTEM!
WHATEVER YOU DO, DON'T TELL THE MAYOR!

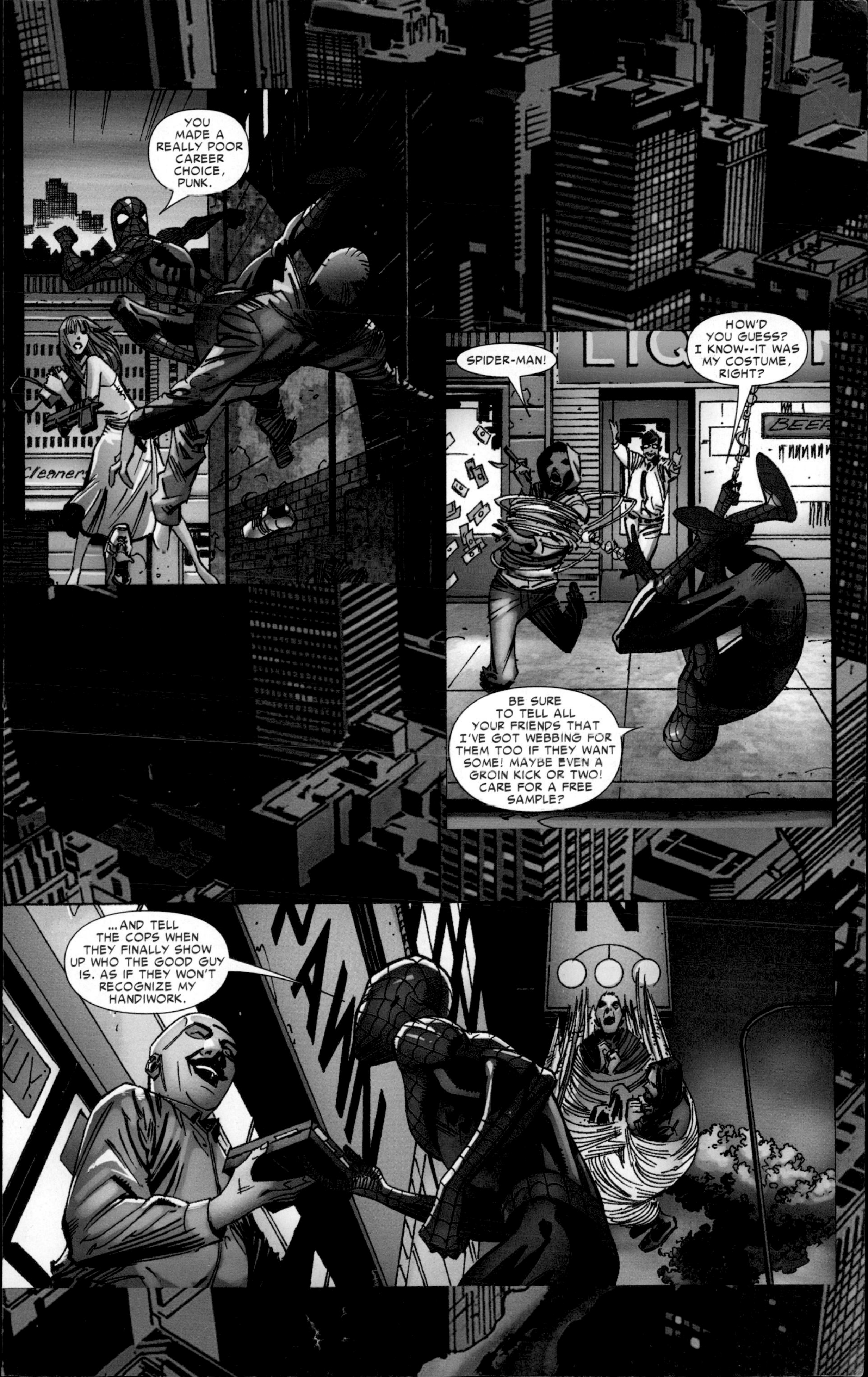
YOU MADE A REALLY POOR CAREER CHOICE, PUNK.
SPIDER-MAN!
HOW'D YOU GUESS? I KNOW--IT WAS MY COSTUME, RIGHT?
BE SURE TO TELL ALL YOUR FRIENDS THAT I'VE GOT WEBBING FOR THEM TOO IF THEY WANT SOME! MAYBE EVEN A GROIN KICK OR TWO! CARE FOR A FREE SAMPLE?
...AND TELL THE COPS WHEN THEY FINALLY SHOW UP WHO THE GOOD GUY IS. AS IF THEY WON'T RECOGNIZE MY HANDIWORK.

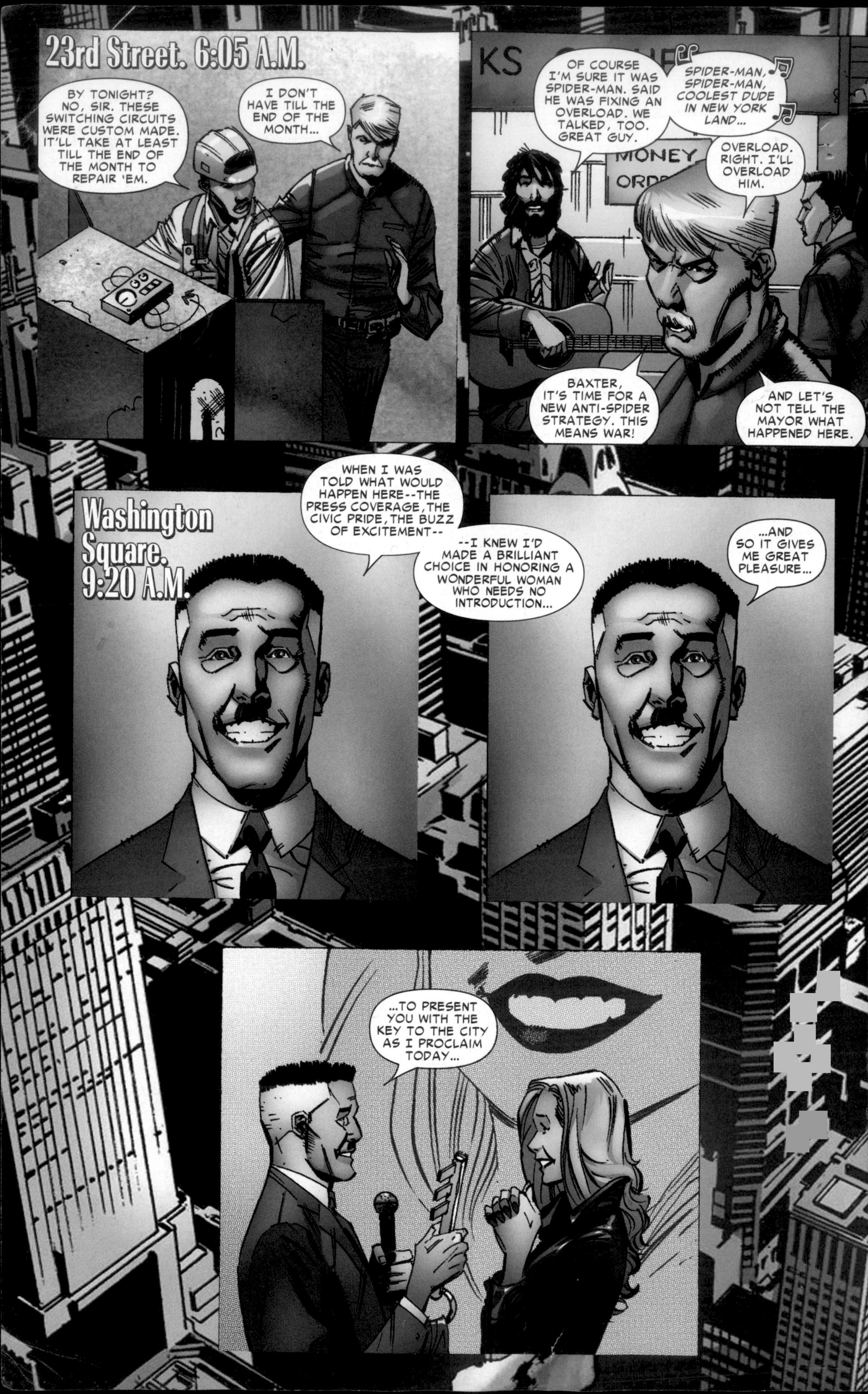
23rd Street. 6:05 A.M.
BY TONIGHT? NO, SIR. THESE SWITCHING CIRCUITS WERE CUSTOM MADE. IT'LL TAKE AT LEAST TILL THE END OF THE MONTH TO REPAIR 'EM.
I DON'T HAVE TILL THE END OF THE MONTH...
KS
OF COURSE I'M SURE IT WAS SPIDER-MAN. SAID HE WAS FIXING AN OVERLOAD. WE TALKED, TOO. GREAT GUY.
SPIDER-MAN, SPIDER-MAN, COOLEST DUDE IN NEW YORK LAND...
MONEY ORD
OVERLOAD. RIGHT. I'LL OVERLOAD HIM.
BAXTER, IT'S TIME FOR A NEW ANTI-SPIDER STRATEGY. THIS MEANS WAR!
AND LET'S NOT TELL THE MAYOR WHAT HAPPENED HERE.
Washington Square. 9:20 A.M.
WHEN I WAS TOLD WHAT WOULD HAPPEN HERE--THE PRESS COVERAGE, THE CIVIC PRIDE, THE BUZZ OF EXCITEMENT--
--I KNEW I'D MADE A BRILLIANT CHOICE IN HONORING A WONDERFUL WOMAN WHO NEEDS NO INTRODUCTION...
...AND SO IT GIVES ME GREAT PLEASURE...
...TO PRESENT YOU WITH THE KEY TO THE CITY AS I PROCLAIM TODAY...

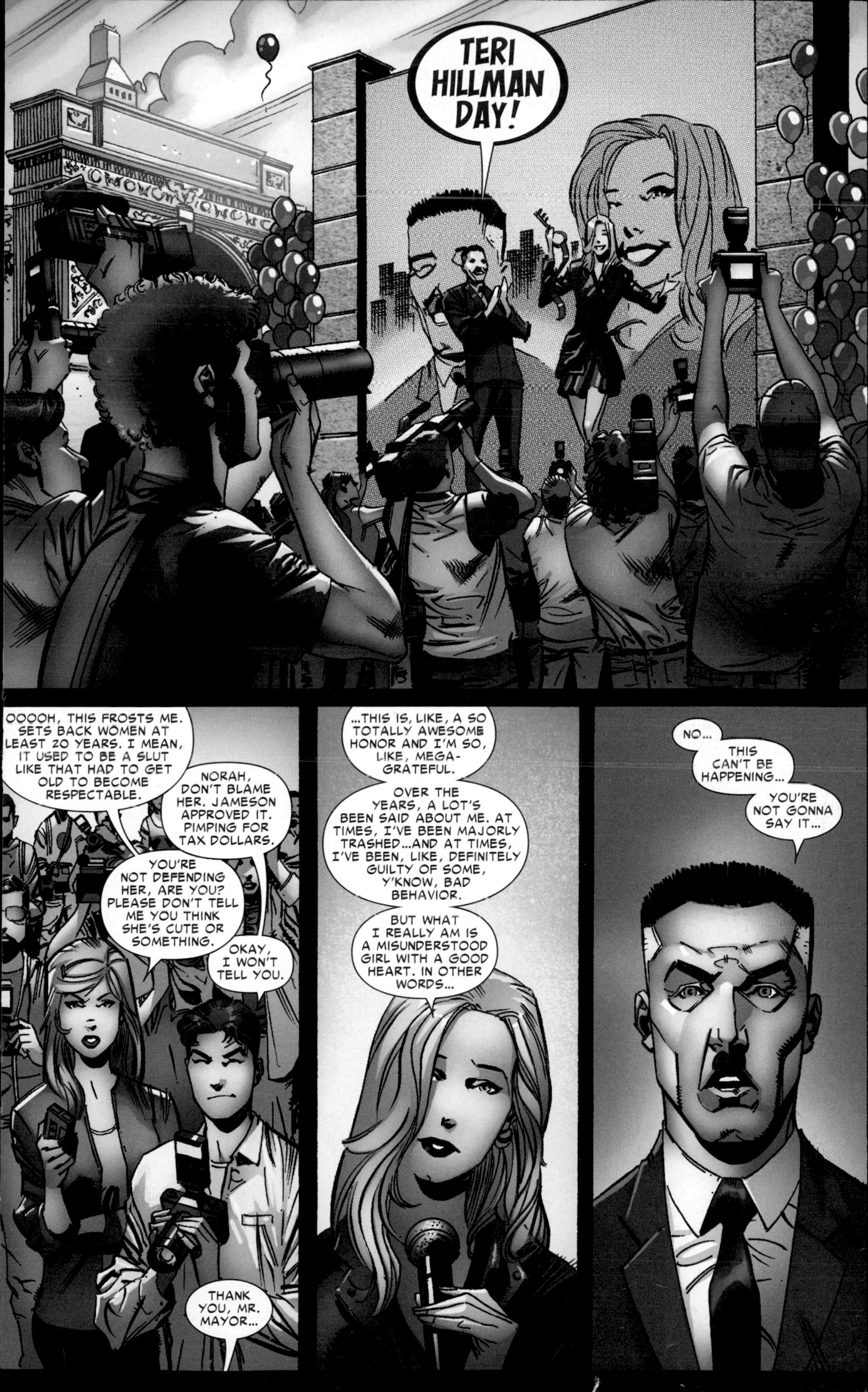
TERI HILLMAN DAY!
OOOOH, THIS FROSTS ME. SETS BACK WOMEN AT LEAST 20 YEARS. I MEAN, IT USED TO BE A SLUT LIKE THAT HAD TO GET OLD TO BECOME RESPECTABLE.
NORAH, DON'T BLAME HER. JAMESON APPROVED IT. PIMPING FOR TAX DOLLARS.
YOU'RE NOT DEFENDING HER, ARE YOU? PLEASE DON'T TELL ME YOU THINK SHE'S CUTE OR SOMETHING.
OKAY, I WON'T TELL YOU.
THANK YOU, MR. MAYOR...
...THIS IS, LIKE, A SO TOTALLY AWESOME HONOR AND I'M SO, LIKE, MEGA-GRATEFUL.
OVER THE YEARS, A LOT'S BEEN SAID ABOUT ME. AT TIMES, I'VE BEEN MAJORLY TRASHED...AND AT TIMES, I'VE BEEN, LIKE, DEFINITELY GUILTY OF SOME, Y'KNOW, BAD BEHAVIOR.
BUT WHAT I REALLY AM IS A MISUNDERSTOOD GIRL WITH A GOOD HEART. IN OTHER WORDS...
NO...
THIS CAN'T BE HAPPENING...
YOU'RE NOT GONNA SAY IT...

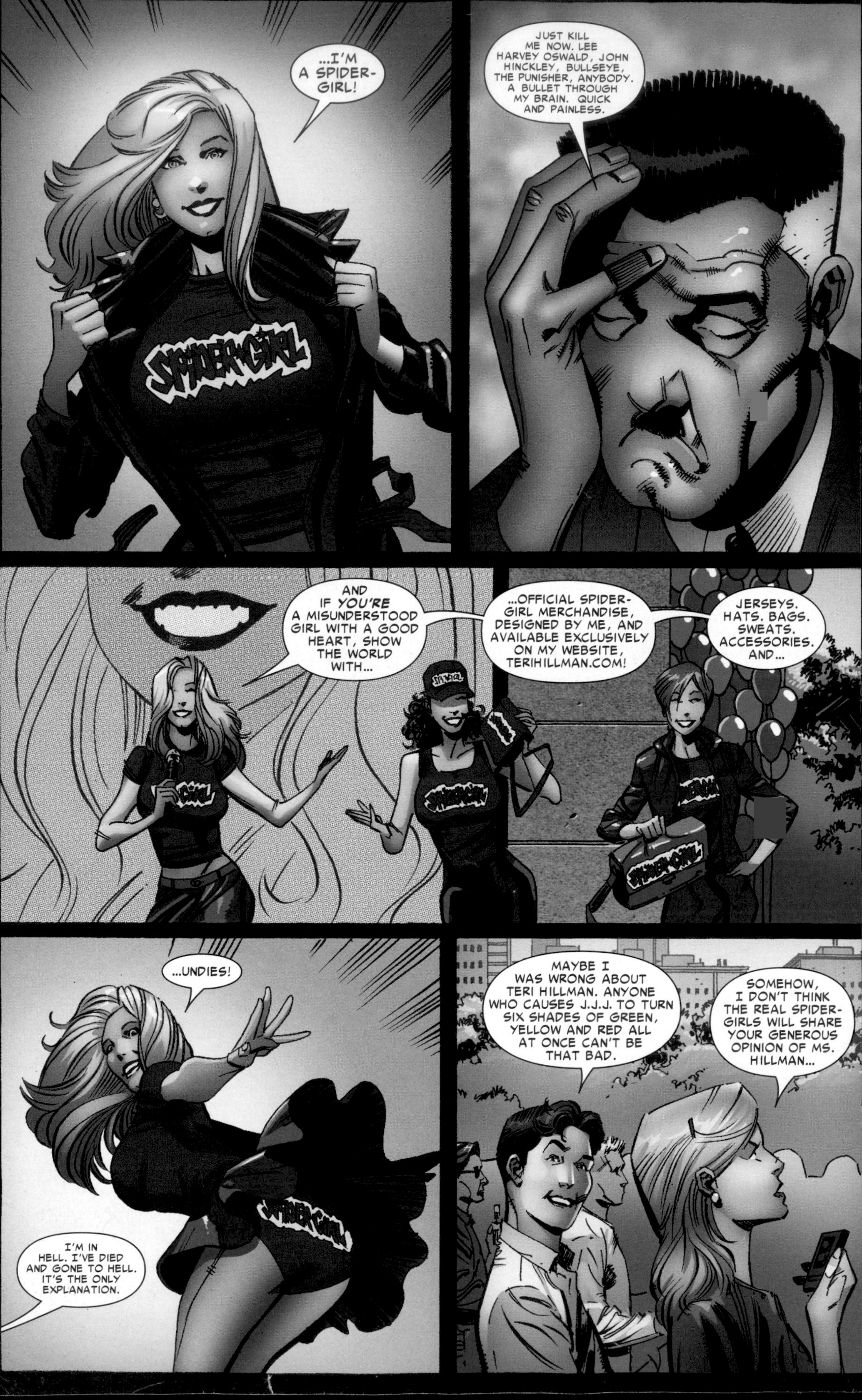
...I'M A SPIDER-GIRL!
JUST KILL ME NOW. LEE HARVEY OSWALD, JOHN HINCKLEY, BULLSEYE, THE PUNISHER, ANYBODY. A BULLET THROUGH MY BRAIN. QUICK AND PAINLESS.
SPIDER-GIRL
AND IF *YOU'RE* A MISUNDERSTOOD GIRL WITH A GOOD HEART, SHOW THE WORLD WITH...
...OFFICIAL SPIDER-GIRL MERCHANDISE, DESIGNED BY ME, AND AVAILABLE EXCLUSIVELY ON MY WEBSITE, TERIHILLMAN.COM!
JERSEYS. HATS. BAGS. SWEATS. ACCESSORIES. AND...
SPIDER-GIRL
...UNDIES!
I'M IN HELL. I'VE DIED AND GONE TO HELL. IT'S THE ONLY EXPLANATION.
SPIDER-GIRL
MAYBE I WAS WRONG ABOUT TERI HILLMAN. ANYONE WHO CAUSES J.J.J. TO TURN SIX SHADES OF GREEN, YELLOW AND RED ALL AT ONCE CAN'T BE THAT BAD.
SOMEHOW, I DON'T THINK THE REAL SPIDER-GIRLS WILL SHARE YOUR GENEROUS OPINION OF MS. HILLMAN...

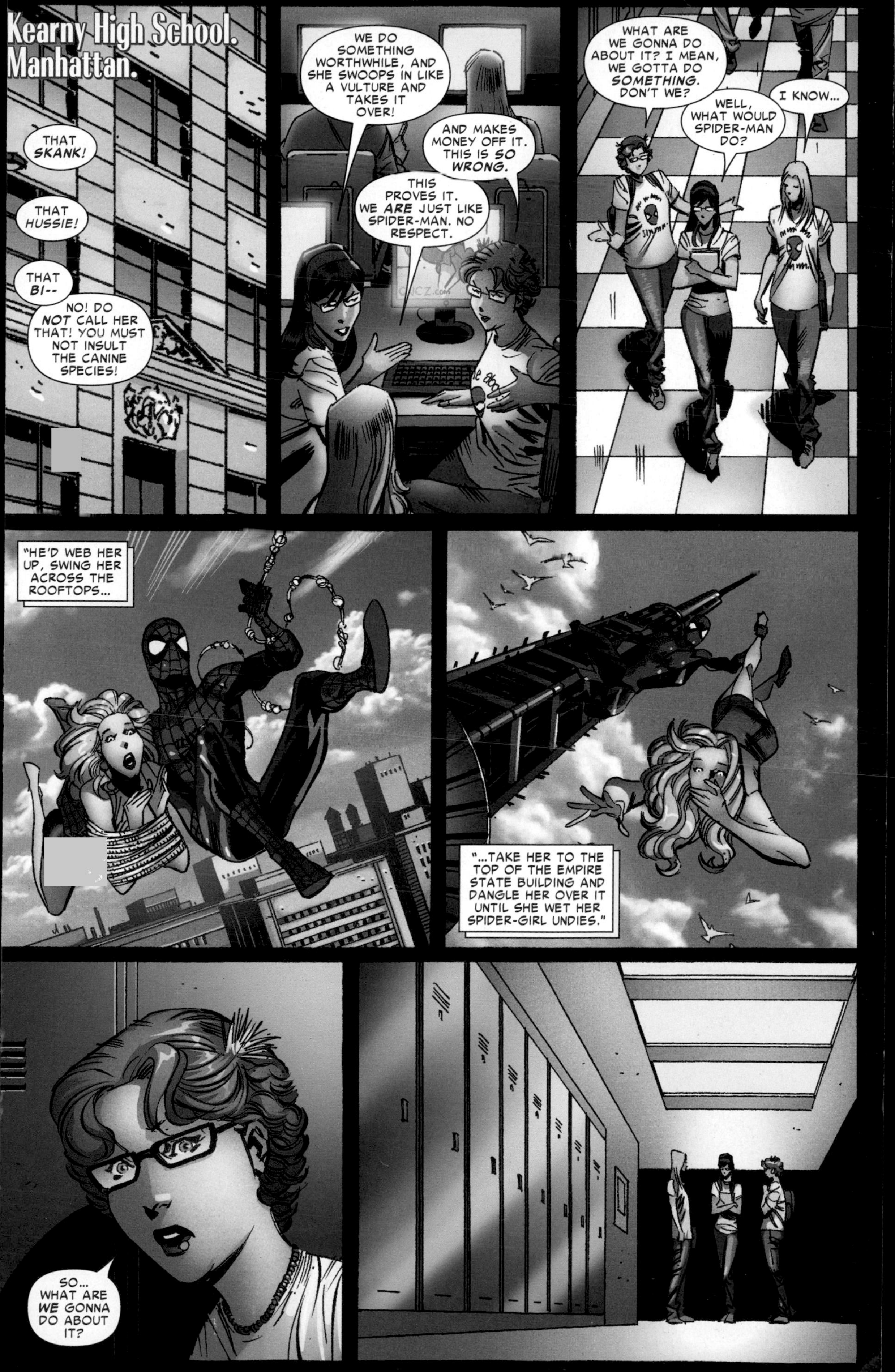
Kearny High School. Manhattan.
THAT SKANK!
THAT HUSSIE!
THAT BI--
NO! DO NOT CALL HER THAT! YOU MUST NOT INSULT THE CANINE SPECIES!
WE DO SOMETHING WORTHWHILE, AND SHE SWOOPS IN LIKE A VULTURE AND TAKES IT OVER!
AND MAKES MONEY OFF IT. THIS IS SO WRONG.
THIS PROVES IT. WE ARE JUST LIKE SPIDER-MAN. NO RESPECT.
WHAT ARE WE GONNA DO ABOUT IT? I MEAN, WE GOTTA DO SOMETHING. DON'T WE?
WELL, WHAT WOULD SPIDER-MAN DO?
I KNOW...
"HE'D WEB HER UP, SWING HER ACROSS THE ROOFTOPS...
"...TAKE HER TO THE TOP OF THE EMPIRE STATE BUILDING AND DANGLE HER OVER IT UNTIL SHE WET HER SPIDER-GIRL UNDIES."
SO... WHAT ARE WE GONNA DO ABOUT IT?

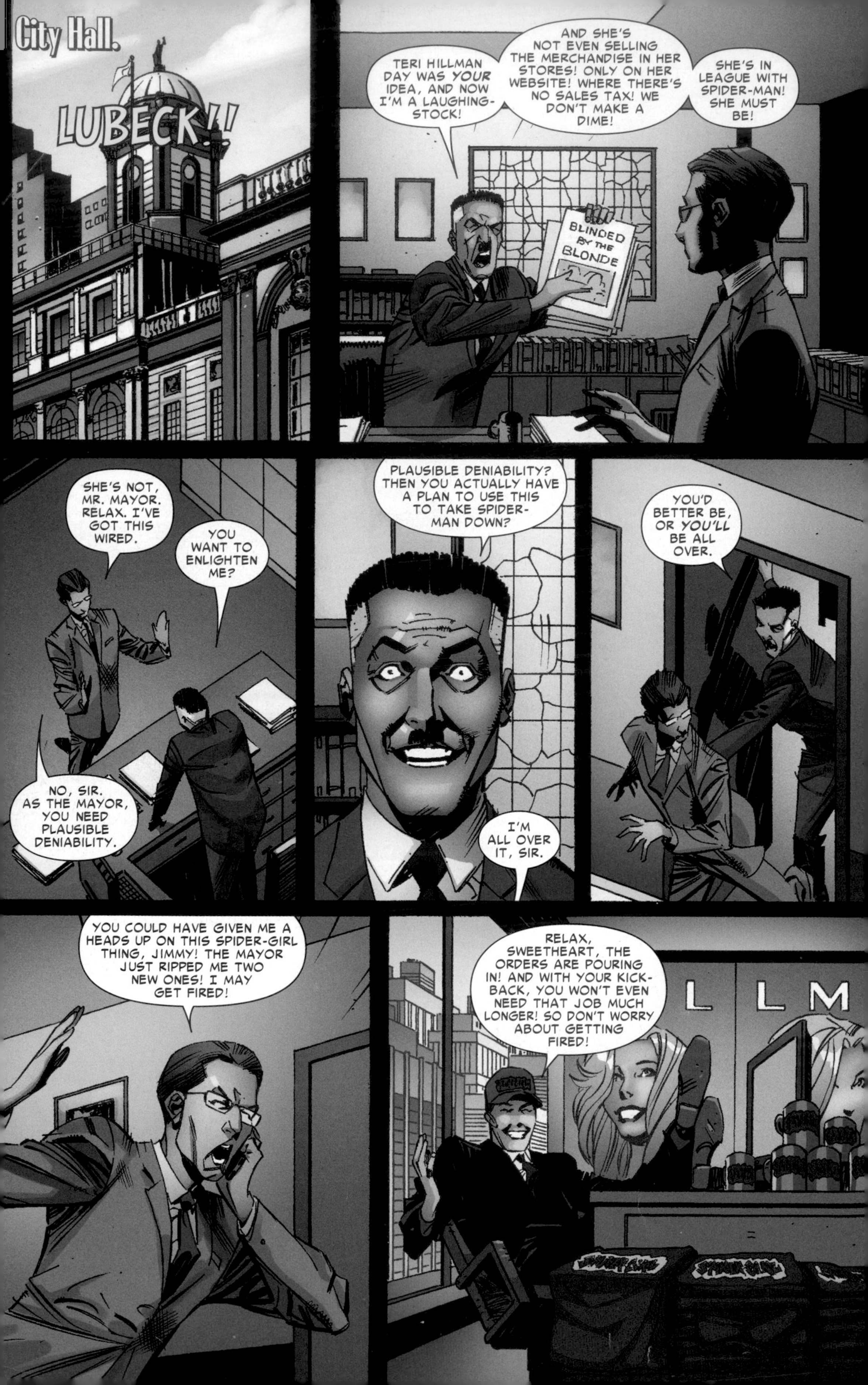
City Hall.
LUBECK!!
TERI HILLMAN DAY WAS *YOUR* IDEA, AND NOW I'M A LAUGHING-STOCK!
AND SHE'S NOT EVEN SELLING THE MERCHANDISE IN HER STORES! ONLY ON HER WEBSITE! WHERE THERE'S NO SALES TAX! WE DON'T MAKE A DIME!
SHE'S IN LEAGUE WITH SPIDER-MAN! SHE MUST BE!
BLINDED BY THE BLONDE
SHE'S NOT, MR. MAYOR. RELAX. I'VE GOT THIS WIRED.
YOU WANT TO ENLIGHTEN ME?
NO, SIR. AS THE MAYOR, YOU NEED PLAUSIBLE DENIABILITY.
PLAUSIBLE DENIABILITY? THEN YOU ACTUALLY HAVE A PLAN TO USE THIS TO TAKE SPIDER-MAN DOWN?
I'M ALL OVER IT, SIR.
YOU'D BETTER BE, OR *YOU'LL* BE ALL OVER.
YOU COULD HAVE GIVEN ME A HEADS UP ON THIS SPIDER-GIRL THING, JIMMY! THE MAYOR JUST RIPPED ME TWO NEW ONES! I MAY GET FIRED!
RELAX, SWEETHEART, THE ORDERS ARE POURING IN! AND WITH YOUR KICK-BACK, YOU WON'T EVEN NEED THAT JOB MUCH LONGER! SO DON'T WORRY ABOUT GETTING FIRED!
L L M

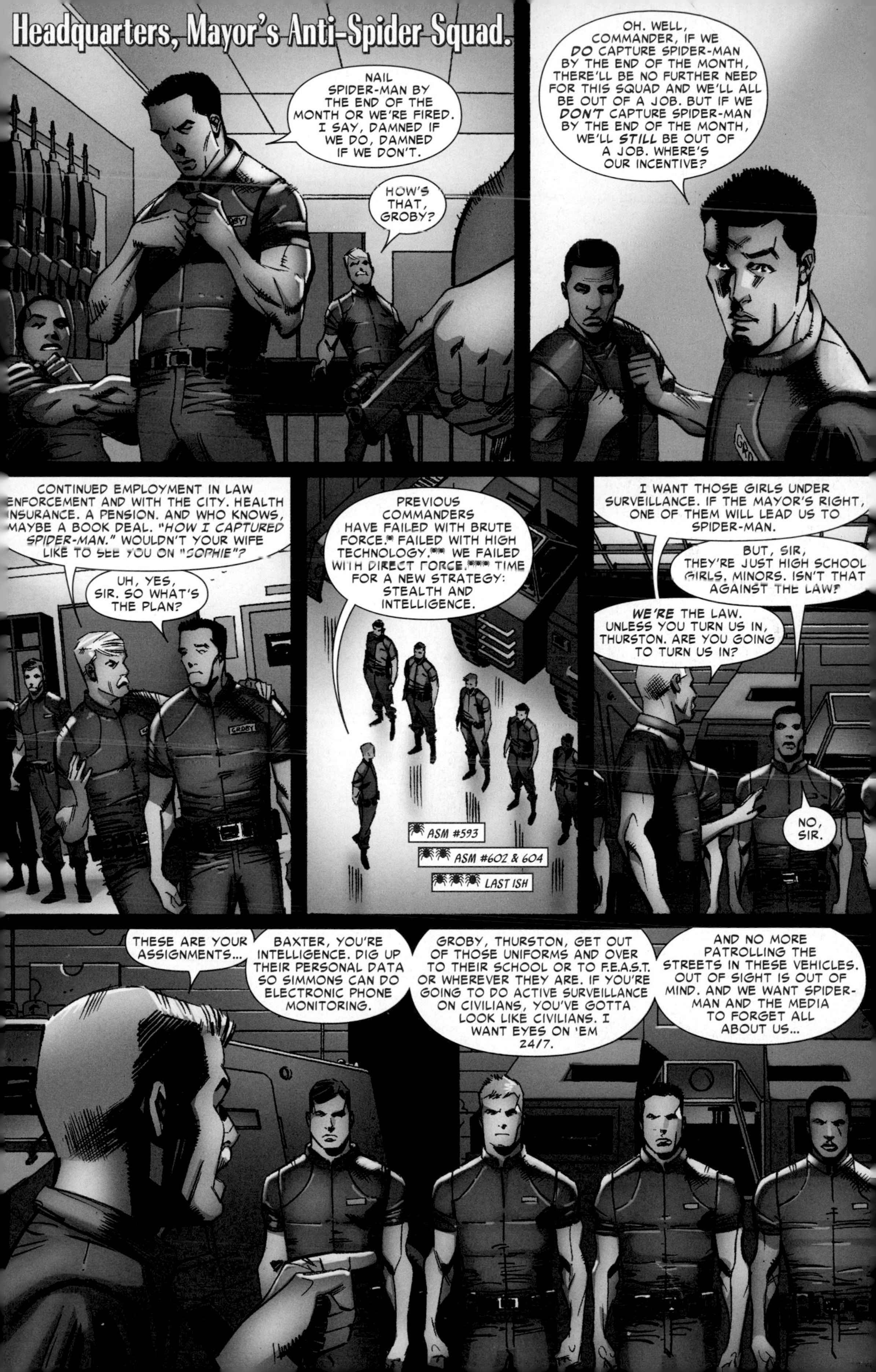
Headquarters, Mayor's Anti-Spider Squad.
NAIL SPIDER-MAN BY THE END OF THE MONTH OR WE'RE FIRED. I SAY, DAMNED IF WE DO, DAMNED IF WE DON'T.
HOW'S THAT, GROBY?
OH. WELL, COMMANDER, IF WE DO CAPTURE SPIDER-MAN BY THE END OF THE MONTH, THERE'LL BE NO FURTHER NEED FOR THIS SQUAD AND WE'LL ALL BE OUT OF A JOB. BUT IF WE DON'T CAPTURE SPIDER-MAN BY THE END OF THE MONTH, WE'LL STILL BE OUT OF A JOB. WHERE'S OUR INCENTIVE?
CONTINUED EMPLOYMENT IN LAW ENFORCEMENT AND WITH THE CITY. HEALTH INSURANCE. A PENSION. AND WHO KNOWS, MAYBE A BOOK DEAL. "HOW I CAPTURED SPIDER-MAN." WOULDN'T YOUR WIFE LIKE TO SEE YOU ON "SOPHIE"?
UH, YES, SIR. SO WHAT'S THE PLAN?
PREVIOUS COMMANDERS HAVE FAILED WITH BRUTE FORCE.* FAILED WITH HIGH TECHNOLOGY.** WE FAILED WITH DIRECT FORCE.*** TIME FOR A NEW STRATEGY: STEALTH AND INTELLIGENCE.
ASM #593
ASM #602 & 604
LAST ISH
I WANT THOSE GIRLS UNDER SURVEILLANCE. IF THE MAYOR'S RIGHT, ONE OF THEM WILL LEAD US TO SPIDER-MAN.
BUT, SIR, THEY'RE JUST HIGH SCHOOL GIRLS. MINORS. ISN'T THAT AGAINST THE LAW?
WE'RE THE LAW. UNLESS YOU TURN US IN, THURSTON. ARE YOU GOING TO TURN US IN?
NO, SIR.
THESE ARE YOUR ASSIGNMENTS...
BAXTER, YOU'RE INTELLIGENCE. DIG UP THEIR PERSONAL DATA SO SIMMONS CAN DO ELECTRONIC PHONE MONITORING.
GROBY, THURSTON, GET OUT OF THOSE UNIFORMS AND OVER TO THEIR SCHOOL OR TO F.E.A.S.T. OR WHEREVER THEY ARE. IF YOU'RE GOING TO DO ACTIVE SURVEILLANCE ON CIVILIANS, YOU'VE GOTTA LOOK LIKE CIVILIANS. I WANT EYES ON 'EM 24/7.
AND NO MORE PATROLLING THE STREETS IN THESE VEHICLES. OUT OF SIGHT IS OUT OF MIND. AND WE WANT SPIDER-MAN AND THE MEDIA TO FORGET ALL ABOUT US...

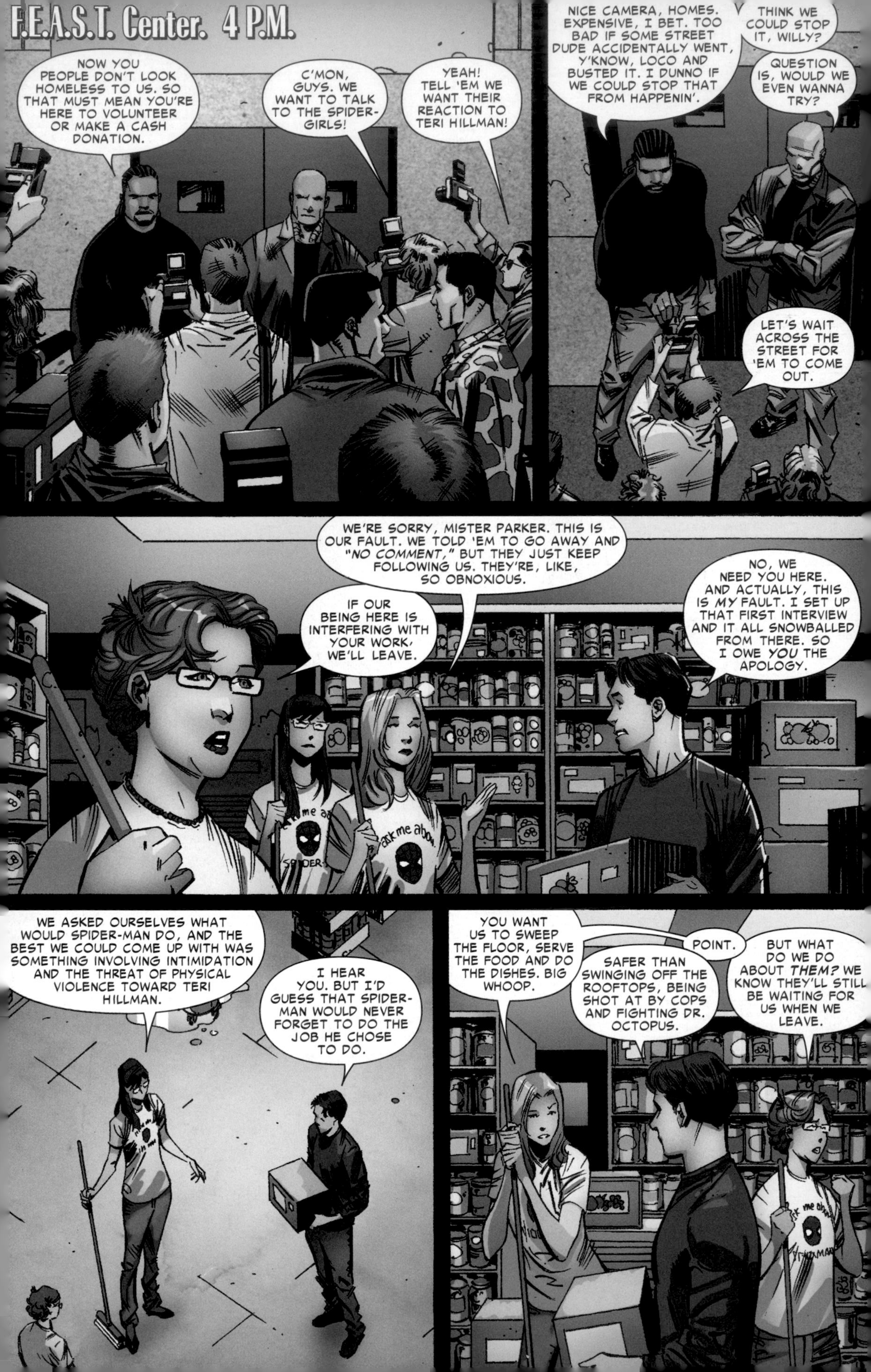
F.E.A.S.T. Center. 4 P.M.
NOW YOU PEOPLE DON'T LOOK HOMELESS TO US. SO THAT MUST MEAN YOU'RE HERE TO VOLUNTEER OR MAKE A CASH DONATION.
C'MON, GUYS. WE WANT TO TALK TO THE SPIDER-GIRLS!
YEAH! TELL 'EM WE WANT THEIR REACTION TO TERI HILLMAN!
NICE CAMERA, HOMES. EXPENSIVE, I BET. TOO BAD IF SOME STREET DUDE ACCIDENTALLY WENT, Y'KNOW, LOCO AND BUSTED IT. I DUNNO IF WE COULD STOP THAT FROM HAPPENIN'.
THINK WE COULD STOP IT, WILLY?
QUESTION IS, WOULD WE EVEN WANNA TRY?
LET'S WAIT ACROSS THE STREET FOR 'EM TO COME OUT.
IF OUR BEING HERE IS INTERFERING WITH YOUR WORK, WE'LL LEAVE.
WE'RE SORRY, MISTER PARKER. THIS IS OUR FAULT. WE TOLD 'EM TO GO AWAY AND "*NO COMMENT,*" BUT THEY JUST KEEP FOLLOWING US. THEY'RE, LIKE, SO OBNOXIOUS.
NO, WE NEED YOU HERE. AND ACTUALLY, THIS IS *MY* FAULT. I SET UP THAT FIRST INTERVIEW AND IT ALL SNOWBALLED FROM THERE. SO I OWE *YOU* THE APOLOGY.
WE ASKED OURSELVES WHAT WOULD SPIDER-MAN DO, AND THE BEST WE COULD COME UP WITH WAS SOMETHING INVOLVING INTIMIDATION AND THE THREAT OF PHYSICAL VIOLENCE TOWARD TERI HILLMAN.
I HEAR YOU. BUT I'D GUESS THAT SPIDER-MAN WOULD NEVER FORGET TO DO THE JOB HE CHOSE TO DO.
YOU WANT US TO SWEEP THE FLOOR, SERVE THE FOOD AND DO THE DISHES. BIG WHOOP.
POINT.
SAFER THAN SWINGING OFF THE ROOFTOPS, BEING SHOT AT BY COPS AND FIGHTING DR. OCTOPUS.
BUT WHAT DO WE DO ABOUT *THEM?* WE KNOW THEY'LL STILL BE WAITING FOR US WHEN WE LEAVE.

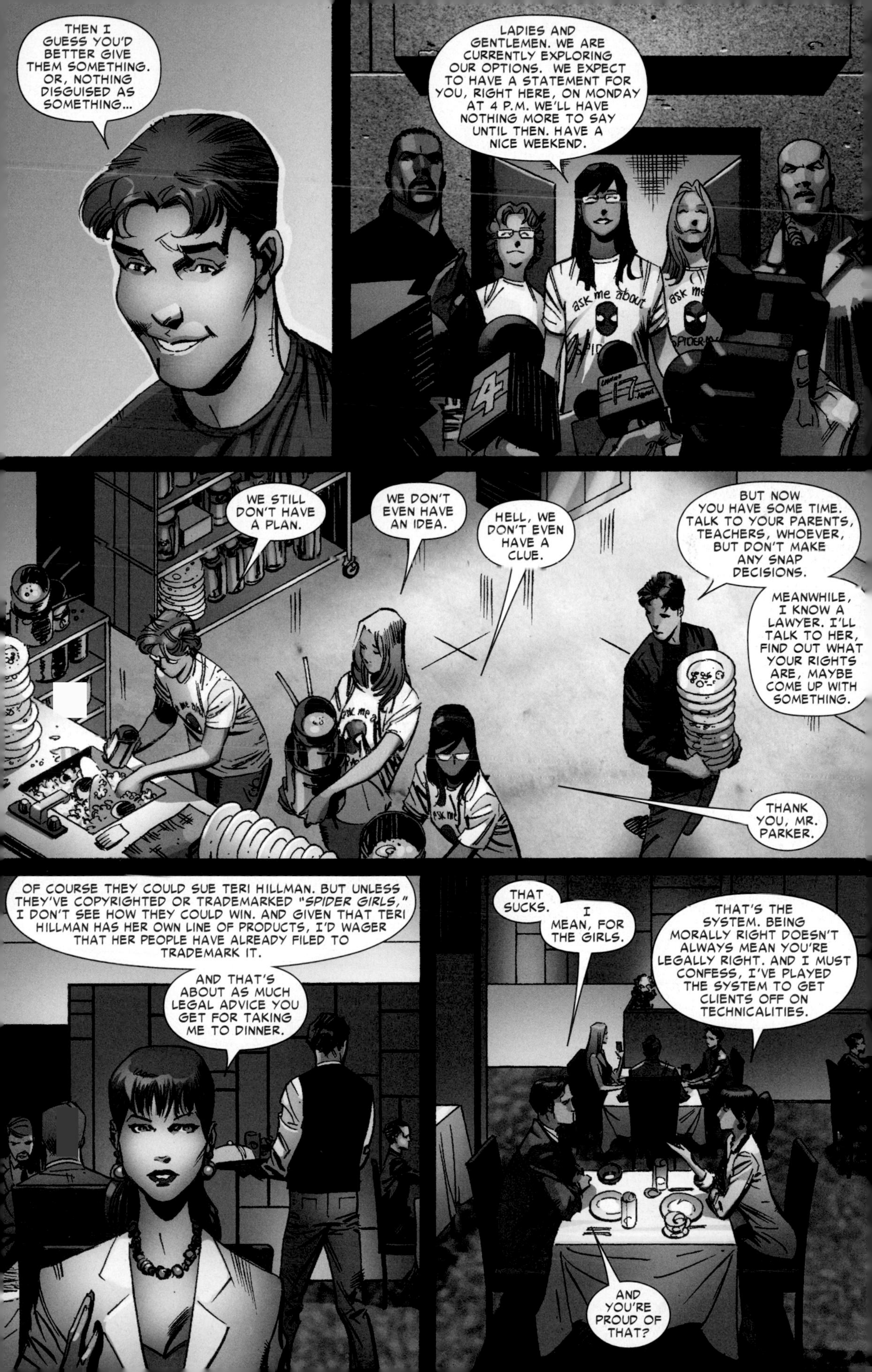
THEN I GUESS YOU'D BETTER GIVE THEM SOMETHING. OR, NOTHING DISGUISED AS SOMETHING...
LADIES AND GENTLEMEN. WE ARE CURRENTLY EXPLORING OUR OPTIONS. WE EXPECT TO HAVE A STATEMENT FOR YOU, RIGHT HERE, ON MONDAY AT 4 P.M. WE'LL HAVE NOTHING MORE TO SAY UNTIL THEN. HAVE A NICE WEEKEND.
ask me about
WE STILL DON'T HAVE A PLAN.
WE DON'T EVEN HAVE AN IDEA.
HELL, WE DON'T EVEN HAVE A CLUE.
BUT NOW YOU HAVE SOME TIME. TALK TO YOUR PARENTS, TEACHERS, WHOEVER, BUT DON'T MAKE ANY SNAP DECISIONS.
MEANWHILE, I KNOW A LAWYER. I'LL TALK TO HER, FIND OUT WHAT YOUR RIGHTS ARE, MAYBE COME UP WITH SOMETHING.
THANK YOU, MR. PARKER.
OF COURSE THEY COULD SUE TERI HILLMAN. BUT UNLESS THEY'VE COPYRIGHTED OR TRADEMARKED "*SPIDER GIRLS*," I DON'T SEE HOW THEY COULD WIN. AND GIVEN THAT TERI HILLMAN HAS HER OWN LINE OF PRODUCTS, I'D WAGER THAT HER PEOPLE HAVE ALREADY FILED TO TRADEMARK IT.
AND THAT'S ABOUT AS MUCH LEGAL ADVICE YOU GET FOR TAKING ME TO DINNER.
THAT SUCKS.
I MEAN, FOR THE GIRLS.
THAT'S THE SYSTEM. BEING MORALLY RIGHT DOESN'T ALWAYS MEAN YOU'RE LEGALLY RIGHT. AND I MUST CONFESS, I'VE PLAYED THE SYSTEM TO GET CLIENTS OFF ON TECHNICALITIES.
AND YOU'RE PROUD OF THAT?

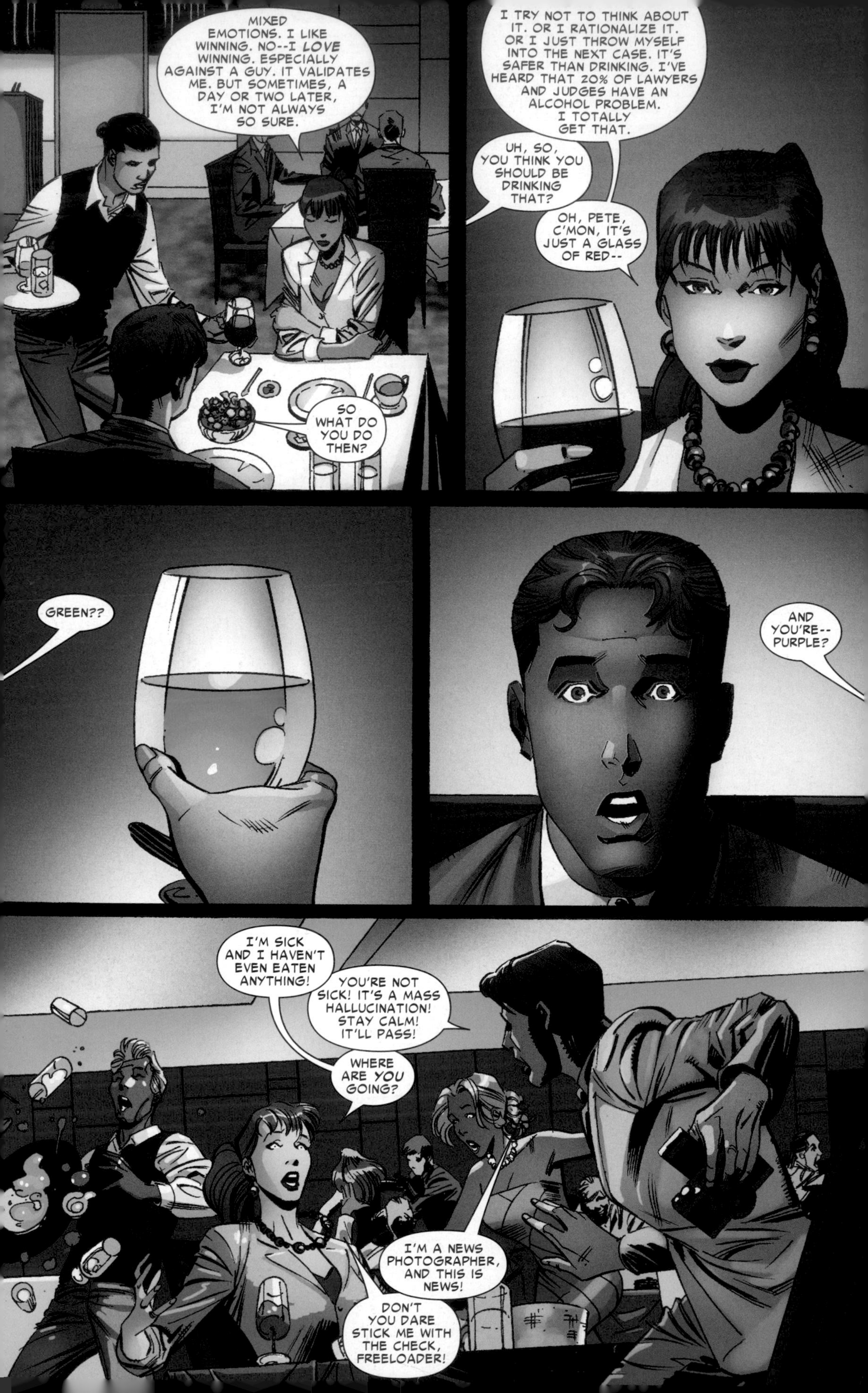
MIXED EMOTIONS. I LIKE WINNING. NO--I *LOVE* WINNING. ESPECIALLY AGAINST A GUY. IT VALIDATES ME. BUT SOMETIMES, A DAY OR TWO LATER, I'M NOT ALWAYS SO SURE.
SO WHAT DO YOU DO THEN?
I TRY NOT TO THINK ABOUT IT. OR I RATIONALIZE IT. OR I JUST THROW MYSELF INTO THE NEXT CASE. IT'S SAFER THAN DRINKING. I'VE HEARD THAT 20% OF LAWYERS AND JUDGES HAVE AN ALCOHOL PROBLEM. I TOTALLY GET THAT.
UH, SO, YOU THINK YOU SHOULD BE DRINKING THAT?
OH, PETE, C'MON, IT'S JUST A GLASS OF RED--
GREEN??
AND YOU'RE--PURPLE?
I'M SICK AND I HAVEN'T EVEN EATEN ANYTHING!
YOU'RE NOT SICK! IT'S A MASS HALLUCINATION! STAY CALM! IT'LL PASS!
WHERE ARE *YOU* GOING?
I'M A NEWS PHOTOGRAPHER, AND THIS IS NEWS!
DON'T YOU DARE STICK ME WITH THE CHECK, FREELOADER!

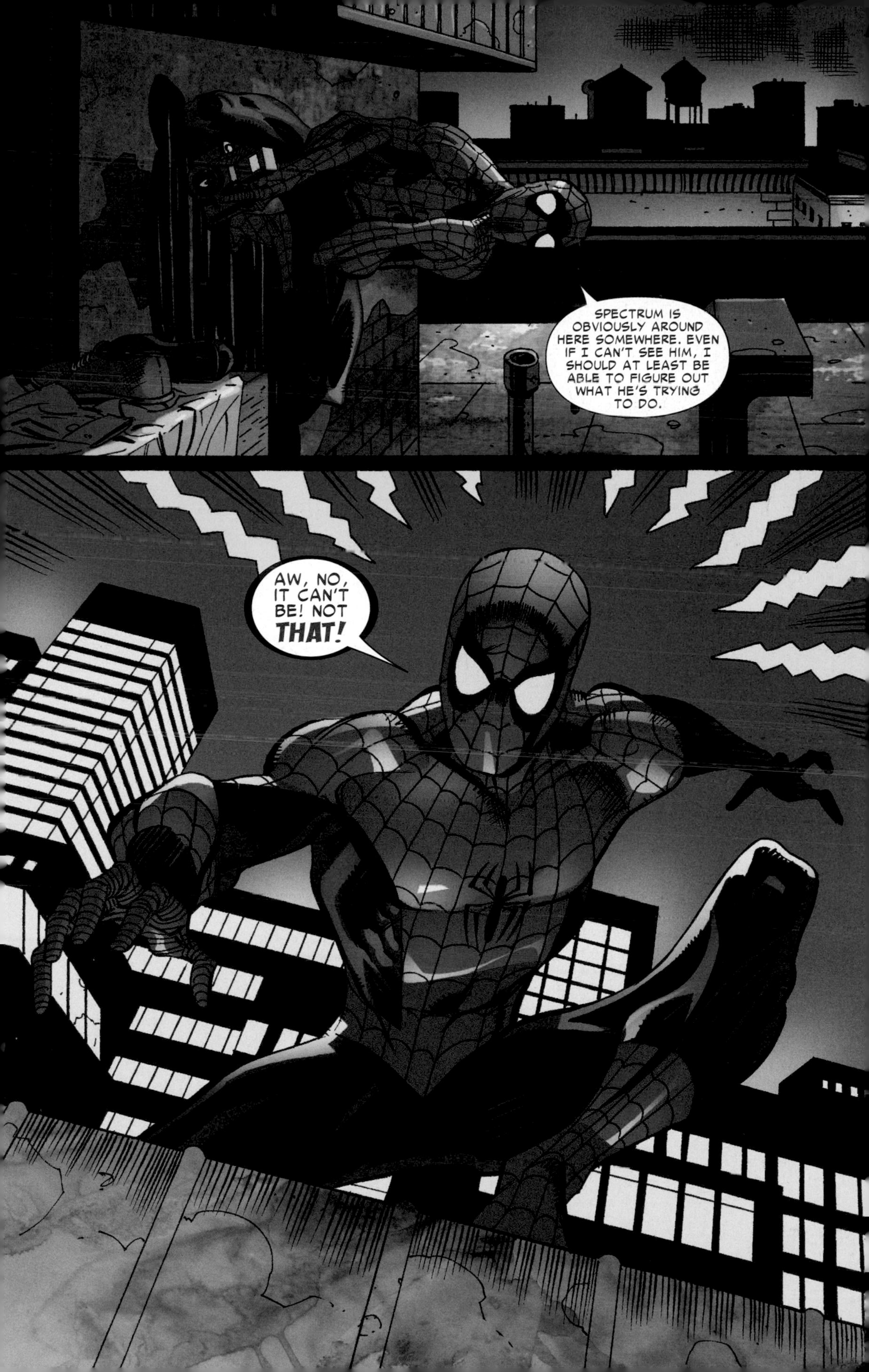
SPECTRUM IS OBVIOUSLY AROUND HERE SOMEWHERE. EVEN IF I CAN'T SEE HIM, I SHOULD AT LEAST BE ABLE TO FIGURE OUT WHAT HE'S TRYING TO DO.
AW, NO, IT CAN'T BE! NOT **THAT!**

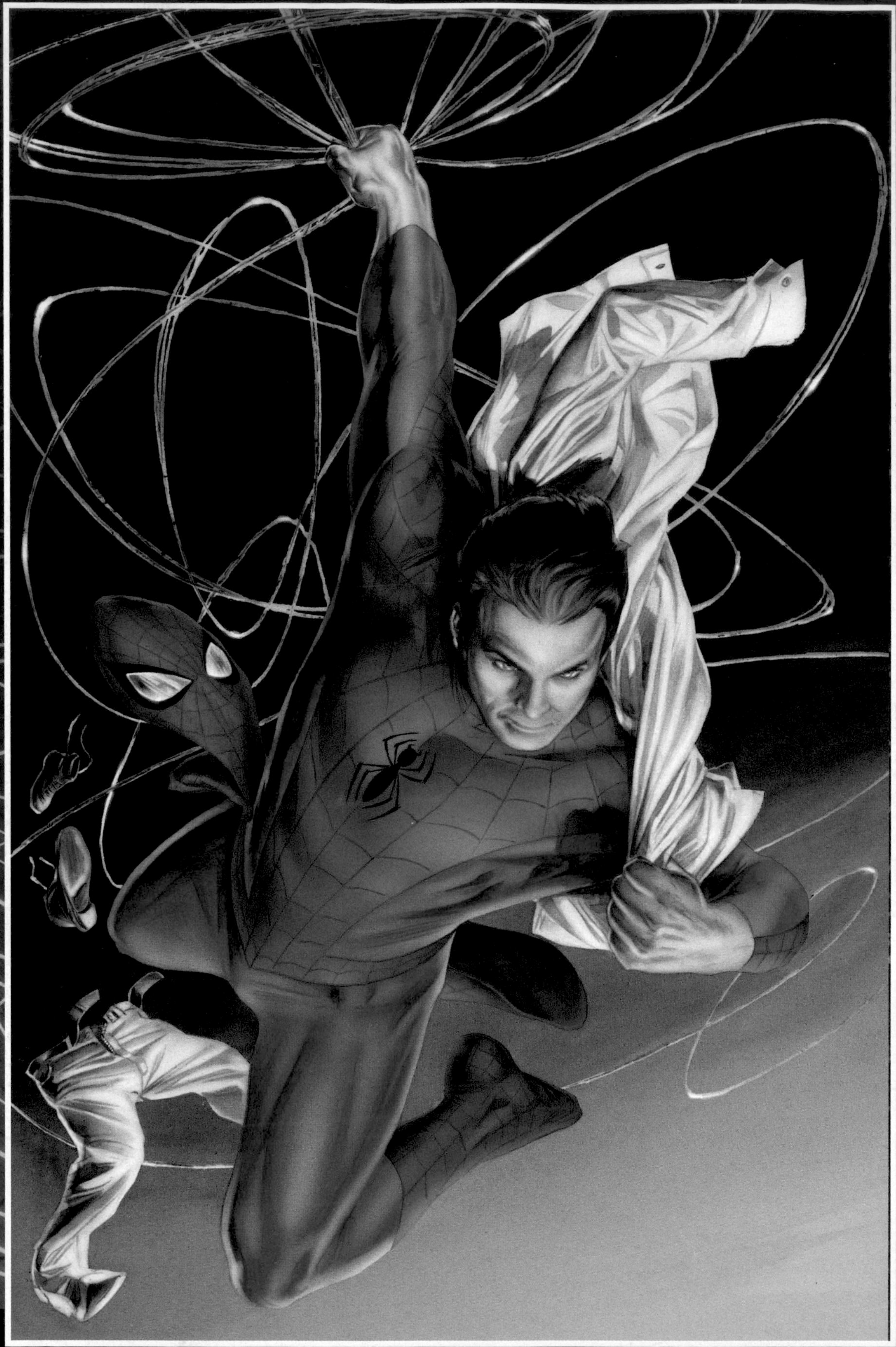

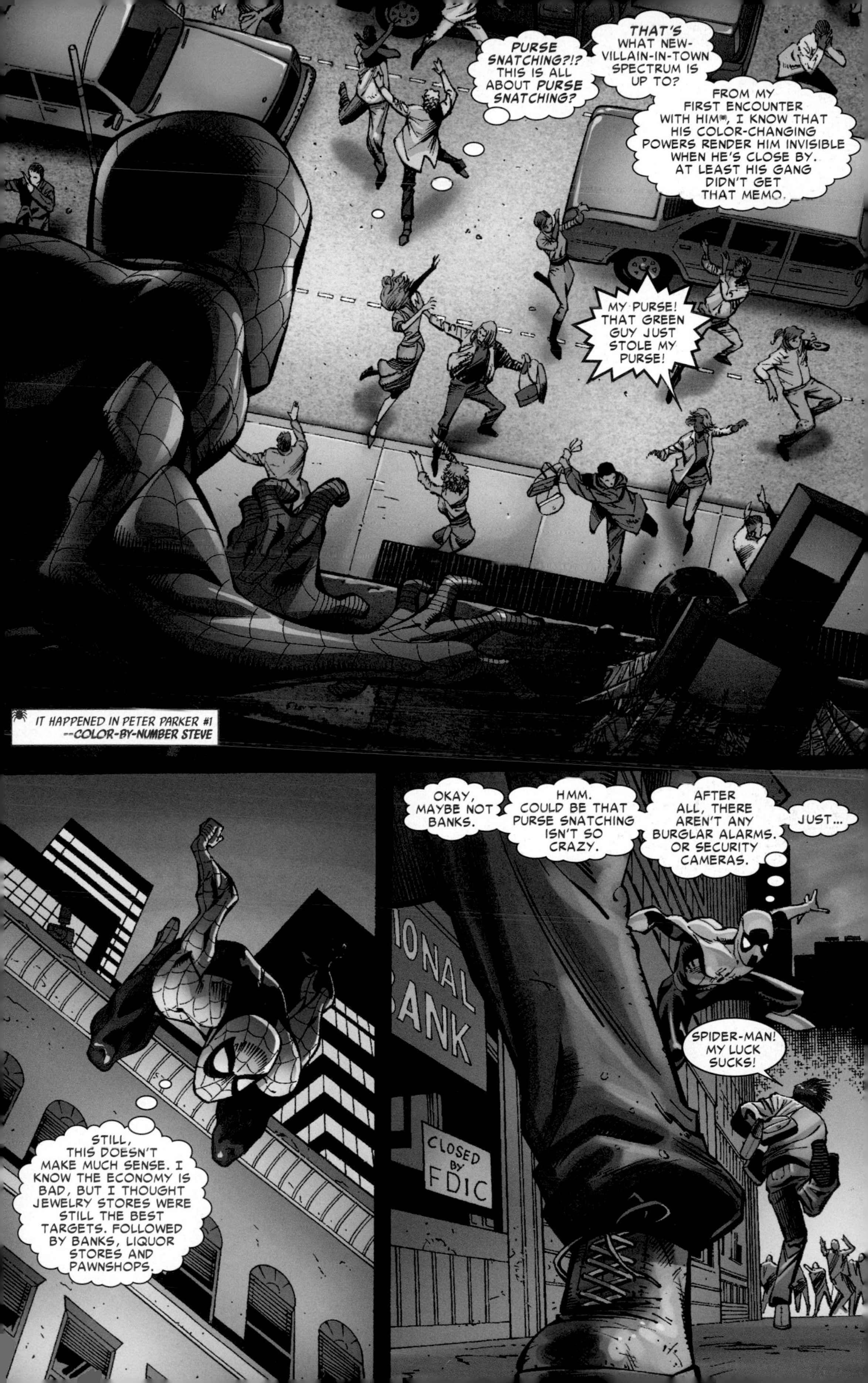
PURSE SNATCHING?!? THIS IS ALL ABOUT PURSE SNATCHING?
THAT'S WHAT NEW-VILLAIN-IN-TOWN SPECTRUM IS UP TO?
FROM MY FIRST ENCOUNTER WITH HIM*, I KNOW THAT HIS COLOR-CHANGING POWERS RENDER HIM INVISIBLE WHEN HE'S CLOSE BY. AT LEAST HIS GANG DIDN'T GET THAT MEMO.
MY PURSE! THAT GREEN GUY JUST STOLE MY PURSE!
*IT HAPPENED IN PETER PARKER #1 --COLOR-BY-NUMBER STEVE
STILL, THIS DOESN'T MAKE MUCH SENSE. I KNOW THE ECONOMY IS BAD, BUT I THOUGHT JEWELRY STORES WERE STILL THE BEST TARGETS. FOLLOWED BY BANKS, LIQUOR STORES AND PAWNSHOPS.
OKAY, MAYBE NOT BANKS.
HMM. COULD BE THAT PURSE SNATCHING ISN'T SO CRAZY.
AFTER ALL, THERE AREN'T ANY BURGLAR ALARMS. OR SECURITY CAMERAS.
JUST...
IONAL BANK
CLOSED BY FDIC
SPIDER-MAN! MY LUCK SUCKS!

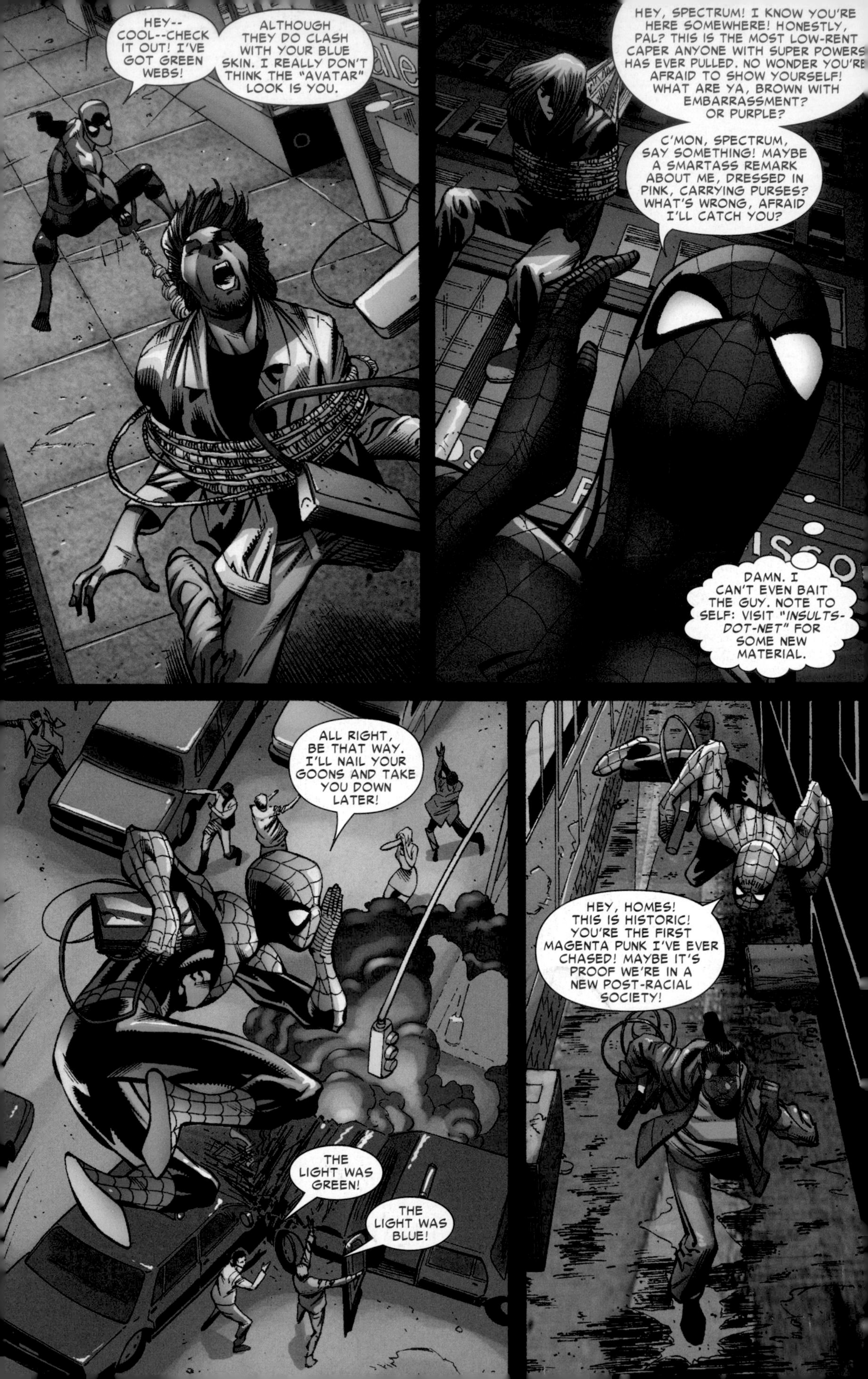
HEY-- COOL--CHECK IT OUT! I'VE GOT GREEN WEBS!
ALTHOUGH THEY DO CLASH WITH YOUR BLUE SKIN. I REALLY DON'T THINK THE "AVATAR" LOOK IS YOU.
HEY, SPECTRUM! I KNOW YOU'RE HERE SOMEWHERE! HONESTLY, PAL? THIS IS THE MOST LOW-RENT CAPER ANYONE WITH SUPER POWERS HAS EVER PULLED. NO WONDER YOU'RE AFRAID TO SHOW YOURSELF! WHAT ARE YA, BROWN WITH EMBARRASSMENT? OR PURPLE?
C'MON, SPECTRUM, SAY SOMETHING! MAYBE A SMARTASS REMARK ABOUT ME, DRESSED IN PINK, CARRYING PURSES? WHAT'S WRONG, AFRAID I'LL CATCH YOU?
DAMN. I CAN'T EVEN BAIT THE GUY. NOTE TO SELF: VISIT *"INSULTS-DOT-NET"* FOR SOME NEW MATERIAL.
ALL RIGHT, BE THAT WAY. I'LL NAIL YOUR GOONS AND TAKE YOU DOWN LATER!
THE LIGHT WAS GREEN!
THE LIGHT WAS BLUE!
HEY, HOMES! THIS IS HISTORIC! YOU'RE THE FIRST MAGENTA PUNK I'VE EVER CHASED! MAYBE IT'S PROOF WE'RE IN A NEW POST-RACIAL SOCIETY!

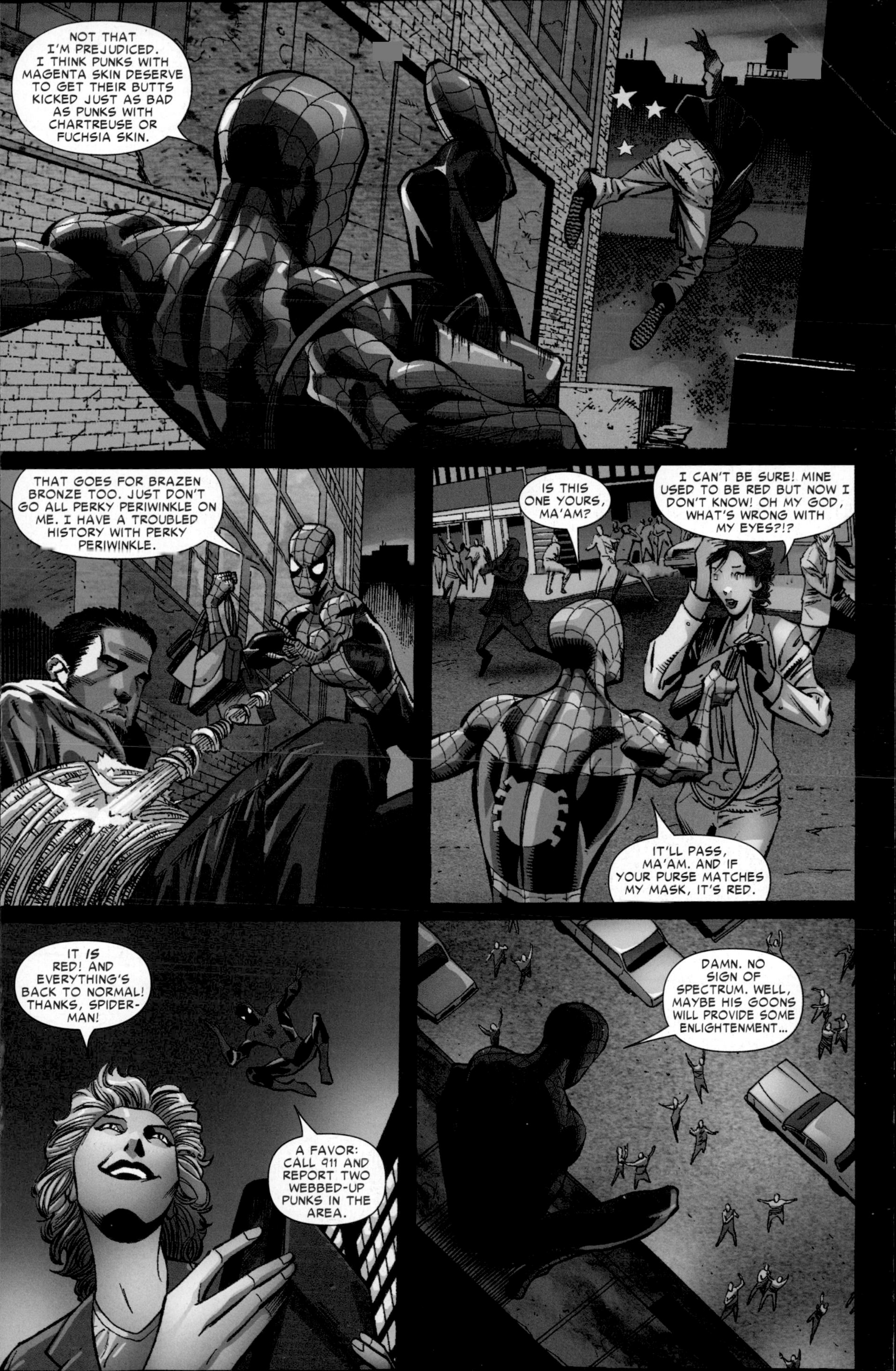
NOT THAT I'M PREJUDICED. I THINK PUNKS WITH MAGENTA SKIN DESERVE TO GET THEIR BUTTS KICKED JUST AS BAD AS PUNKS WITH CHARTREUSE OR FUCHSIA SKIN.
THAT GOES FOR BRAZEN BRONZE TOO. JUST DON'T GO ALL PERKY PERIWINKLE ON ME. I HAVE A TROUBLED HISTORY WITH PERKY PERIWINKLE.
IS THIS ONE YOURS, MA'AM?
I CAN'T BE SURE! MINE USED TO BE RED BUT NOW I DON'T KNOW! OH MY GOD, WHAT'S WRONG WITH MY EYES?!?
IT'LL PASS, MA'AM. AND IF YOUR PURSE MATCHES MY MASK, IT'S RED.
IT IS RED! AND EVERYTHING'S BACK TO NORMAL! THANKS, SPIDER-MAN!
A FAVOR: CALL 911 AND REPORT TWO WEBBED-UP PUNKS IN THE AREA.
DAMN. NO SIGN OF SPECTRUM. WELL, MAYBE HIS GOONS WILL PROVIDE SOME ENLIGHTENMENT...

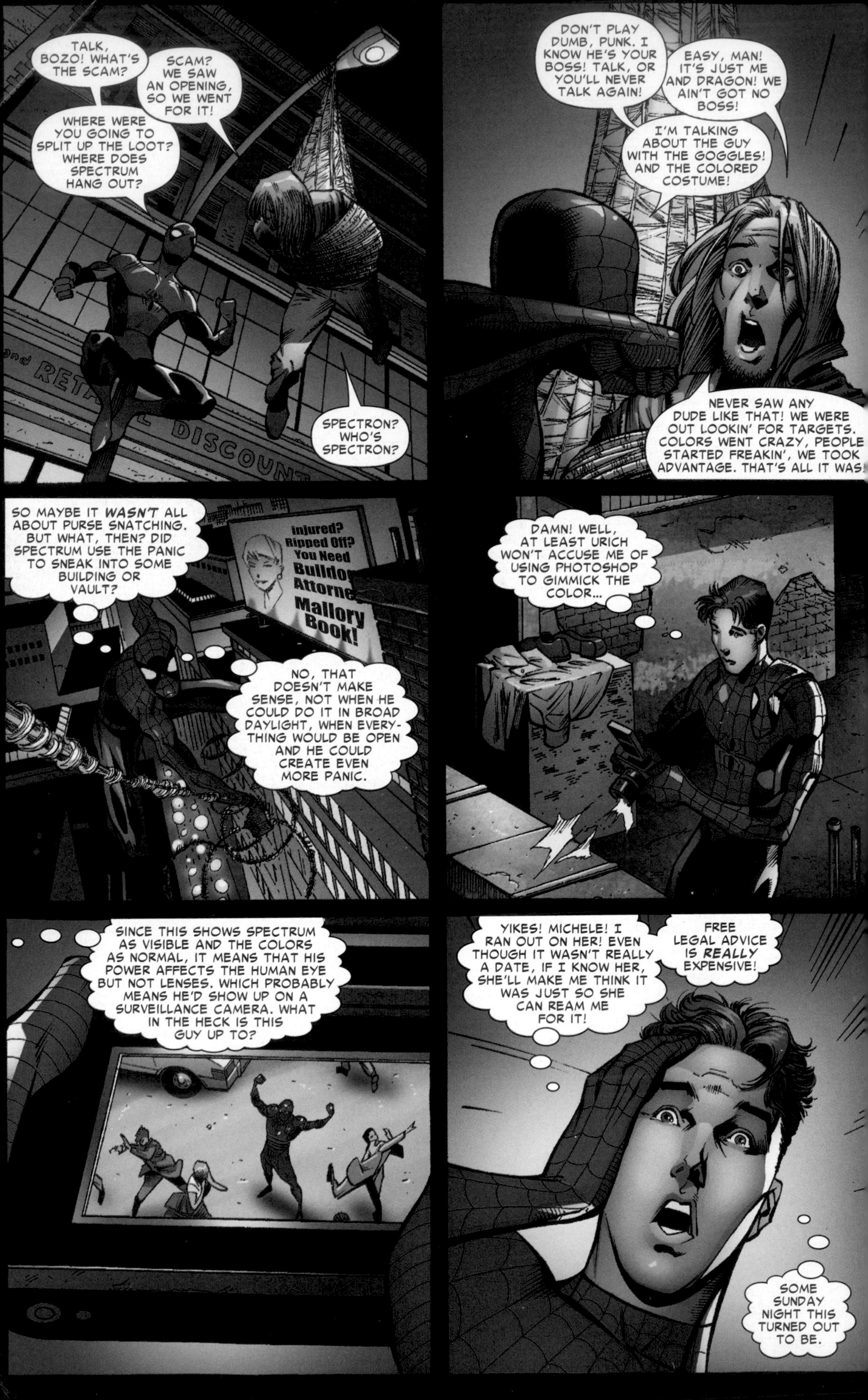
TALK, BOZO! WHAT'S THE SCAM?
SCAM? WE SAW AN OPENING, SO WE WENT FOR IT!
WHERE WERE YOU GOING TO SPLIT UP THE LOOT? WHERE DOES SPECTRUM HANG OUT?
SPECTRON? WHO'S SPECTRON?
DON'T PLAY DUMB, PUNK. I KNOW HE'S YOUR BOSS! TALK, OR YOU'LL NEVER TALK AGAIN!
EASY, MAN! IT'S JUST ME AND DRAGON! WE AIN'T GOT NO BOSS!
I'M TALKING ABOUT THE GUY WITH THE GOGGLES! AND THE COLORED COSTUME!
NEVER SAW ANY DUDE LIKE THAT! WE WERE OUT LOOKIN' FOR TARGETS. COLORS WENT CRAZY, PEOPLE STARTED FREAKIN', WE TOOK ADVANTAGE. THAT'S ALL IT WAS!
SO MAYBE IT WASN'T ALL ABOUT PURSE SNATCHING. BUT WHAT, THEN? DID SPECTRUM USE THE PANIC TO SNEAK INTO SOME BUILDING OR VAULT?
injured? Ripped Off? You Need
Mallory Book!
NO, THAT DOESN'T MAKE SENSE, NOT WHEN HE COULD DO IT IN BROAD DAYLIGHT, WHEN EVERYTHING WOULD BE OPEN AND HE COULD CREATE EVEN MORE PANIC.
DAMN! WELL, AT LEAST URICH WON'T ACCUSE ME OF USING PHOTOSHOP TO GIMMICK THE COLOR...
SINCE THIS SHOWS SPECTRUM AS VISIBLE AND THE COLORS AS NORMAL, IT MEANS THAT HIS POWER AFFECTS THE HUMAN EYE BUT NOT LENSES. WHICH PROBABLY MEANS HE'D SHOW UP ON A SURVEILLANCE CAMERA. WHAT IN THE HECK IS THIS GUY UP TO?
YIKES! MICHELE! I RAN OUT ON HER! EVEN THOUGH IT WASN'T REALLY A DATE, IF I KNOW HER, SHE'LL MAKE ME THINK IT WAS JUST SO SHE CAN REAM ME FOR IT!
FREE LEGAL ADVICE IS REALLY EXPENSIVE!
SOME SUNDAY NIGHT THIS TURNED OUT TO BE.

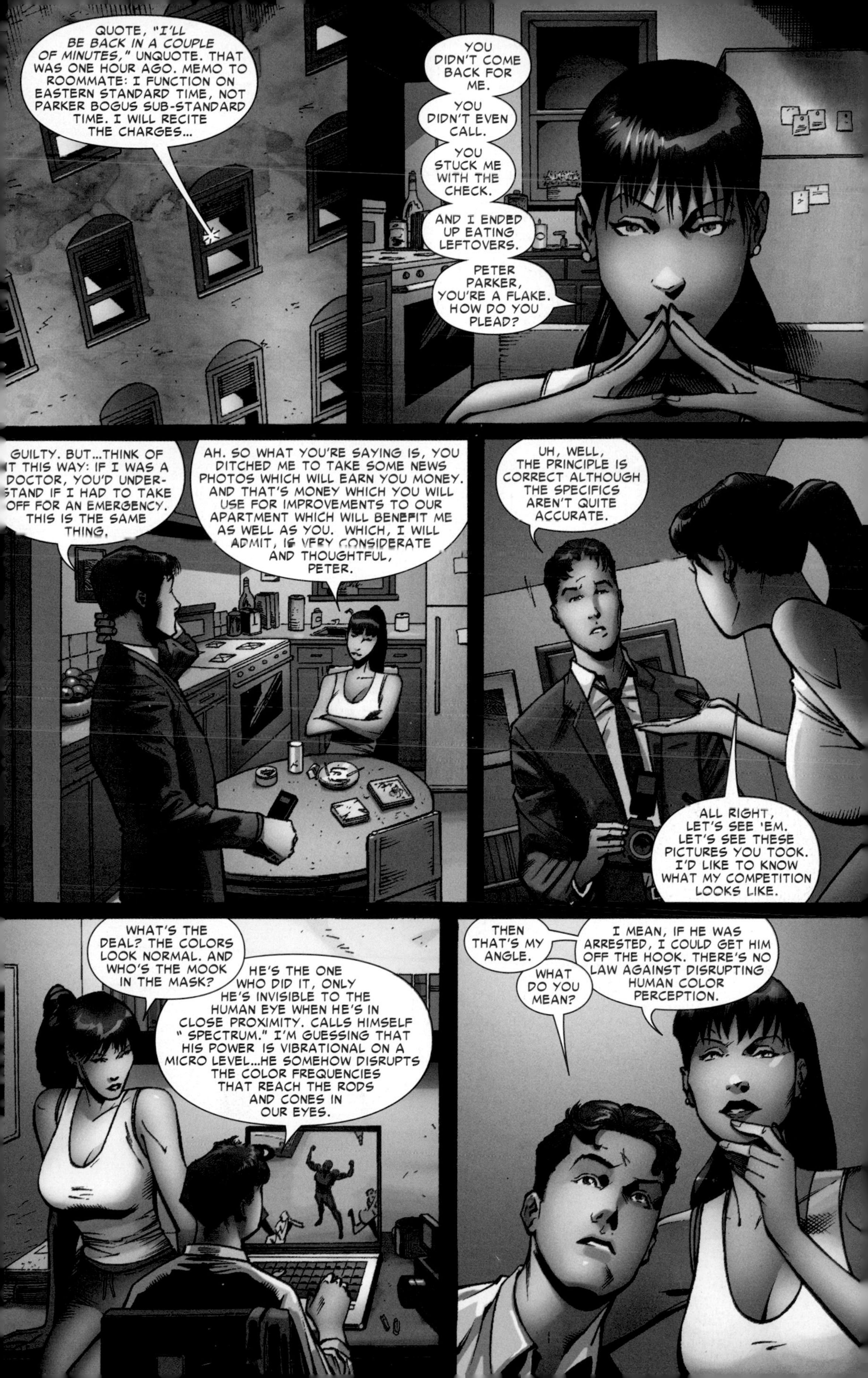
QUOTE, "I'LL BE BACK IN A COUPLE OF MINUTES," UNQUOTE. THAT WAS ONE HOUR AGO. MEMO TO ROOMMATE: I FUNCTION ON EASTERN STANDARD TIME, NOT PARKER BOGUS SUB-STANDARD TIME. I WILL RECITE THE CHARGES...
YOU DIDN'T COME BACK FOR ME.
YOU DIDN'T EVEN CALL.
YOU STUCK ME WITH THE CHECK.
AND I ENDED UP EATING LEFTOVERS.
PETER PARKER, YOU'RE A FLAKE. HOW DO YOU PLEAD?
GUILTY. BUT...THINK OF IT THIS WAY: IF I WAS A DOCTOR, YOU'D UNDERSTAND IF I HAD TO TAKE OFF FOR AN EMERGENCY. THIS IS THE SAME THING.
AH. SO WHAT YOU'RE SAYING IS, YOU DITCHED ME TO TAKE SOME NEWS PHOTOS WHICH WILL EARN YOU MONEY. AND THAT'S MONEY WHICH YOU WILL USE FOR IMPROVEMENTS TO OUR APARTMENT WHICH WILL BENEFIT ME AS WELL AS YOU. WHICH, I WILL ADMIT, IS VERY CONSIDERATE AND THOUGHTFUL, PETER.
UH, WELL, THE PRINCIPLE IS CORRECT ALTHOUGH THE SPECIFICS AREN'T QUITE ACCURATE.
ALL RIGHT, LET'S SEE 'EM. LET'S SEE THESE PICTURES YOU TOOK. I'D LIKE TO KNOW WHAT MY COMPETITION LOOKS LIKE.
WHAT'S THE DEAL? THE COLORS LOOK NORMAL. AND WHO'S THE MOOK IN THE MASK?
HE'S THE ONE WHO DID IT, ONLY HE'S INVISIBLE TO THE HUMAN EYE WHEN HE'S IN CLOSE PROXIMITY. CALLS HIMSELF "SPECTRUM." I'M GUESSING THAT HIS POWER IS VIBRATIONAL ON A MICRO LEVEL...HE SOMEHOW DISRUPTS THE COLOR FREQUENCIES THAT REACH THE RODS AND CONES IN OUR EYES.
THEN THAT'S MY ANGLE.
WHAT DO YOU MEAN?
I MEAN, IF HE WAS ARRESTED, I COULD GET HIM OFF THE HOOK. THERE'S NO LAW AGAINST DISRUPTING HUMAN COLOR PERCEPTION.

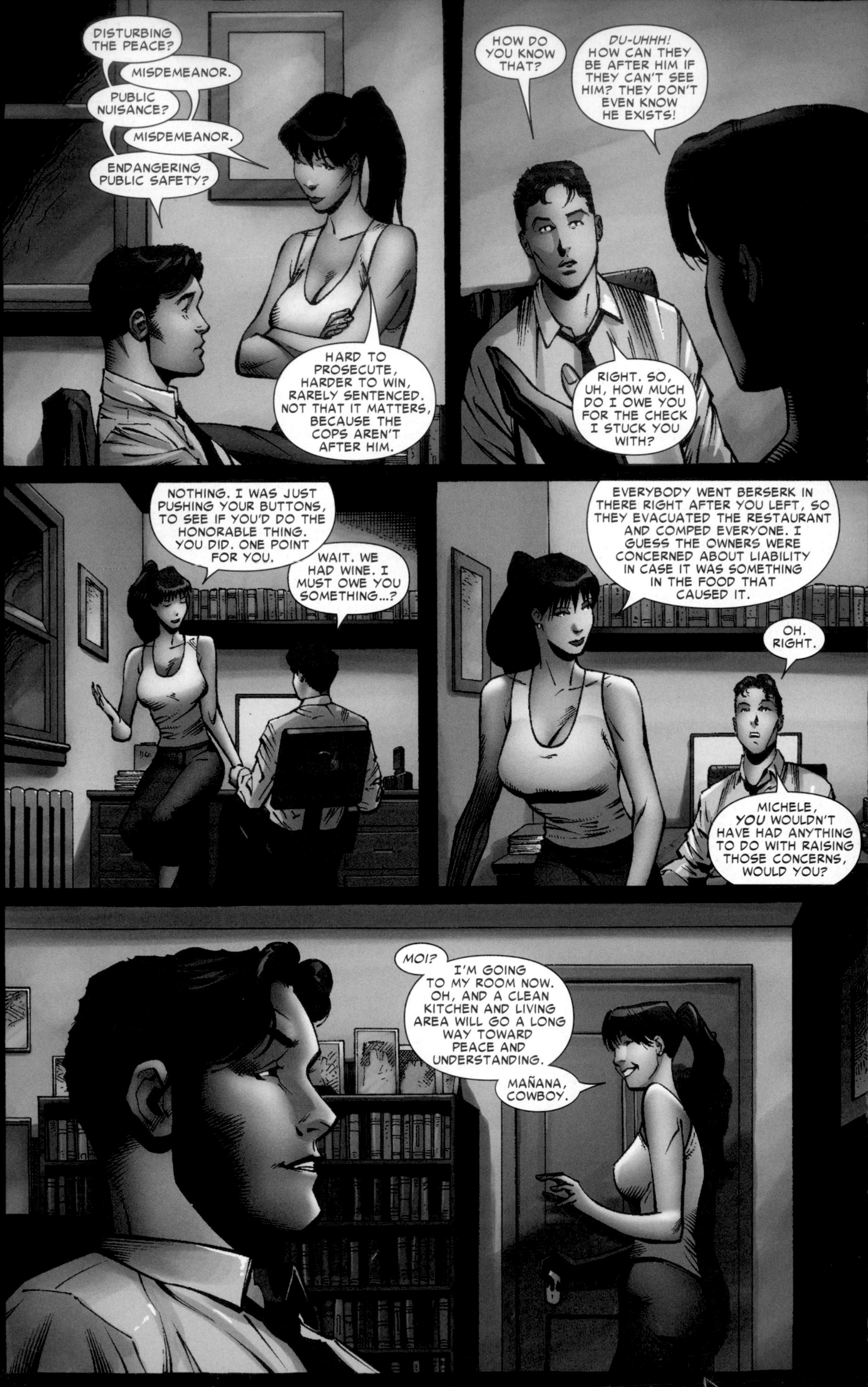
DISTURBING THE PEACE?
MISDEMEANOR.
PUBLIC NUISANCE?
MISDEMEANOR.
ENDANGERING PUBLIC SAFETY?
HARD TO PROSECUTE, HARDER TO WIN, RARELY SENTENCED. NOT THAT IT MATTERS, BECAUSE THE COPS AREN'T AFTER HIM.
HOW DO YOU KNOW THAT?
DU-UHHH! HOW CAN THEY BE AFTER HIM IF THEY CAN'T SEE HIM? THEY DON'T EVEN KNOW HE EXISTS!
RIGHT. SO, UH, HOW MUCH DO I OWE YOU FOR THE CHECK I STUCK YOU WITH?
NOTHING. I WAS JUST PUSHING YOUR BUTTONS, TO SEE IF YOU'D DO THE HONORABLE THING. YOU DID. ONE POINT FOR YOU.
WAIT. WE HAD WINE. I MUST OWE YOU SOMETHING...?
EVERYBODY WENT BERSERK IN THERE RIGHT AFTER YOU LEFT, SO THEY EVACUATED THE RESTAURANT AND COMPED EVERYONE. I GUESS THE OWNERS WERE CONCERNED ABOUT LIABILITY IN CASE IT WAS SOMETHING IN THE FOOD THAT CAUSED IT.
OH. RIGHT.
MICHELE, YOU WOULDN'T HAVE HAD ANYTHING TO DO WITH RAISING THOSE CONCERNS, WOULD YOU?
MOI?
I'M GOING TO MY ROOM NOW. OH, AND A CLEAN KITCHEN AND LIVING AREA WILL GO A LONG WAY TOWARD PEACE AND UNDERSTANDING.
MAÑANA, COWBOY.

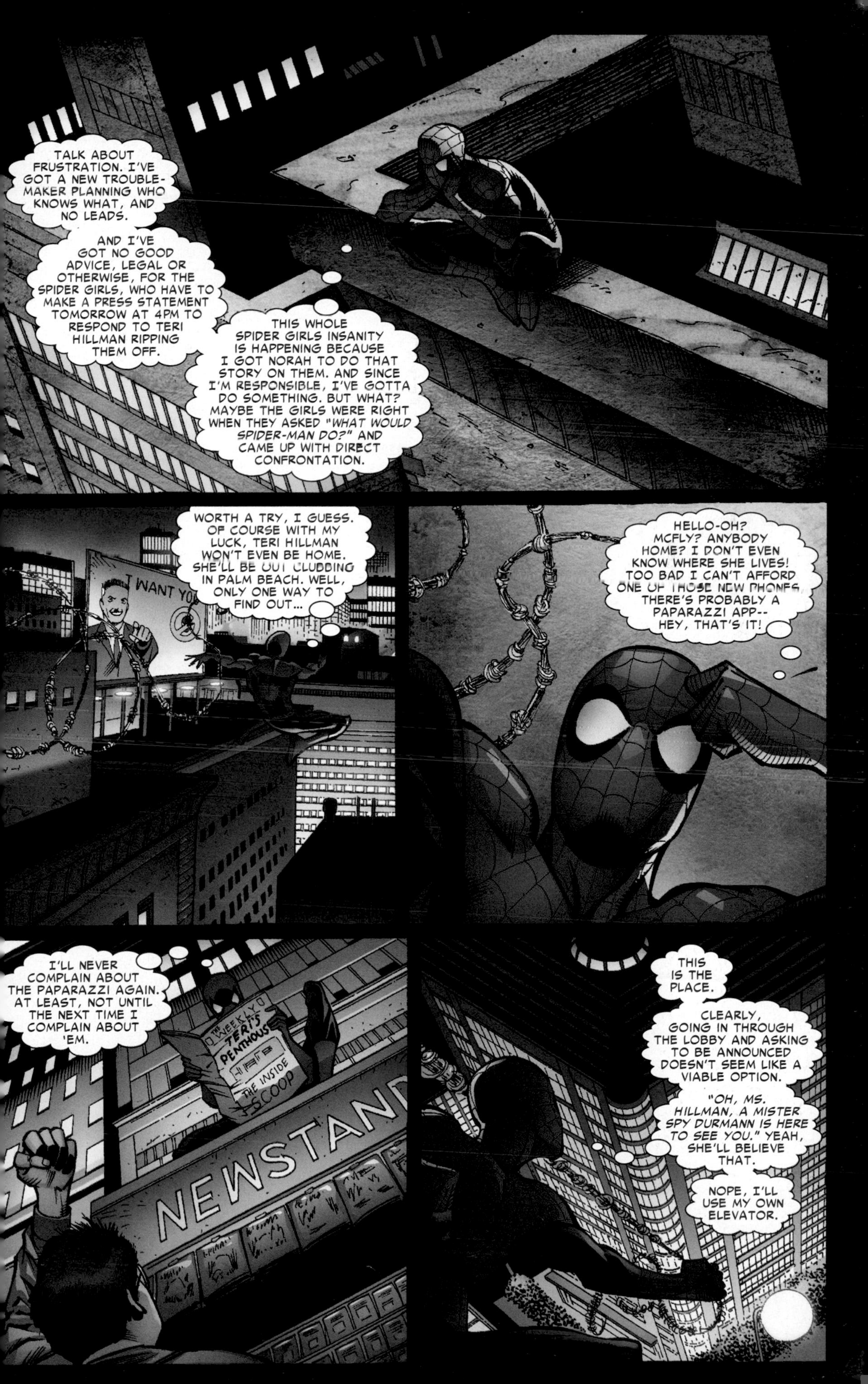
TALK ABOUT FRUSTRATION. I'VE GOT A NEW TROUBLE-MAKER PLANNING WHO KNOWS WHAT, AND NO LEADS.
AND I'VE GOT NO GOOD ADVICE, LEGAL OR OTHERWISE, FOR THE SPIDER GIRLS, WHO HAVE TO MAKE A PRESS STATEMENT TOMORROW AT 4PM TO RESPOND TO TERI HILLMAN RIPPING THEM OFF.
THIS WHOLE SPIDER GIRLS INSANITY IS HAPPENING BECAUSE I GOT NORAH TO DO THAT STORY ON THEM. AND SINCE I'M RESPONSIBLE, I'VE GOTTA DO SOMETHING. BUT WHAT? MAYBE THE GIRLS WERE RIGHT WHEN THEY ASKED "*WHAT WOULD SPIDER-MAN DO?*" AND CAME UP WITH DIRECT CONFRONTATION.
I WANT YO
WORTH A TRY, I GUESS. OF COURSE WITH MY LUCK, TERI HILLMAN WON'T EVEN BE HOME. SHE'LL BE OUT CLUBBING IN PALM BEACH. WELL, ONLY ONE WAY TO FIND OUT...
HELLO-OH? MCFLY? ANYBODY HOME? I DON'T EVEN KNOW WHERE SHE LIVES! TOO BAD I CAN'T AFFORD ONE OF THOSE NEW PHONES. THERE'S PROBABLY A PAPARAZZI APP-- HEY, THAT'S IT!
I'LL NEVER COMPLAIN ABOUT THE PAPARAZZI AGAIN. AT LEAST, NOT UNTIL THE NEXT TIME I COMPLAIN ABOUT 'EM.
THE WEEKLY
TERI'S PENTHOUSE
THE INSIDE SCOOP
NEWSTAND
THIS IS THE PLACE.
CLEARLY, GOING IN THROUGH THE LOBBY AND ASKING TO BE ANNOUNCED DOESN'T SEEM LIKE A VIABLE OPTION.
"*OH, MS. HILLMAN, A MISTER SPY DURMANN IS HERE TO SEE YOU.*" YEAH, SHE'LL BELIEVE THAT.
NOPE, I'LL USE MY OWN ELEVATOR.

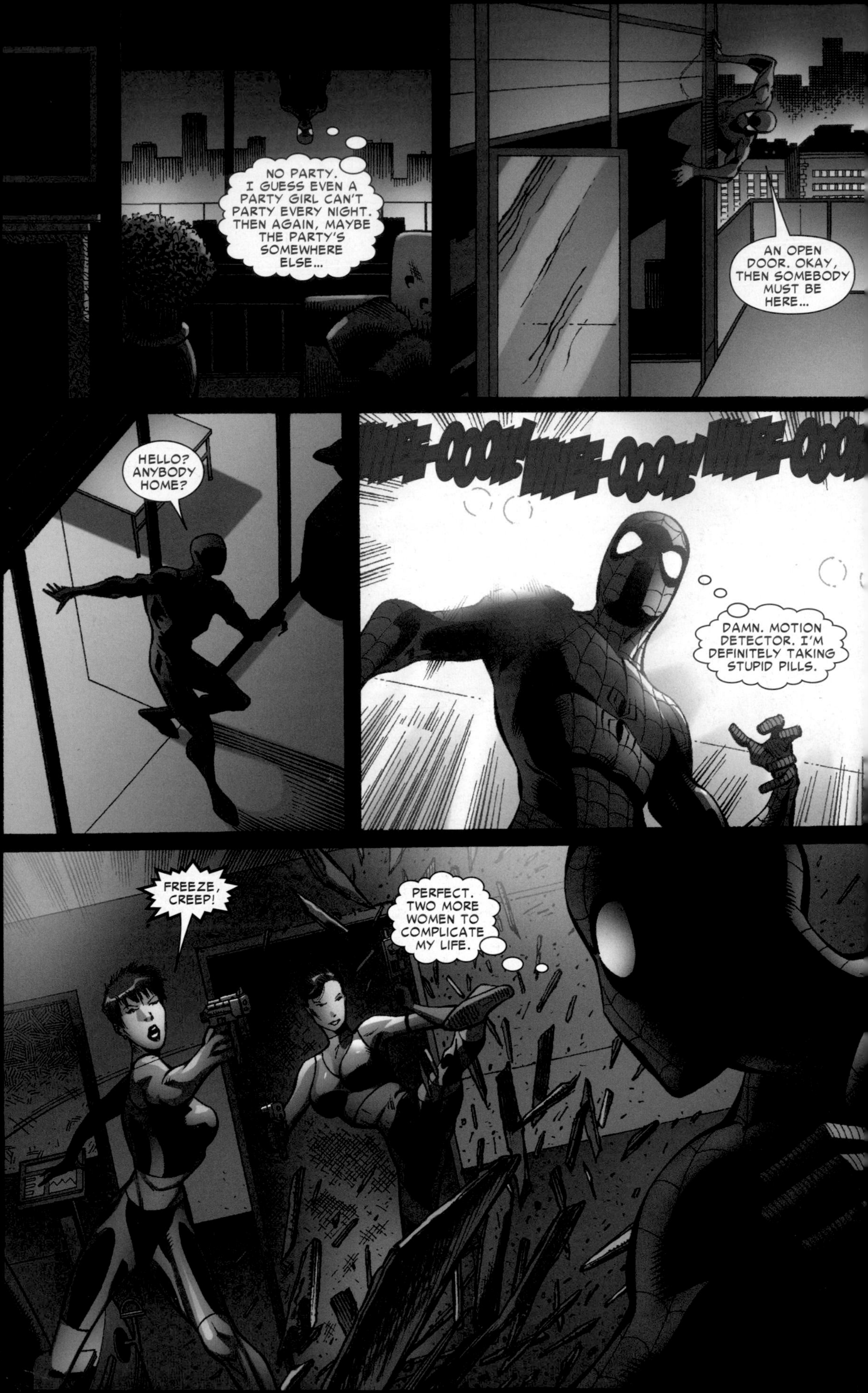
NO PARTY. I GUESS EVEN A PARTY GIRL CAN'T PARTY EVERY NIGHT. THEN AGAIN, MAYBE THE PARTY'S SOMEWHERE ELSE...
AN OPEN DOOR. OKAY, THEN SOMEBODY MUST BE HERE...
HELLO? ANYBODY HOME?
WHEE-OOOH! WHEE-OOOH! WHEE-OOOH
DAMN. MOTION DETECTOR. I'M DEFINITELY TAKING STUPID PILLS.
FREEZE, CREEP!
PERFECT. TWO MORE WOMEN TO COMPLICATE MY LIFE.

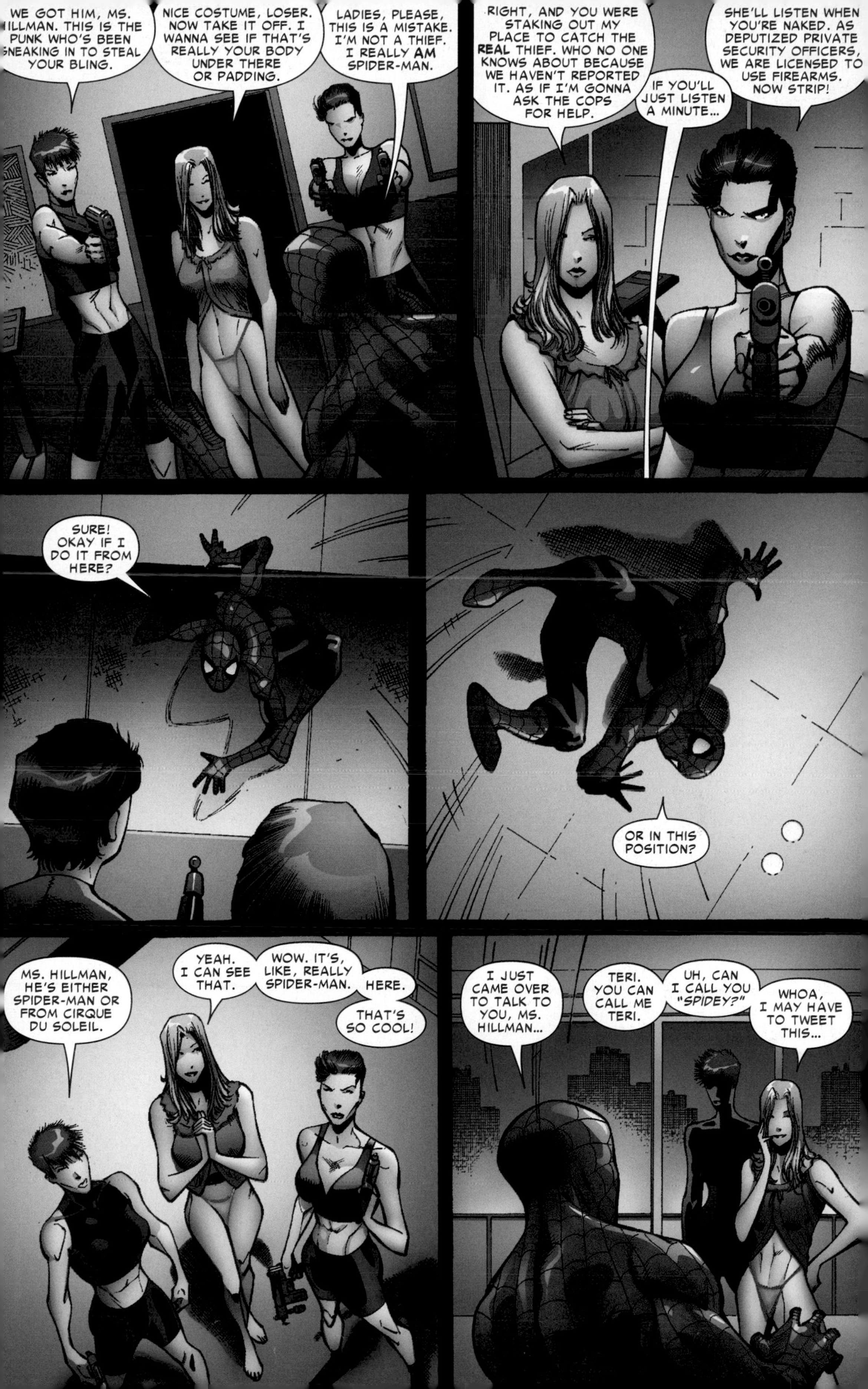
WE GOT HIM, MS. HILLMAN. THIS IS THE PUNK WHO'S BEEN SNEAKING IN TO STEAL YOUR BLING.
NICE COSTUME, LOSER. NOW TAKE IT OFF. I WANNA SEE IF THAT'S REALLY YOUR BODY UNDER THERE OR PADDING.
LADIES, PLEASE, THIS IS A MISTAKE. I'M NOT A THIEF. I REALLY **AM** SPIDER-MAN.
RIGHT, AND YOU WERE STAKING OUT MY PLACE TO CATCH THE **REAL** THIEF. WHO NO ONE KNOWS ABOUT BECAUSE WE HAVEN'T REPORTED IT. AS IF I'M GONNA ASK THE COPS FOR HELP.
IF YOU'LL JUST LISTEN A MINUTE...
SHE'LL LISTEN WHEN YOU'RE NAKED. AS DEPUTIZED PRIVATE SECURITY OFFICERS, WE ARE LICENSED TO USE FIREARMS. NOW STRIP!
SURE! OKAY IF I DO IT FROM HERE?
OR IN THIS POSITION?
MS. HILLMAN, HE'S EITHER SPIDER-MAN OR FROM CIRQUE DU SOLEIL.
YEAH. I CAN SEE THAT.
WOW. IT'S, LIKE, REALLY SPIDER-MAN.
HERE.
THAT'S SO COOL!
I JUST CAME OVER TO TALK TO YOU, MS. HILLMAN...
TERI. YOU CAN CALL ME TERI.
UH, CAN I CALL YOU *"SPIDEY?"*
WHOA, I MAY HAVE TO TWEET THIS...

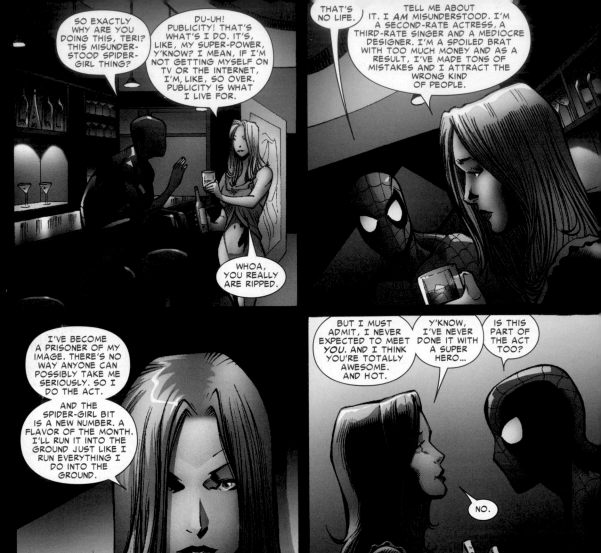

SO EXACTLY WHY ARE YOU DOING THIS, TERI? THIS MISUNDERSTOOD SPIDER-GIRL THING?

DU-UH! PUBLICITY! THAT'S WHAT'S I DO. IT'S, LIKE, MY SUPER-POWER, Y'KNOW? I MEAN, IF I'M NOT GETTING MYSELF ON TV OR THE INTERNET, I'M, LIKE, SO OVER. PUBLICITY IS WHAT I LIVE FOR.

WHOA, YOU REALLY ARE RIPPED.

THAT'S NO LIFE.

TELL ME ABOUT IT. I AM MISUNDERSTOOD. I'M A SECOND-RATE ACTRESS, A THIRD-RATE SINGER AND A MEDIOCRE DESIGNER. I'M A SPOILED BRAT WITH TOO MUCH MONEY AND AS A RESULT, I'VE MADE TONS OF MISTAKES AND I ATTRACT THE WRONG KIND OF PEOPLE.

I'VE BECOME A PRISONER OF MY IMAGE. THERE'S NO WAY ANYONE CAN POSSIBLY TAKE ME SERIOUSLY. SO I DO THE ACT.

AND THE SPIDER-GIRL BIT IS A NEW NUMBER. A FLAVOR OF THE MONTH. I'LL RUN IT INTO THE GROUND JUST LIKE I RUN EVERYTHING I DO INTO THE GROUND.

BUT I MUST ADMIT, I NEVER EXPECTED TO MEET YOU. AND I THINK YOU'RE TOTALLY AWESOME. AND HOT.

Y'KNOW, I'VE NEVER DONE IT WITH A SUPER HERO...

IS THIS PART OF THE ACT TOO?

NO.

TERI, YOU'RE HURTING THE THREE VERY DECENT GIRLS WHO STARTED THIS.

BIG WHOOP. SO I'M STEALING THEIR MOMENT IN THE SUN. THEY'LL GET OVER IT. ANYWAY, THAT'S WHAT I DO. THAT'S WHAT PEOPLE EXPECT. WHAT DO YOU WANT ME TO DO, SPIDEY, GO OUT AND TRASH YOU INSTEAD?

WELL... NO...

TRUTH IS, IF I DROP THIS SPIDER-GIRLS THING NOW, I'LL LOOK LIKE A BIGGER IDIOT THAN PEOPLE ALREADY THINK I AM. AND I'M NOT AN IDIOT, EVEN THOUGH I PLAY ONE ON TV.

I'M STARTING TO REALIZE THAT...

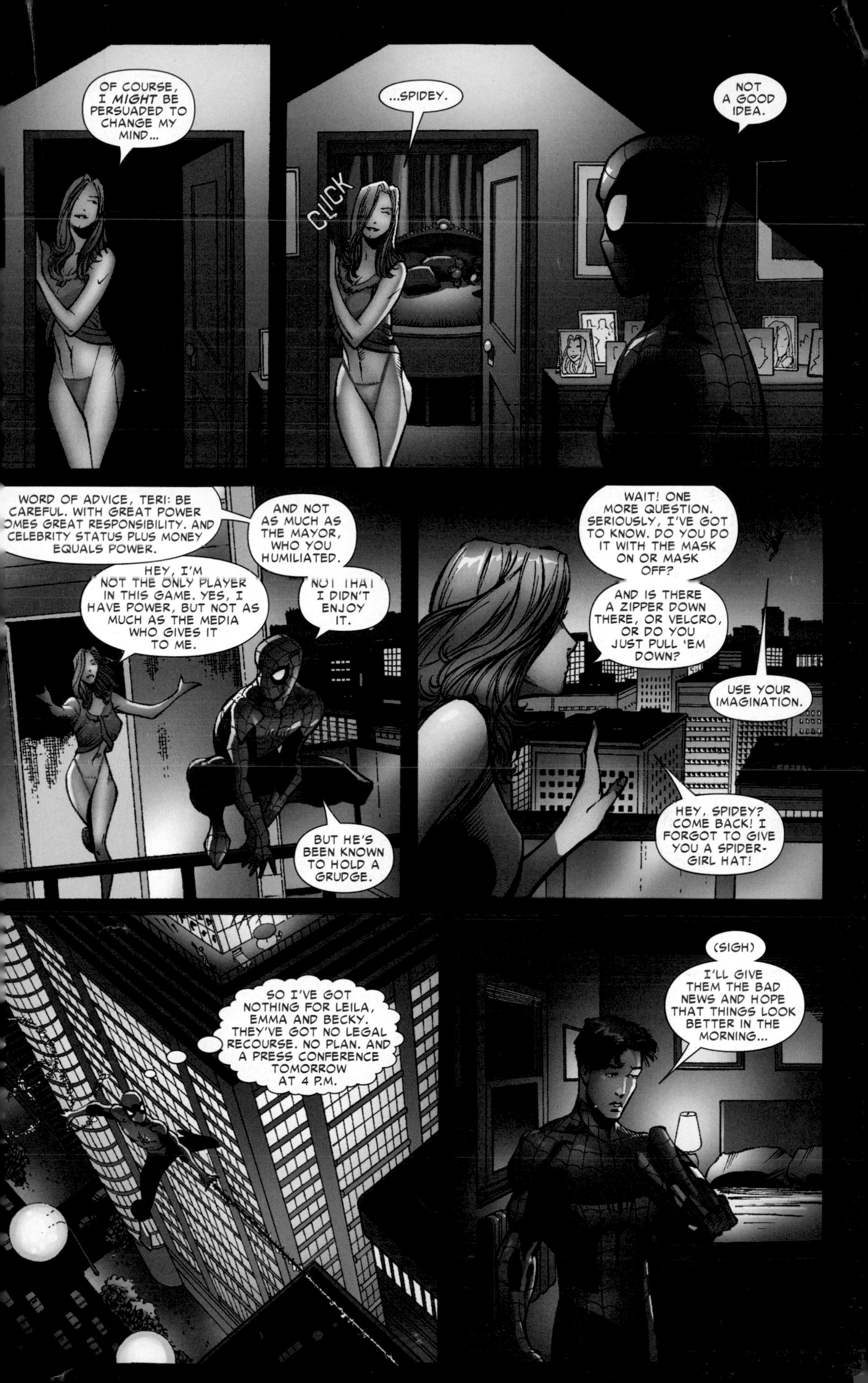
OF COURSE, I MIGHT BE PERSUADED TO CHANGE MY MIND...
...SPIDEY.
CLICK
NOT A GOOD IDEA.
WORD OF ADVICE, TERI: BE CAREFUL. WITH GREAT POWER OMES GREAT RESPONSIBILITY. AND CELEBRITY STATUS PLUS MONEY EQUALS POWER.
HEY, I'M NOT THE ONLY PLAYER IN THIS GAME. YES, I HAVE POWER, BUT NOT AS MUCH AS THE MEDIA WHO GIVES IT TO ME.
AND NOT AS MUCH AS THE MAYOR, WHO YOU HUMILIATED.
NOT THAT I DIDN'T ENJOY IT.
BUT HE'S BEEN KNOWN TO HOLD A GRUDGE.
WAIT! ONE MORE QUESTION. SERIOUSLY, I'VE GOT TO KNOW. DO YOU DO IT WITH THE MASK ON OR MASK OFF?
AND IS THERE A ZIPPER DOWN THERE, OR VELCRO, OR DO YOU JUST PULL 'EM DOWN?
USE YOUR IMAGINATION.
HEY, SPIDEY? COME BACK! I FORGOT TO GIVE YOU A SPIDER-GIRL HAT!
SO I'VE GOT NOTHING FOR LEILA, EMMA AND BECKY. THEY'VE GOT NO LEGAL RECOURSE. NO PLAN. AND A PRESS CONFERENCE TOMORROW AT 4 P.M.
(SIGH)
I'LL GIVE THEM THE BAD NEWS AND HOPE THAT THINGS LOOK BETTER IN THE MORNING...

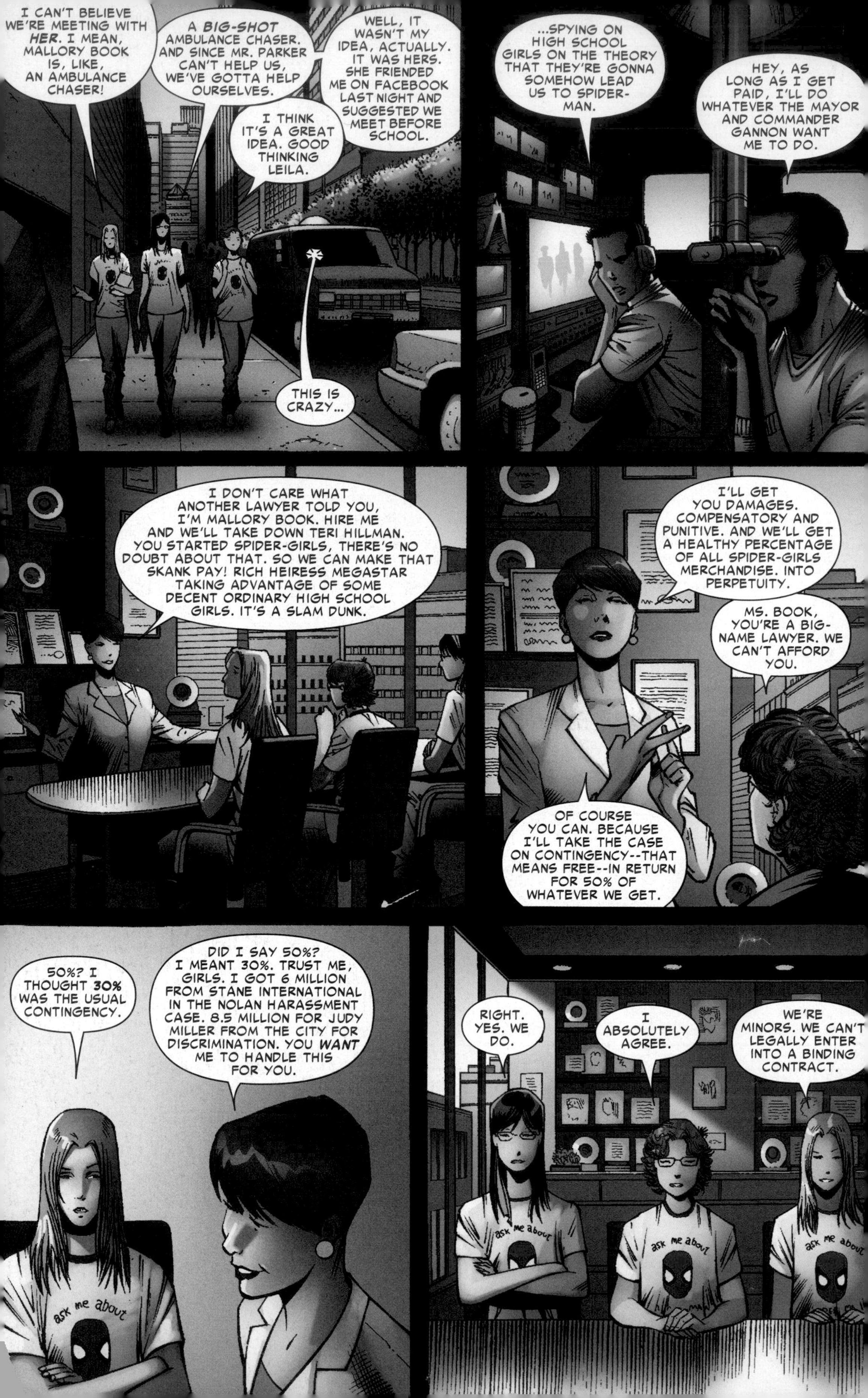
I CAN'T BELIEVE WE'RE MEETING WITH *HER*. I MEAN, MALLORY BOOK IS, LIKE, AN AMBULANCE CHASER!
A *BIG-SHOT* AMBULANCE CHASER. AND SINCE MR. PARKER CAN'T HELP US, WE'VE GOTTA HELP OURSELVES.
I THINK IT'S A GREAT IDEA. GOOD THINKING LEILA.
WELL, IT WASN'T MY IDEA, ACTUALLY. IT WAS HERS. SHE FRIENDED ME ON FACEBOOK LAST NIGHT AND SUGGESTED WE MEET BEFORE SCHOOL.
THIS IS CRAZY...
...SPYING ON HIGH SCHOOL GIRLS ON THE THEORY THAT THEY'RE GONNA SOMEHOW LEAD US TO SPIDER-MAN.
HEY, AS LONG AS I GET PAID, I'LL DO WHATEVER THE MAYOR AND COMMANDER GANNON WANT ME TO DO.
I DON'T CARE WHAT ANOTHER LAWYER TOLD YOU, I'M MALLORY BOOK. HIRE ME AND WE'LL TAKE DOWN TERI HILLMAN. YOU STARTED SPIDER-GIRLS, THERE'S NO DOUBT ABOUT THAT. SO WE CAN MAKE THAT SKANK PAY! RICH HEIRESS MEGASTAR TAKING ADVANTAGE OF SOME DECENT ORDINARY HIGH SCHOOL GIRLS. IT'S A SLAM DUNK.
I'LL GET YOU DAMAGES. COMPENSATORY AND PUNITIVE. AND WE'LL GET A HEALTHY PERCENTAGE OF ALL SPIDER-GIRLS MERCHANDISE. INTO PERPETUITY.
MS. BOOK, YOU'RE A BIG-NAME LAWYER. WE CAN'T AFFORD YOU.
OF COURSE YOU CAN. BECAUSE I'LL TAKE THE CASE ON CONTINGENCY--THAT MEANS FREE--IN RETURN FOR 50% OF WHATEVER WE GET.
50%? I THOUGHT **30%** WAS THE USUAL CONTINGENCY.
DID I SAY 50%? I MEANT 30%. TRUST ME, GIRLS. I GOT 6 MILLION FROM STANE INTERNATIONAL IN THE NOLAN HARASSMENT CASE. 8.5 MILLION FOR JUDY MILLER FROM THE CITY FOR DISCRIMINATION. YOU *WANT* ME TO HANDLE THIS FOR YOU.
ask me about
RIGHT. YES. WE DO.
I ABSOLUTELY AGREE.
WE'RE MINORS. WE CAN'T LEGALLY ENTER INTO A BINDING CONTRACT.
ask me about
ask me about
ask me about

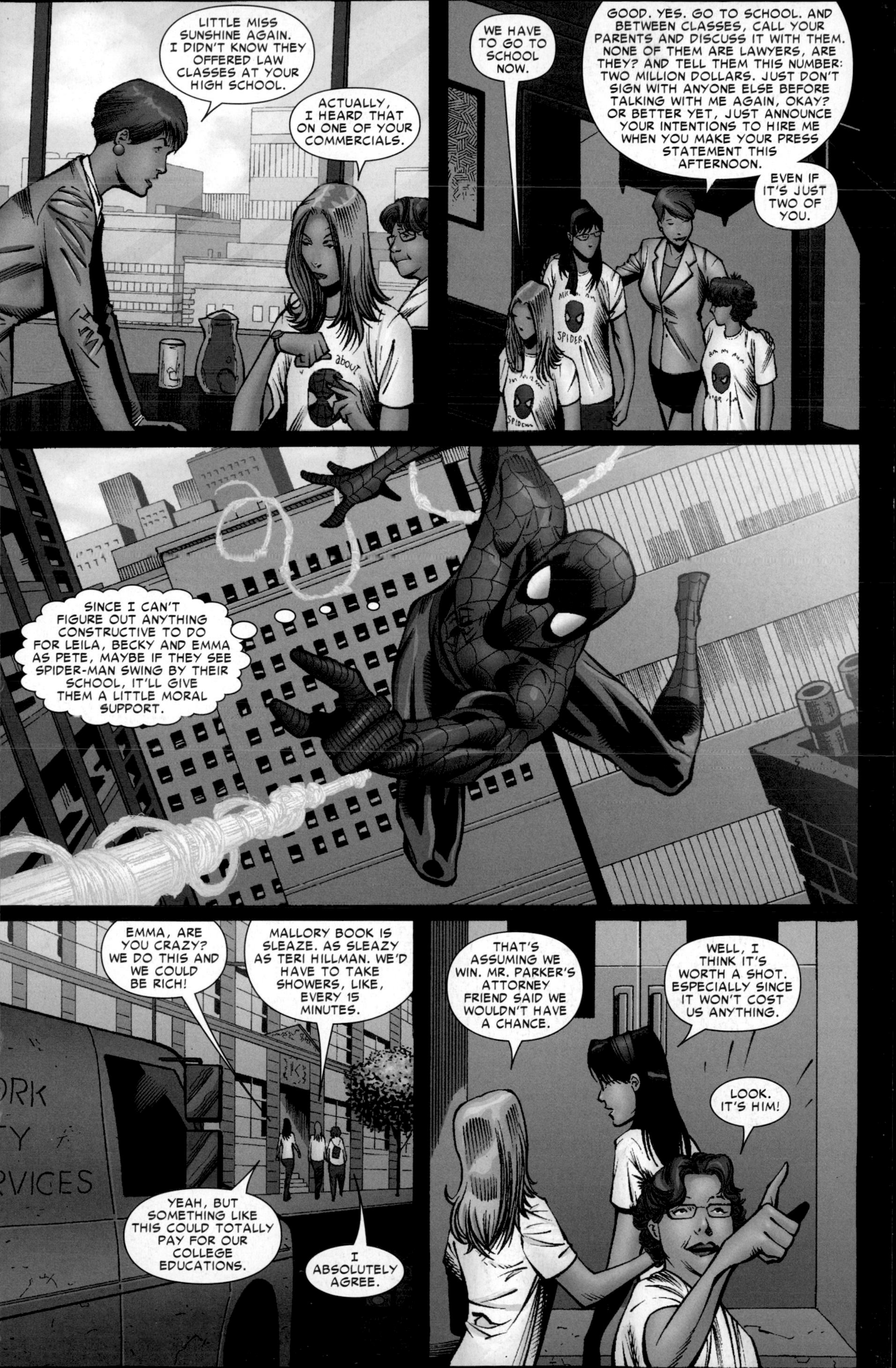

LITTLE MISS SUNSHINE AGAIN. I DIDN'T KNOW THEY OFFERED LAW CLASSES AT YOUR HIGH SCHOOL.
ACTUALLY, I HEARD THAT ON ONE OF YOUR COMMERCIALS.
WE HAVE TO GO TO SCHOOL NOW.
GOOD. YES. GO TO SCHOOL. AND BETWEEN CLASSES, CALL YOUR PARENTS AND DISCUSS IT WITH THEM. NONE OF THEM ARE LAWYERS, ARE THEY? AND TELL THEM THIS NUMBER: TWO MILLION DOLLARS. JUST DON'T SIGN WITH ANYONE ELSE BEFORE TALKING WITH ME AGAIN, OKAY? OR BETTER YET, JUST ANNOUNCE YOUR INTENTIONS TO HIRE ME WHEN YOU MAKE YOUR PRESS STATEMENT THIS AFTERNOON.
EVEN IF IT'S JUST TWO OF YOU.
SINCE I CAN'T FIGURE OUT ANYTHING CONSTRUCTIVE TO DO FOR LEILA, BECKY AND EMMA AS PETE, MAYBE IF THEY SEE SPIDER-MAN SWING BY THEIR SCHOOL, IT'LL GIVE THEM A LITTLE MORAL SUPPORT.
EMMA, ARE YOU CRAZY? WE DO THIS AND WE COULD BE RICH!
MALLORY BOOK IS SLEAZE. AS SLEAZY AS TERI HILLMAN. WE'D HAVE TO TAKE SHOWERS, LIKE, EVERY 15 MINUTES.
YEAH, BUT SOMETHING LIKE THIS COULD TOTALLY PAY FOR OUR COLLEGE EDUCATIONS.
I ABSOLUTELY AGREE.
THAT'S ASSUMING WE WIN. MR. PARKER'S ATTORNEY FRIEND SAID WE WOULDN'T HAVE A CHANCE.
WELL, I THINK IT'S WORTH A SHOT. ESPECIALLY SINCE IT WON'T COST US ANYTHING.
LOOK. IT'S HIM!

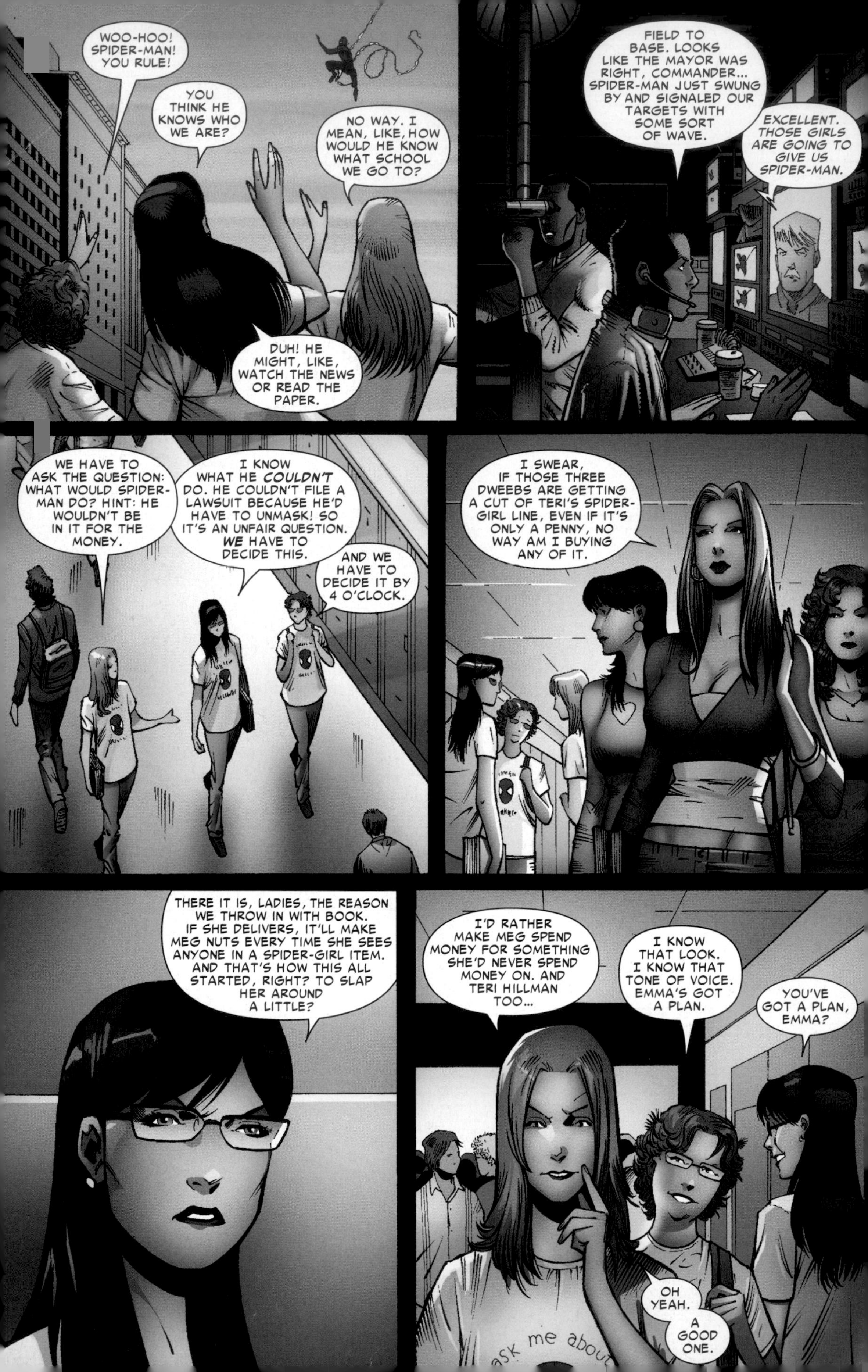
WOO-HOO! SPIDER-MAN! YOU RULE!
YOU THINK HE KNOWS WHO WE ARE?
NO WAY. I MEAN, LIKE, HOW WOULD HE KNOW WHAT SCHOOL WE GO TO?
DUH! HE MIGHT, LIKE, WATCH THE NEWS OR READ THE PAPER.
FIELD TO BASE. LOOKS LIKE THE MAYOR WAS RIGHT, COMMANDER... SPIDER-MAN JUST SWUNG BY AND SIGNALED OUR TARGETS WITH SOME SORT OF WAVE.
EXCELLENT. THOSE GIRLS ARE GOING TO GIVE US SPIDER-MAN.
WE HAVE TO ASK THE QUESTION: WHAT WOULD SPIDER-MAN DO? HINT: HE WOULDN'T BE IN IT FOR THE MONEY.
I KNOW WHAT HE *COULDN'T* DO. HE COULDN'T FILE A LAWSUIT BECAUSE HE'D HAVE TO UNMASK! SO IT'S AN UNFAIR QUESTION. ***WE*** HAVE TO DECIDE THIS.
AND WE HAVE TO DECIDE IT BY 4 O'CLOCK.
I SWEAR, IF THOSE THREE DWEEBS ARE GETTING A CUT OF TERI'S SPIDER-GIRL LINE, EVEN IF IT'S ONLY A PENNY, NO WAY AM I BUYING ANY OF IT.
THERE IT IS, LADIES, THE REASON WE THROW IN WITH BOOK. IF SHE DELIVERS, IT'LL MAKE MEG NUTS EVERY TIME SHE SEES ANYONE IN A SPIDER-GIRL ITEM. AND THAT'S HOW THIS ALL STARTED, RIGHT? TO SLAP HER AROUND A LITTLE?
I'D RATHER MAKE MEG SPEND MONEY FOR SOMETHING SHE'D NEVER SPEND MONEY ON. AND TERI HILLMAN TOO...
I KNOW THAT LOOK. I KNOW THAT TONE OF VOICE. EMMA'S GOT A PLAN.
YOU'VE GOT A PLAN, EMMA?
OH YEAH.
A GOOD ONE.
ask me about

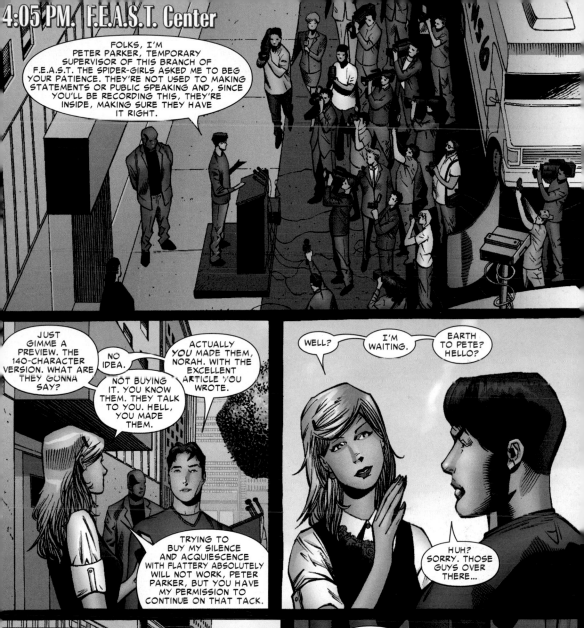

FOLKS, I'M PETER PARKER, TEMPORARY SUPERVISOR OF THIS BRANCH OF F.E.A.S.T. THE SPIDER-GIRLS ASKED ME TO BEG YOUR PATIENCE. THEY'RE NOT USED TO MAKING STATEMENTS OR PUBLIC SPEAKING AND, SINCE YOU'LL BE RECORDING THIS, THEY'RE INSIDE, MAKING SURE THEY HAVE IT RIGHT.

JUST GIMME A PREVIEW. THE 140-CHARACTER VERSION. WHAT ARE THEY GONNA SAY?

NO IDEA.

NOT BUYING IT. YOU KNOW THEM. THEY TALK TO YOU. HELL, YOU MADE THEM.

ACTUALLY YOU MADE THEM, NORAH. WITH THE EXCELLENT ARTICLE YOU WROTE.

TRYING TO BUY MY SILENCE AND ACQUIESCENCE WITH FLATTERY ABSOLUTELY WILL NOT WORK, PETER PARKER, BUT YOU HAVE MY PERMISSION TO CONTINUE ON THAT TACK.

WELL?

I'M WAITING.

EARTH TO PETE? HELLO?

HUH? SORRY. THOSE GUYS OVER THERE...

"...THEY SEEM MORE LIKE STALKERS THAN REPORTERS."

INTERNET PAPARAZZI. THEY'RE ALL STALKERS.

SO, YOU KNOW 'EM?

NO. BUT I KNOW THE TYPE.

HERE THEY COME! HERE COME THE SPIDER-GIRLS!

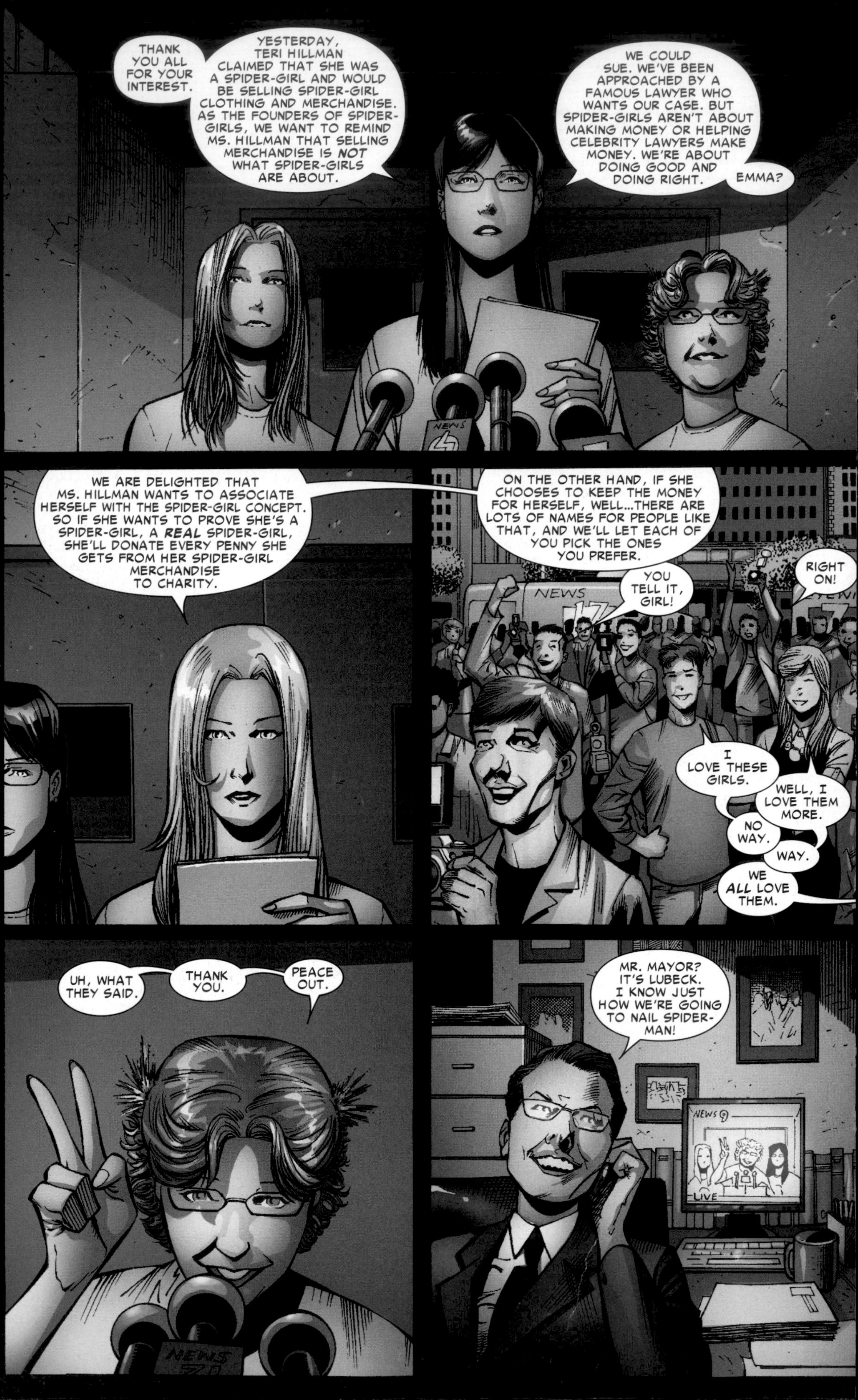
THANK YOU ALL FOR YOUR INTEREST.
YESTERDAY, TERI HILLMAN CLAIMED THAT SHE WAS A SPIDER-GIRL AND WOULD BE SELLING SPIDER-GIRL CLOTHING AND MERCHANDISE. AS THE FOUNDERS OF SPIDER-GIRLS, WE WANT TO REMIND MS. HILLMAN THAT SELLING MERCHANDISE IS *NOT* WHAT SPIDER-GIRLS ARE ABOUT.
WE COULD SUE. WE'VE BEEN APPROACHED BY A FAMOUS LAWYER WHO WANTS OUR CASE. BUT SPIDER-GIRLS AREN'T ABOUT MAKING MONEY OR HELPING CELEBRITY LAWYERS MAKE MONEY. WE'RE ABOUT DOING GOOD AND DOING RIGHT.
EMMA?
NEWS
WE ARE DELIGHTED THAT MS. HILLMAN WANTS TO ASSOCIATE HERSELF WITH THE SPIDER-GIRL CONCEPT. SO IF SHE WANTS TO PROVE SHE'S A SPIDER-GIRL, A *REAL* SPIDER-GIRL, SHE'LL DONATE EVERY PENNY SHE GETS FROM HER SPIDER-GIRL MERCHANDISE TO CHARITY.
ON THE OTHER HAND, IF SHE CHOOSES TO KEEP THE MONEY FOR HERSELF, WELL...THERE ARE LOTS OF NAMES FOR PEOPLE LIKE THAT, AND WE'LL LET EACH OF YOU PICK THE ONES YOU PREFER.
NEWS
YOU TELL IT, GIRL!
RIGHT ON!
I LOVE THESE GIRLS.
WELL, I LOVE THEM MORE.
NO WAY.
WAY.
WE *ALL* LOVE THEM.
UH, WHAT THEY SAID.
THANK YOU.
PEACE OUT.
NEWS
MR. MAYOR? IT'S LUBECK. I KNOW JUST HOW WE'RE GOING TO NAIL SPIDER-MAN!
NEWS
LIVE

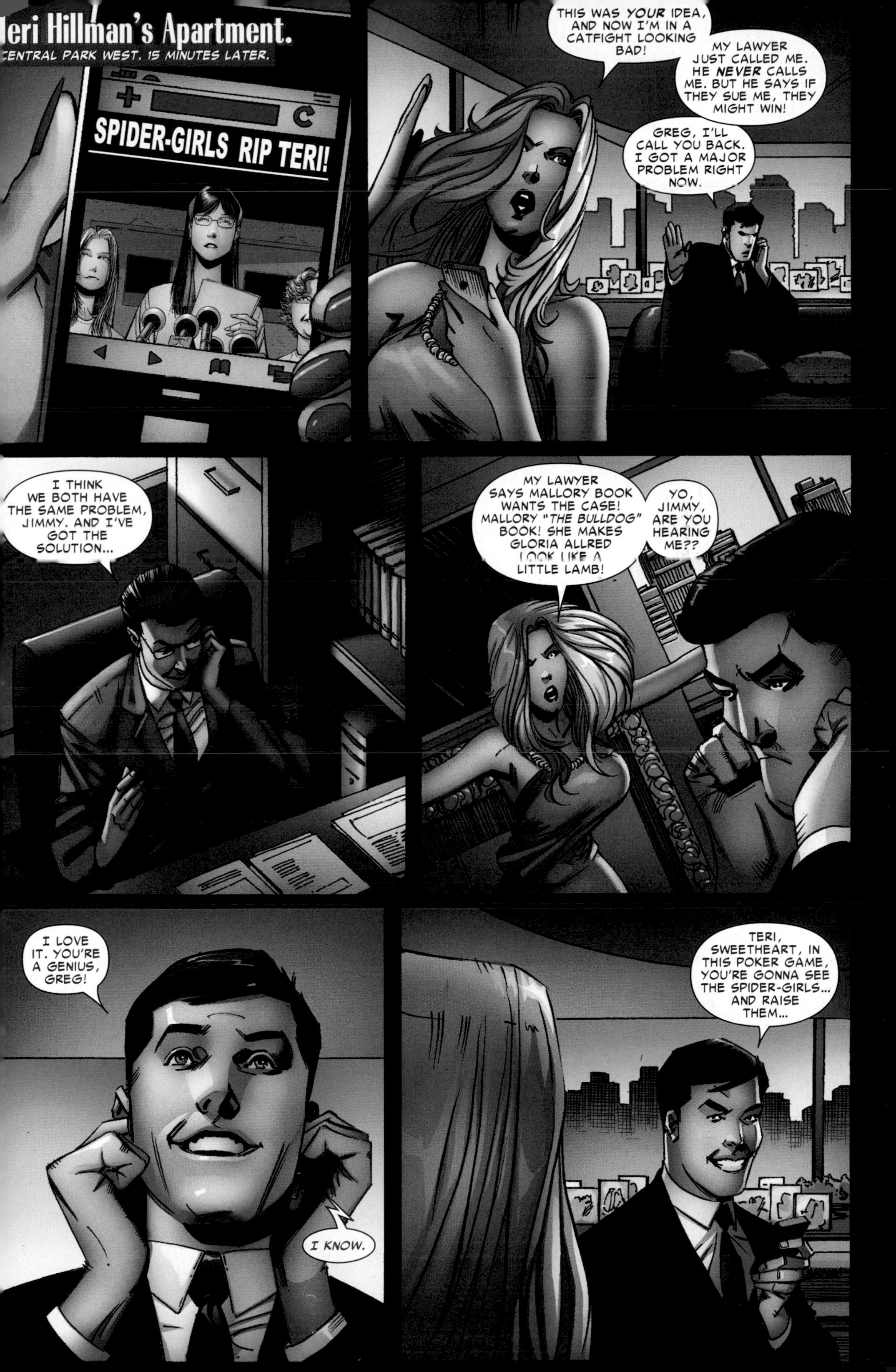
Teri Hillman's Apartment.
CENTRAL PARK WEST. 15 MINUTES LATER.
SPIDER-GIRLS RIP TERI!
THIS WAS YOUR IDEA, AND NOW I'M IN A CATFIGHT LOOKING BAD!
MY LAWYER JUST CALLED ME. HE NEVER CALLS ME. BUT HE SAYS IF THEY SUE ME, THEY MIGHT WIN!
GREG, I'LL CALL YOU BACK. I GOT A MAJOR PROBLEM RIGHT NOW.
I THINK WE BOTH HAVE THE SAME PROBLEM, JIMMY. AND I'VE GOT THE SOLUTION...
MY LAWYER SAYS MALLORY BOOK WANTS THE CASE! MALLORY "THE BULLDOG" BOOK! SHE MAKES GLORIA ALLRED LOOK LIKE A LITTLE LAMB!
YO, JIMMY, ARE YOU HEARING ME??
I LOVE IT. YOU'RE A GENIUS, GREG!
I KNOW.
TERI, SWEETHEART, IN THIS POKER GAME, YOU'RE GONNA SEE THE SPIDER-GIRLS... AND RAISE THEM...

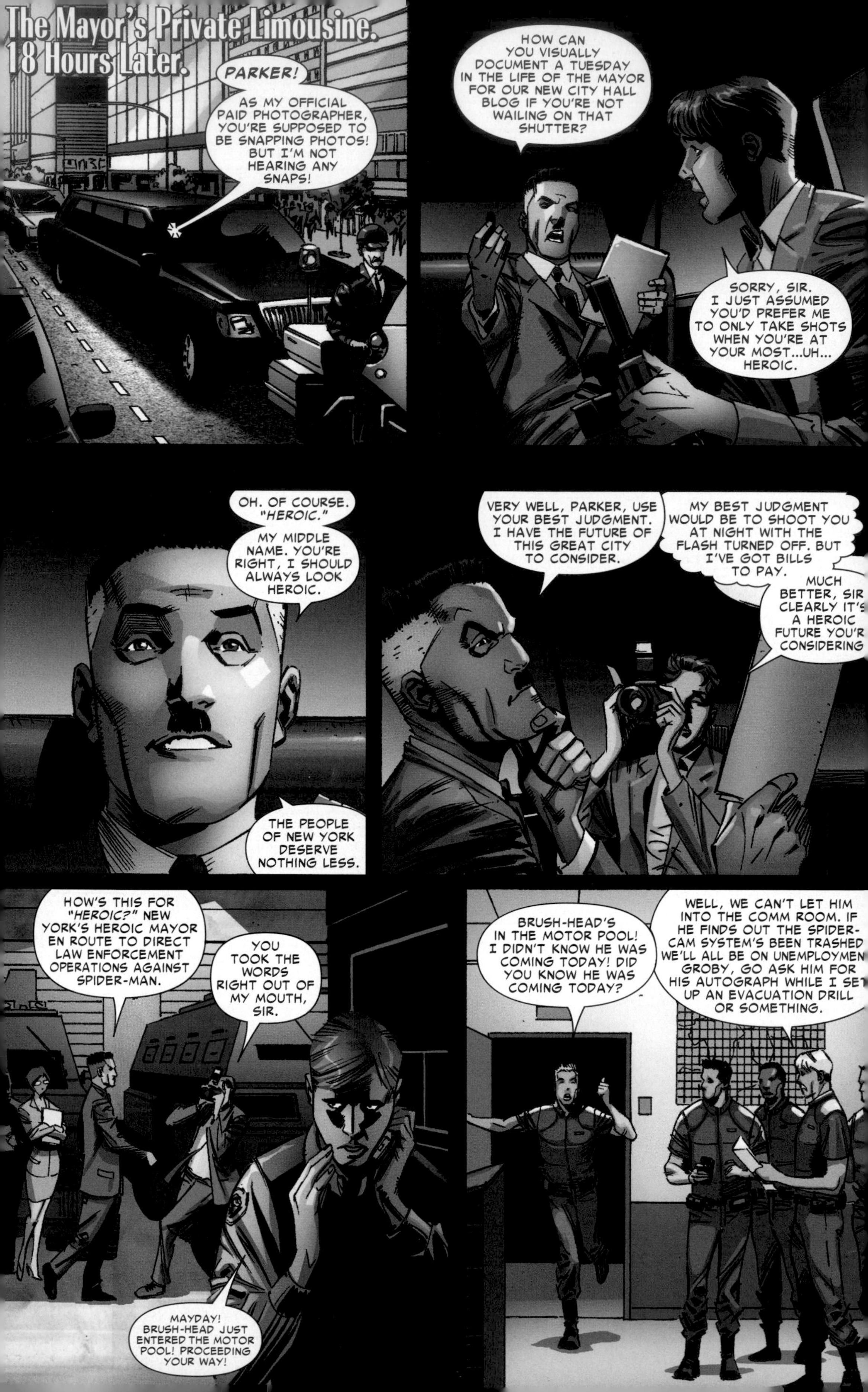
The Mayor's Private Limousine. 18 Hours Later.
PARKER!
AS MY OFFICIAL PAID PHOTOGRAPHER, YOU'RE SUPPOSED TO BE SNAPPING PHOTOS! BUT I'M NOT HEARING ANY SNAPS!
HOW CAN YOU VISUALLY DOCUMENT A TUESDAY IN THE LIFE OF THE MAYOR FOR OUR NEW CITY HALL BLOG IF YOU'RE NOT WAILING ON THAT SHUTTER?
SORRY, SIR. I JUST ASSUMED YOU'D PREFER ME TO ONLY TAKE SHOTS WHEN YOU'RE AT YOUR MOST...UH... HEROIC.
OH. OF COURSE. "HEROIC."
MY MIDDLE NAME. YOU'RE RIGHT, I SHOULD ALWAYS LOOK HEROIC.
THE PEOPLE OF NEW YORK DESERVE NOTHING LESS.
VERY WELL, PARKER, USE YOUR BEST JUDGMENT. I HAVE THE FUTURE OF THIS GREAT CITY TO CONSIDER.
MY BEST JUDGMENT WOULD BE TO SHOOT YOU AT NIGHT WITH THE FLASH TURNED OFF. BUT I'VE GOT BILLS TO PAY.
MUCH BETTER, SIR CLEARLY IT'S A HEROIC FUTURE YOU'R CONSIDERING
HOW'S THIS FOR "HEROIC?" NEW YORK'S HEROIC MAYOR EN ROUTE TO DIRECT LAW ENFORCEMENT OPERATIONS AGAINST SPIDER-MAN.
YOU TOOK THE WORDS RIGHT OUT OF MY MOUTH, SIR.
MAYDAY! BRUSH-HEAD JUST ENTERED THE MOTOR POOL! PROCEEDING YOUR WAY!
BRUSH-HEAD'S IN THE MOTOR POOL! I DIDN'T KNOW HE WAS COMING TODAY! DID YOU KNOW HE WAS COMING TODAY?
WELL, WE CAN'T LET HIM INTO THE COMM ROOM. IF HE FINDS OUT THE SPIDER-CAM SYSTEM'S BEEN TRASHED WE'LL ALL BE ON UNEMPLOYMEN GROBY, GO ASK HIM FOR HIS AUTOGRAPH WHILE I SET UP AN EVACUATION DRILL OR SOMETHING.

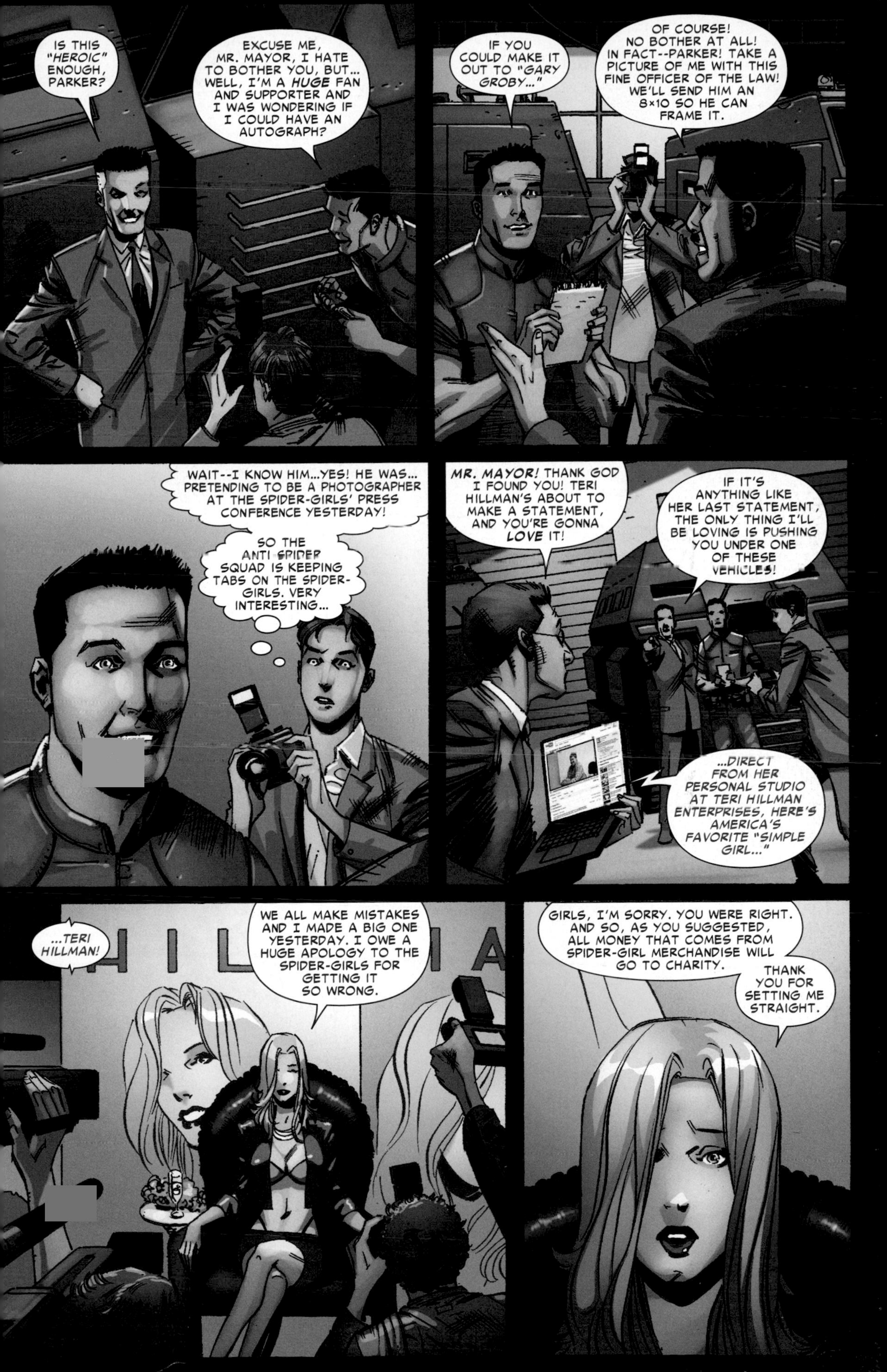
IS THIS "HEROIC" ENOUGH, PARKER?
EXCUSE ME, MR. MAYOR, I HATE TO BOTHER YOU, BUT... WELL, I'M A HUGE FAN AND SUPPORTER AND I WAS WONDERING IF I COULD HAVE AN AUTOGRAPH?
IF YOU COULD MAKE IT OUT TO "GARY GROBY..."
OF COURSE! NO BOTHER AT ALL! IN FACT--PARKER! TAKE A PICTURE OF ME WITH THIS FINE OFFICER OF THE LAW! WE'LL SEND HIM AN 8×10 SO HE CAN FRAME IT.
WAIT--I KNOW HIM...YES! HE WAS... PRETENDING TO BE A PHOTOGRAPHER AT THE SPIDER-GIRLS' PRESS CONFERENCE YESTERDAY!
SO THE ANTI SPIDER SQUAD IS KEEPING TABS ON THE SPIDER-GIRLS. VERY INTERESTING...
MR. MAYOR! THANK GOD I FOUND YOU! TERI HILLMAN'S ABOUT TO MAKE A STATEMENT, AND YOU'RE GONNA LOVE IT!
IF IT'S ANYTHING LIKE HER LAST STATEMENT, THE ONLY THING I'LL BE LOVING IS PUSHING YOU UNDER ONE OF THESE VEHICLES!
...DIRECT FROM HER PERSONAL STUDIO AT TERI HILLMAN ENTERPRISES, HERE'S AMERICA'S FAVORITE "SIMPLE GIRL..."
...TERI HILLMAN!
WE ALL MAKE MISTAKES AND I MADE A BIG ONE YESTERDAY. I OWE A HUGE APOLOGY TO THE SPIDER-GIRLS FOR GETTING IT SO WRONG.
GIRLS, I'M SORRY. YOU WERE RIGHT. AND SO, AS YOU SUGGESTED, ALL MONEY THAT COMES FROM SPIDER-GIRL MERCHANDISE WILL GO TO CHARITY.
THANK YOU FOR SETTING ME STRAIGHT.

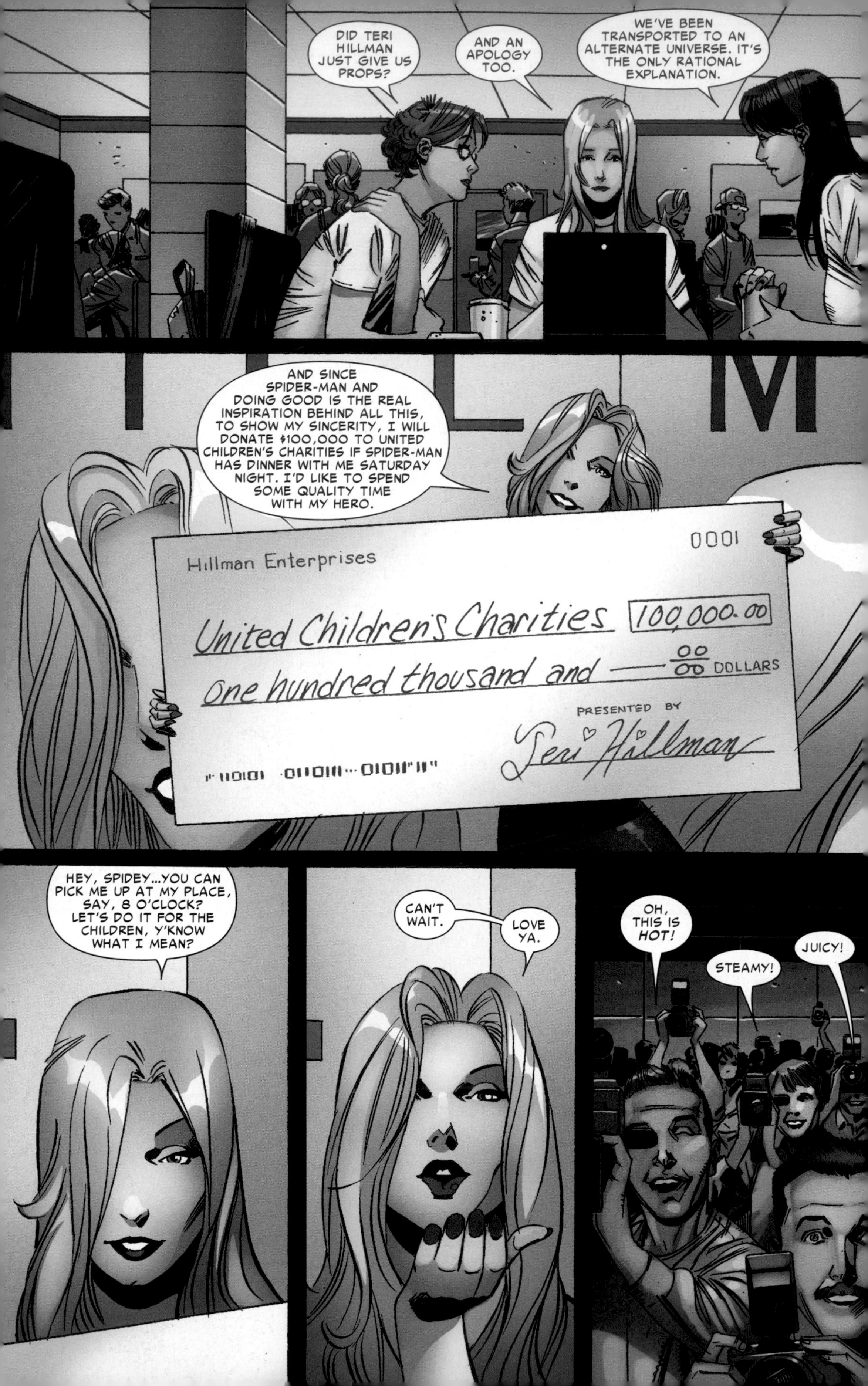
DID TERI HILLMAN JUST GIVE US PROPS?
AND AN APOLOGY TOO.
WE'VE BEEN TRANSPORTED TO AN ALTERNATE UNIVERSE. IT'S THE ONLY RATIONAL EXPLANATION.
AND SINCE SPIDER-MAN AND DOING GOOD IS THE REAL INSPIRATION BEHIND ALL THIS, TO SHOW MY SINCERITY, I WILL DONATE $100,000 TO UNITED CHILDREN'S CHARITIES IF SPIDER-MAN HAS DINNER WITH ME SATURDAY NIGHT. I'D LIKE TO SPEND SOME QUALITY TIME WITH MY HERO.
0001
Hillman Enterprises
United Children's Charities
100,000.00
One hundred thousand and 00/00 DOLLARS
PRESENTED BY
Teri Hillman
HEY, SPIDEY...YOU CAN PICK ME UP AT MY PLACE, SAY, 8 O'CLOCK? LET'S DO IT FOR THE CHILDREN, Y'KNOW WHAT I MEAN?
CAN'T WAIT.
LOVE YA.
OH, THIS IS HOT!
STEAMY!
JUICY!

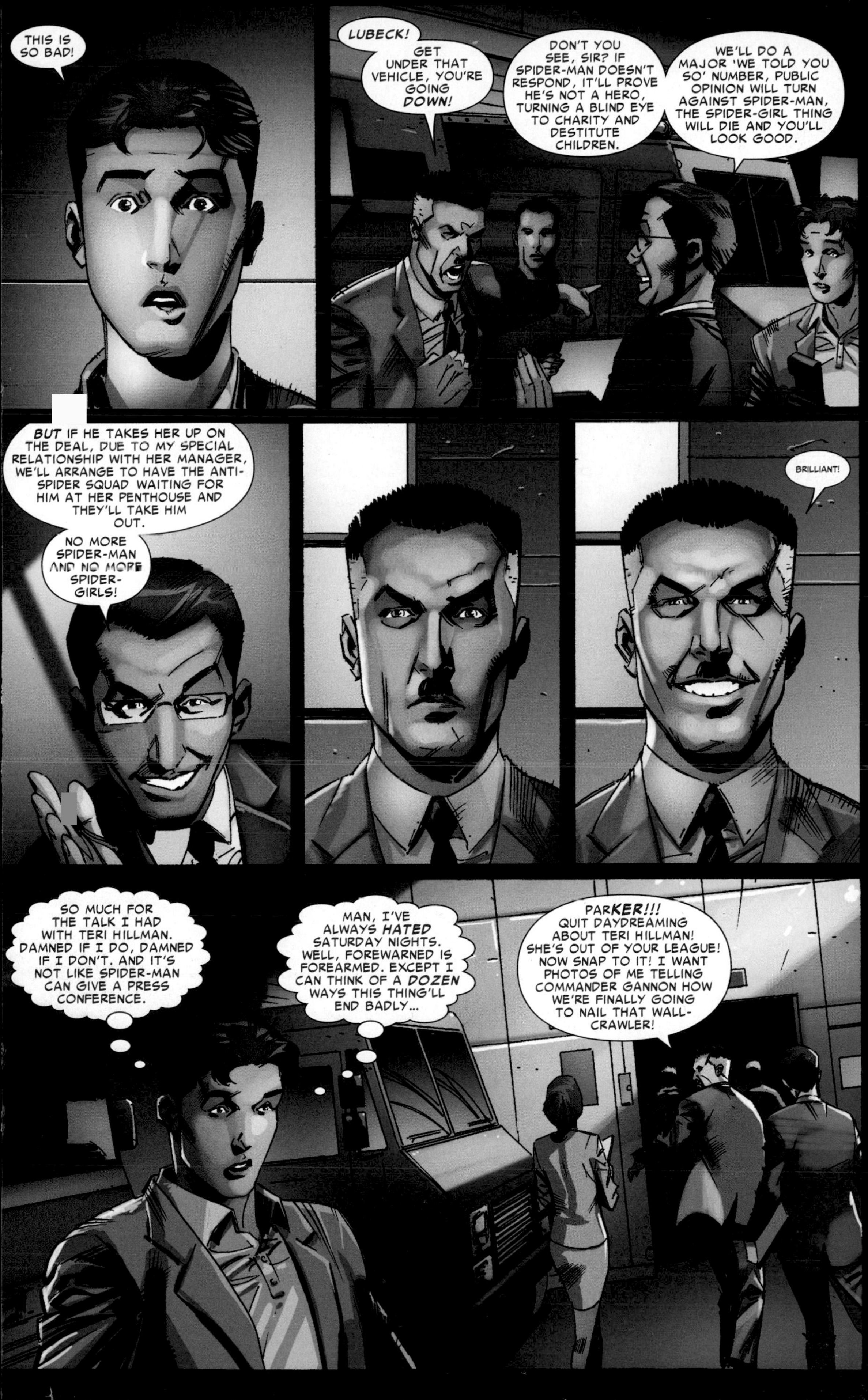
THIS IS SO BAD!
LUBECK!
GET UNDER THAT VEHICLE, YOU'RE GOING *DOWN!*
DON'T YOU SEE, SIR? IF SPIDER-MAN DOESN'T RESPOND, IT'LL PROVE HE'S NOT A HERO, TURNING A BLIND EYE TO CHARITY AND DESTITUTE CHILDREN.
WE'LL DO A MAJOR 'WE TOLD YOU SO' NUMBER, PUBLIC OPINION WILL TURN AGAINST SPIDER-MAN, THE SPIDER-GIRL THING WILL DIE AND YOU'LL LOOK GOOD.
BUT IF HE TAKES HER UP ON THE DEAL, DUE TO MY SPECIAL RELATIONSHIP WITH HER MANAGER, WE'LL ARRANGE TO HAVE THE ANTI-SPIDER SQUAD WAITING FOR HIM AT HER PENTHOUSE AND THEY'LL TAKE HIM OUT.
NO MORE SPIDER-MAN AND NO MORE SPIDER-GIRLS!
BRILLIANT!
SO MUCH FOR THE TALK I HAD WITH TERI HILLMAN. DAMNED IF I DO, DAMNED IF I DON'T. AND IT'S NOT LIKE SPIDER-MAN CAN GIVE A PRESS CONFERENCE.
MAN, I'VE ALWAYS *HATED* SATURDAY NIGHTS. WELL, FOREWARNED IS FOREARMED. EXCEPT I CAN THINK OF A *DOZEN* WAYS THIS THING'LL END BADLY...
PAR*KER!!!* QUIT DAYDREAMING ABOUT TERI HILLMAN! SHE'S OUT OF YOUR LEAGUE! NOW SNAP TO IT! I WANT PHOTOS OF ME TELLING COMMANDER GANNON HOW WE'RE FINALLY GOING TO NAIL THAT WALL-CRAWLER!

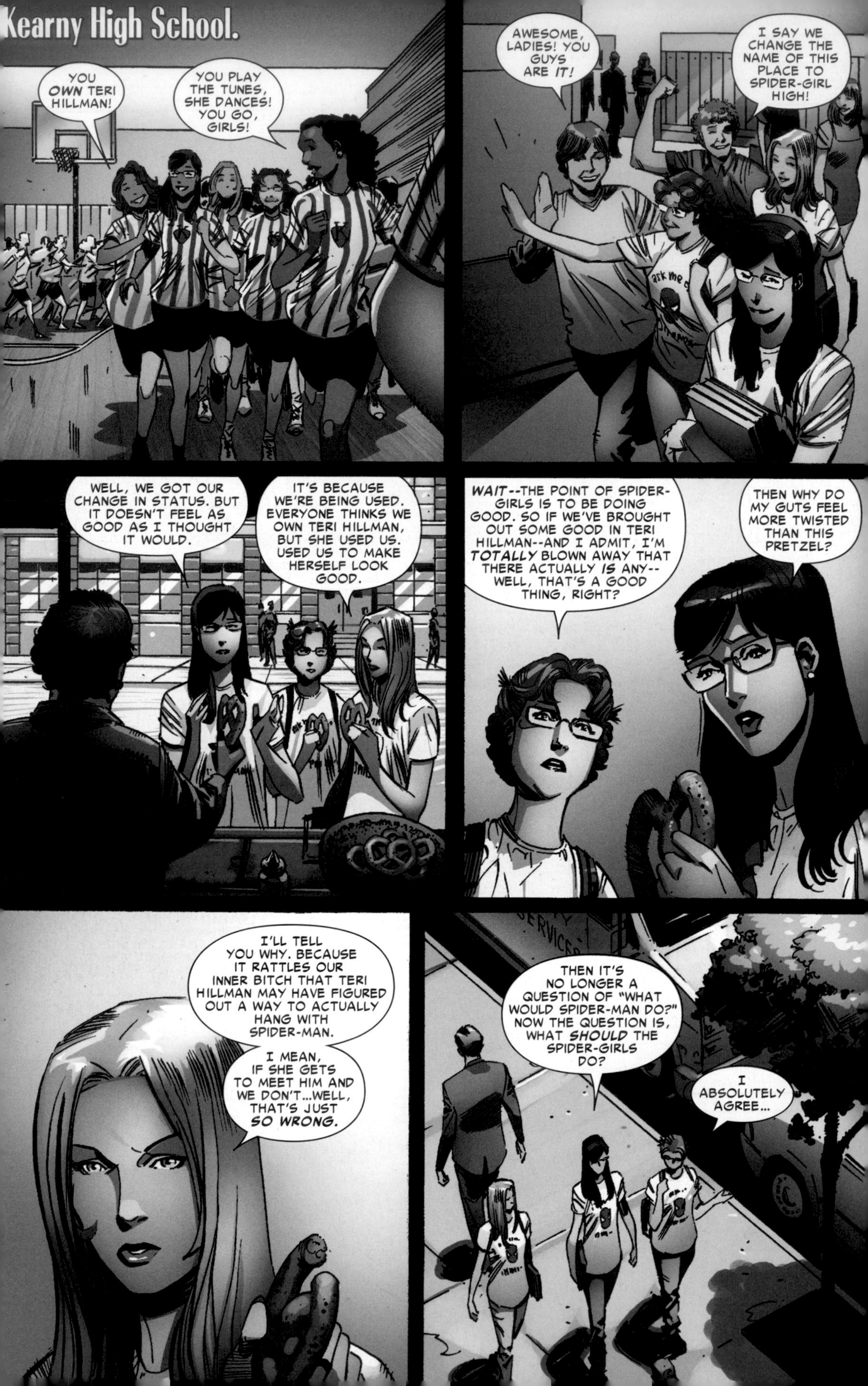
Kearny High School.
YOU OWN TERI HILLMAN!
YOU PLAY THE TUNES, SHE DANCES! YOU GO, GIRLS!
AWESOME, LADIES! YOU GUYS ARE IT!
I SAY WE CHANGE THE NAME OF THIS PLACE TO SPIDER-GIRL HIGH!
WELL, WE GOT OUR CHANGE IN STATUS. BUT IT DOESN'T FEEL AS GOOD AS I THOUGHT IT WOULD.
IT'S BECAUSE WE'RE BEING USED. EVERYONE THINKS WE OWN TERI HILLMAN, BUT SHE USED US. USED US TO MAKE HERSELF LOOK GOOD.
WAIT--THE POINT OF SPIDER-GIRLS IS TO BE DOING GOOD. SO IF WE'VE BROUGHT OUT SOME GOOD IN TERI HILLMAN--AND I ADMIT, I'M TOTALLY BLOWN AWAY THAT THERE ACTUALLY IS ANY--WELL, THAT'S A GOOD THING, RIGHT?
THEN WHY DO MY GUTS FEEL MORE TWISTED THAN THIS PRETZEL?
I'LL TELL YOU WHY. BECAUSE IT RATTLES OUR INNER BITCH THAT TERI HILLMAN MAY HAVE FIGURED OUT A WAY TO ACTUALLY HANG WITH SPIDER-MAN.
I MEAN, IF SHE GETS TO MEET HIM AND WE DON'T...WELL, THAT'S JUST SO WRONG.
THEN IT'S NO LONGER A QUESTION OF "WHAT WOULD SPIDER-MAN DO?" NOW THE QUESTION IS, WHAT SHOULD THE SPIDER-GIRLS DO?
I ABSOLUTELY AGREE...

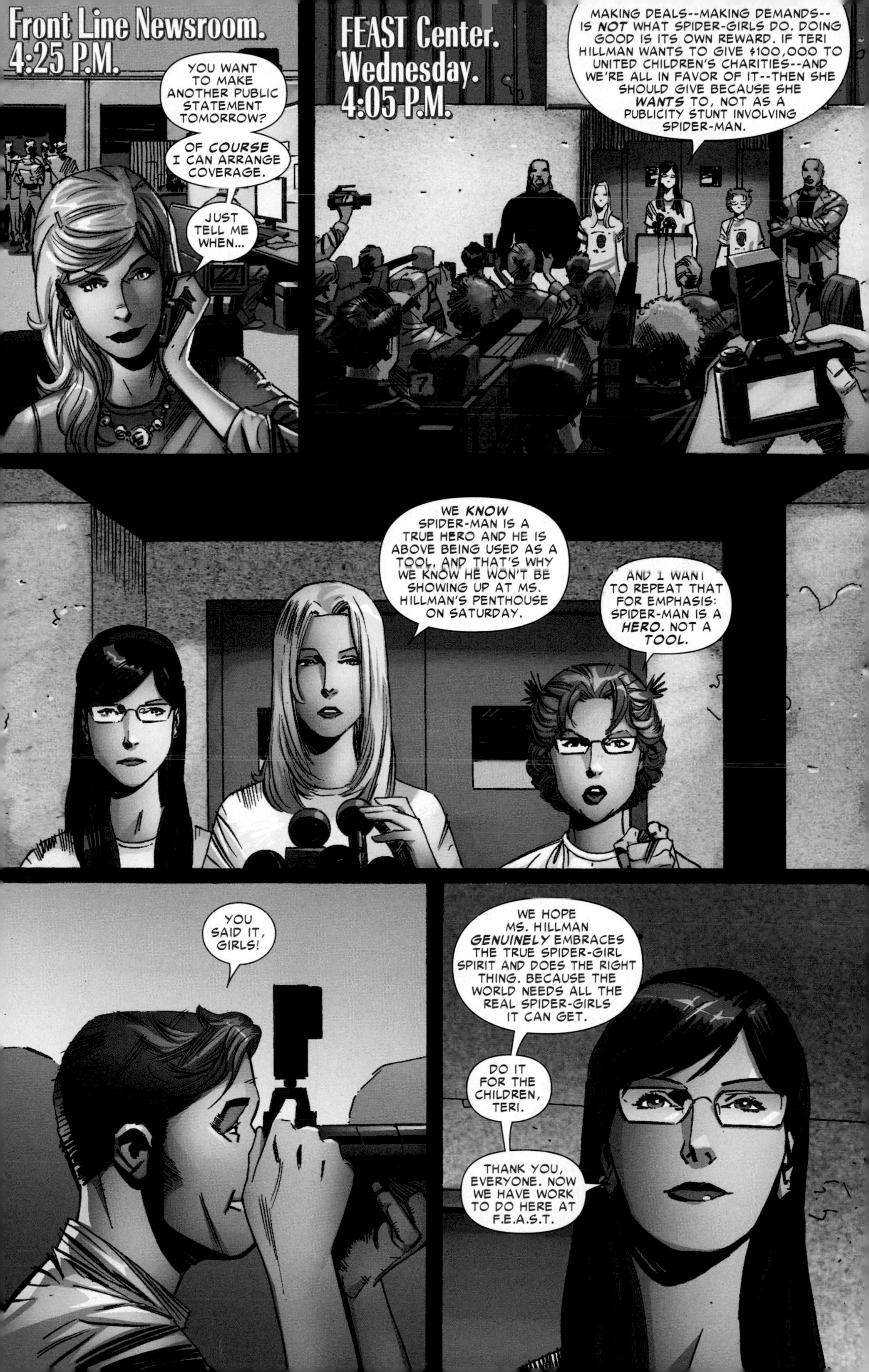

Front Line Newsroom. 4:25 P.M.
YOU WANT TO MAKE ANOTHER PUBLIC STATEMENT TOMORROW?
OF COURSE I CAN ARRANGE COVERAGE.
JUST TELL ME WHEN...
FEAST Center. Wednesday. 4:05 P.M.
MAKING DEALS--MAKING DEMANDS--IS NOT WHAT SPIDER-GIRLS DO. DOING GOOD IS ITS OWN REWARD. IF TERI HILLMAN WANTS TO GIVE $100,000 TO UNITED CHILDREN'S CHARITIES--AND WE'RE ALL IN FAVOR OF IT--THEN SHE SHOULD GIVE BECAUSE SHE WANTS TO, NOT AS A PUBLICITY STUNT INVOLVING SPIDER-MAN.
WE KNOW SPIDER-MAN IS A TRUE HERO AND HE IS ABOVE BEING USED AS A TOOL, AND THAT'S WHY WE KNOW HE WON'T BE SHOWING UP AT MS. HILLMAN'S PENTHOUSE ON SATURDAY.
AND I WANT TO REPEAT THAT FOR EMPHASIS: SPIDER-MAN IS A HERO. NOT A TOOL.
YOU SAID IT, GIRLS!
WE HOPE MS. HILLMAN GENUINELY EMBRACES THE TRUE SPIDER-GIRL SPIRIT AND DOES THE RIGHT THING. BECAUSE THE WORLD NEEDS ALL THE REAL SPIDER-GIRLS IT CAN GET.
DO IT FOR THE CHILDREN, TERI.
THANK YOU, EVERYONE. NOW WE HAVE WORK TO DO HERE AT F.E.A.S.T.

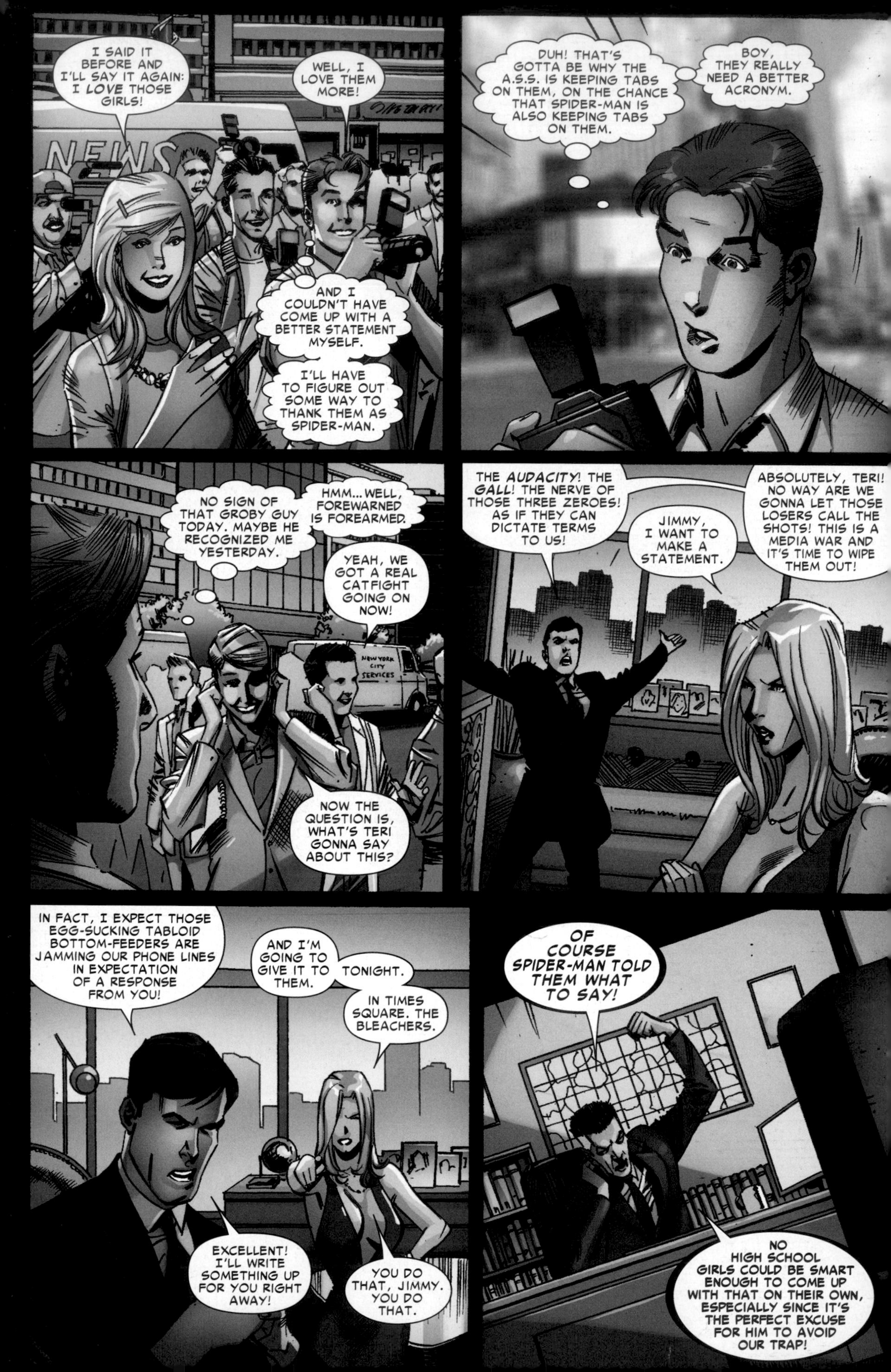
I SAID IT BEFORE AND I'LL SAY IT AGAIN: I *LOVE* THOSE GIRLS!
WELL, I LOVE THEM MORE!
AND I COULDN'T HAVE COME UP WITH A BETTER STATEMENT MYSELF.
I'LL HAVE TO FIGURE OUT SOME WAY TO THANK THEM AS SPIDER-MAN.
DUH! THAT'S GOTTA BE WHY THE A.S.S. IS KEEPING TABS ON THEM, ON THE CHANCE THAT SPIDER-MAN IS ALSO KEEPING TABS ON THEM.
BOY, THEY REALLY NEED A BETTER ACRONYM.
NO SIGN OF THAT GROBY GUY TODAY. MAYBE HE RECOGNIZED ME YESTERDAY.
HMM...WELL, FOREWARNED IS FOREARMED.
YEAH, WE GOT A REAL CATFIGHT GOING ON NOW!
NEW YORK CITY SERVICES
NOW THE QUESTION IS, WHAT'S TERI GONNA SAY ABOUT THIS?
THE *AUDACITY*! THE *GALL*! THE NERVE OF THOSE THREE ZEROES! AS IF THEY CAN DICTATE TERMS TO US!
JIMMY, I WANT TO MAKE A STATEMENT.
ABSOLUTELY, TERI! NO WAY ARE WE GONNA LET THOSE LOSERS CALL THE SHOTS! THIS IS A MEDIA WAR AND IT'S TIME TO WIPE THEM OUT!
IN FACT, I EXPECT THOSE EGG-SUCKING TABLOID BOTTOM-FEEDERS ARE JAMMING OUR PHONE LINES IN EXPECTATION OF A RESPONSE FROM YOU!
AND I'M GOING TO GIVE IT TO THEM.
TONIGHT.
IN TIMES SQUARE. THE BLEACHERS.
EXCELLENT! I'LL WRITE SOMETHING UP FOR YOU RIGHT AWAY!
YOU DO THAT, JIMMY. YOU DO THAT.
OF COURSE SPIDER-MAN TOLD THEM WHAT TO SAY!
NO HIGH SCHOOL GIRLS COULD BE SMART ENOUGH TO COME UP WITH THAT ON THEIR OWN, ESPECIALLY SINCE IT'S THE PERFECT EXCUSE FOR HIM TO AVOID OUR TRAP!

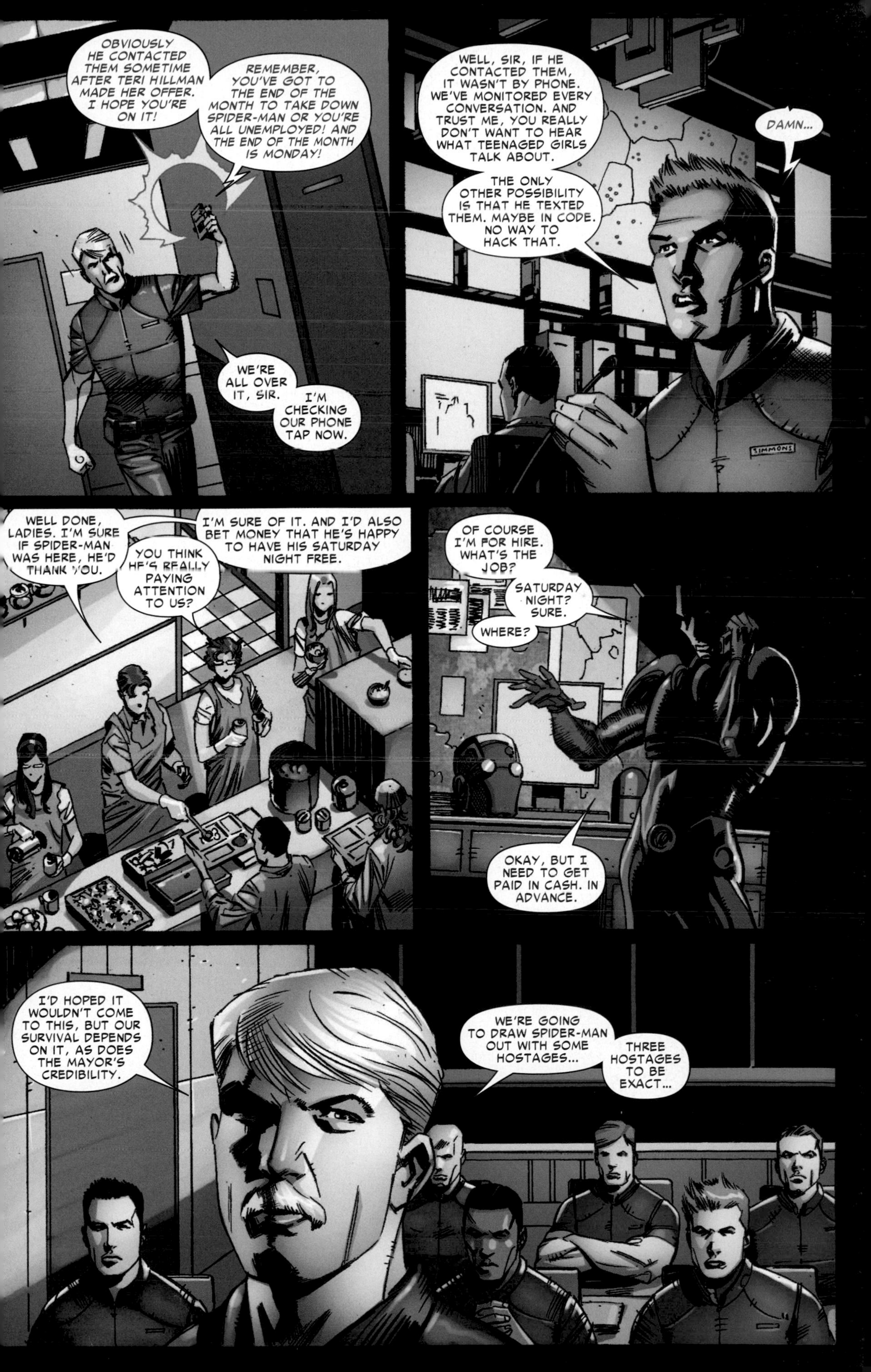
OBVIOUSLY HE CONTACTED THEM SOMETIME AFTER TERI HILLMAN MADE HER OFFER. I HOPE YOU'RE ON IT!
REMEMBER, YOU'VE GOT TO THE END OF THE MONTH TO TAKE DOWN SPIDER-MAN OR YOU'RE ALL UNEMPLOYED! AND THE END OF THE MONTH IS MONDAY!
WE'RE ALL OVER IT, SIR.
I'M CHECKING OUR PHONE TAP NOW.
WELL, SIR, IF HE CONTACTED THEM, IT WASN'T BY PHONE. WE'VE MONITORED EVERY CONVERSATION. AND TRUST ME, YOU REALLY DON'T WANT TO HEAR WHAT TEENAGED GIRLS TALK ABOUT.
THE ONLY OTHER POSSIBILITY IS THAT HE TEXTED THEM. MAYBE IN CODE. NO WAY TO HACK THAT.
DAMN...
SIMMONS
WELL DONE, LADIES. I'M SURE IF SPIDER-MAN WAS HERE, HE'D THANK YOU.
YOU THINK HE'S REALLY PAYING ATTENTION TO US?
I'M SURE OF IT. AND I'D ALSO BET MONEY THAT HE'S HAPPY TO HAVE HIS SATURDAY NIGHT FREE.
OF COURSE I'M FOR HIRE. WHAT'S THE JOB?
SATURDAY NIGHT? SURE.
WHERE?
OKAY, BUT I NEED TO GET PAID IN CASH. IN ADVANCE.
I'D HOPED IT WOULDN'T COME TO THIS, BUT OUR SURVIVAL DEPENDS ON IT, AS DOES THE MAYOR'S CREDIBILITY.
WE'RE GOING TO DRAW SPIDER-MAN OUT WITH SOME HOSTAGES...
THREE HOSTAGES TO BE EXACT...

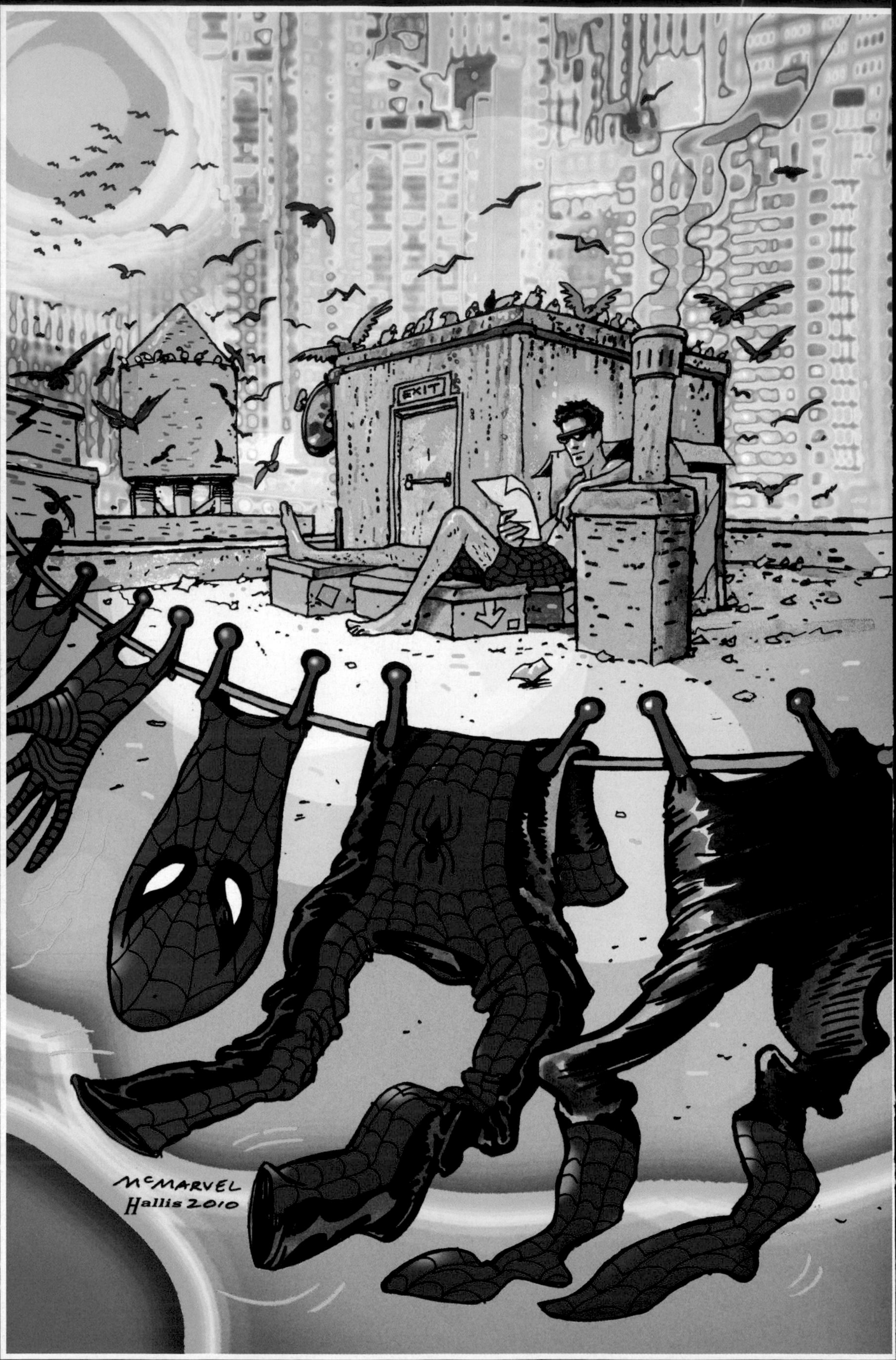
EXIT
McMARVEL
Hallis 2010

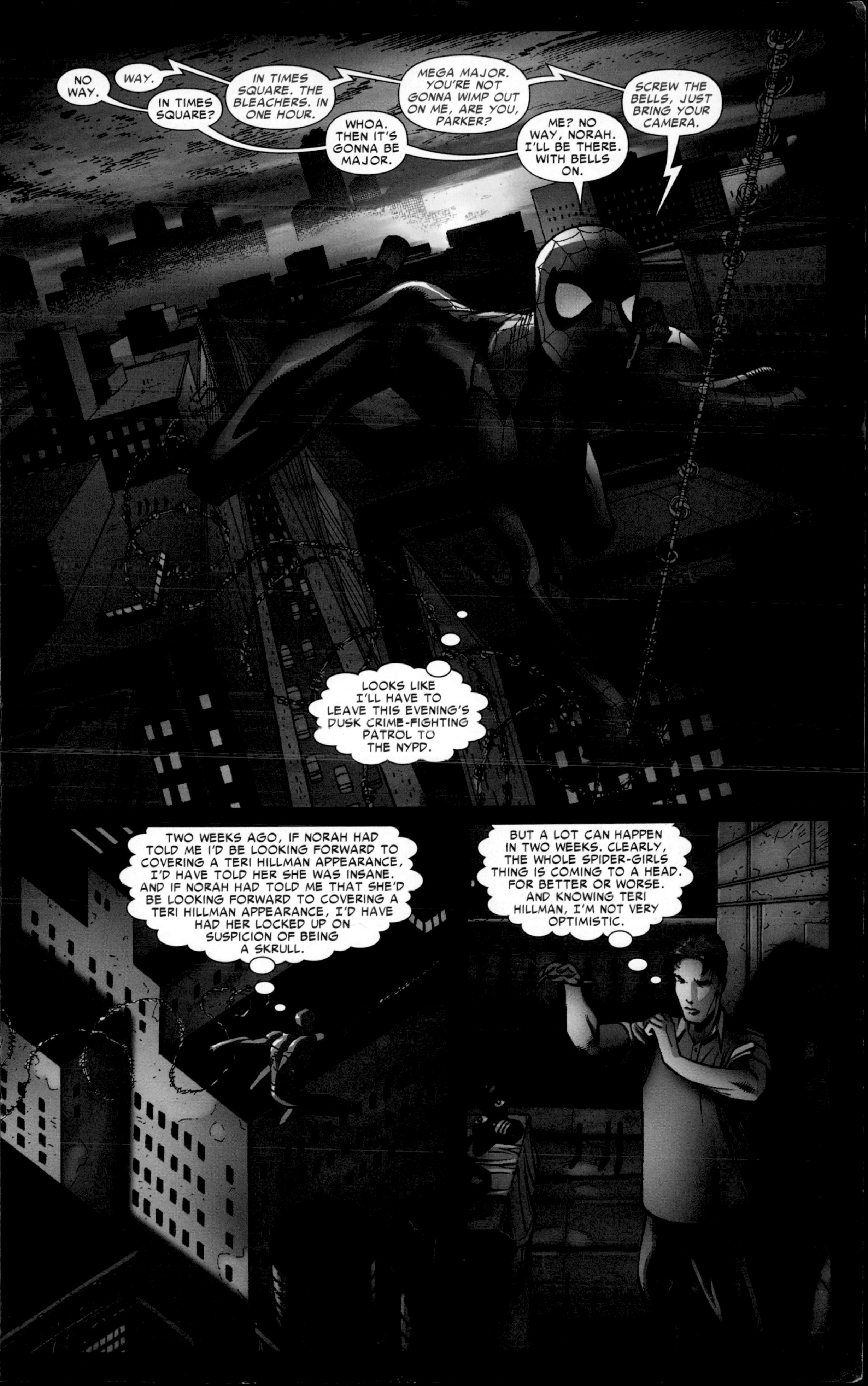
NO WAY.
WAY.
IN TIMES SQUARE?
IN TIMES SQUARE. THE BLEACHERS. IN ONE HOUR.
WHOA. THEN IT'S GONNA BE MAJOR.
MEGA MAJOR. YOU'RE NOT GONNA WIMP OUT ON ME, ARE YOU, PARKER?
ME? NO WAY, NORAH. I'LL BE THERE. WITH BELLS ON.
SCREW THE BELLS, JUST BRING YOUR CAMERA.
LOOKS LIKE I'LL HAVE TO LEAVE THIS EVENING'S DUSK CRIME-FIGHTING PATROL TO THE NYPD.
TWO WEEKS AGO, IF NORAH HAD TOLD ME I'D BE LOOKING FORWARD TO COVERING A TERI HILLMAN APPEARANCE, I'D HAVE TOLD HER SHE WAS INSANE. AND IF NORAH HAD TOLD ME THAT SHE'D BE LOOKING FORWARD TO COVERING A TERI HILLMAN APPEARANCE, I'D HAVE HAD HER LOCKED UP ON SUSPICION OF BEING A SKRULL.
BUT A LOT CAN HAPPEN IN TWO WEEKS. CLEARLY, THE WHOLE SPIDER-GIRLS THING IS COMING TO A HEAD. FOR BETTER OR WORSE. AND KNOWING TERI HILLMAN, I'M NOT VERY OPTIMISTIC.

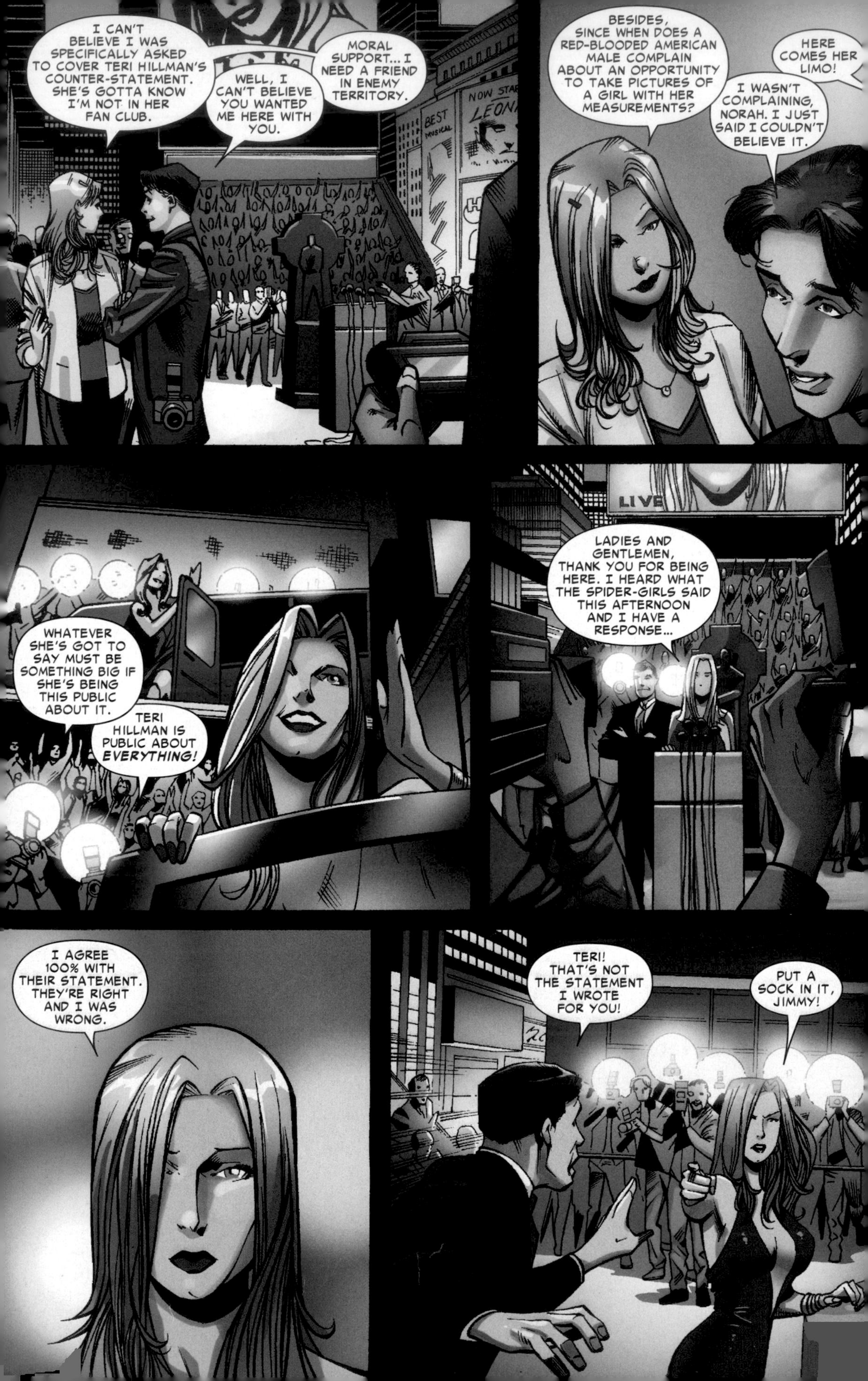
I CAN'T BELIEVE I WAS SPECIFICALLY ASKED TO COVER TERI HILLMAN'S COUNTER-STATEMENT. SHE'S GOTTA KNOW I'M NOT IN HER FAN CLUB.
WELL, I CAN'T BELIEVE YOU WANTED ME HERE WITH YOU.
MORAL SUPPORT... I NEED A FRIEND IN ENEMY TERRITORY.
NOW STAR
LEON
BEST MUSICAL
BESIDES, SINCE WHEN DOES A RED-BLOODED AMERICAN MALE COMPLAIN ABOUT AN OPPORTUNITY TO TAKE PICTURES OF A GIRL WITH HER MEASUREMENTS?
HERE COMES HER LIMO!
I WASN'T COMPLAINING, NORAH. I JUST SAID I COULDN'T BELIEVE IT.
WHATEVER SHE'S GOT TO SAY MUST BE SOMETHING BIG IF SHE'S BEING THIS PUBLIC ABOUT IT.
TERI HILLMAN IS PUBLIC ABOUT *EVERYTHING!*
LIVE
LADIES AND GENTLEMEN, THANK YOU FOR BEING HERE. I HEARD WHAT THE SPIDER-GIRLS SAID THIS AFTERNOON AND I HAVE A RESPONSE...
I AGREE 100% WITH THEIR STATEMENT. THEY'RE RIGHT AND I WAS WRONG.
TERI! THAT'S NOT THE STATEMENT I WROTE FOR YOU!
PUT A SOCK IN IT, JIMMY!

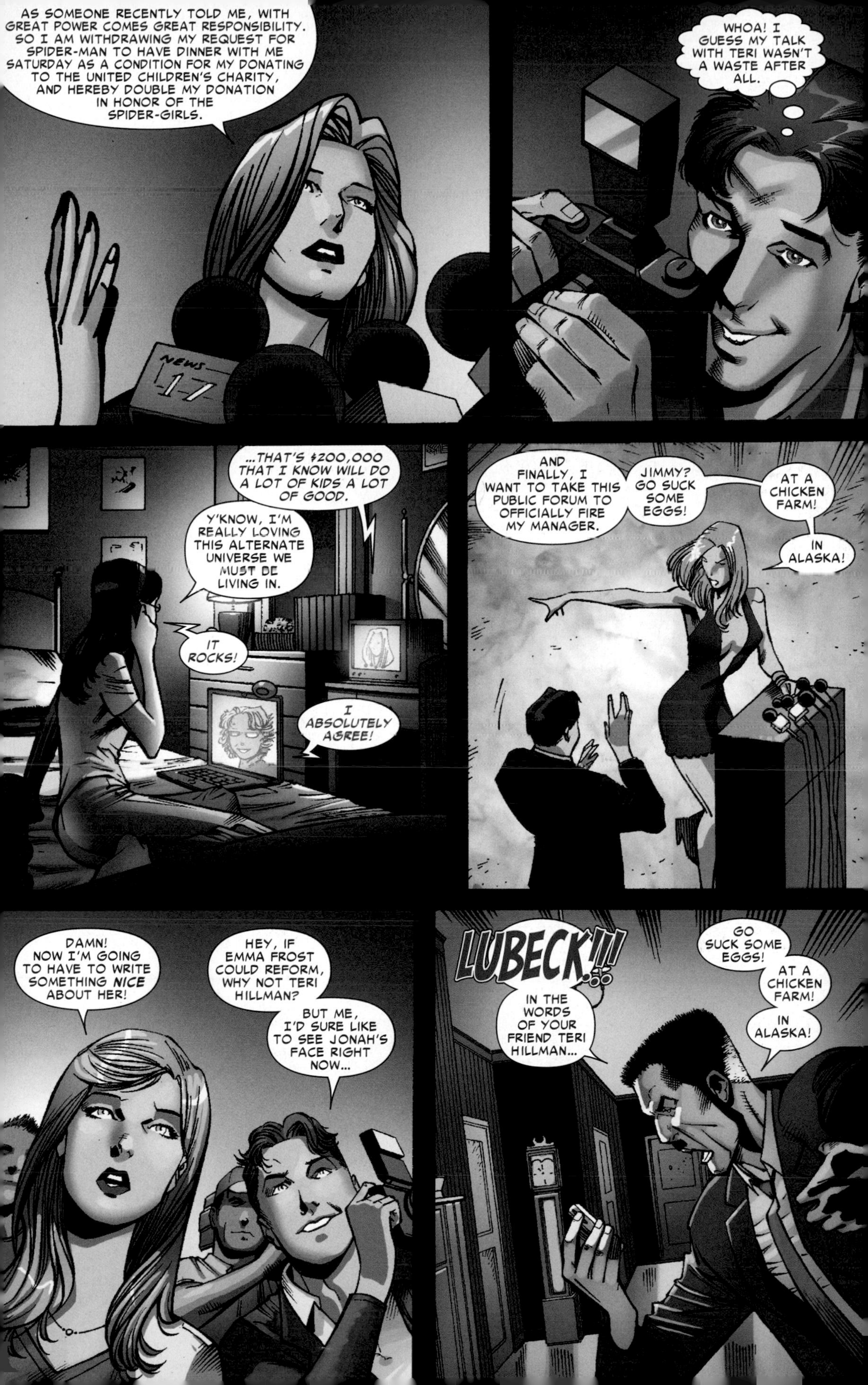
AS SOMEONE RECENTLY TOLD ME, WITH GREAT POWER COMES GREAT RESPONSIBILITY. SO I AM WITHDRAWING MY REQUEST FOR SPIDER-MAN TO HAVE DINNER WITH ME SATURDAY AS A CONDITION FOR MY DONATING TO THE UNITED CHILDREN'S CHARITY, AND HEREBY DOUBLE MY DONATION IN HONOR OF THE SPIDER-GIRLS.
NEWS 17
WHOA! I GUESS MY TALK WITH TERI WASN'T A WASTE AFTER ALL.
...THAT'S $200,000 THAT I KNOW WILL DO A LOT OF KIDS A LOT OF GOOD.
Y'KNOW, I'M REALLY LOVING THIS ALTERNATE UNIVERSE WE MUST BE LIVING IN.
IT ROCKS!
I ABSOLUTELY AGREE!
AND FINALLY, I WANT TO TAKE THIS PUBLIC FORUM TO OFFICIALLY FIRE MY MANAGER.
JIMMY? GO SUCK SOME EGGS!
AT A CHICKEN FARM!
IN ALASKA!
DAMN! NOW I'M GOING TO HAVE TO WRITE SOMETHING *NICE* ABOUT HER!
HEY, IF EMMA FROST COULD REFORM, WHY NOT TERI HILLMAN?
BUT ME, I'D SURE LIKE TO SEE JONAH'S FACE RIGHT NOW...
LUBECK!!!
IN THE WORDS OF YOUR FRIEND TERI HILLMAN...
GO SUCK SOME EGGS!
AT A CHICKEN FARM!
IN ALASKA!

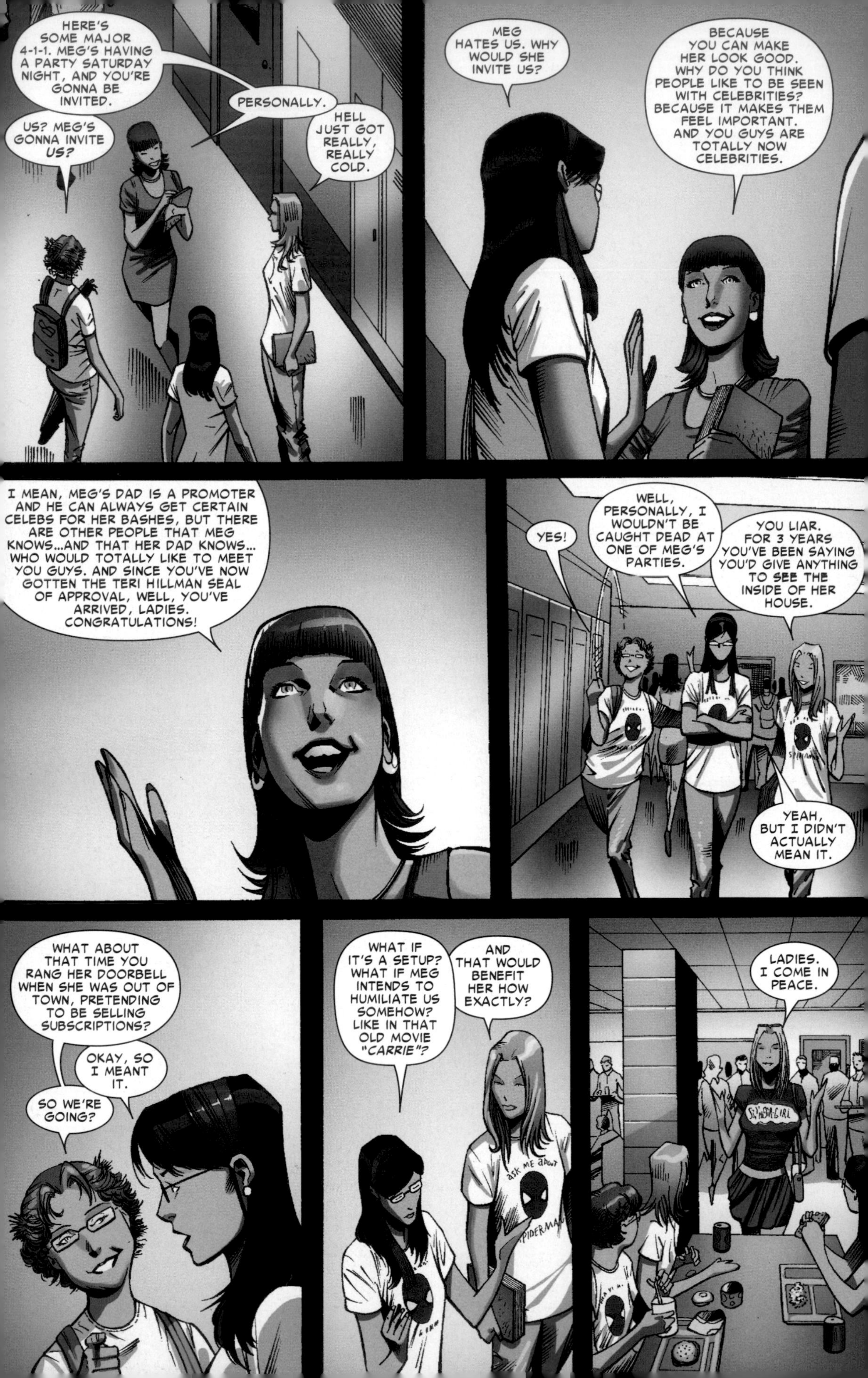
HERE'S SOME MAJOR 4-1-1. MEG'S HAVING A PARTY SATURDAY NIGHT, AND YOU'RE GONNA BE INVITED.
US? MEG'S GONNA INVITE *US?*
PERSONALLY.
HELL JUST GOT REALLY, REALLY COLD.
MEG HATES US. WHY WOULD SHE INVITE US?
BECAUSE YOU CAN MAKE HER LOOK GOOD. WHY DO YOU THINK PEOPLE LIKE TO BE SEEN WITH CELEBRITIES? BECAUSE IT MAKES THEM FEEL IMPORTANT. AND YOU GUYS ARE TOTALLY NOW CELEBRITIES.
I MEAN, MEG'S DAD IS A PROMOTER AND HE CAN ALWAYS GET CERTAIN CELEBS FOR HER BASHES, BUT THERE ARE OTHER PEOPLE THAT MEG KNOWS...AND THAT HER DAD KNOWS... WHO WOULD TOTALLY LIKE TO MEET YOU GUYS. AND SINCE YOU'VE NOW GOTTEN THE TERI HILLMAN SEAL OF APPROVAL, WELL, YOU'VE ARRIVED, LADIES. CONGRATULATIONS!
YES!
WELL, PERSONALLY, I WOULDN'T BE CAUGHT DEAD AT ONE OF MEG'S PARTIES.
YOU LIAR. FOR 3 YEARS YOU'VE BEEN SAYING YOU'D GIVE ANYTHING TO SEE THE INSIDE OF HER HOUSE.
YEAH, BUT I DIDN'T ACTUALLY MEAN IT.
WHAT ABOUT THAT TIME YOU RANG HER DOORBELL WHEN SHE WAS OUT OF TOWN, PRETENDING TO BE SELLING SUBSCRIPTIONS?
OKAY, SO I MEANT IT.
SO WE'RE GOING?
WHAT IF IT'S A SETUP? WHAT IF MEG INTENDS TO HUMILIATE US SOMEHOW? LIKE IN THAT OLD MOVIE *"CARRIE"?*
AND THAT WOULD BENEFIT HER HOW EXACTLY?
LADIES. I COME IN PEACE.

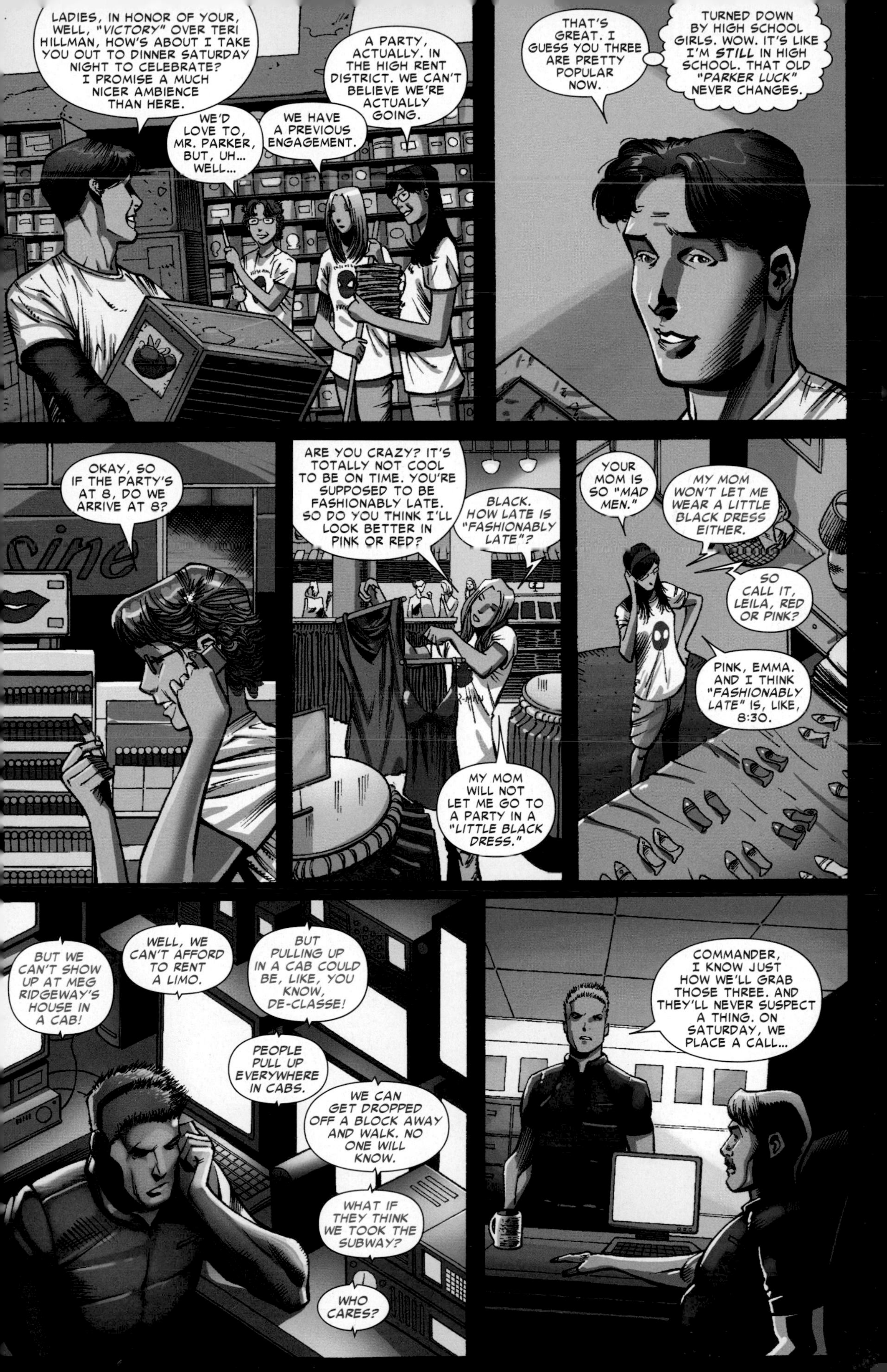

LADIES, IN HONOR OF YOUR, WELL, "VICTORY" OVER TERI HILLMAN, HOW'S ABOUT I TAKE YOU OUT TO DINNER SATURDAY NIGHT TO CELEBRATE? I PROMISE A MUCH NICER AMBIENCE THAN HERE.
WE'D LOVE TO, MR. PARKER, BUT, UH... WELL...
WE HAVE A PREVIOUS ENGAGEMENT.
A PARTY, ACTUALLY. IN THE HIGH RENT DISTRICT. WE CAN'T BELIEVE WE'RE ACTUALLY GOING.
THAT'S GREAT. I GUESS YOU THREE ARE PRETTY POPULAR NOW.
TURNED DOWN BY HIGH SCHOOL GIRLS. WOW. IT'S LIKE I'M STILL IN HIGH SCHOOL. THAT OLD "PARKER LUCK" NEVER CHANGES.
OKAY, SO IF THE PARTY'S AT 8, DO WE ARRIVE AT 8?
ARE YOU CRAZY? IT'S TOTALLY NOT COOL TO BE ON TIME. YOU'RE SUPPOSED TO BE FASHIONABLY LATE. SO DO YOU THINK I'LL LOOK BETTER IN PINK OR RED?
BLACK. HOW LATE IS "FASHIONABLY LATE"?
MY MOM WILL NOT LET ME GO TO A PARTY IN A "LITTLE BLACK DRESS."
YOUR MOM IS SO "MAD MEN."
MY MOM WON'T LET ME WEAR A LITTLE BLACK DRESS EITHER.
SO CALL IT, LEILA, RED OR PINK?
PINK, EMMA. AND I THINK "FASHIONABLY LATE" IS, LIKE, 8:30.
BUT WE CAN'T SHOW UP AT MEG RIDGEWAY'S HOUSE IN A CAB!
WELL, WE CAN'T AFFORD TO RENT A LIMO.
BUT PULLING UP IN A CAB COULD BE, LIKE, YOU KNOW, DE-CLASSE!
PEOPLE PULL UP EVERYWHERE IN CABS.
WE CAN GET DROPPED OFF A BLOCK AWAY AND WALK. NO ONE WILL KNOW.
WHAT IF THEY THINK WE TOOK THE SUBWAY?
WHO CARES?
COMMANDER, I KNOW JUST HOW WE'LL GRAB THOSE THREE. AND THEY'LL NEVER SUSPECT A THING. ON SATURDAY, WE PLACE A CALL...

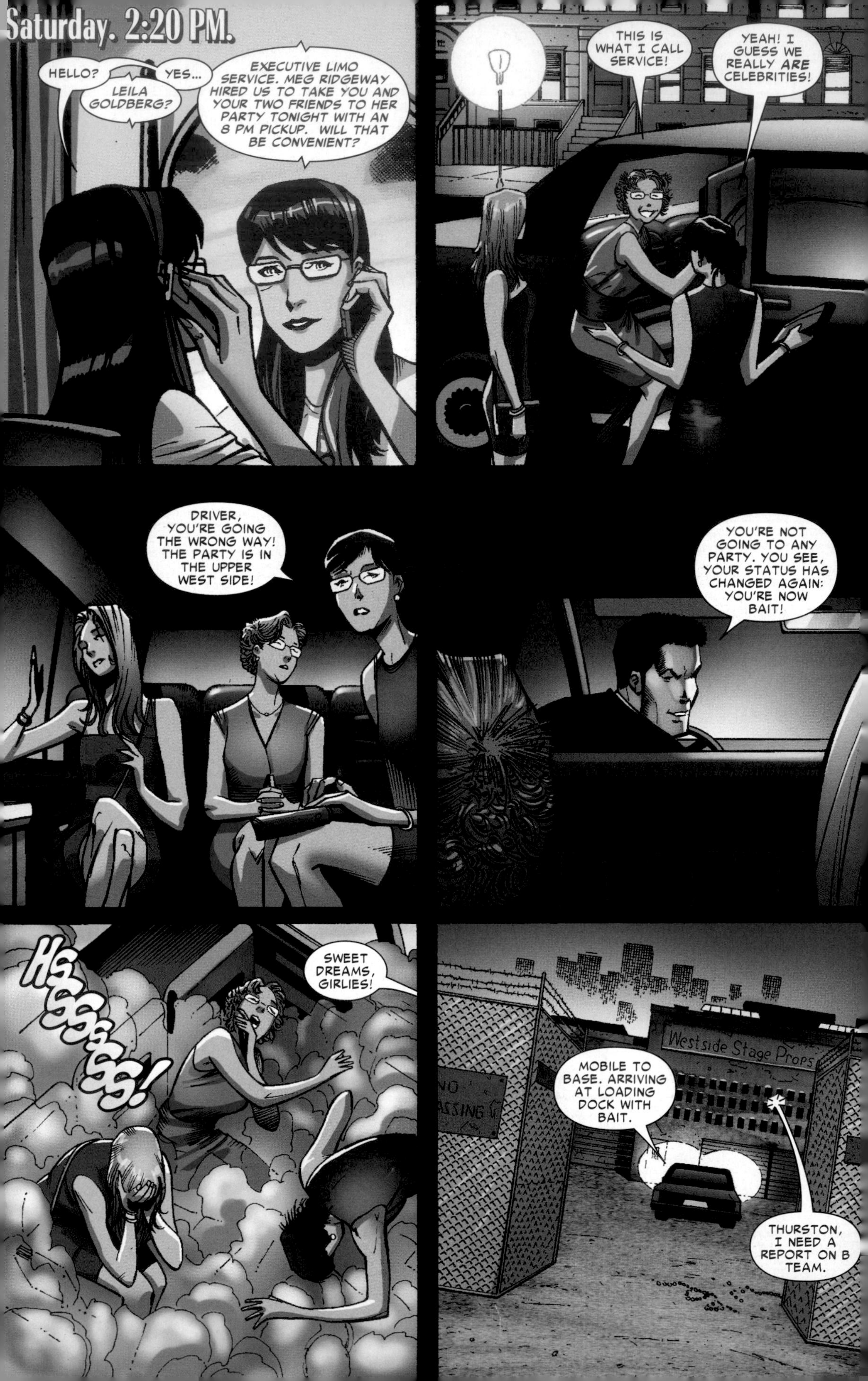
Saturday. 2:20 PM.
HELLO?
LEILA GOLDBERG?
YES...
EXECUTIVE LIMO SERVICE. MEG RIDGEWAY HIRED US TO TAKE YOU AND YOUR TWO FRIENDS TO HER PARTY TONIGHT WITH AN 8 PM PICKUP. WILL THAT BE CONVENIENT?
THIS IS WHAT I CALL SERVICE!
YEAH! I GUESS WE REALLY ARE CELEBRITIES!
DRIVER, YOU'RE GOING THE WRONG WAY! THE PARTY IS IN THE UPPER WEST SIDE!
YOU'RE NOT GOING TO ANY PARTY. YOU SEE, YOUR STATUS HAS CHANGED AGAIN: YOU'RE NOW BAIT!
HSSSSSSS!
SWEET DREAMS, GIRLIES!
Westside Stage Props
MOBILE TO BASE. ARRIVING AT LOADING DOCK WITH BAIT.
THURSTON, I NEED A REPORT ON B TEAM.

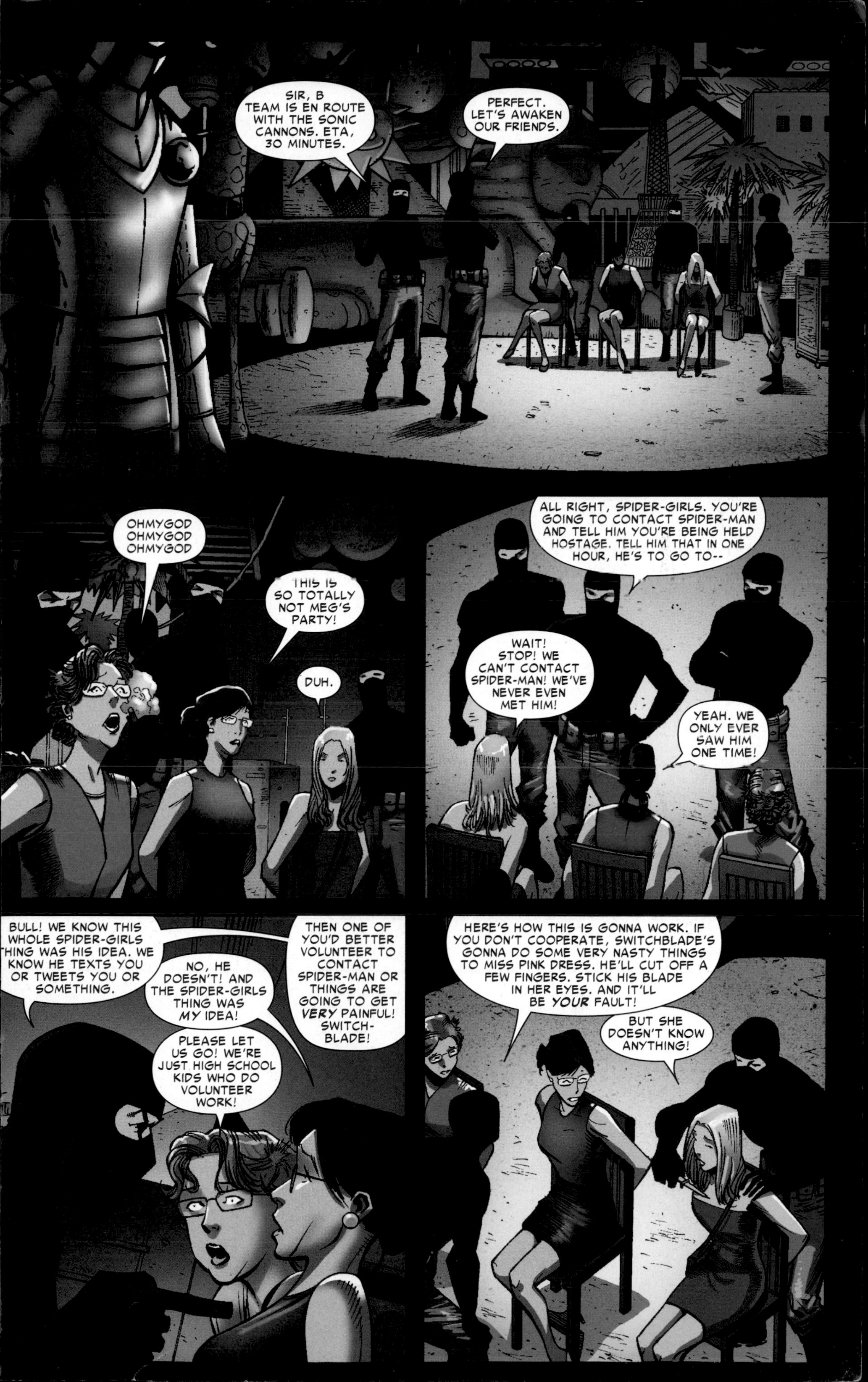
SIR, B TEAM IS EN ROUTE WITH THE SONIC CANNONS. ETA, 30 MINUTES.
PERFECT. LET'S AWAKEN OUR FRIENDS.
OHMYGOD OHMYGOD OHMYGOD
THIS IS SO TOTALLY NOT MEG'S PARTY!
DUH.
ALL RIGHT, SPIDER-GIRLS. YOU'RE GOING TO CONTACT SPIDER-MAN AND TELL HIM YOU'RE BEING HELD HOSTAGE. TELL HIM THAT IN ONE HOUR, HE'S TO GO TO--
WAIT! STOP! WE CAN'T CONTACT SPIDER-MAN! WE'VE NEVER EVEN MET HIM!
YEAH. WE ONLY EVER SAW HIM ONE TIME!
BULL! WE KNOW THIS WHOLE SPIDER-GIRLS THING WAS HIS IDEA. WE KNOW HE TEXTS YOU OR TWEETS YOU OR SOMETHING.
NO, HE DOESN'T! AND THE SPIDER-GIRLS THING WAS MY IDEA!
THEN ONE OF YOU'D BETTER VOLUNTEER TO CONTACT SPIDER-MAN OR THINGS ARE GOING TO GET VERY PAINFUL! SWITCH-BLADE!
PLEASE LET US GO! WE'RE JUST HIGH SCHOOL KIDS WHO DO VOLUNTEER WORK!
HERE'S HOW THIS IS GONNA WORK. IF YOU DON'T COOPERATE, SWITCHBLADE'S GONNA DO SOME VERY NASTY THINGS TO MISS PINK DRESS. HE'LL CUT OFF A FEW FINGERS. STICK HIS BLADE IN HER EYES. AND IT'LL BE YOUR FAULT!
BUT SHE DOESN'T KNOW ANYTHING!

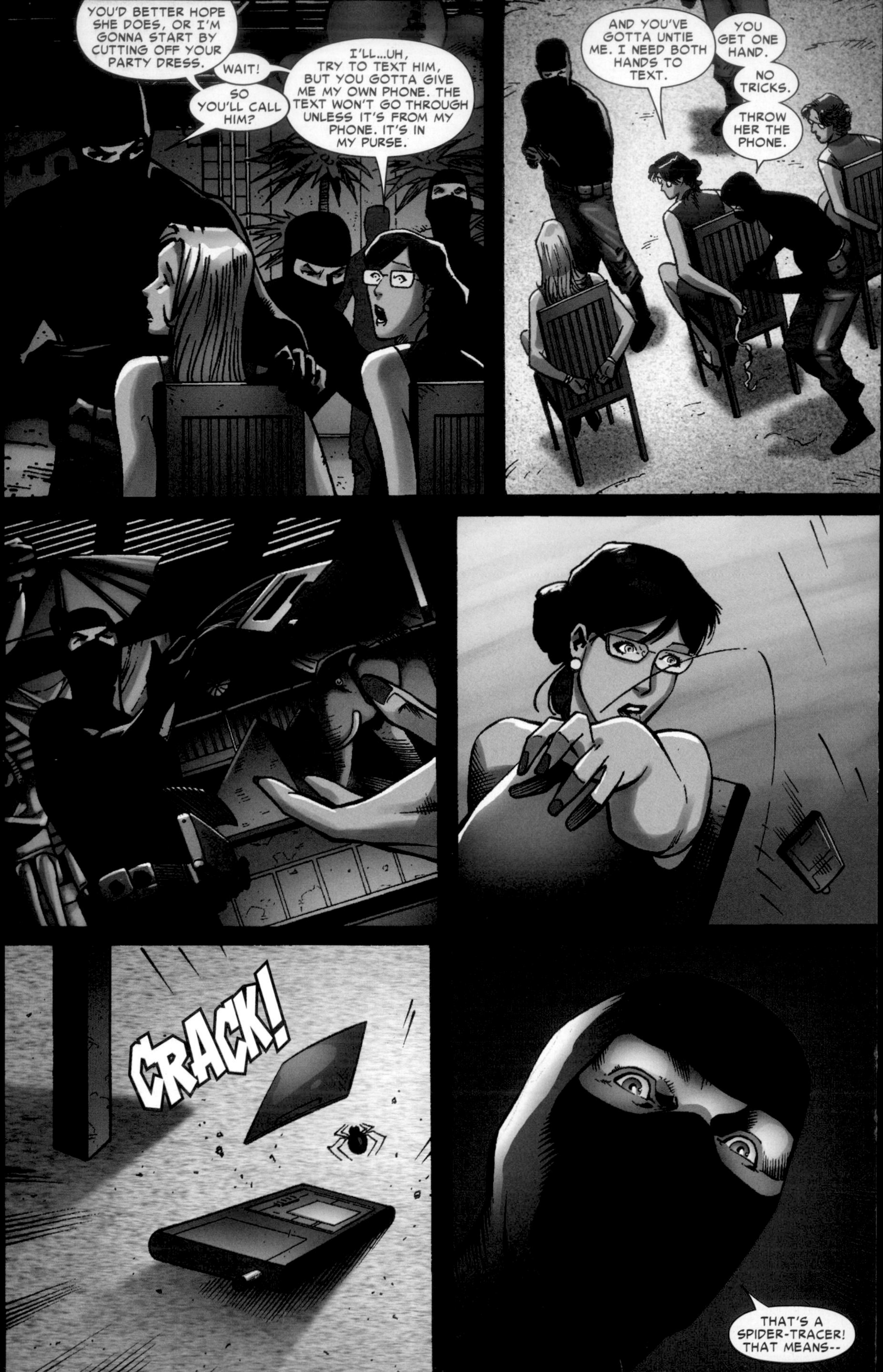
YOU'D BETTER HOPE SHE DOES, OR I'M GONNA START BY CUTTING OFF YOUR PARTY DRESS.
WAIT!
SO YOU'LL CALL HIM?
I'LL...UH, TRY TO TEXT HIM, BUT YOU GOTTA GIVE ME MY OWN PHONE. THE TEXT WON'T GO THROUGH UNLESS IT'S FROM MY PHONE. IT'S IN MY PURSE.
AND YOU'VE GOTTA UNTIE ME. I NEED BOTH HANDS TO TEXT.
YOU GET ONE HAND.
NO TRICKS.
THROW HER THE PHONE.
CRACK!
THAT'S A SPIDER-TRACER! THAT MEANS--

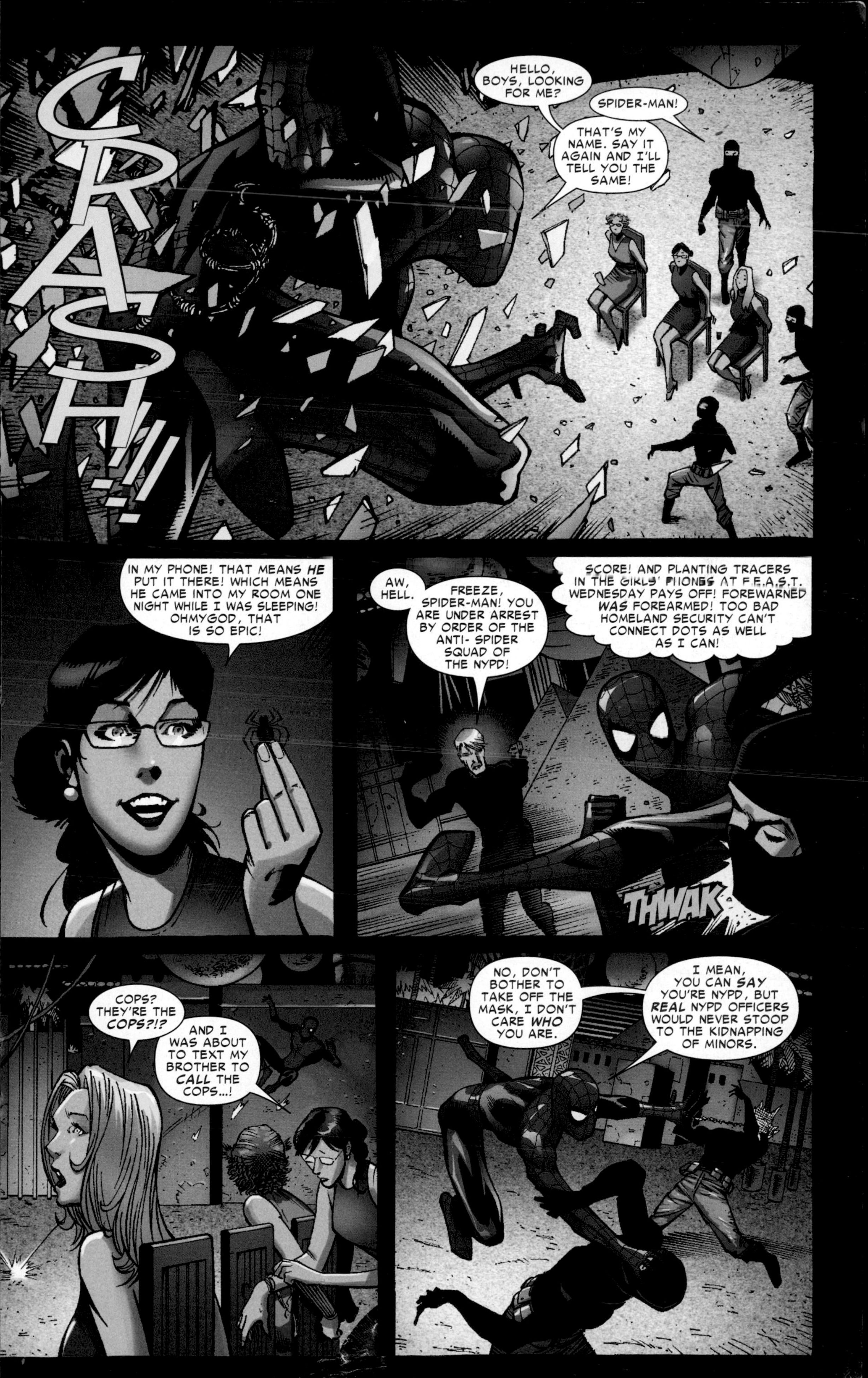
CRASH!!!
HELLO, BOYS, LOOKING FOR ME?
SPIDER-MAN!
THAT'S MY NAME. SAY IT AGAIN AND I'LL TELL YOU THE SAME!
IN MY PHONE! THAT MEANS HE PUT IT THERE! WHICH MEANS HE CAME INTO MY ROOM ONE NIGHT WHILE I WAS SLEEPING! OHMYGOD, THAT IS SO EPIC!
AW, HELL.
FREEZE, SPIDER-MAN! YOU ARE UNDER ARREST BY ORDER OF THE ANTI- SPIDER SQUAD OF THE NYPD!
SCORE! AND PLANTING TRACERS IN THE GIRLS' PHONES AT F.E.A.S.T. WEDNESDAY PAYS OFF! FOREWARNED WAS FOREARMED! TOO BAD HOMELAND SECURITY CAN'T CONNECT DOTS AS WELL AS I CAN!
THWAK
COPS? THEY'RE THE COPS?!?
AND I WAS ABOUT TO TEXT MY BROTHER TO CALL THE COPS...!
NO, DON'T BOTHER TO TAKE OFF THE MASK, I DON'T CARE WHO YOU ARE.
I MEAN, YOU CAN SAY YOU'RE NYPD, BUT REAL NYPD OFFICERS WOULD NEVER STOOP TO THE KIDNAPPING OF MINORS.

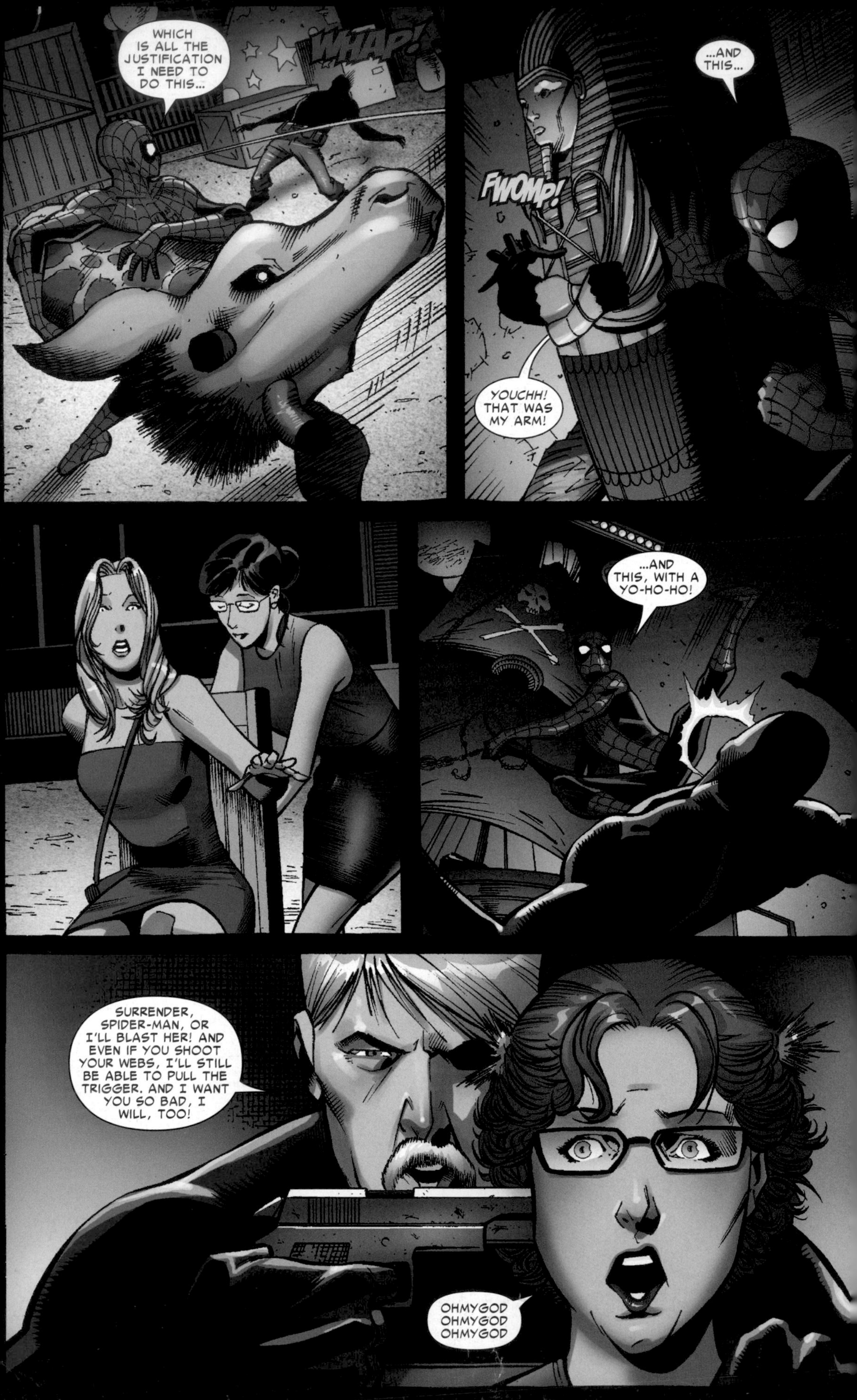
WHICH IS ALL THE JUSTIFICATION I NEED TO DO THIS...
WHAP!
...AND THIS...
FWOMP!
YOUCHH! THAT WAS MY ARM!
...AND THIS, WITH A YO-HO-HO!
SURRENDER, SPIDER-MAN, OR I'LL BLAST HER! AND EVEN IF YOU SHOOT YOUR WEBS, I'LL STILL BE ABLE TO PULL THE TRIGGER. AND I WANT YOU SO BAD, I WILL, TOO!
OHMYGOD OHMYGOD OHMYGOD

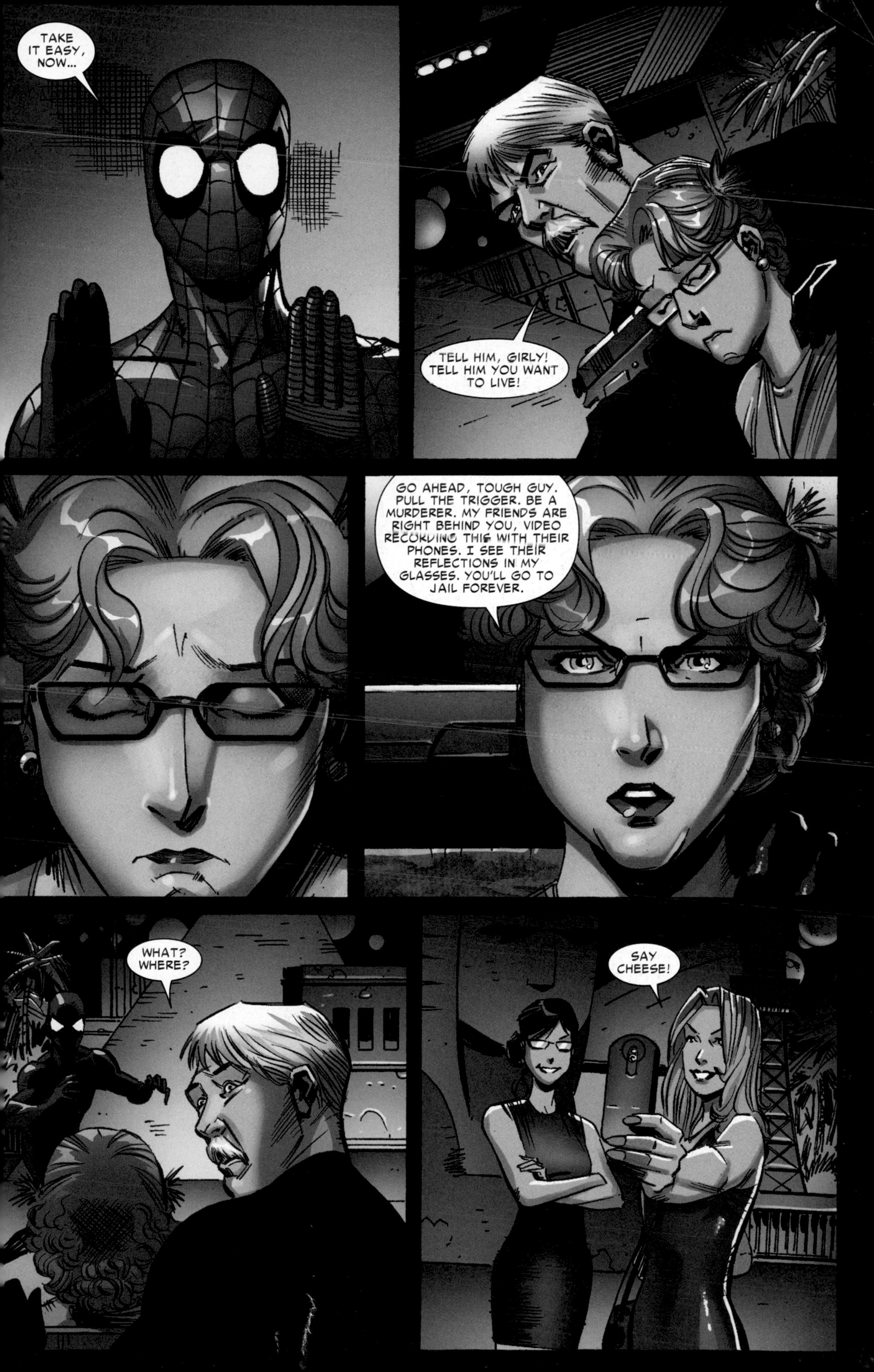
TAKE IT EASY, NOW...
TELL HIM, GIRLY! TELL HIM YOU WANT TO LIVE!
GO AHEAD, TOUGH GUY. PULL THE TRIGGER. BE A MURDERER. MY FRIENDS ARE RIGHT BEHIND YOU, VIDEO RECORDING THIS WITH THEIR PHONES. I SEE THEIR REFLECTIONS IN MY GLASSES. YOU'LL GO TO JAIL FOREVER.
WHAT? WHERE?
SAY CHEESE!

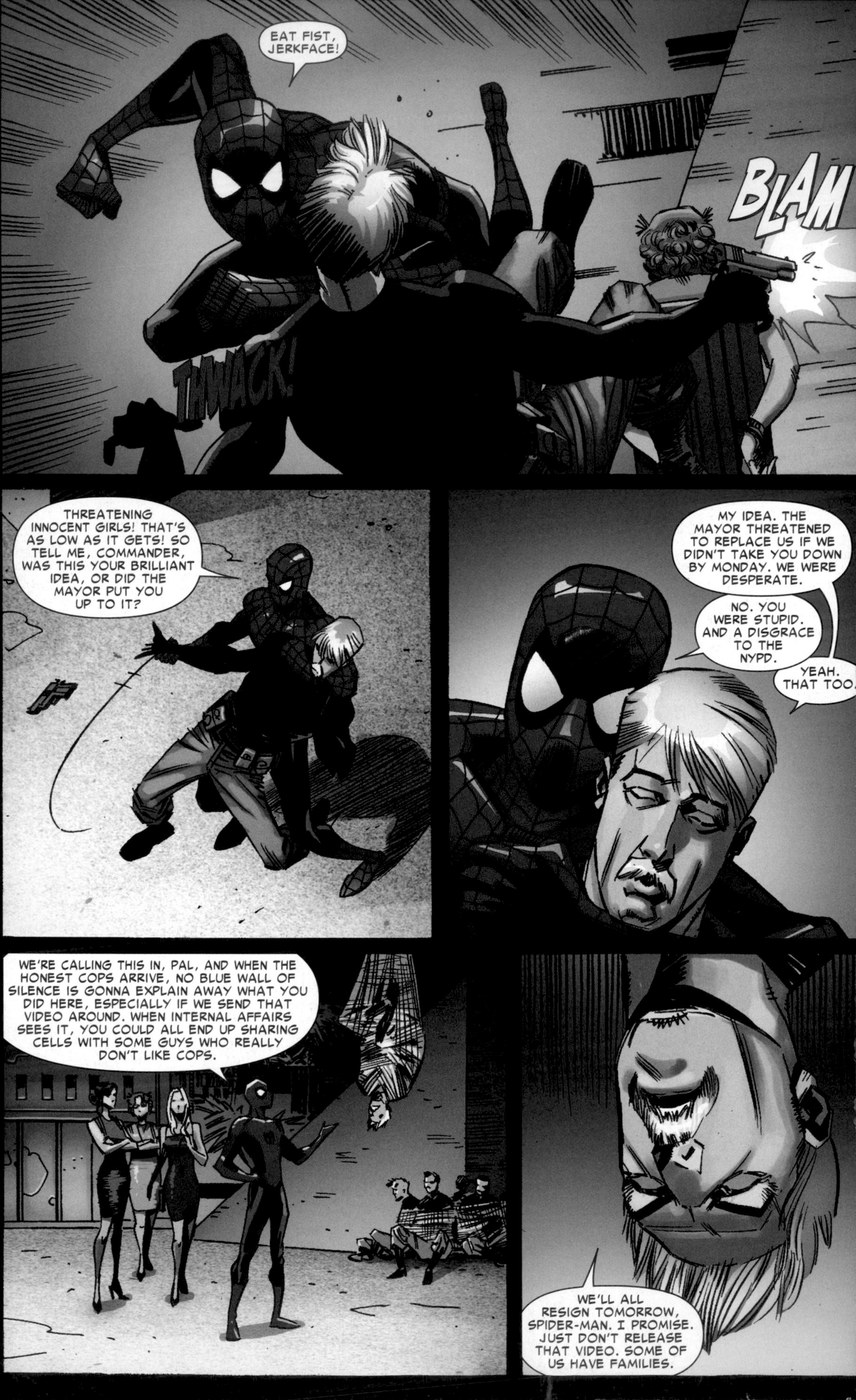
EAT FIST, JERKFACE!
BLAM
THWACK!
THREATENING INNOCENT GIRLS! THAT'S AS LOW AS IT GETS! SO TELL ME, COMMANDER, WAS THIS YOUR BRILLIANT IDEA, OR DID THE MAYOR PUT YOU UP TO IT?
MY IDEA. THE MAYOR THREATENED TO REPLACE US IF WE DIDN'T TAKE YOU DOWN BY MONDAY. WE WERE DESPERATE.
NO. YOU WERE STUPID. AND A DISGRACE TO THE NYPD.
YEAH. THAT TOO.
WE'RE CALLING THIS IN, PAL, AND WHEN THE HONEST COPS ARRIVE, NO BLUE WALL OF SILENCE IS GONNA EXPLAIN AWAY WHAT YOU DID HERE, ESPECIALLY IF WE SEND THAT VIDEO AROUND. WHEN INTERNAL AFFAIRS SEES IT, YOU COULD ALL END UP SHARING CELLS WITH SOME GUYS WHO REALLY DON'T LIKE COPS.
WE'LL ALL RESIGN TOMORROW, SPIDER-MAN. I PROMISE. JUST DON'T RELEASE THAT VIDEO. SOME OF US HAVE FAMILIES.

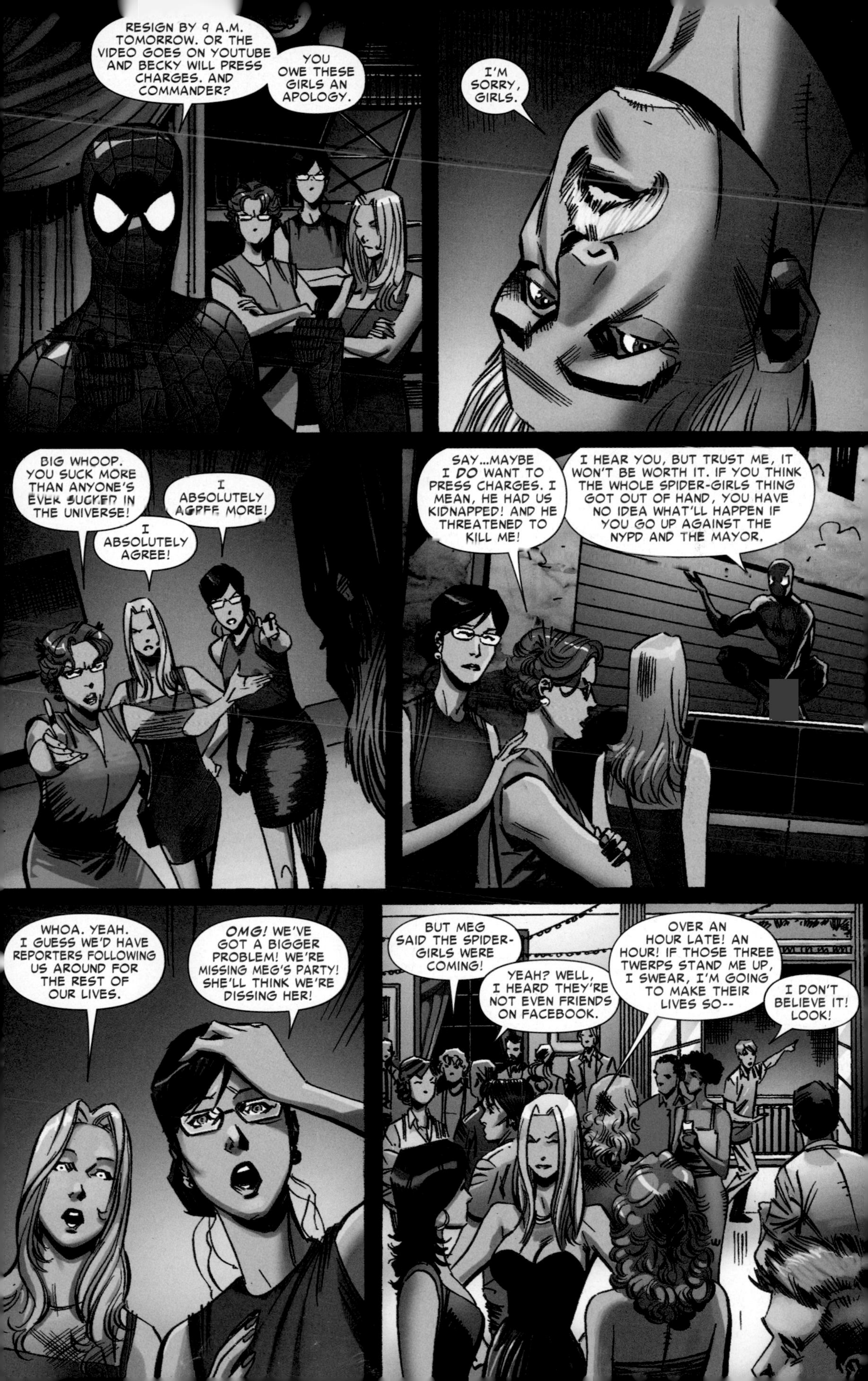

RESIGN BY 9 A.M. TOMORROW. OR THE VIDEO GOES ON YOUTUBE AND BECKY WILL PRESS CHARGES. AND COMMANDER?
YOU OWE THESE GIRLS AN APOLOGY.
I'M SORRY, GIRLS.
BIG WHOOP. YOU SUCK MORE THAN ANYONE'S EVER SUCKED IN THE UNIVERSE!
I ABSOLUTELY AGREE!
I ABSOLUTELY AGREE MORE!
SAY...MAYBE I *DO* WANT TO PRESS CHARGES. I MEAN, HE HAD US KIDNAPPED! AND HE THREATENED TO KILL ME!
I HEAR YOU, BUT TRUST ME, IT WON'T BE WORTH IT. IF YOU THINK THE WHOLE SPIDER-GIRLS THING GOT OUT OF HAND, YOU HAVE NO IDEA WHAT'LL HAPPEN IF YOU GO UP AGAINST THE NYPD AND THE MAYOR.
WHOA. YEAH. I GUESS WE'D HAVE REPORTERS FOLLOWING US AROUND FOR THE REST OF OUR LIVES.
OMG! WE'VE GOT A BIGGER PROBLEM! WE'RE MISSING MEG'S PARTY! SHE'LL THINK WE'RE DISSING HER!
BUT MEG SAID THE SPIDER-GIRLS WERE COMING!
YEAH? WELL, I HEARD THEY'RE NOT EVEN FRIENDS ON FACEBOOK.
OVER AN HOUR LATE! AN HOUR! IF THOSE THREE TWERPS STAND ME UP, I SWEAR, I'M GOING TO MAKE THEIR LIVES SO--
I DON'T BELIEVE IT! LOOK!

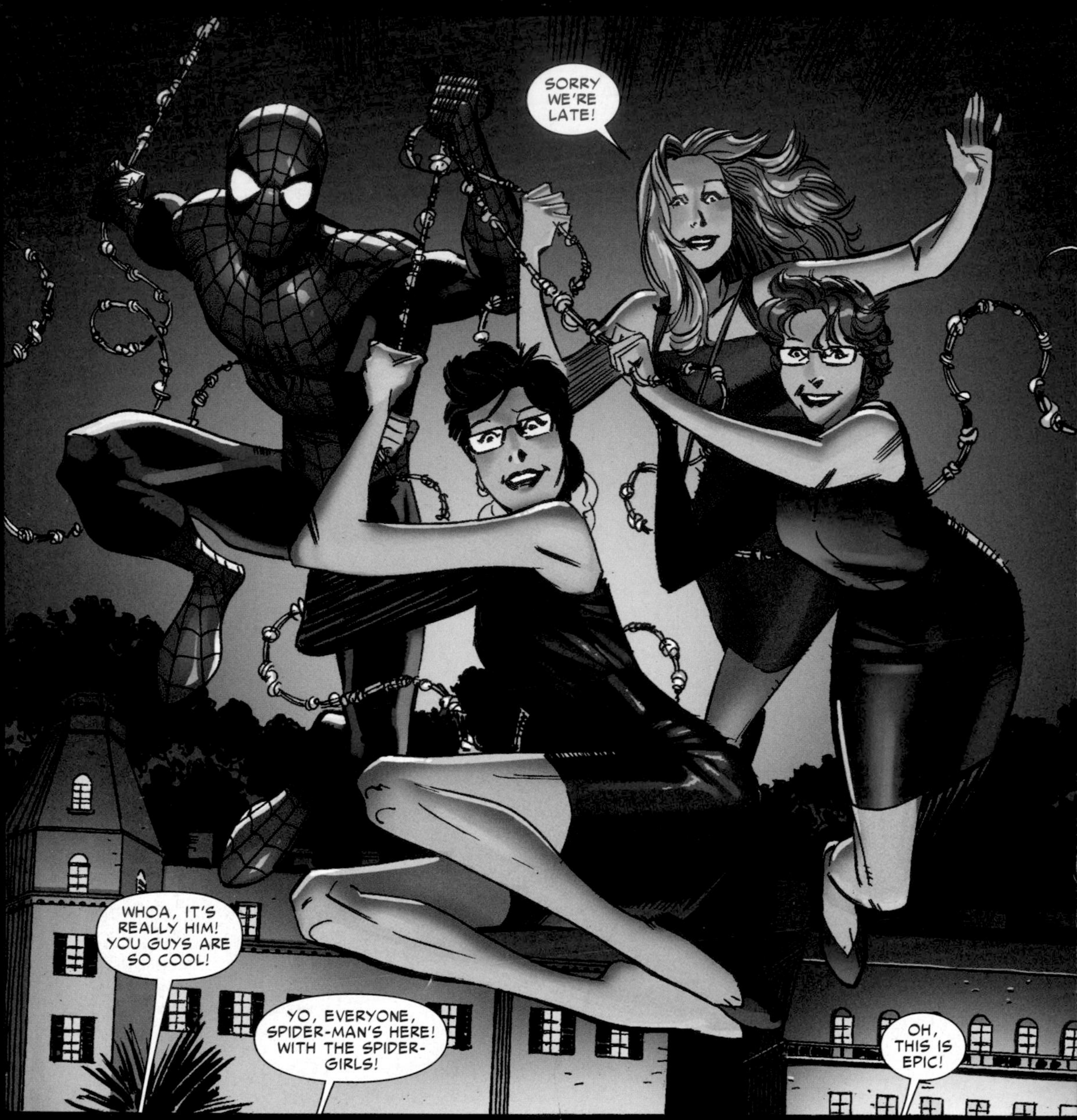
SORRY WE'RE LATE!
WHOA, IT'S REALLY HIM! YOU GUYS ARE SO COOL!
YO, EVERYONE, SPIDER-MAN'S HERE! WITH THE SPIDER-GIRLS!
OH, THIS IS EPIC!

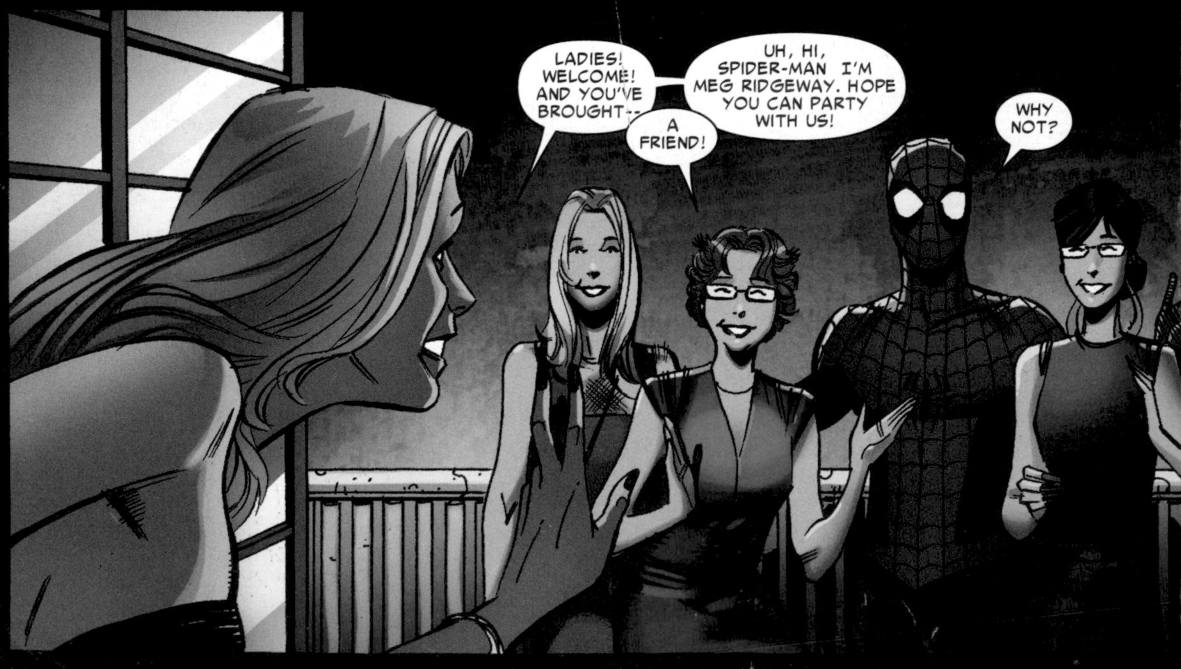
LADIES! WELCOME! AND YOU'VE BROUGHT--
A FRIEND!
UH, HI, SPIDER-MAN I'M MEG RIDGEWAY. HOPE YOU CAN PARTY WITH US!
WHY NOT?

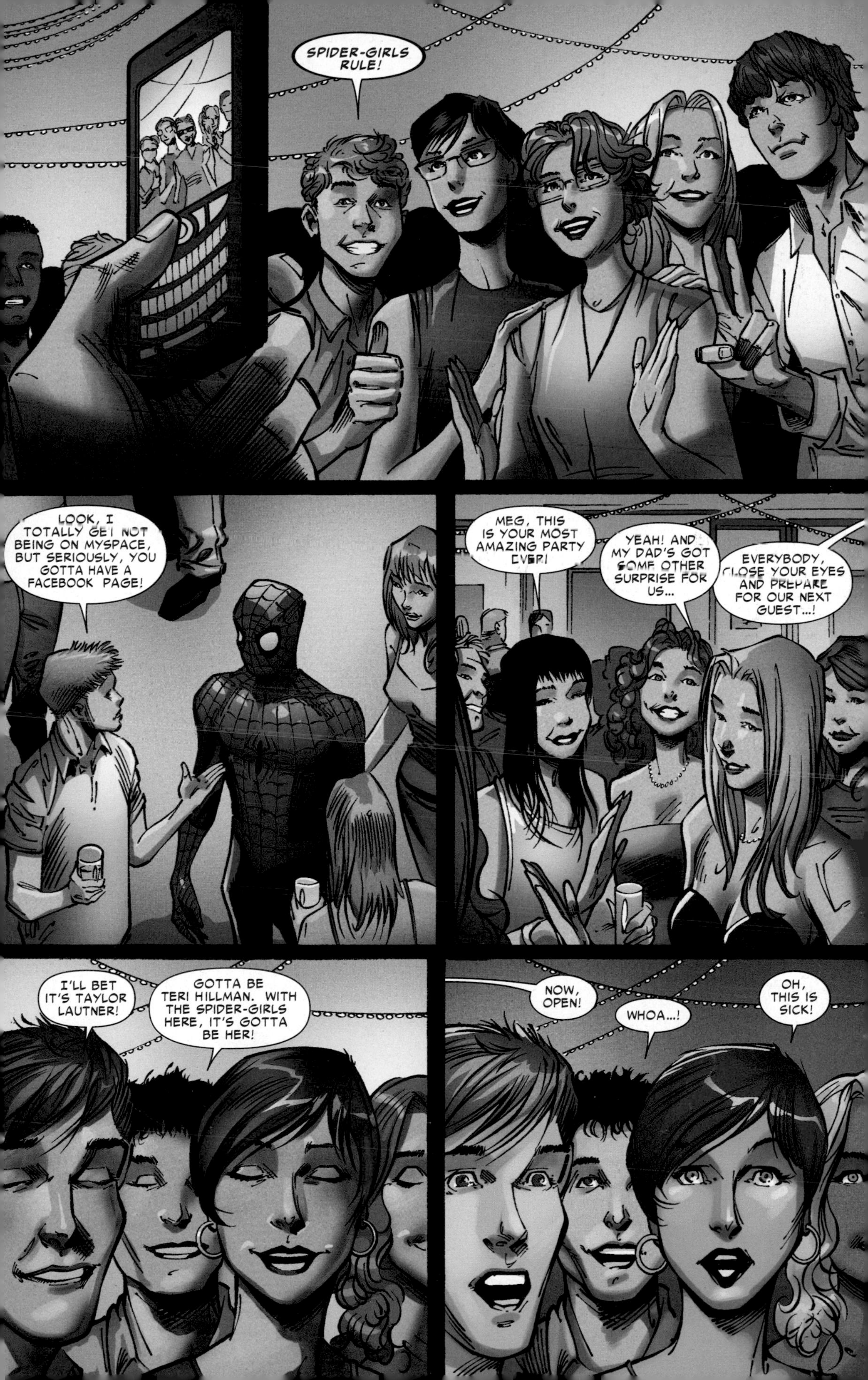
SPIDER-GIRLS RULE!
LOOK, I TOTALLY GET NOT BEING ON MYSPACE, BUT SERIOUSLY, YOU GOTTA HAVE A FACEBOOK PAGE!
MEG, THIS IS YOUR MOST AMAZING PARTY EVER!
YEAH! AND MY DAD'S GOT SOME OTHER SURPRISE FOR US...
EVERYBODY, CLOSE YOUR EYES AND PREPARE FOR OUR NEXT GUEST...!
I'LL BET IT'S TAYLOR LAUTNER!
GOTTA BE TERI HILLMAN. WITH THE SPIDER-GIRLS HERE, IT'S GOTTA BE HER!
NOW, OPEN!
WHOA...!
OH, THIS IS SICK!

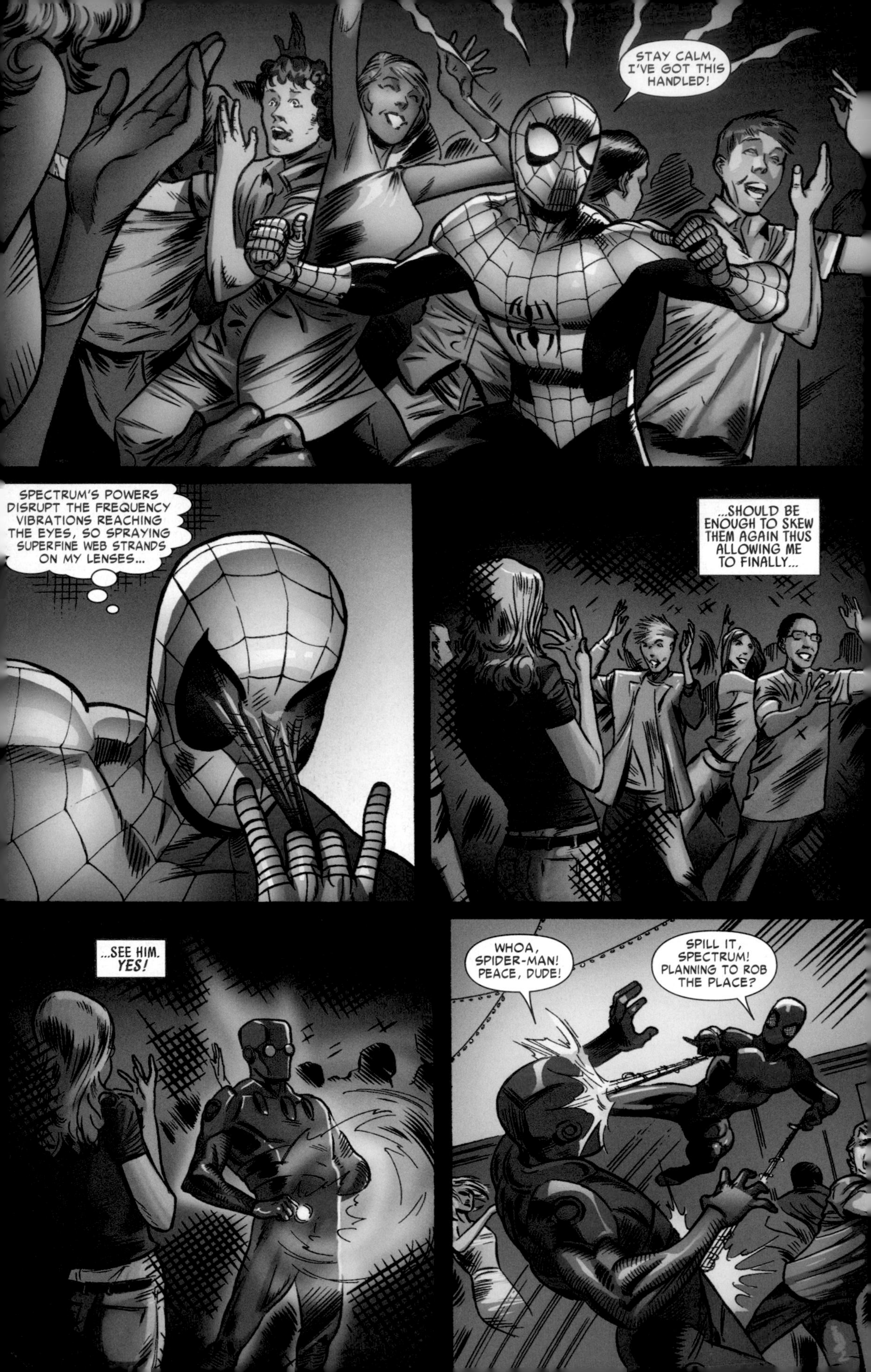

STAY CALM, I'VE GOT THIS HANDLED!
SPECTRUM'S POWERS DISRUPT THE FREQUENCY VIBRATIONS REACHING THE EYES, SO SPRAYING SUPERFINE WEB STRANDS ON MY LENSES...
...SHOULD BE ENOUGH TO SKEW THEM AGAIN THUS ALLOWING ME TO FINALLY...
...SEE HIM. YES!
WHOA, SPIDER-MAN! PEACE, DUDE!
SPILL IT, SPECTRUM! PLANNING TO ROB THE PLACE?

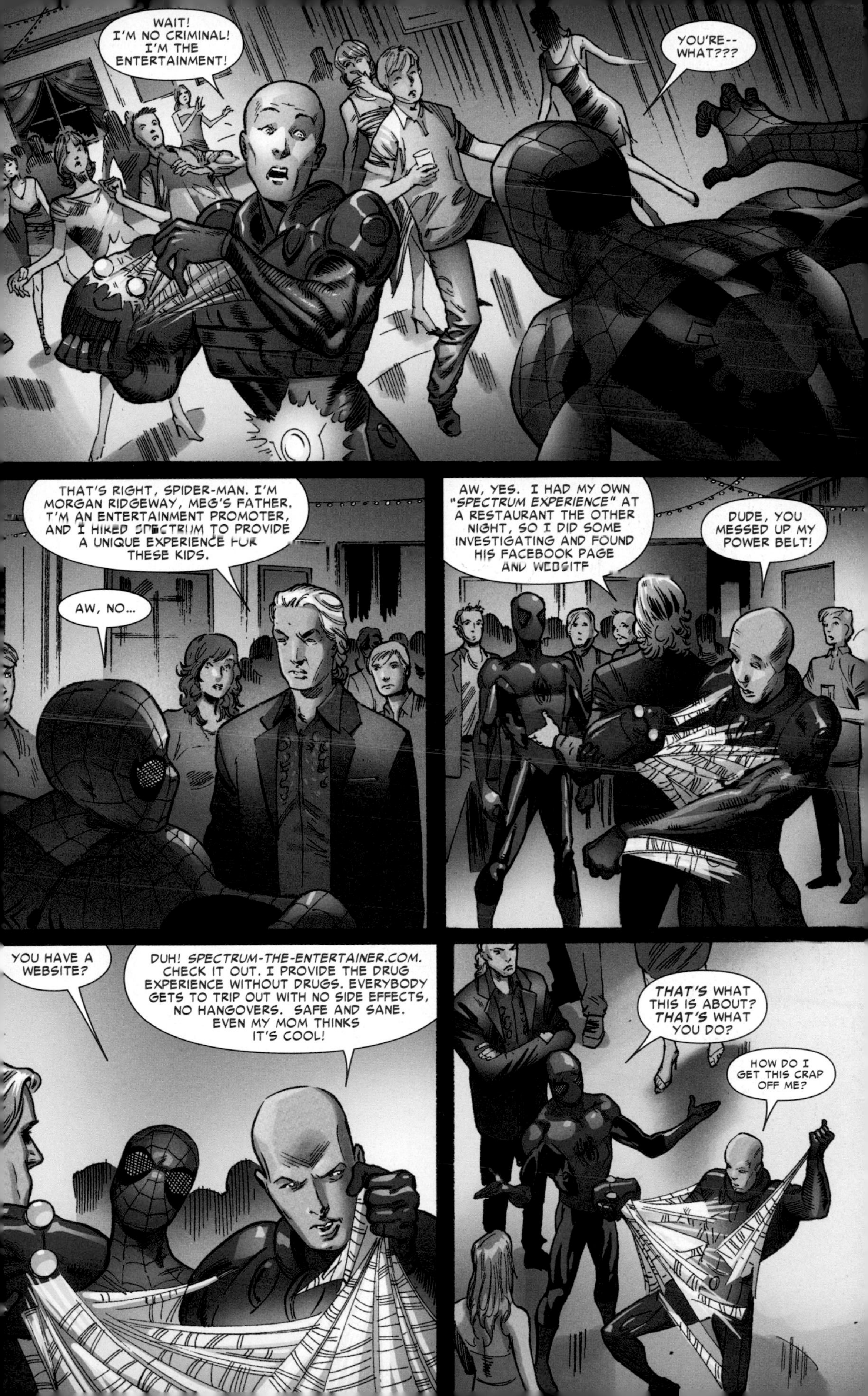
WAIT! I'M NO CRIMINAL! I'M THE ENTERTAINMENT!
YOU'RE-- WHAT???
THAT'S RIGHT, SPIDER-MAN. I'M MORGAN RIDGEWAY, MEG'S FATHER. I'M AN ENTERTAINMENT PROMOTER, AND I HIRED SPECTRUM TO PROVIDE A UNIQUE EXPERIENCE FOR THESE KIDS.
AW, NO...
AW, YES. I HAD MY OWN "SPECTRUM EXPERIENCE" AT A RESTAURANT THE OTHER NIGHT, SO I DID SOME INVESTIGATING AND FOUND HIS FACEBOOK PAGE AND WEBSITE.
DUDE, YOU MESSED UP MY POWER BELT!
YOU HAVE A WEBSITE?
DUH! SPECTRUM-THE-ENTERTAINER.COM. CHECK IT OUT. I PROVIDE THE DRUG EXPERIENCE WITHOUT DRUGS. EVERYBODY GETS TO TRIP OUT WITH NO SIDE EFFECTS, NO HANGOVERS. SAFE AND SANE. EVEN MY MOM THINKS IT'S COOL!
THAT'S WHAT THIS IS ABOUT? THAT'S WHAT YOU DO?
HOW DO I GET THIS CRAP OFF ME?

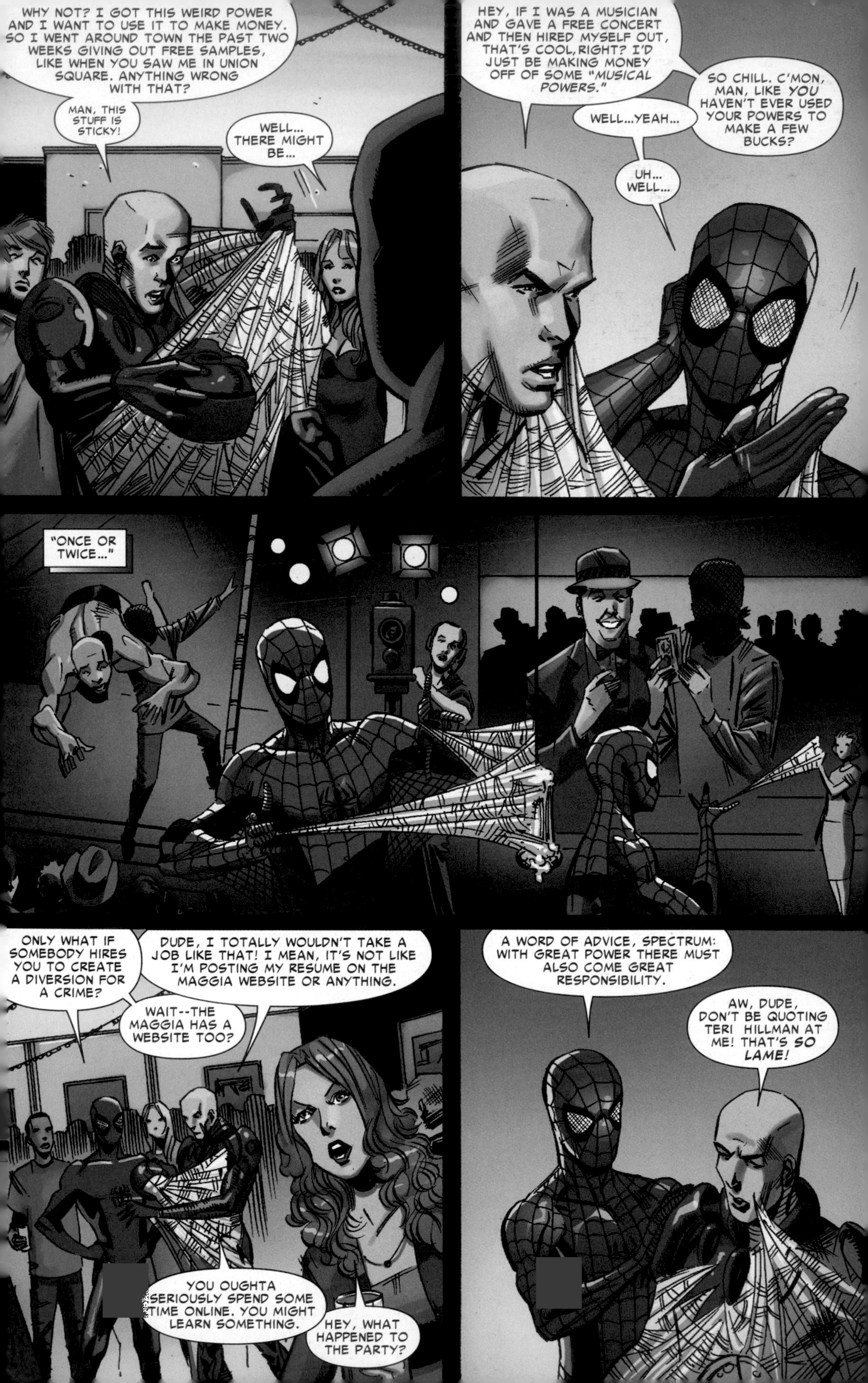
WHY NOT? I GOT THIS WEIRD POWER AND I WANT TO USE IT TO MAKE MONEY. SO I WENT AROUND TOWN THE PAST TWO WEEKS GIVING OUT FREE SAMPLES, LIKE WHEN YOU SAW ME IN UNION SQUARE. ANYTHING WRONG WITH THAT?
MAN, THIS STUFF IS STICKY!
WELL... THERE MIGHT BE...
HEY, IF I WAS A MUSICIAN AND GAVE A FREE CONCERT AND THEN HIRED MYSELF OUT, THAT'S COOL, RIGHT? I'D JUST BE MAKING MONEY OFF OF SOME "*MUSICAL POWERS.*"
WELL...YEAH...
SO CHILL. C'MON, MAN, LIKE *YOU* HAVEN'T EVER USED YOUR POWERS TO MAKE A FEW BUCKS?
UH... WELL...
"ONCE OR TWICE..."
ONLY WHAT IF SOMEBODY HIRES YOU TO CREATE A DIVERSION FOR A CRIME?
DUDE, I TOTALLY WOULDN'T TAKE A JOB LIKE THAT! I MEAN, IT'S NOT LIKE I'M POSTING MY RESUME ON THE MAGGIA WEBSITE OR ANYTHING.
WAIT--THE MAGGIA HAS A WEBSITE TOO?
YOU OUGHTA SERIOUSLY SPEND SOME TIME ONLINE. YOU MIGHT LEARN SOMETHING.
HEY, WHAT HAPPENED TO THE PARTY?
A WORD OF ADVICE, SPECTRUM: WITH GREAT POWER THERE MUST ALSO COME GREAT RESPONSIBILITY.
AW, DUDE, DON'T BE QUOTING TERI HILLMAN AT ME! THAT'S *SO LAME!*

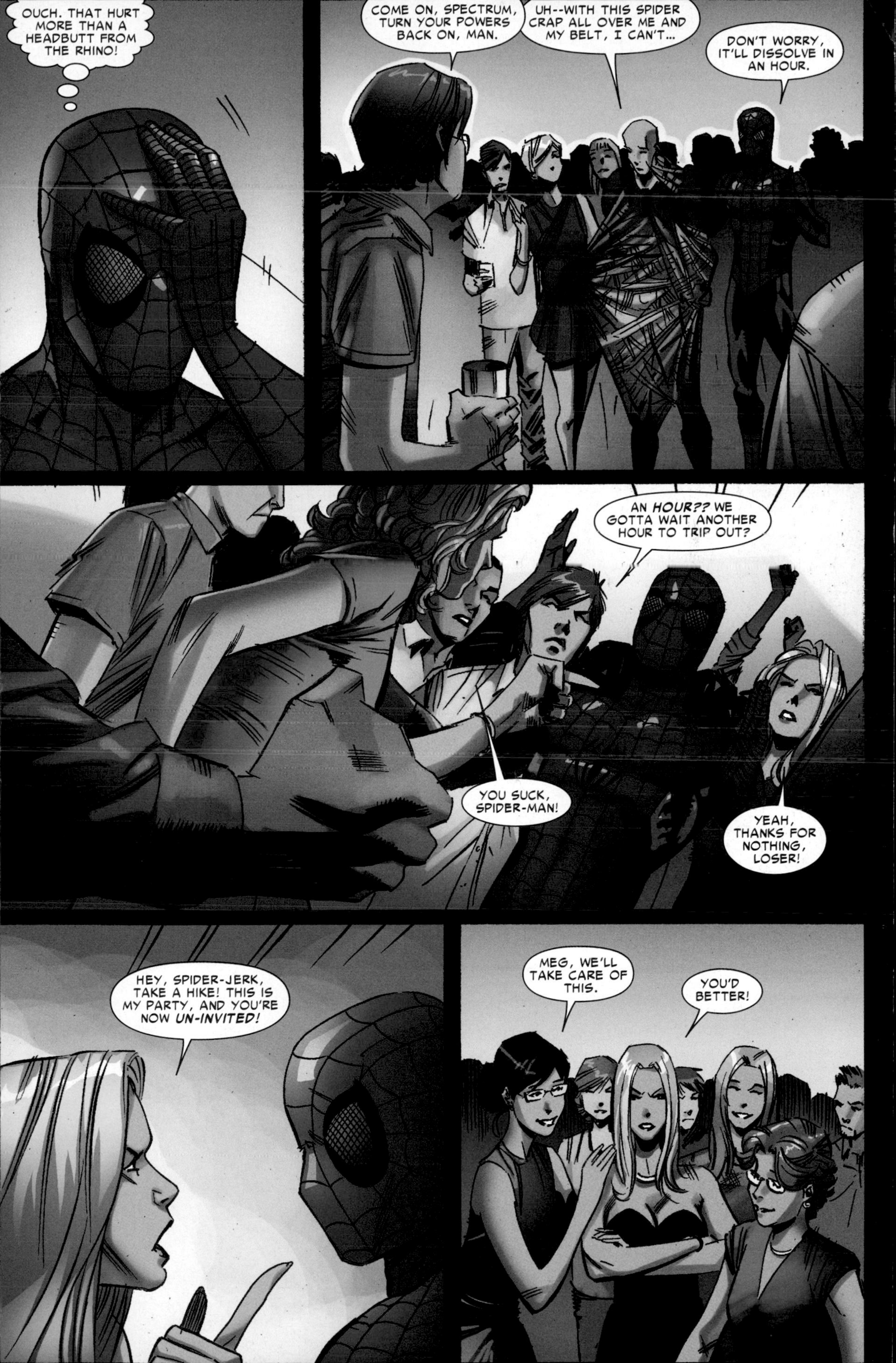
OUCH. THAT HURT MORE THAN A HEADBUTT FROM THE RHINO!
COME ON, SPECTRUM, TURN YOUR POWERS BACK ON, MAN.
UH--WITH THIS SPIDER CRAP ALL OVER ME AND MY BELT, I CAN'T...
DON'T WORRY, IT'LL DISSOLVE IN AN HOUR.
AN HOUR?? WE GOTTA WAIT ANOTHER HOUR TO TRIP OUT?
YOU SUCK, SPIDER-MAN!
YEAH, THANKS FOR NOTHING, LOSER!
HEY, SPIDER-JERK, TAKE A HIKE! THIS IS MY PARTY, AND YOU'RE NOW UN-INVITED!
MEG, WE'LL TAKE CARE OF THIS.
YOU'D BETTER!

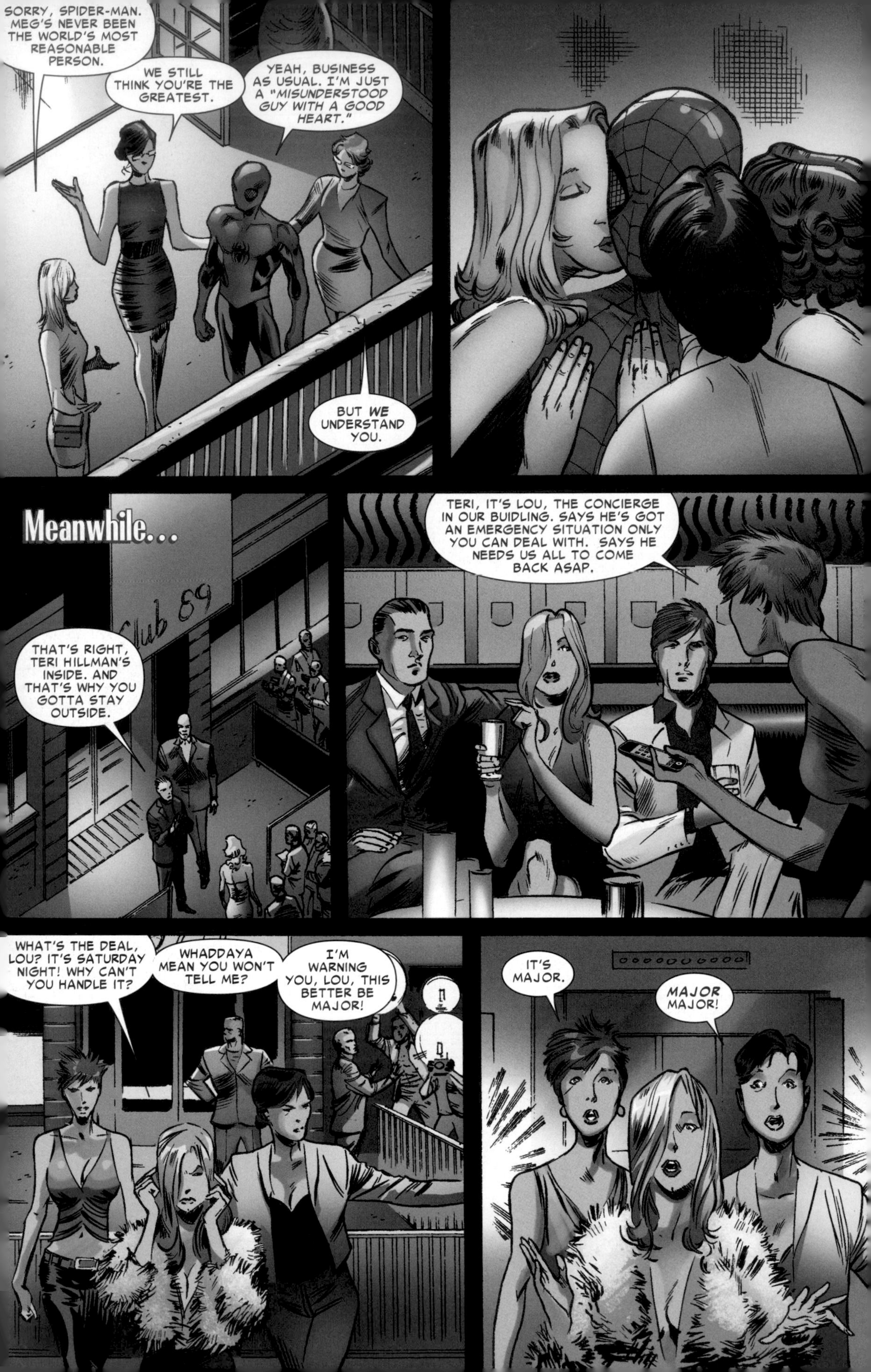
SORRY, SPIDER-MAN. MEG'S NEVER BEEN THE WORLD'S MOST REASONABLE PERSON.
WE STILL THINK YOU'RE THE GREATEST.
YEAH, BUSINESS AS USUAL. I'M JUST A "MISUNDERSTOOD GUY WITH A GOOD HEART."
BUT WE UNDERSTAND YOU.
Meanwhile...
Club 89
THAT'S RIGHT, TERI HILLMAN'S INSIDE. AND THAT'S WHY YOU GOTTA STAY OUTSIDE.
TERI, IT'S LOU, THE CONCIERGE IN OUR BUIDLING. SAYS HE'S GOT AN EMERGENCY SITUATION ONLY YOU CAN DEAL WITH. SAYS HE NEEDS US ALL TO COME BACK ASAP.
WHAT'S THE DEAL, LOU? IT'S SATURDAY NIGHT! WHY CAN'T YOU HANDLE IT?
WHADDAYA MEAN YOU WON'T TELL ME?
I'M WARNING YOU, LOU, THIS BETTER BE MAJOR!
IT'S MAJOR.
MAJOR MAJOR!

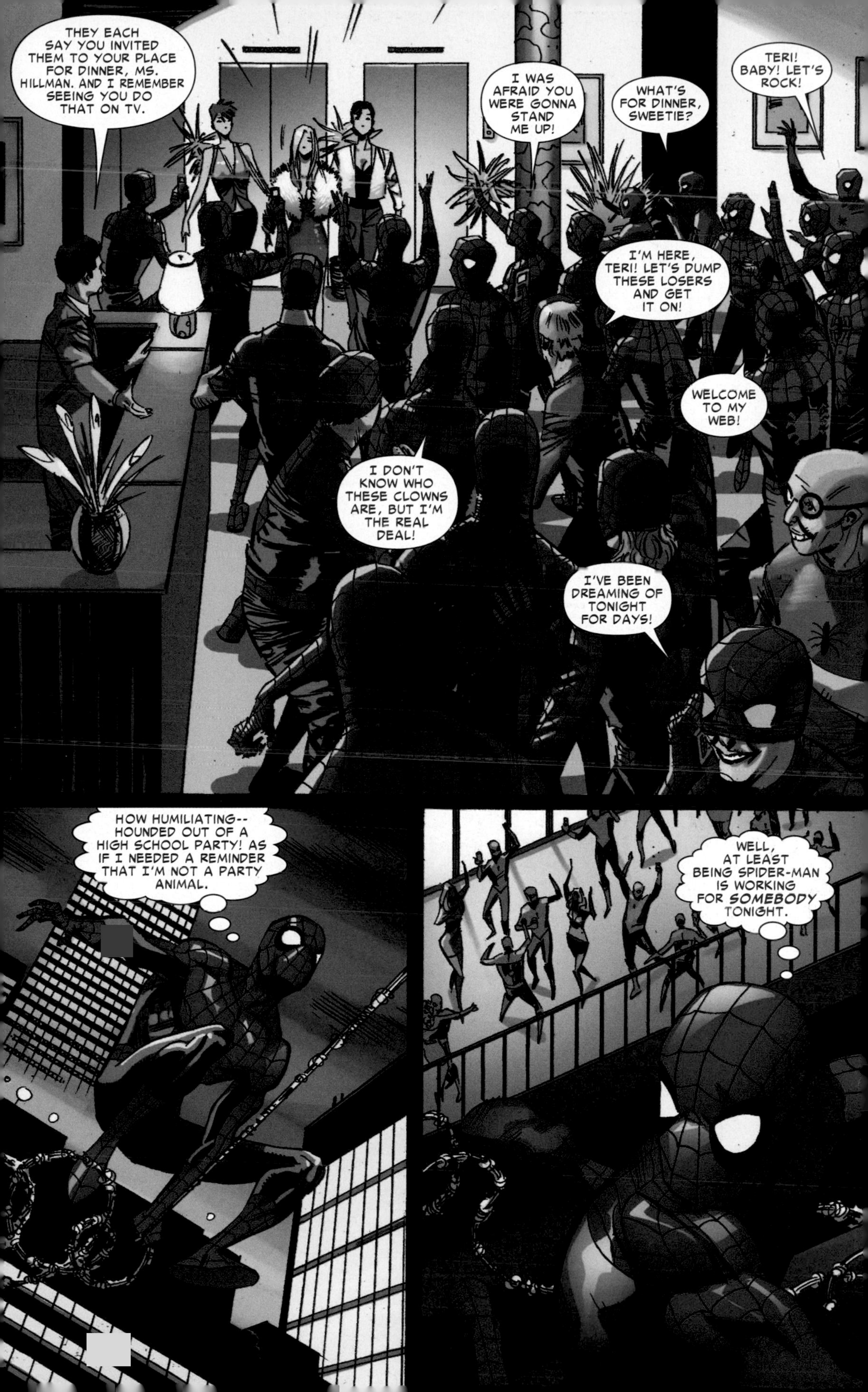
THEY EACH SAY YOU INVITED THEM TO YOUR PLACE FOR DINNER, MS. HILLMAN. AND I REMEMBER SEEING YOU DO THAT ON TV.
I WAS AFRAID YOU WERE GONNA STAND ME UP!
WHAT'S FOR DINNER, SWEETIE?
TERI! BABY! LET'S ROCK!
I'M HERE, TERI! LET'S DUMP THESE LOSERS AND GET IT ON!
WELCOME TO MY WEB!
I DON'T KNOW WHO THESE CLOWNS ARE, BUT I'M THE REAL DEAL!
I'VE BEEN DREAMING OF TONIGHT FOR DAYS!
HOW HUMILIATING-- HOUNDED OUT OF A HIGH SCHOOL PARTY! AS IF I NEEDED A REMINDER THAT I'M NOT A PARTY ANIMAL.
WELL, AT LEAST BEING SPIDER-MAN IS WORKING FOR *SOMEBODY* TONIGHT.

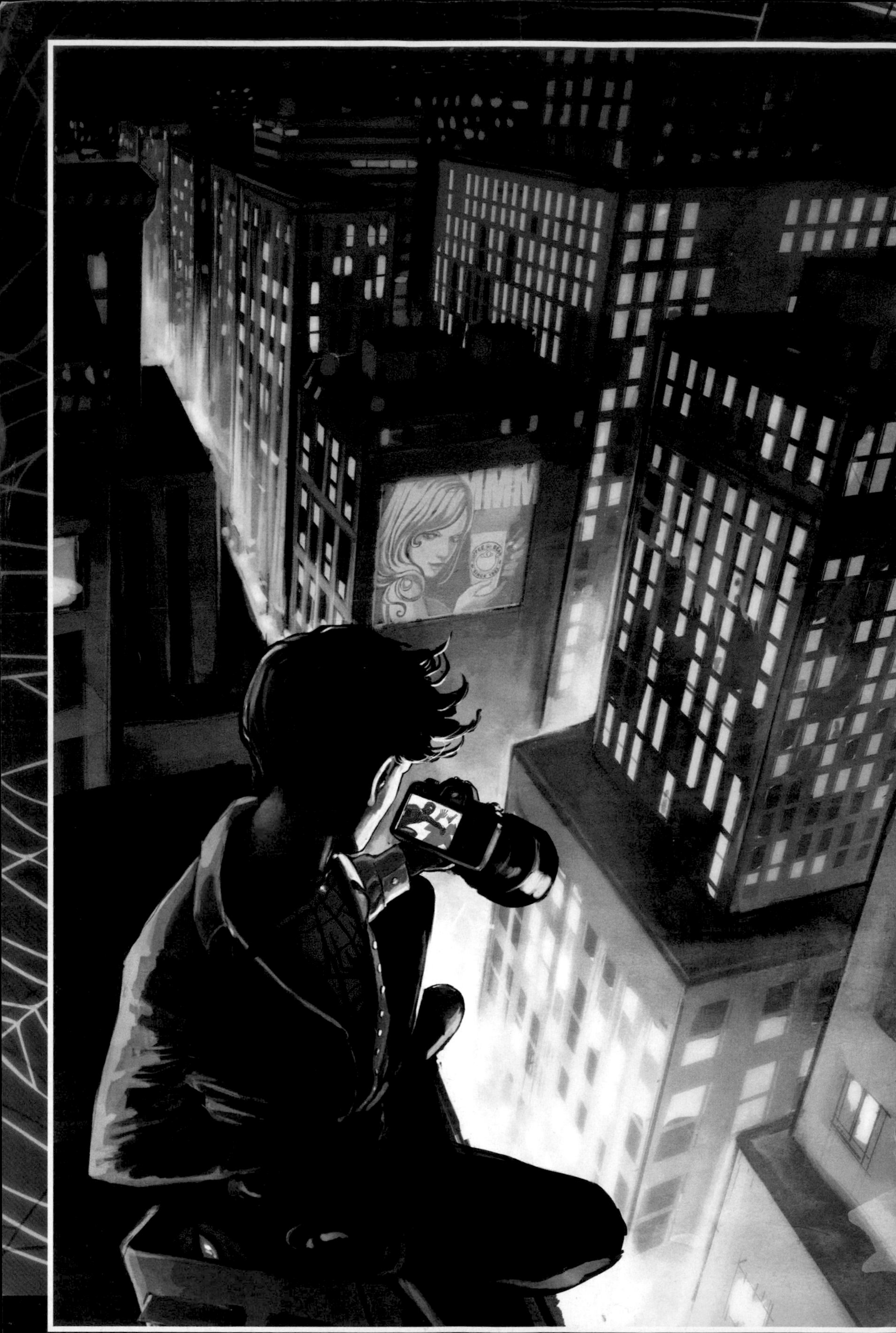

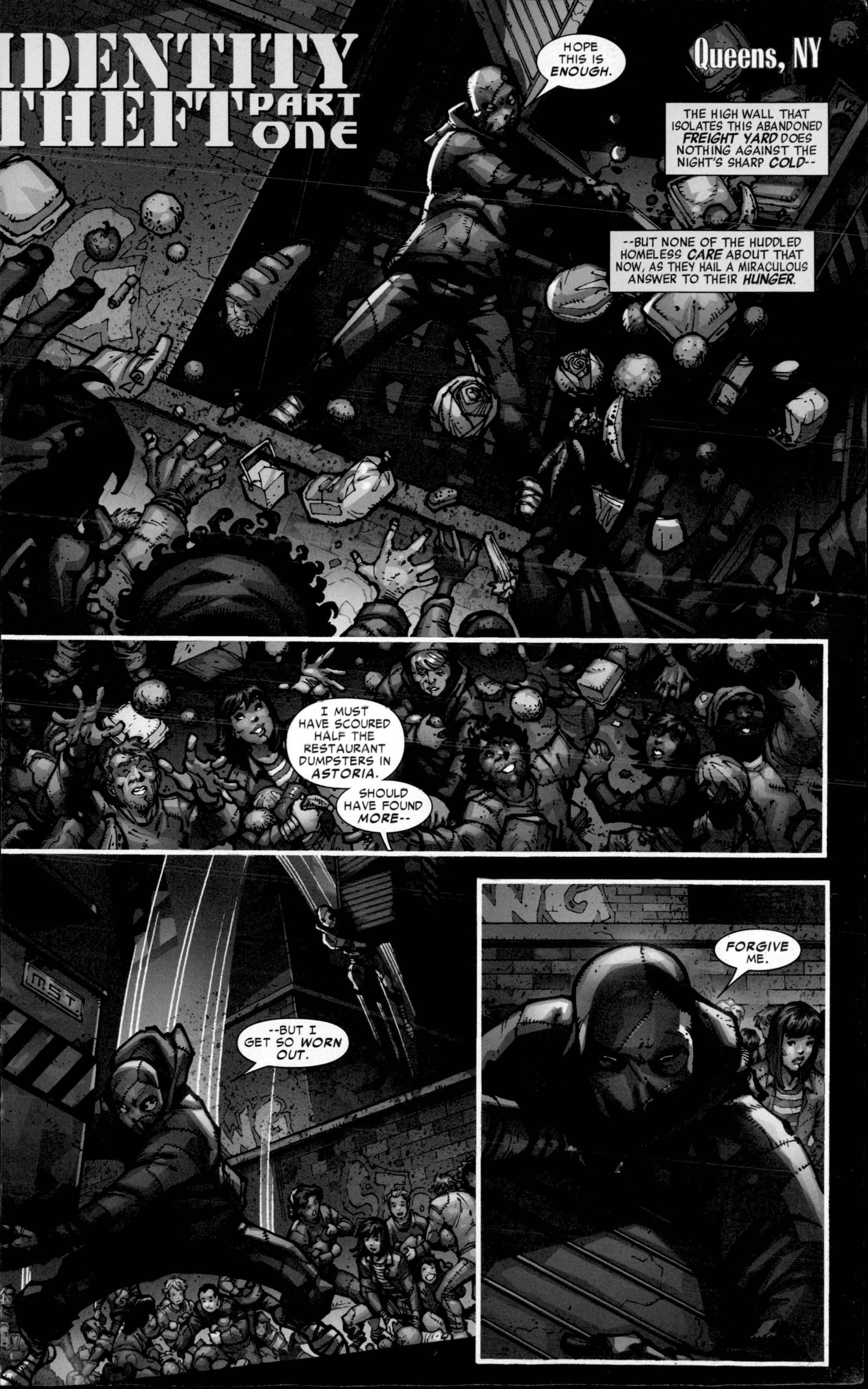
IDENTITY THEFT PART ONE
HOPE THIS IS ENOUGH.
Queens, NY
THE HIGH WALL THAT ISOLATES THIS ABANDONED FREIGHT YARD DOES NOTHING AGAINST THE NIGHT'S SHARP COLD--
--BUT NONE OF THE HUDDLED HOMELESS CARE ABOUT THAT NOW, AS THEY HAIL A MIRACULOUS ANSWER TO THEIR HUNGER.
I MUST HAVE SCOURED HALF THE RESTAURANT DUMPSTERS IN ASTORIA.
SHOULD HAVE FOUND MORE--
--BUT I GET SO WORN OUT.
FORGIVE ME.

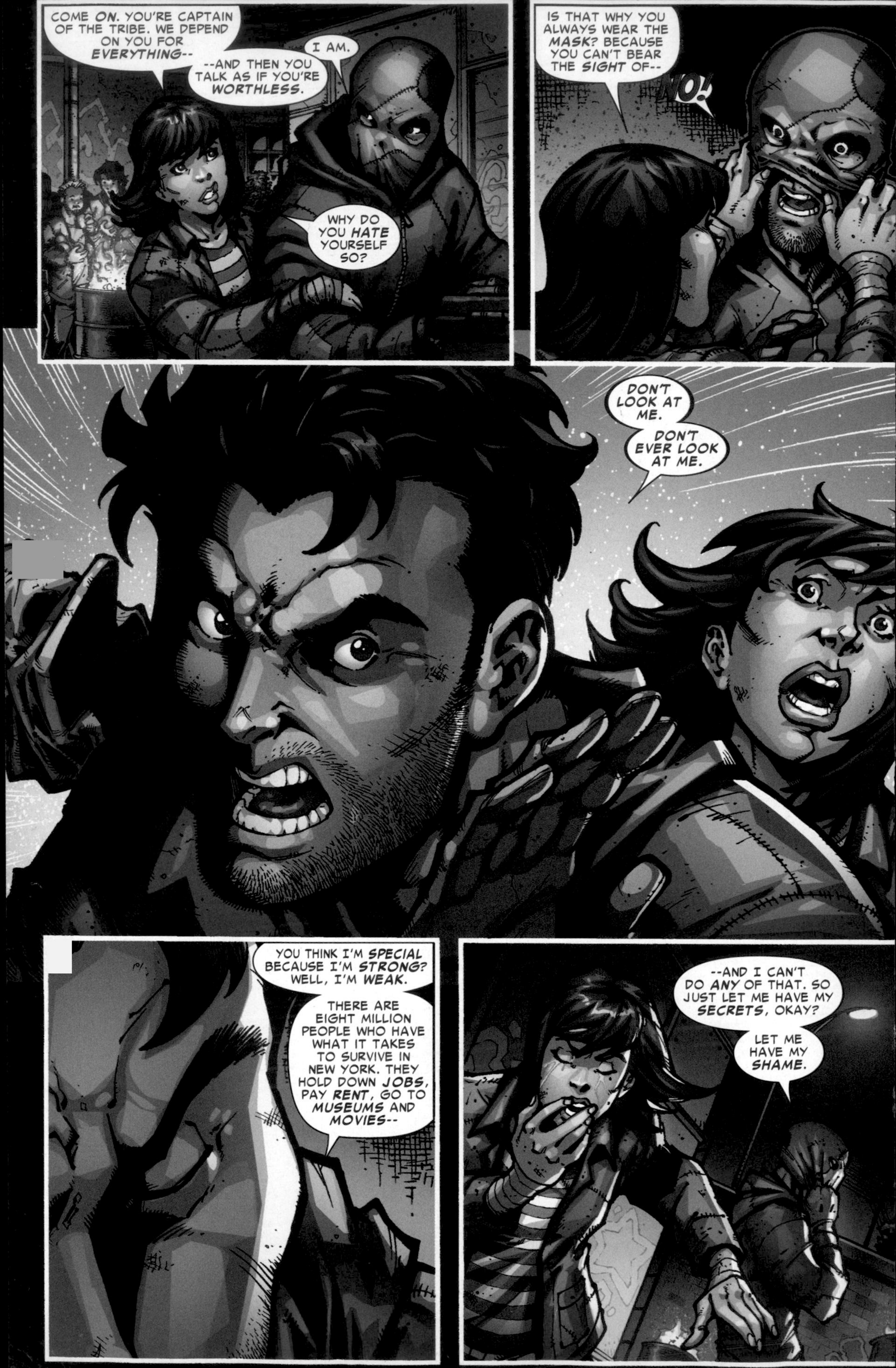
COME ON. YOU'RE CAPTAIN OF THE TRIBE. WE DEPEND ON YOU FOR EVERYTHING--
I AM.
--AND THEN YOU TALK AS IF YOU'RE WORTHLESS.
WHY DO YOU HATE YOURSELF SO?
IS THAT WHY YOU ALWAYS WEAR THE MASK? BECAUSE YOU CAN'T BEAR THE SIGHT OF--
NO!
DON'T LOOK AT ME.
DON'T EVER LOOK AT ME.
YOU THINK I'M SPECIAL BECAUSE I'M STRONG? WELL, I'M WEAK.
THERE ARE EIGHT MILLION PEOPLE WHO HAVE WHAT IT TAKES TO SURVIVE IN NEW YORK. THEY HOLD DOWN JOBS, PAY RENT, GO TO MUSEUMS AND MOVIES--
--AND I CAN'T DO ANY OF THAT. SO JUST LET ME HAVE MY SECRETS, OKAY?
LET ME HAVE MY SHAME.

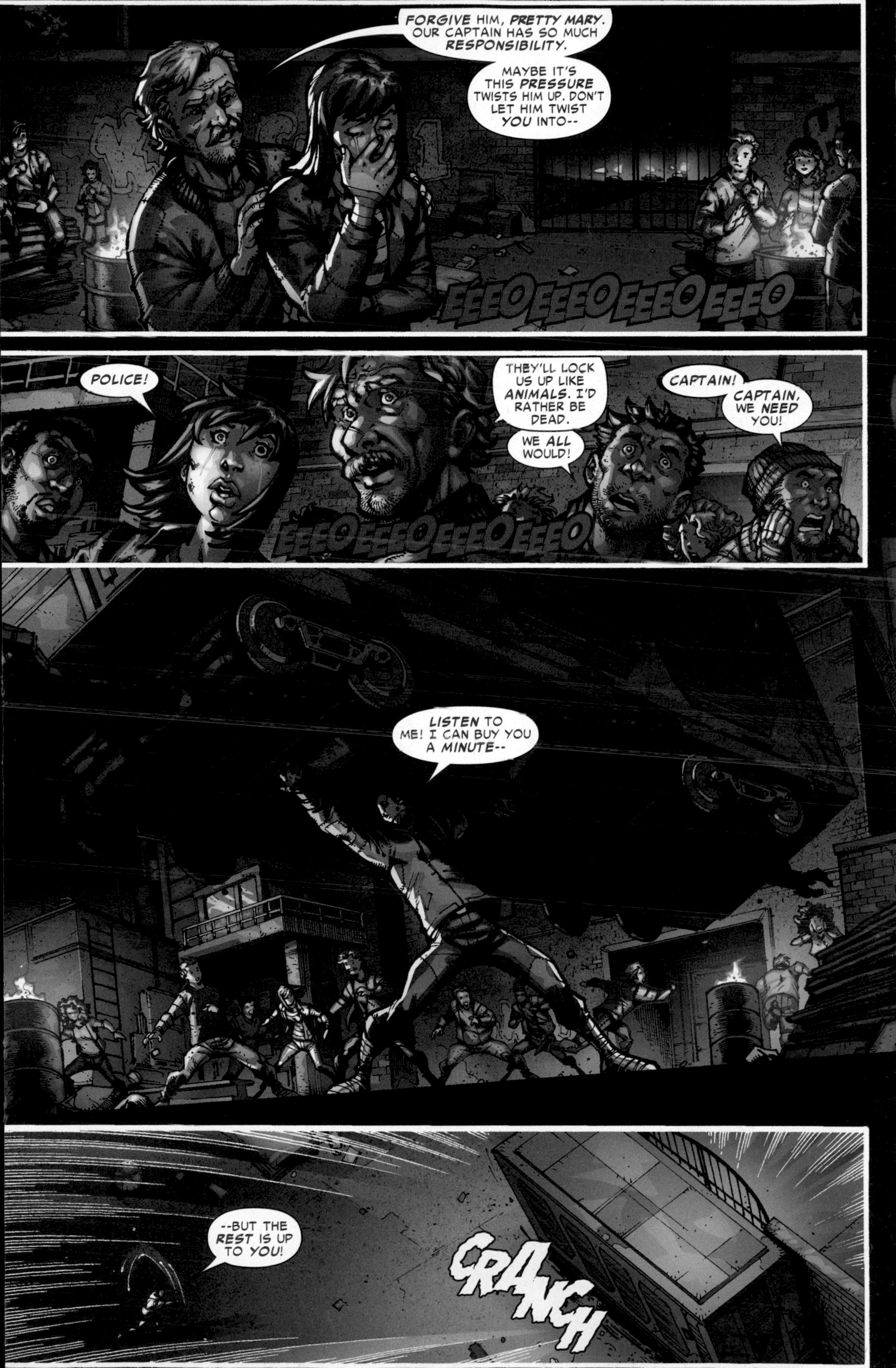
FORGIVE HIM, PRETTY MARY. OUR CAPTAIN HAS SO MUCH RESPONSIBILITY.
MAYBE IT'S THIS PRESSURE TWISTS HIM UP. DON'T LET HIM TWIST YOU INTO--
EEEOEEEOEEEOEEEO
POLICE!
THEY'LL LOCK US UP LIKE ANIMALS. I'D RATHER BE DEAD.
WE ALL WOULD!
CAPTAIN!
CAPTAIN, WE NEED YOU!
EEEOEEEOEEEOEEEO
LISTEN TO ME! I CAN BUY YOU A MINUTE--
--BUT THE REST IS UP TO YOU!
CRANCH

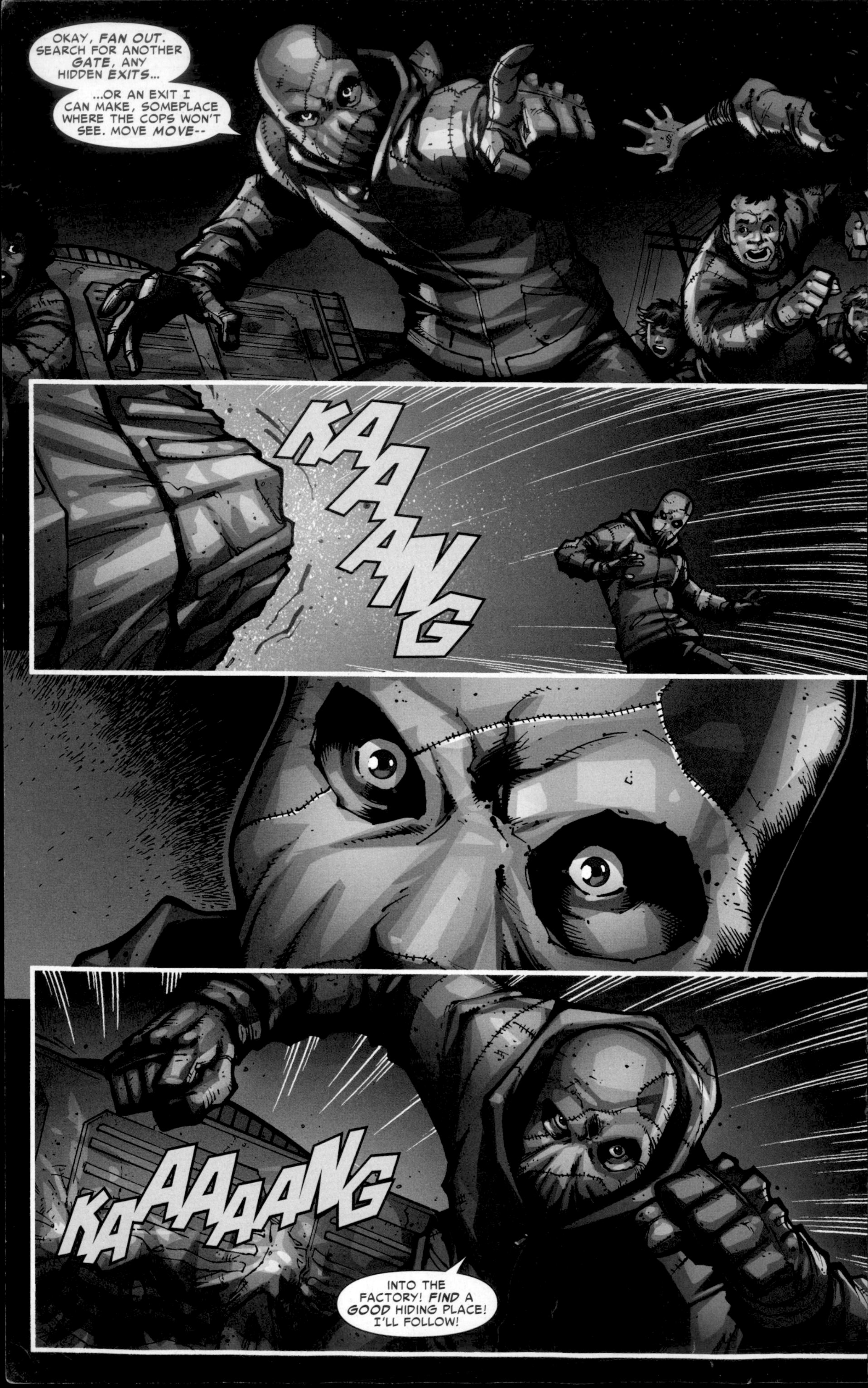
OKAY, FAN OUT. SEARCH FOR ANOTHER GATE, ANY HIDDEN EXITS...
...OR AN EXIT I CAN MAKE, SOMEPLACE WHERE THE COPS WON'T SEE. MOVE MOVE--
KAAAANG
KAAAAANG
INTO THE FACTORY! FIND A GOOD HIDING PLACE! I'LL FOLLOW!

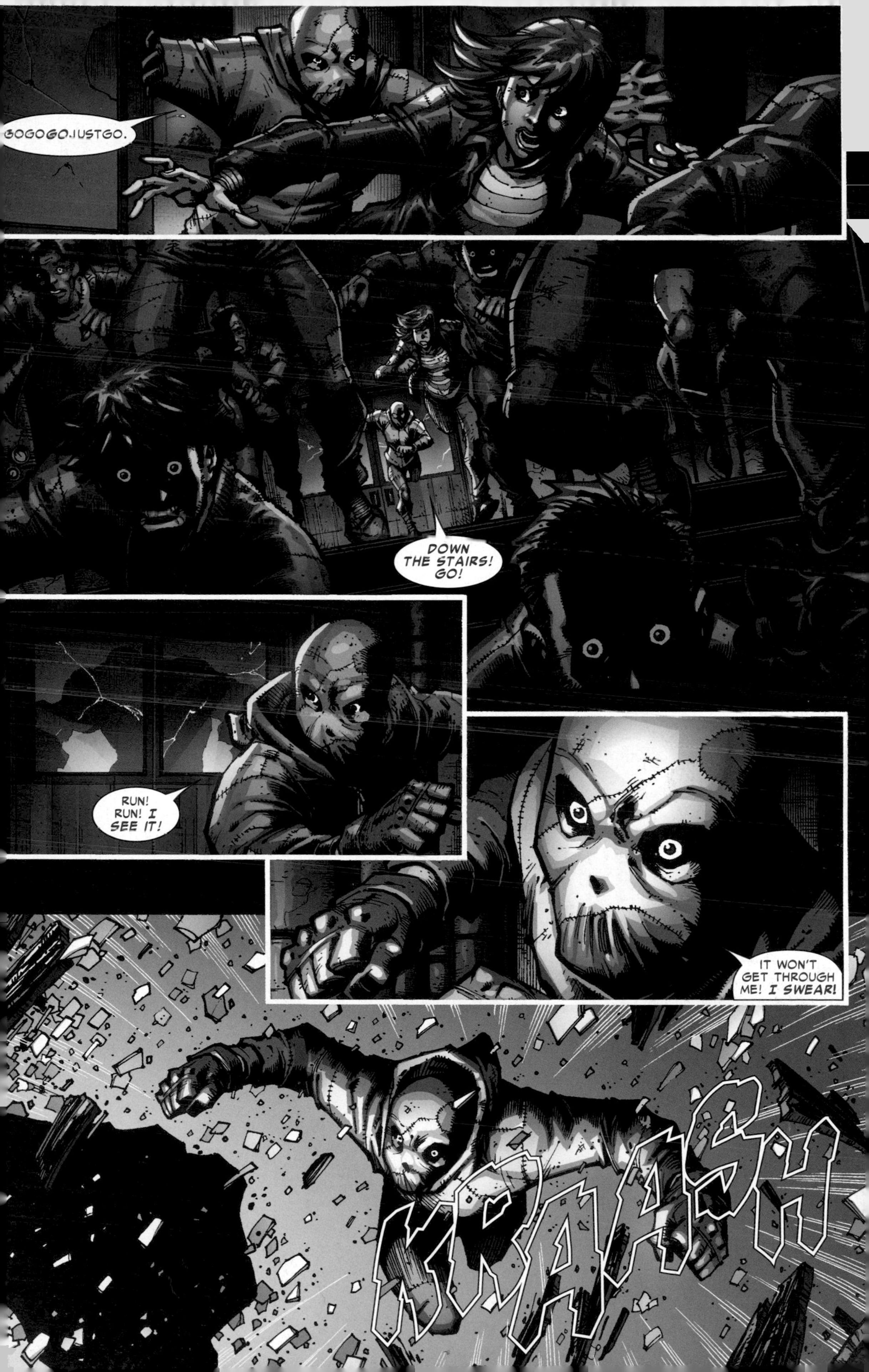
GOGOGO.JUSTGO.
DOWN THE STAIRS! GO!
RUN! RUN! I SEE IT!
IT WON'T GET THROUGH ME! I SWEAR!
KRAASH

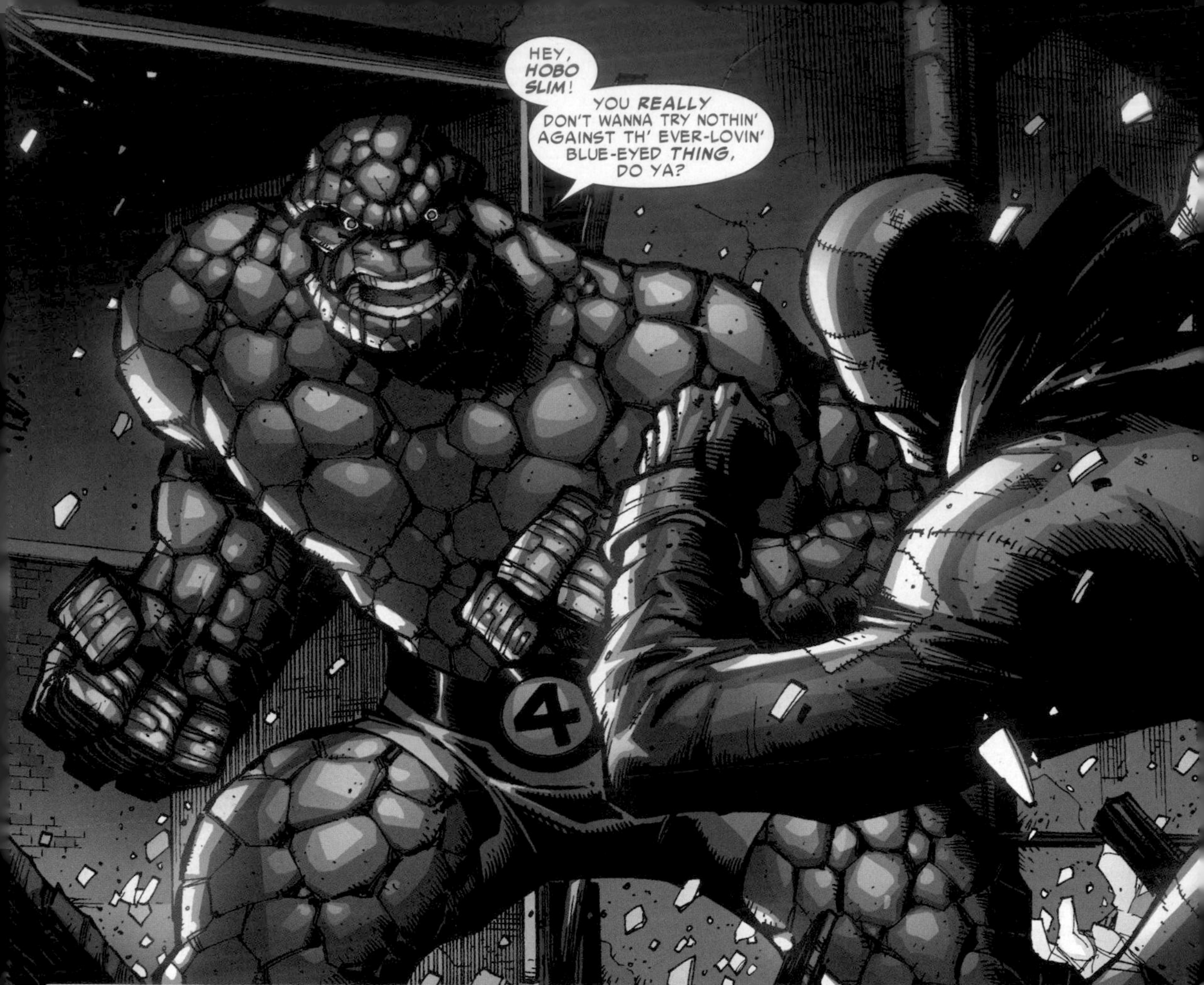
HEY, HOBO SLIM!
YOU REALLY DON'T WANNA TRY NOTHIN' AGAINST TH' EVER-LOVIN' BLUE-EYED THING, DO YA?
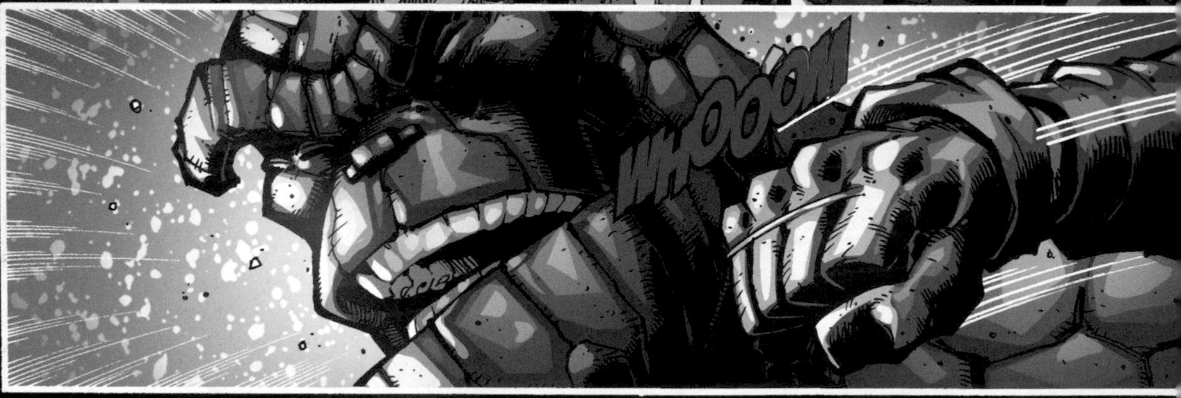
WHOOOM
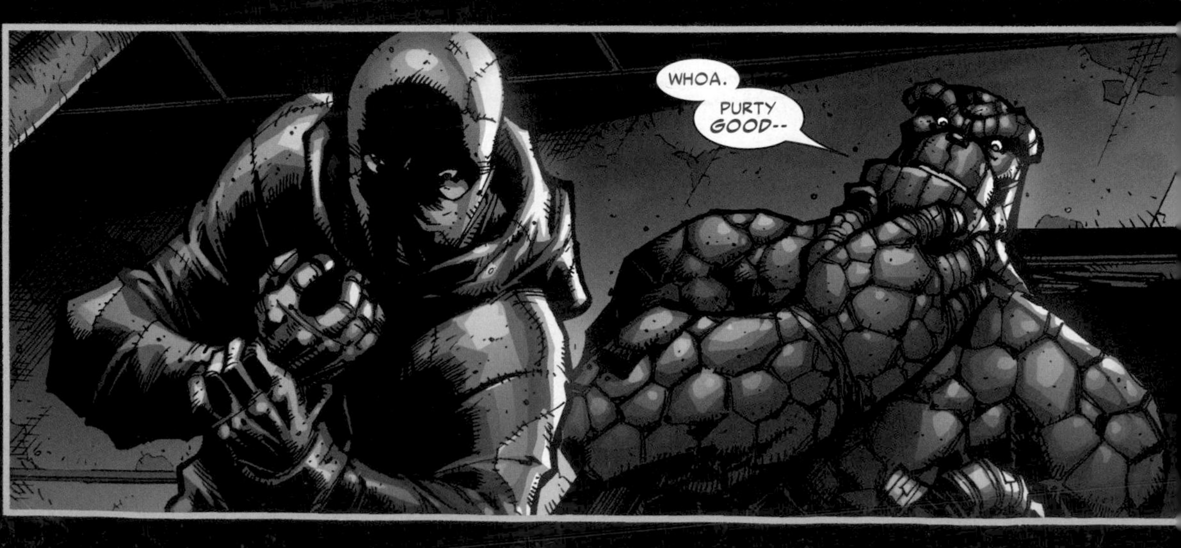
WHOA.
PURTY GOOD--

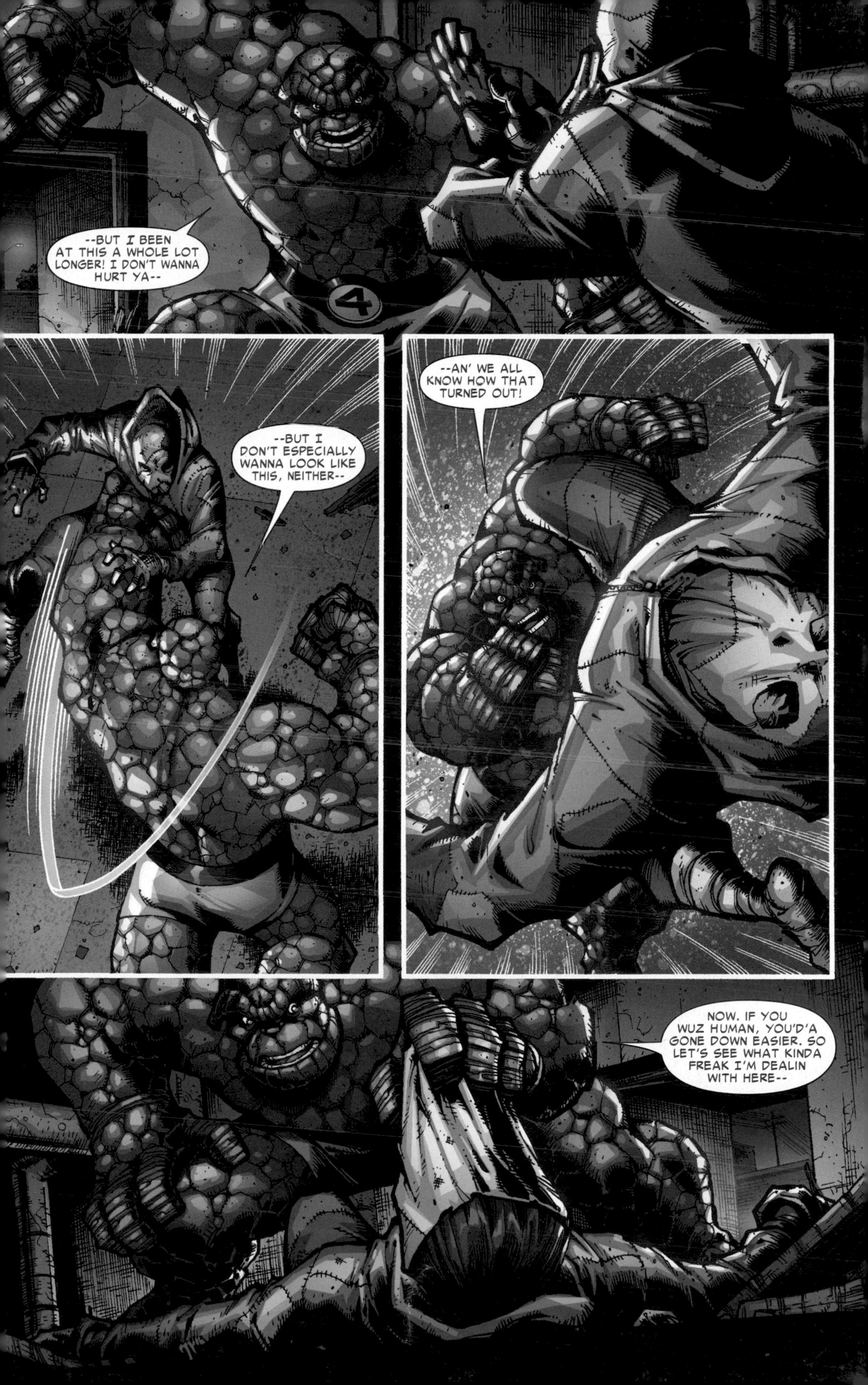
--BUT I BEEN AT THIS A WHOLE LOT LONGER! I DON'T WANNA HURT YA--
4
--BUT I DON'T ESPECIALLY WANNA LOOK LIKE THIS, NEITHER--
--AN' WE ALL KNOW HOW THAT TURNED OUT!
NOW. IF YOU WUZ HUMAN, YOU'D'A GONE DOWN EASIER. SO LET'S SEE WHAT KINDA FREAK I'M DEALIN WITH HERE--

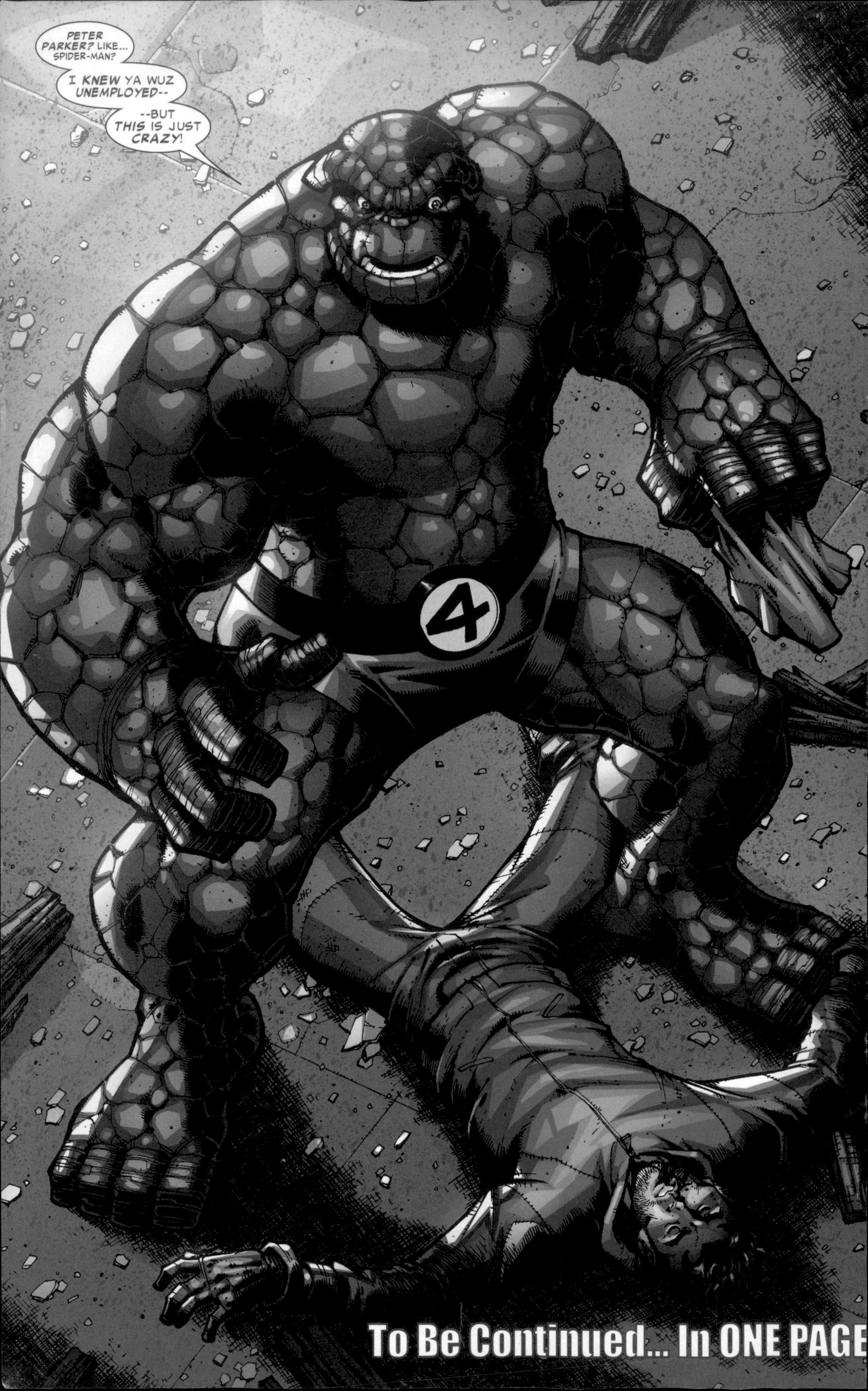
PETER PARKER? LIKE... SPIDER-MAN?
I KNEW YA WUZ UNEMPLOYED--
--BUT THIS IS JUST CRAZY!
To Be Continued... In ONE PAGE

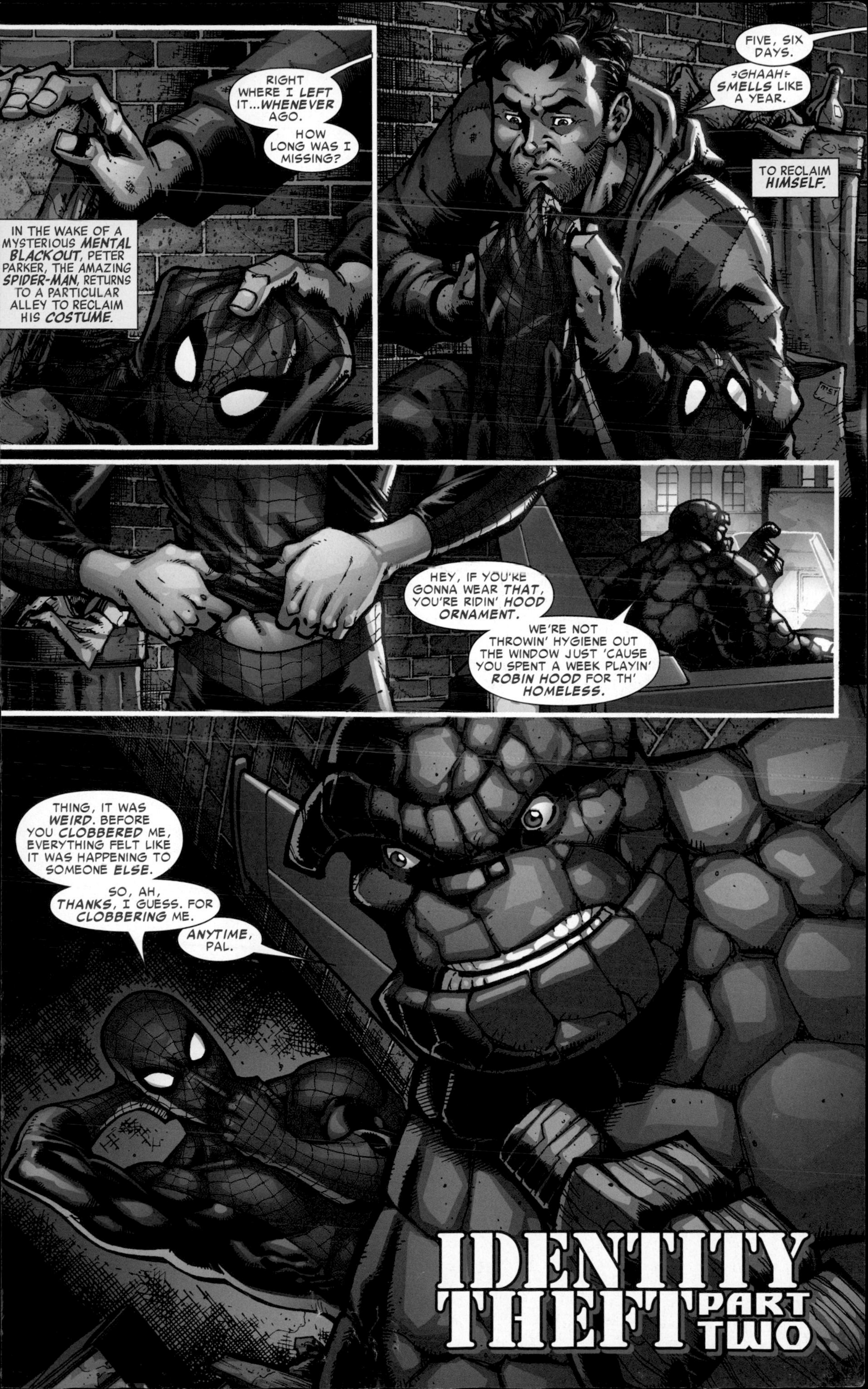
IN THE WAKE OF A MYSTERIOUS MENTAL BLACKOUT, PETER PARKER, THE AMAZING SPIDER-MAN, RETURNS TO A PARTICULAR ALLEY TO RECLAIM HIS COSTUME.
RIGHT WHERE I LEFT IT...WHENEVER AGO.
HOW LONG WAS I MISSING?
FIVE, SIX DAYS.
GHAAH SMELLS LIKE A YEAR.
TO RECLAIM HIMSELF.
HEY, IF YOU'RE GONNA WEAR THAT, YOU'RE RIDIN' HOOD ORNAMENT.
WE'RE NOT THROWIN' HYGIENE OUT THE WINDOW JUST 'CAUSE YOU SPENT A WEEK PLAYIN' ROBIN HOOD FOR TH' HOMELESS.
THING, IT WAS WEIRD. BEFORE YOU CLOBBERED ME, EVERYTHING FELT LIKE IT WAS HAPPENING TO SOMEONE ELSE.
SO, AH, THANKS, I GUESS. FOR CLOBBERING ME.
ANYTIME, PAL.
IDENTITY THEFT PART TWO

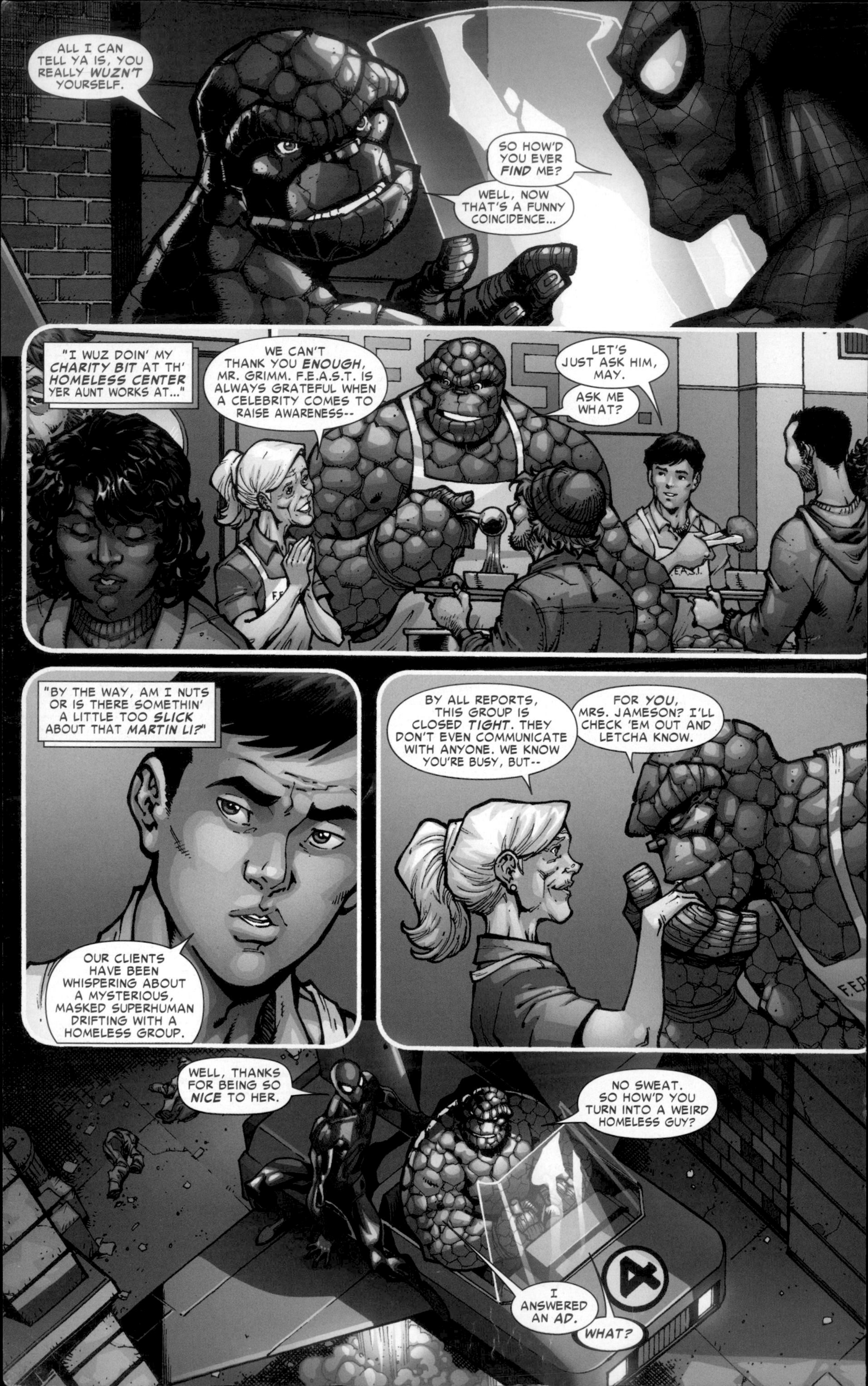
ALL I CAN TELL YA IS, YOU REALLY WUZN'T YOURSELF.
SO HOW'D YOU EVER FIND ME?
WELL, NOW THAT'S A FUNNY COINCIDENCE...
"I WUZ DOIN' MY CHARITY BIT AT TH' HOMELESS CENTER YER AUNT WORKS AT..."
WE CAN'T THANK YOU ENOUGH, MR. GRIMM. F.E.A.S.T. IS ALWAYS GRATEFUL WHEN A CELEBRITY COMES TO RAISE AWARENESS--
LET'S JUST ASK HIM, MAY.
ASK ME WHAT?
"BY THE WAY, AM I NUTS OR IS THERE SOMETHIN' A LITTLE TOO SLICK ABOUT THAT MARTIN LI?"
OUR CLIENTS HAVE BEEN WHISPERING ABOUT A MYSTERIOUS, MASKED SUPERHUMAN DRIFTING WITH A HOMELESS GROUP.
BY ALL REPORTS, THIS GROUP IS CLOSED TIGHT. THEY DON'T EVEN COMMUNICATE WITH ANYONE. WE KNOW YOU'RE BUSY, BUT--
FOR YOU, MRS. JAMESON? I'LL CHECK 'EM OUT AND LETCHA KNOW.
WELL, THANKS FOR BEING SO NICE TO HER.
NO SWEAT. SO HOW'D YOU TURN INTO A WEIRD HOMELESS GUY?
I ANSWERED AN AD.
WHAT?

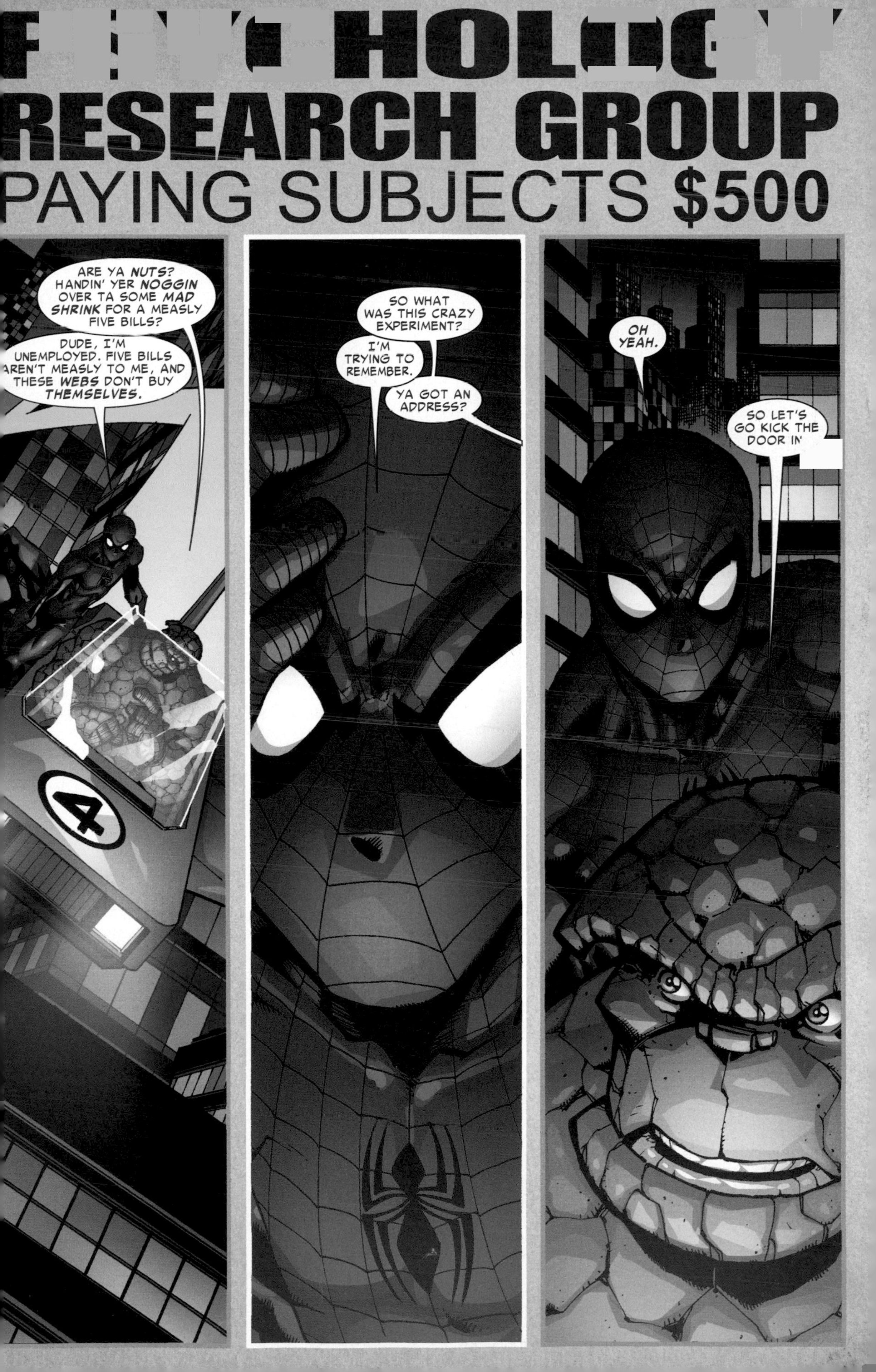
RESEARCH GROUP
PAYING SUBJECTS $500
ARE YA NUTS? HANDIN' YER NOGGIN OVER TA SOME MAD SHRINK FOR A MEASLY FIVE BILLS?
DUDE, I'M UNEMPLOYED. FIVE BILLS AREN'T MEASLY TO ME, AND THESE WEBS DON'T BUY THEMSELVES.
SO WHAT WAS THIS CRAZY EXPERIMENT?
I'M TRYING TO REMEMBER.
YA GOT AN ADDRESS?
OH YEAH.
SO LET'S GO KICK THE DOOR IN
4

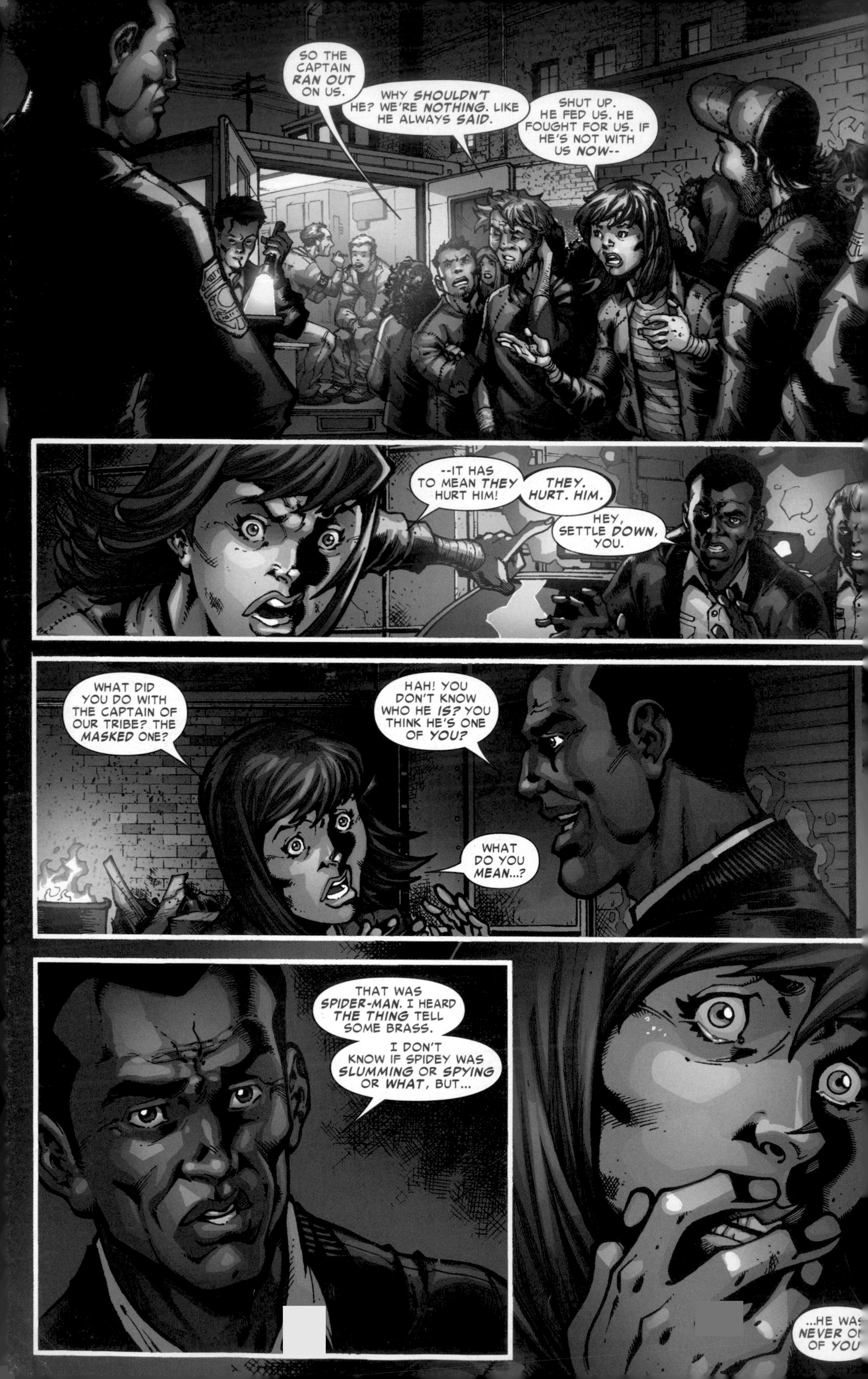
SO THE CAPTAIN RAN OUT ON US.
WHY SHOULDN'T HE? WE'RE NOTHING. LIKE HE ALWAYS SAID.
SHUT UP. HE FED US. HE FOUGHT FOR US. IF HE'S NOT WITH US NOW--
--IT HAS TO MEAN THEY HURT HIM!
THEY. HURT. HIM.
HEY, SETTLE DOWN, YOU.
WHAT DID YOU DO WITH THE CAPTAIN OF OUR TRIBE? THE MASKED ONE?
HAH! YOU DON'T KNOW WHO HE IS? YOU THINK HE'S ONE OF YOU?
WHAT DO YOU MEAN...?
THAT WAS SPIDER-MAN. I HEARD THE THING TELL SOME BRASS.
I DON'T KNOW IF SPIDEY WAS SLUMMING OR SPYING OR WHAT, BUT...
...HE WAS NEVER O OF YOU

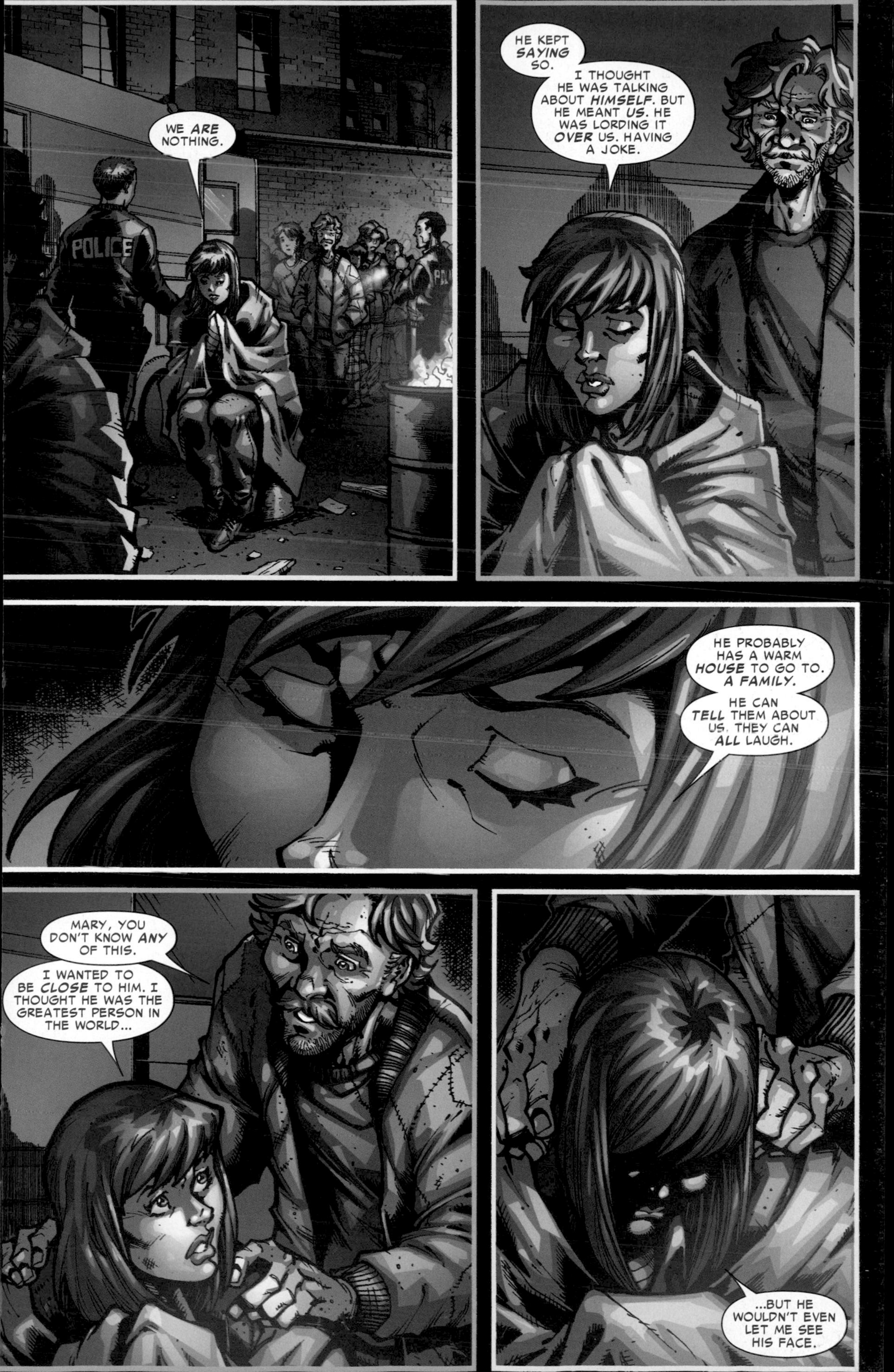
WE ARE NOTHING.
HE KEPT SAYING SO.
I THOUGHT HE WAS TALKING ABOUT HIMSELF. BUT HE MEANT US. HE WAS LORDING IT OVER US. HAVING A JOKE.
HE PROBABLY HAS A WARM HOUSE TO GO TO. A FAMILY.
HE CAN TELL THEM ABOUT US. THEY CAN ALL LAUGH.
MARY, YOU DON'T KNOW ANY OF THIS.
I WANTED TO BE CLOSE TO HIM. I THOUGHT HE WAS THE GREATEST PERSON IN THE WORLD...
...BUT HE WOULDN'T EVEN LET ME SEE HIS FACE.

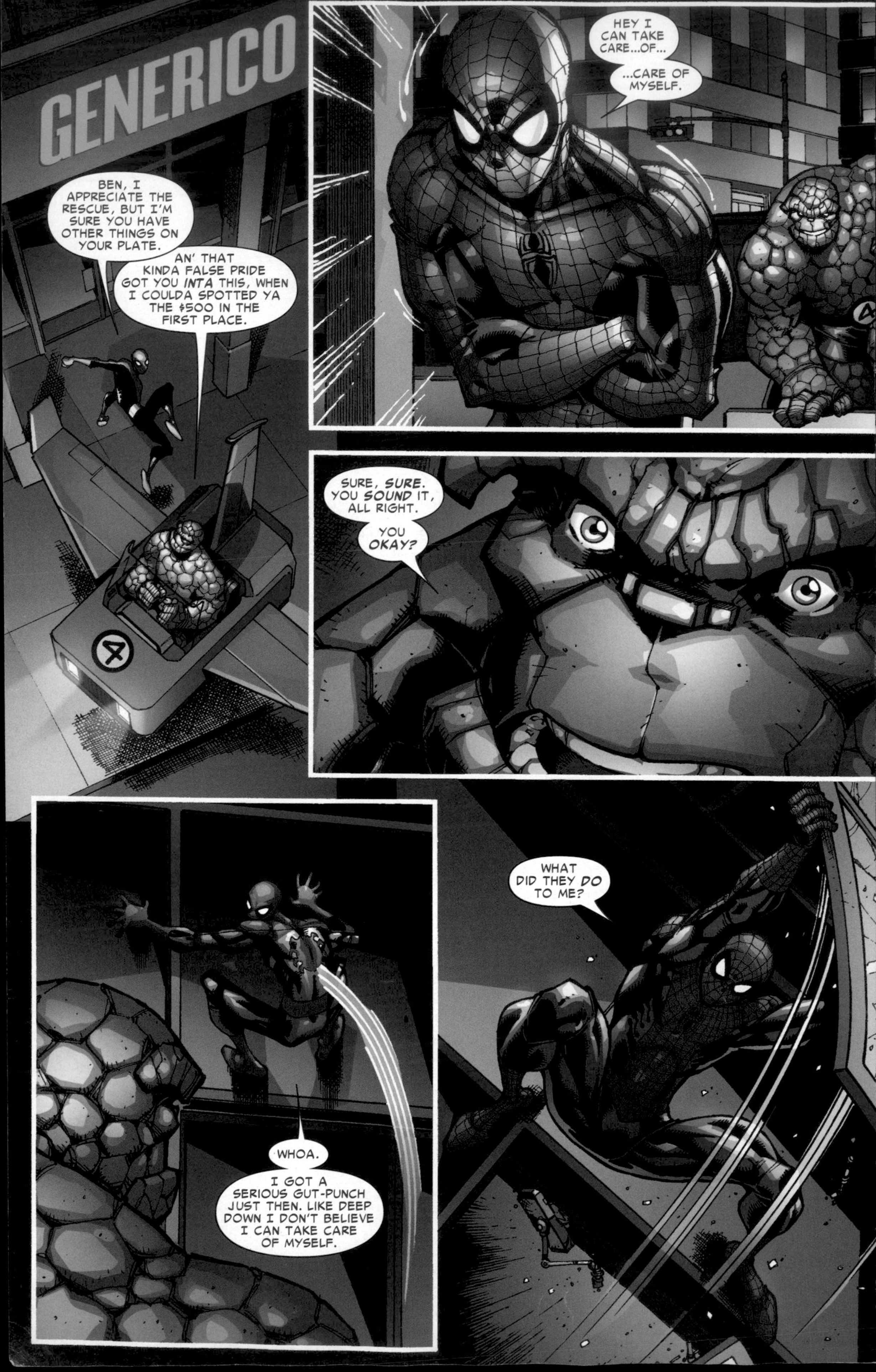
GENERICO
BEN, I APPRECIATE THE RESCUE, BUT I'M SURE YOU HAVE OTHER THINGS ON YOUR PLATE.
AN' THAT KINDA FALSE PRIDE GOT YOU INTA THIS, WHEN I COULDA SPOTTED YA THE $500 IN THE FIRST PLACE.
HEY I CAN TAKE CARE...OF...
...CARE OF MYSELF.
SURE, SURE. YOU SOUND IT, ALL RIGHT.
YOU OKAY?
WHOA.
I GOT A SERIOUS GUT-PUNCH JUST THEN. LIKE DEEP DOWN I DON'T BELIEVE I CAN TAKE CARE OF MYSELF.
WHAT DID THEY DO TO ME?

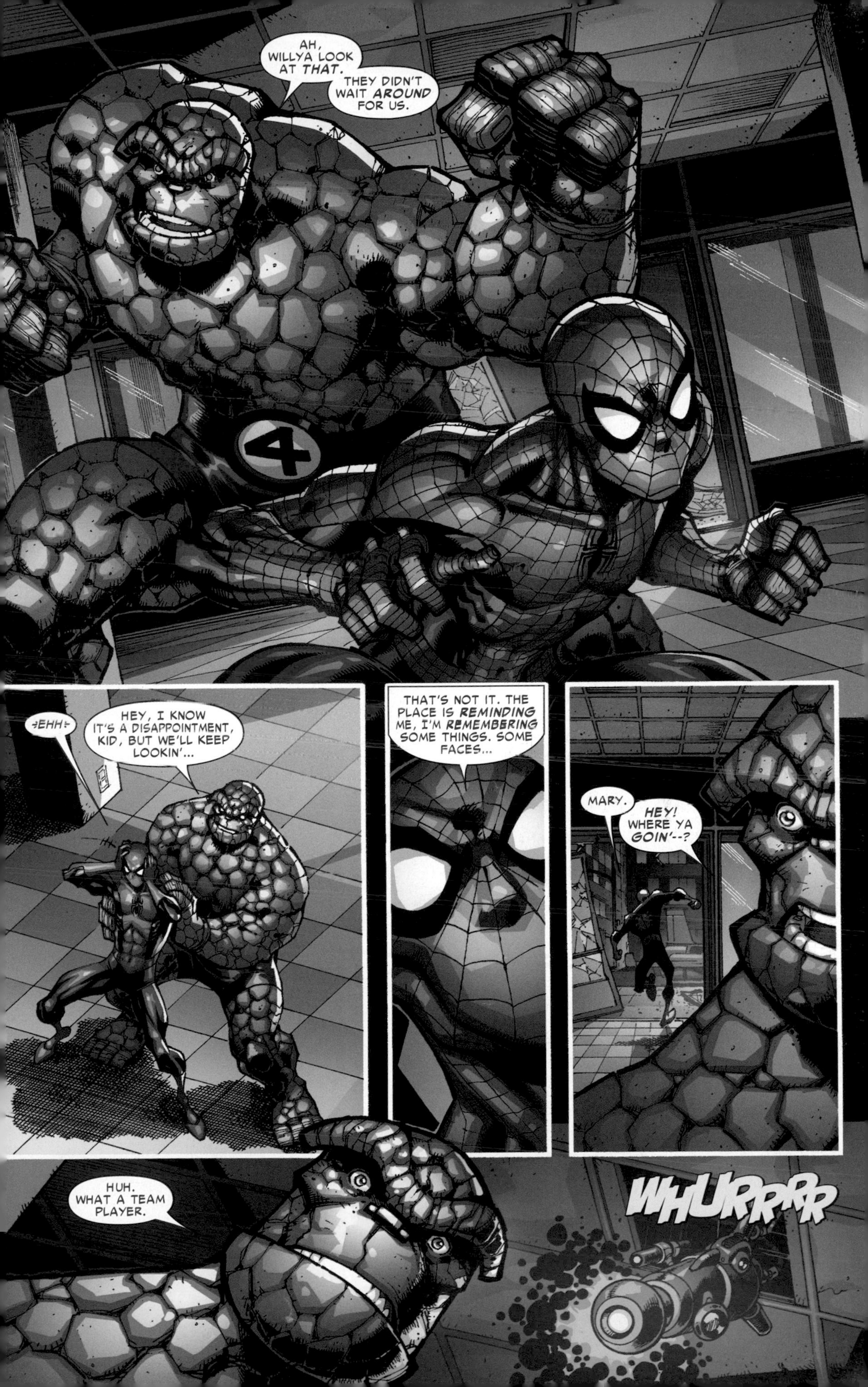
AH, WILLYA LOOK AT *THAT*.
THEY DIDN'T WAIT *AROUND* FOR US.
EHH
HEY, I KNOW IT'S A DISAPPOINTMENT, KID, BUT WE'LL KEEP LOOKIN'...
THAT'S NOT IT. THE PLACE IS *REMINDING* ME, I'M *REMEMBERING* SOME THINGS. SOME FACES...
MARY.
HEY! WHERE YA *GOIN'*--?
HUH. WHAT A TEAM PLAYER.
WHURRRR

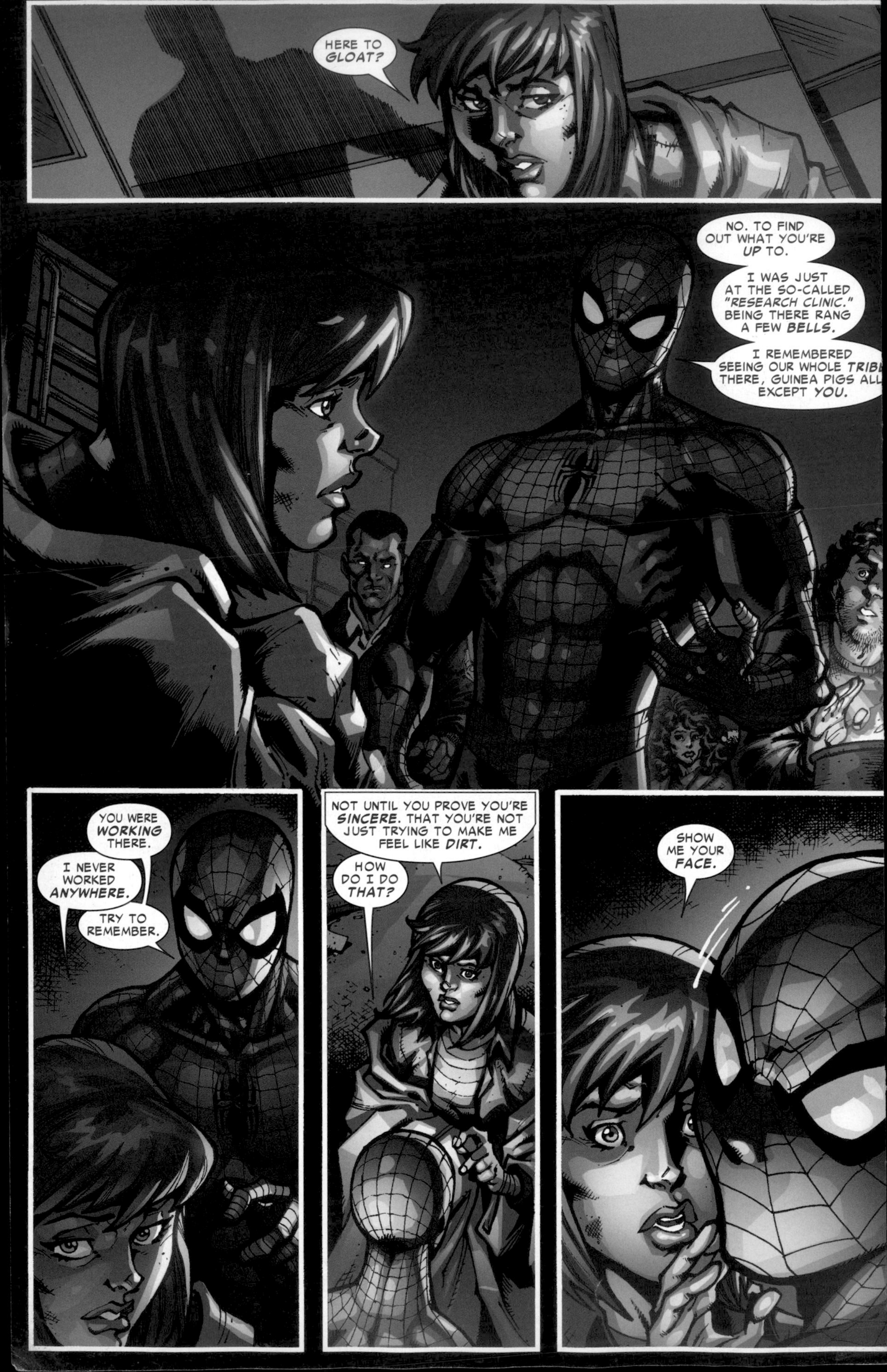
HERE TO GLOAT?
NO. TO FIND OUT WHAT YOU'RE UP TO.
I WAS JUST AT THE SO-CALLED "RESEARCH CLINIC." BEING THERE RANG A FEW BELLS.
I REMEMBERED SEEING OUR WHOLE TRIBE THERE, GUINEA PIGS ALL EXCEPT YOU.
YOU WERE WORKING THERE.
I NEVER WORKED ANYWHERE.
TRY TO REMEMBER.
NOT UNTIL YOU PROVE YOU'RE SINCERE. THAT YOU'RE NOT JUST TRYING TO MAKE ME FEEL LIKE DIRT.
HOW DO I DO THAT?
SHOW ME YOUR FACE.

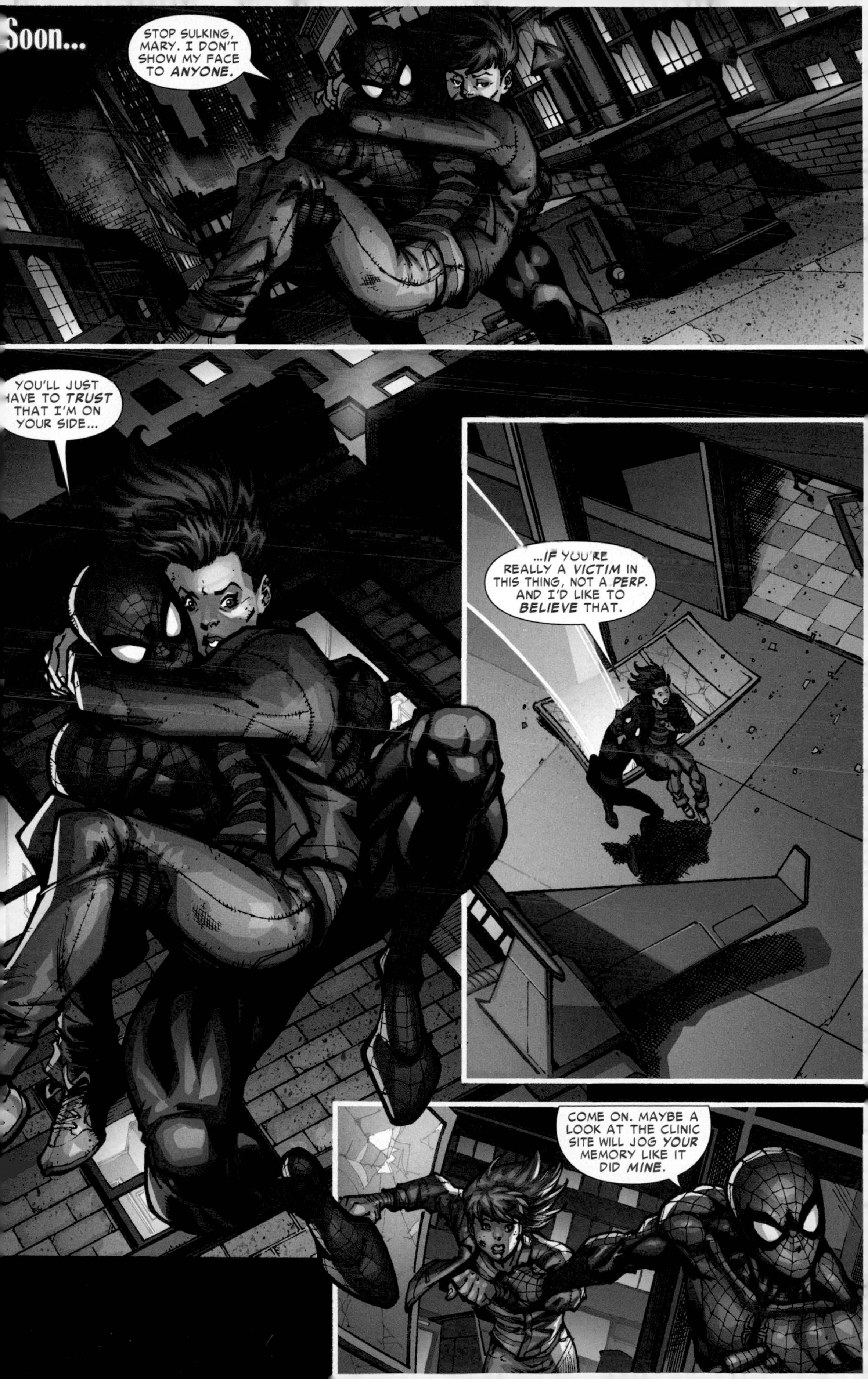
Soon...
STOP SULKING, MARY. I DON'T SHOW MY FACE TO ANYONE.
YOU'LL JUST HAVE TO TRUST THAT I'M ON YOUR SIDE...
...IF YOU'RE REALLY A VICTIM IN THIS THING, NOT A PERP. AND I'D LIKE TO BELIEVE THAT.
COME ON. MAYBE A LOOK AT THE CLINIC SITE WILL JOG YOUR MEMORY LIKE IT DID MINE.

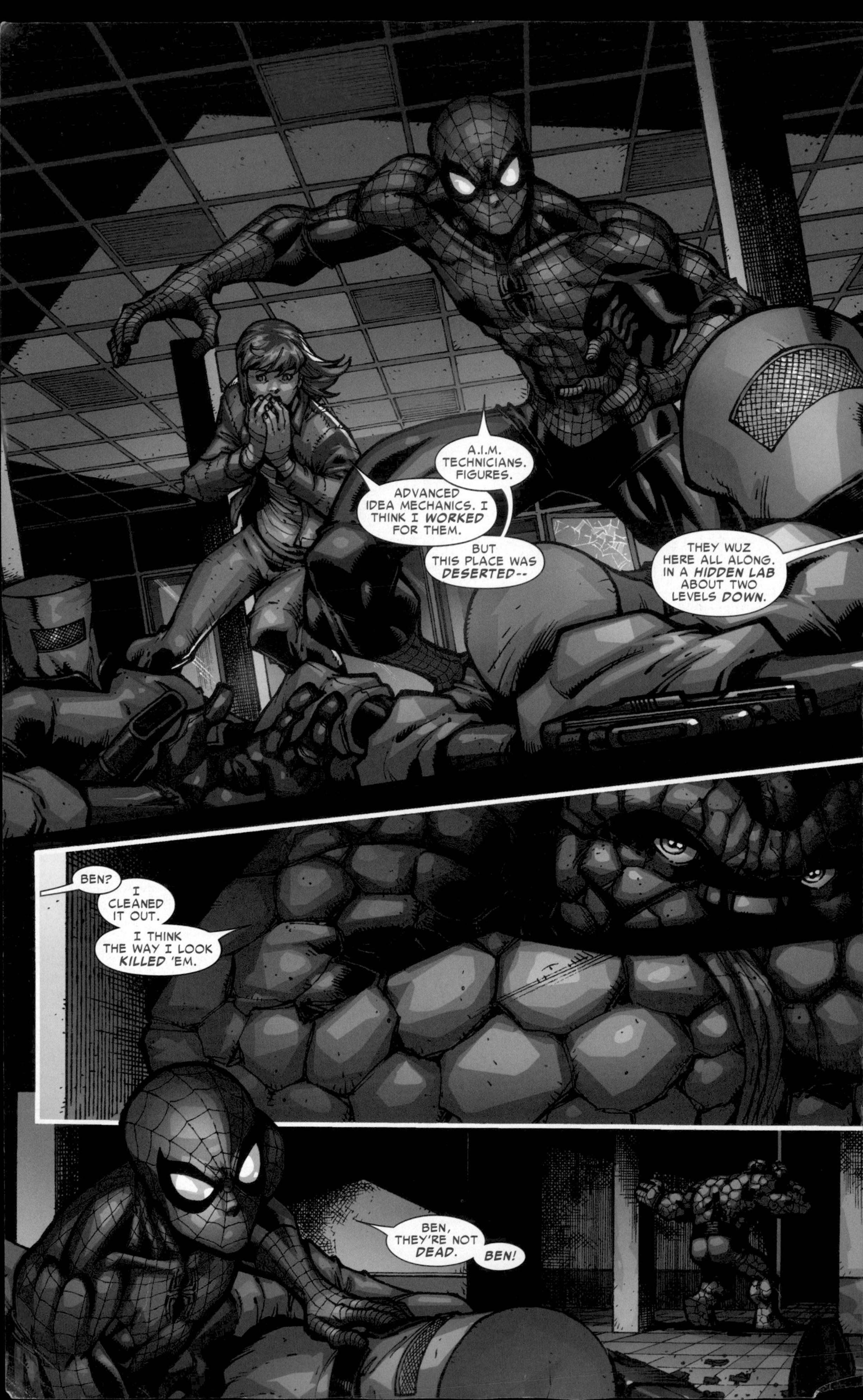
ADVANCED IDEA MECHANICS. I THINK I *WORKED* FOR THEM.
A.I.M. TECHNICIANS. FIGURES.
BUT THIS PLACE WAS *DESERTED*--
THEY WUZ HERE ALL ALONG. IN A *HIDDEN LAB* ABOUT TWO LEVELS *DOWN*.
BEN?
I CLEANED IT OUT.
I THINK THE WAY I LOOK *KILLED* 'EM.
BEN, THEY'RE NOT *DEAD*.
BEN!

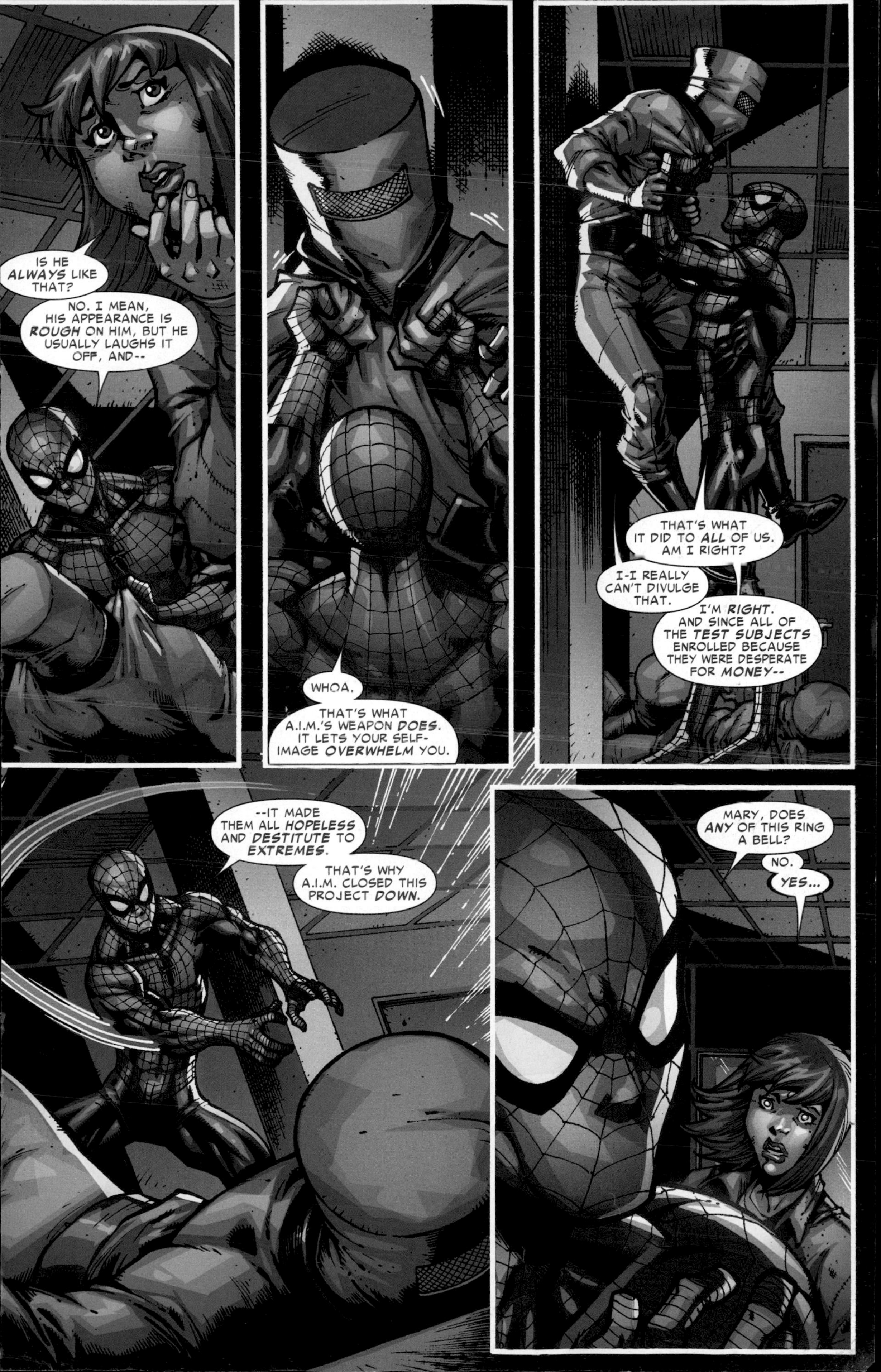
IS HE ALWAYS LIKE THAT?
NO. I MEAN, HIS APPEARANCE IS ROUGH ON HIM, BUT HE USUALLY LAUGHS IT OFF, AND--
WHOA.
THAT'S WHAT A.I.M.'S WEAPON DOES. IT LETS YOUR SELF-IMAGE OVERWHELM YOU.
THAT'S WHAT IT DID TO ALL OF US. AM I RIGHT?
I-I REALLY CAN'T DIVULGE THAT.
I'M RIGHT. AND SINCE ALL OF THE TEST SUBJECTS ENROLLED BECAUSE THEY WERE DESPERATE FOR MONEY--
--IT MADE THEM ALL HOPELESS AND DESTITUTE TO EXTREMES.
THAT'S WHY A.I.M. CLOSED THIS PROJECT DOWN.
MARY, DOES ANY OF THIS RING A BELL?
NO.
YES...

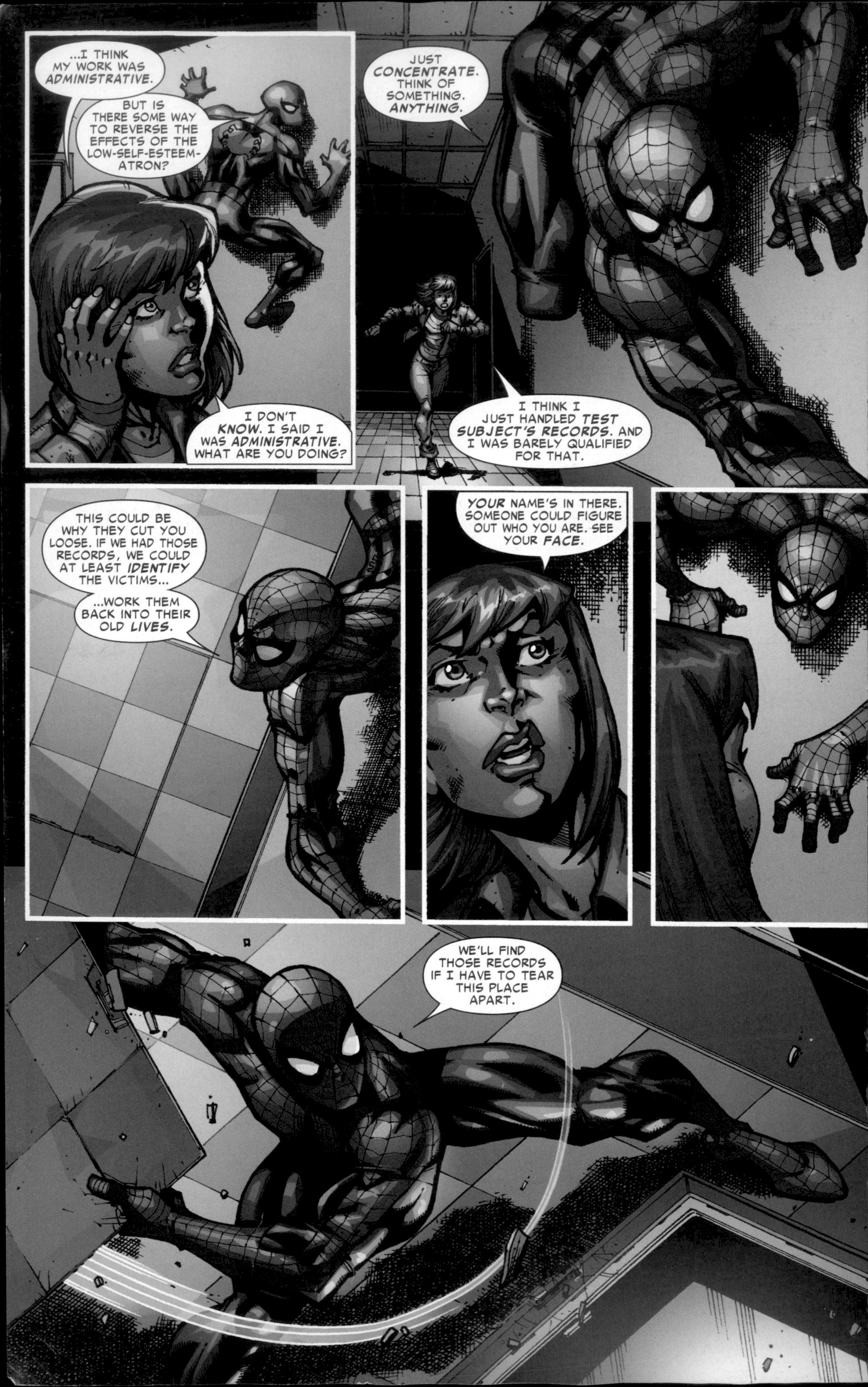

...I THINK MY WORK WAS *ADMINISTRATIVE*.
BUT IS THERE SOME WAY TO REVERSE THE EFFECTS OF THE LOW-SELF-ESTEEM-ATRON?
I DON'T *KNOW*. I SAID I WAS *ADMINISTRATIVE*. WHAT ARE YOU DOING?
JUST *CONCENTRATE*. THINK OF SOMETHING. *ANYTHING*.
I THINK I JUST HANDLED *TEST SUBJECT'S RECORDS*. AND I WAS BARELY QUALIFIED FOR THAT.
THIS COULD BE WHY THEY CUT YOU LOOSE. IF WE HAD THOSE RECORDS, WE COULD AT LEAST *IDENTIFY* THE VICTIMS...
...WORK THEM BACK INTO THEIR OLD *LIVES*.
YOUR NAME'S IN THERE. SOMEONE COULD FIGURE OUT WHO YOU ARE. SEE YOUR *FACE*.
WE'LL FIND THOSE RECORDS IF I HAVE TO TEAR THIS PLACE APART.

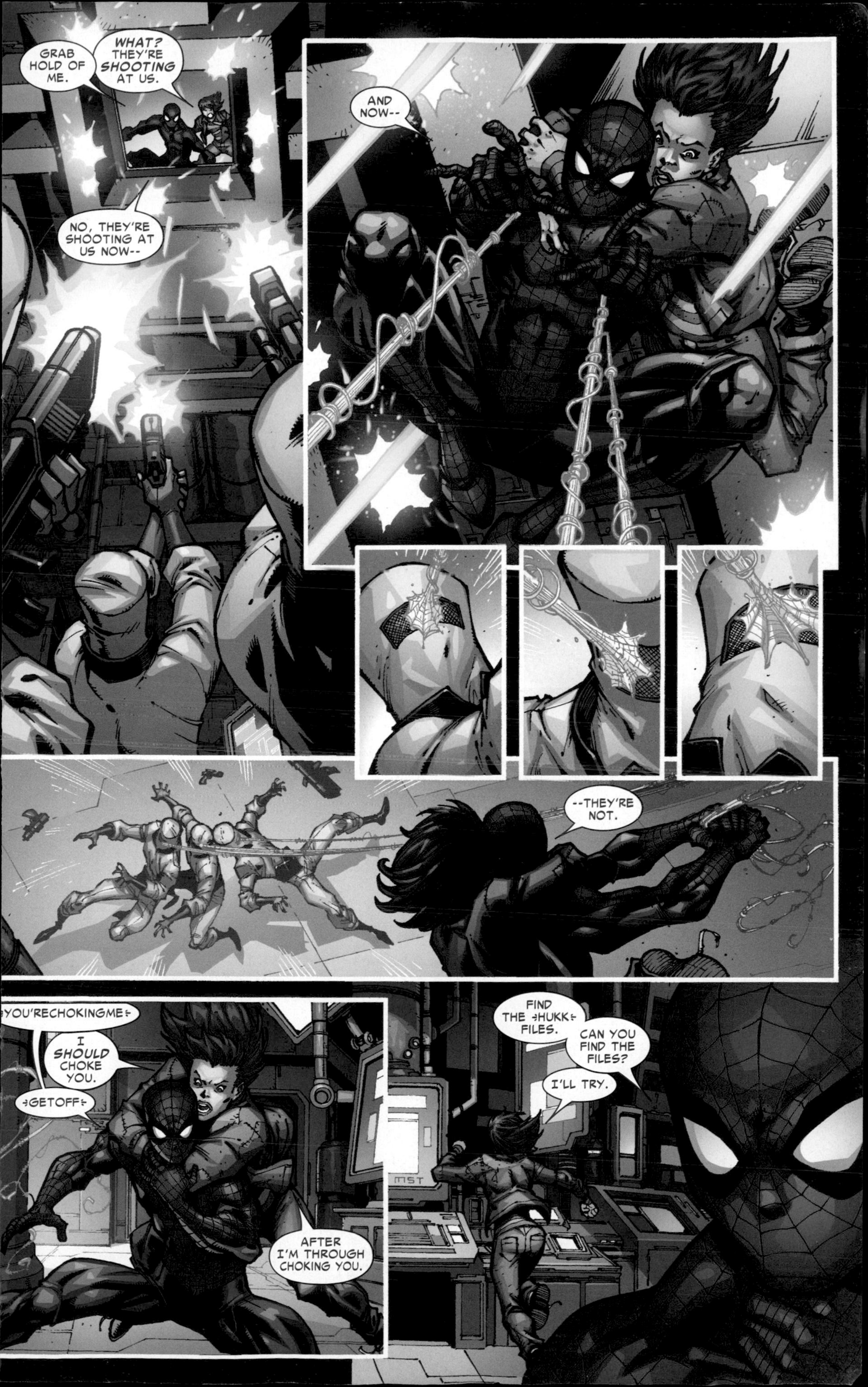

GRAB HOLD OF ME.
WHAT? THEY'RE SHOOTING AT US.
NO, THEY'RE SHOOTING AT US NOW--
AND NOW--
--THEY'RE NOT.
-YOU'RECHOKINGME-
I SHOULD CHOKE YOU.
-GETOFF-
AFTER I'M THROUGH CHOKING YOU.
MST
FIND THE -HUKK- FILES.
CAN YOU FIND THE FILES?
I'LL TRY.

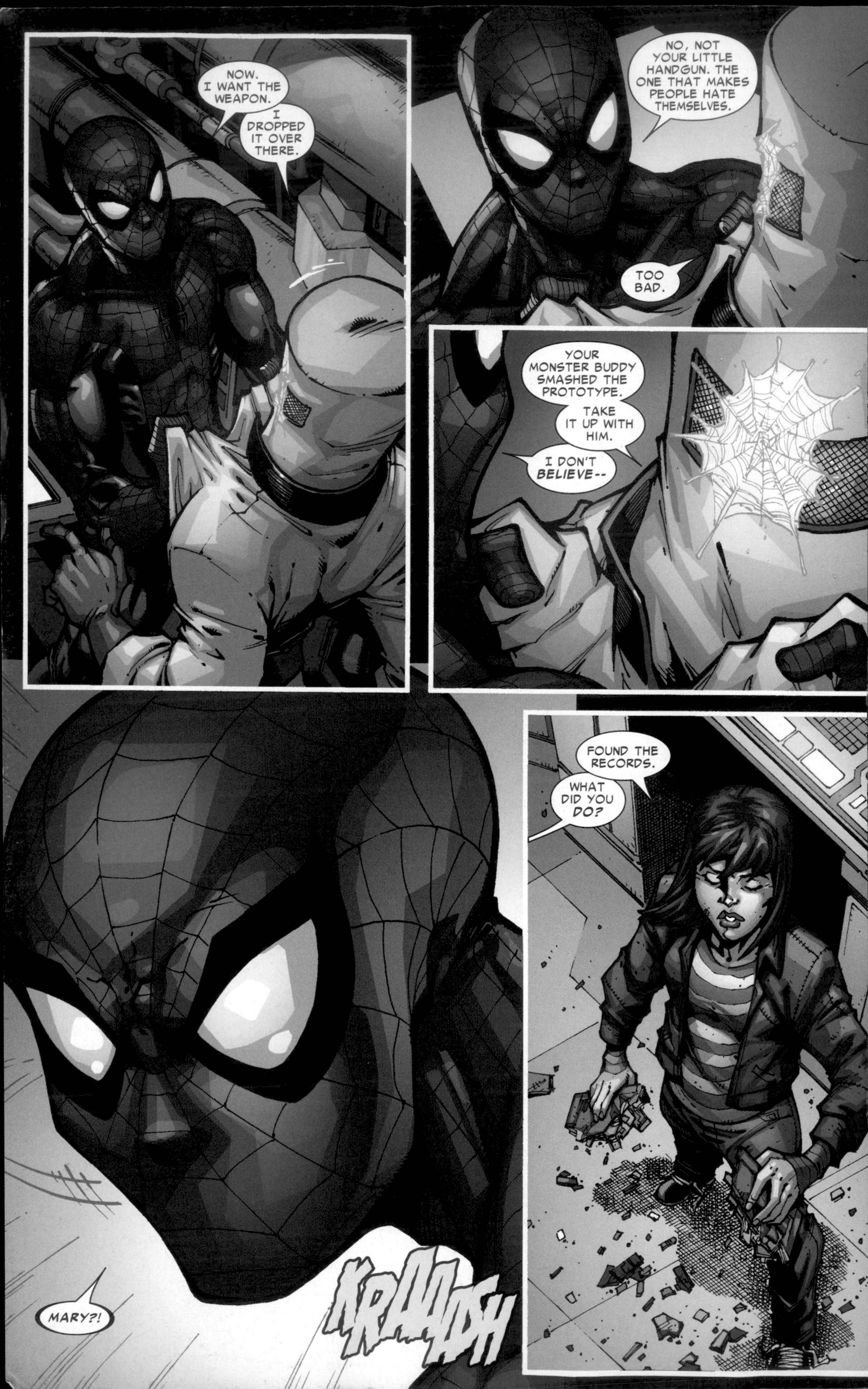
NOW. I WANT THE WEAPON.
I DROPPED IT OVER THERE.
NO, NOT YOUR LITTLE HANDGUN. THE ONE THAT MAKES PEOPLE HATE THEMSELVES.
TOO BAD.
YOUR MONSTER BUDDY SMASHED THE PROTOTYPE.
TAKE IT UP WITH HIM.
I DON'T *BELIEVE*--
MARY?!
KRAASH
FOUND THE RECORDS.
WHAT DID YOU *DO?*

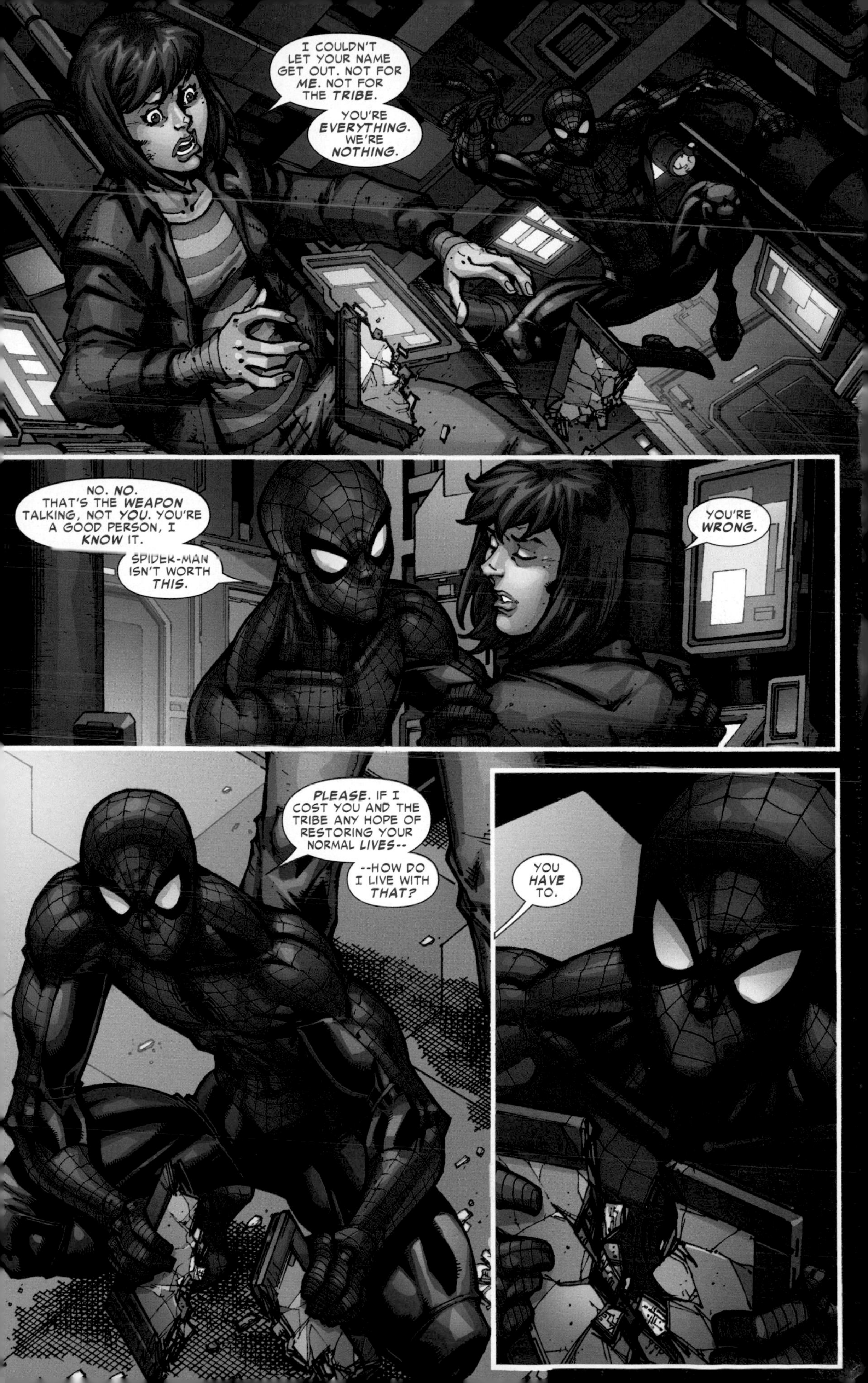
I COULDN'T LET YOUR NAME GET OUT. NOT FOR ME. NOT FOR THE TRIBE.
YOU'RE EVERYTHING. WE'RE NOTHING.
NO. NO. THAT'S THE WEAPON TALKING, NOT YOU. YOU'RE A GOOD PERSON, I KNOW IT.
SPIDER-MAN ISN'T WORTH THIS.
YOU'RE WRONG.
PLEASE. IF I COST YOU AND THE TRIBE ANY HOPE OF RESTORING YOUR NORMAL LIVES--
--HOW DO I LIVE WITH THAT?
YOU HAVE TO.

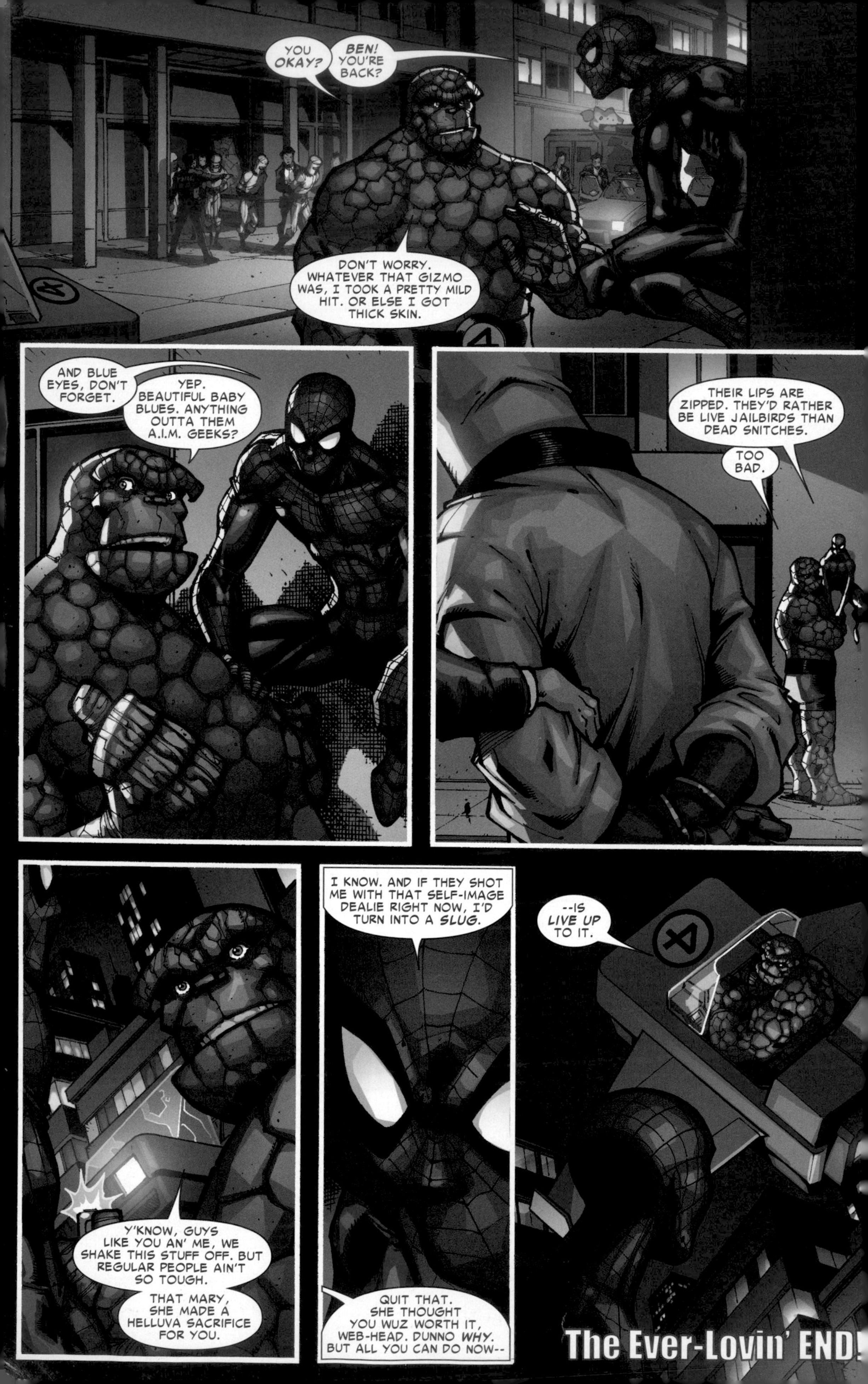
YOU OKAY?
BEN! YOU'RE BACK?
DON'T WORRY. WHATEVER THAT GIZMO WAS, I TOOK A PRETTY MILD HIT. OR ELSE I GOT THICK SKIN.
AND BLUE EYES, DON'T FORGET.
YEP. BEAUTIFUL BABY BLUES. ANYTHING OUTTA THEM A.I.M. GEEKS?
THEIR LIPS ARE ZIPPED. THEY'D RATHER BE LIVE JAILBIRDS THAN DEAD SNITCHES.
TOO BAD.
Y'KNOW, GUYS LIKE YOU AN' ME, WE SHAKE THIS STUFF OFF. BUT REGULAR PEOPLE AIN'T SO TOUGH.
THAT MARY, SHE MADE A HELLUVA SACRIFICE FOR YOU.
I KNOW. AND IF THEY SHOT ME WITH THAT SELF-IMAGE DEALIE RIGHT NOW, I'D TURN INTO A SLUG.
QUIT THAT. SHE THOUGHT YOU WUZ WORTH IT, WEB-HEAD. DUNNO WHY. BUT ALL YOU CAN DO NOW--
--IS LIVE UP TO IT.
The Ever-Lovin' END!

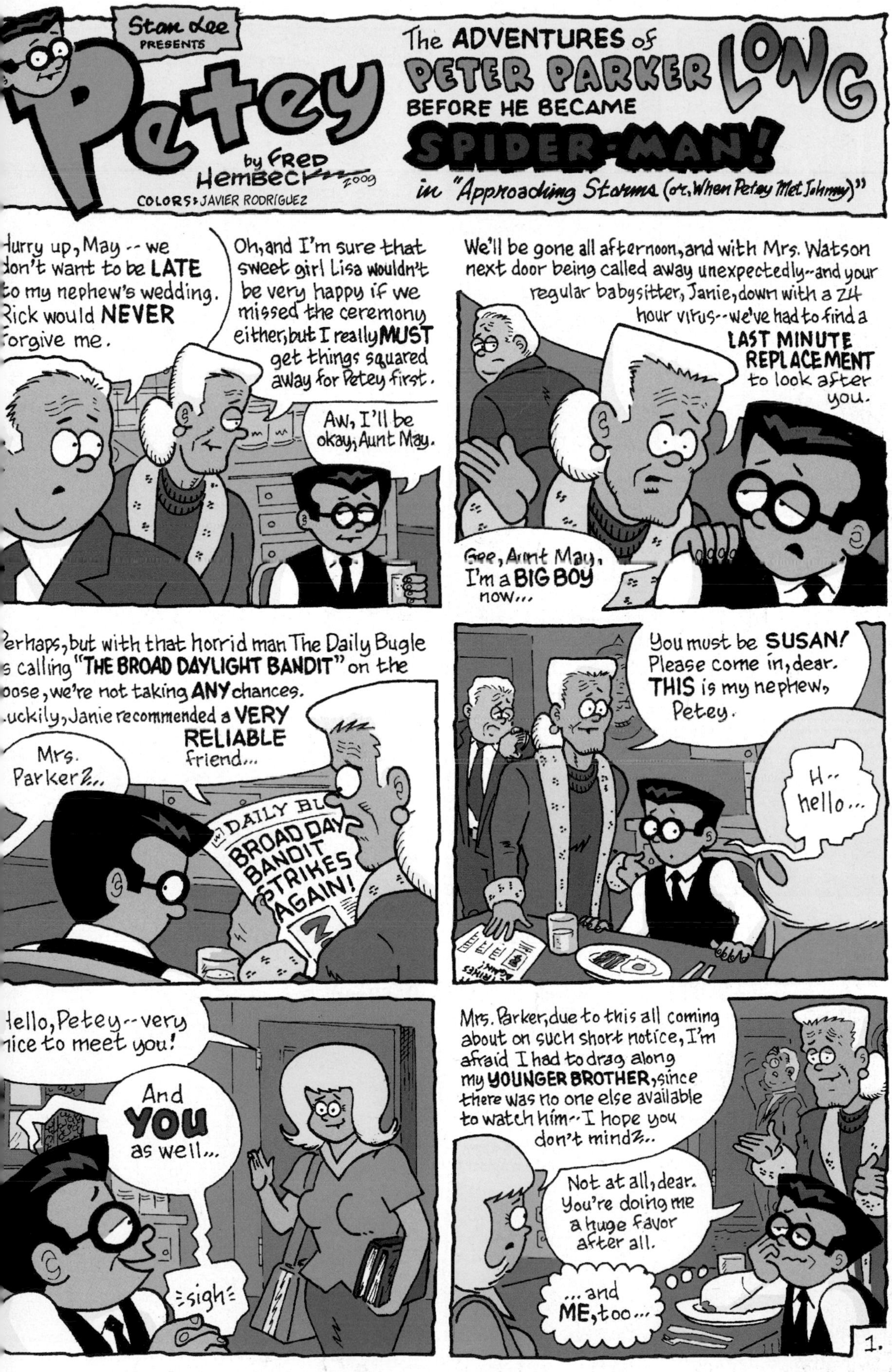

Stan Lee PRESENTS
Petey
by FRED HEMBECK 2009
COLORS: JAVIER RODRIGUEZ
The ADVENTURES of PETER PARKER LONG BEFORE HE BECAME SPIDER-MAN!
in "Approaching Storms (or, When Petey Met Johnny)"
Hurry up, May -- we don't want to be LATE to my nephew's wedding. Rick would NEVER forgive me.
Oh, and I'm sure that sweet girl Lisa wouldn't be very happy if we missed the ceremony either, but I really MUST get things squared away for Petey first.
Aw, I'll be okay, Aunt May.
We'll be gone all afternoon, and with Mrs. Watson next door being called away unexpectedly--and your regular babysitter, Janie, down with a 24 hour virus--we've had to find a LAST MINUTE REPLACEMENT to look after you.
Gee, Aunt May, I'm a BIG BOY now...
Perhaps, but with that horrid man The Daily Bugle is calling "THE BROAD DAYLIGHT BANDIT" on the loose, we're not taking ANY chances. Luckily, Janie recommended a VERY RELIABLE friend...
Mrs. Parker?...
DAILY BU
BROAD DAY BANDIT STRIKES AGAIN!
You must be SUSAN! Please come in, dear. THIS is my nephew, Petey.
H.. hello...
Hello, Petey--very nice to meet you!
And YOU as well...
sigh
Mrs. Parker, due to this all coming about on such short notice, I'm afraid I had to drag along my YOUNGER BROTHER, since there was no one else available to watch him--I hope you don't mind?..
Not at all, dear. You're doing me a huge favor after all.
...and ME, too...

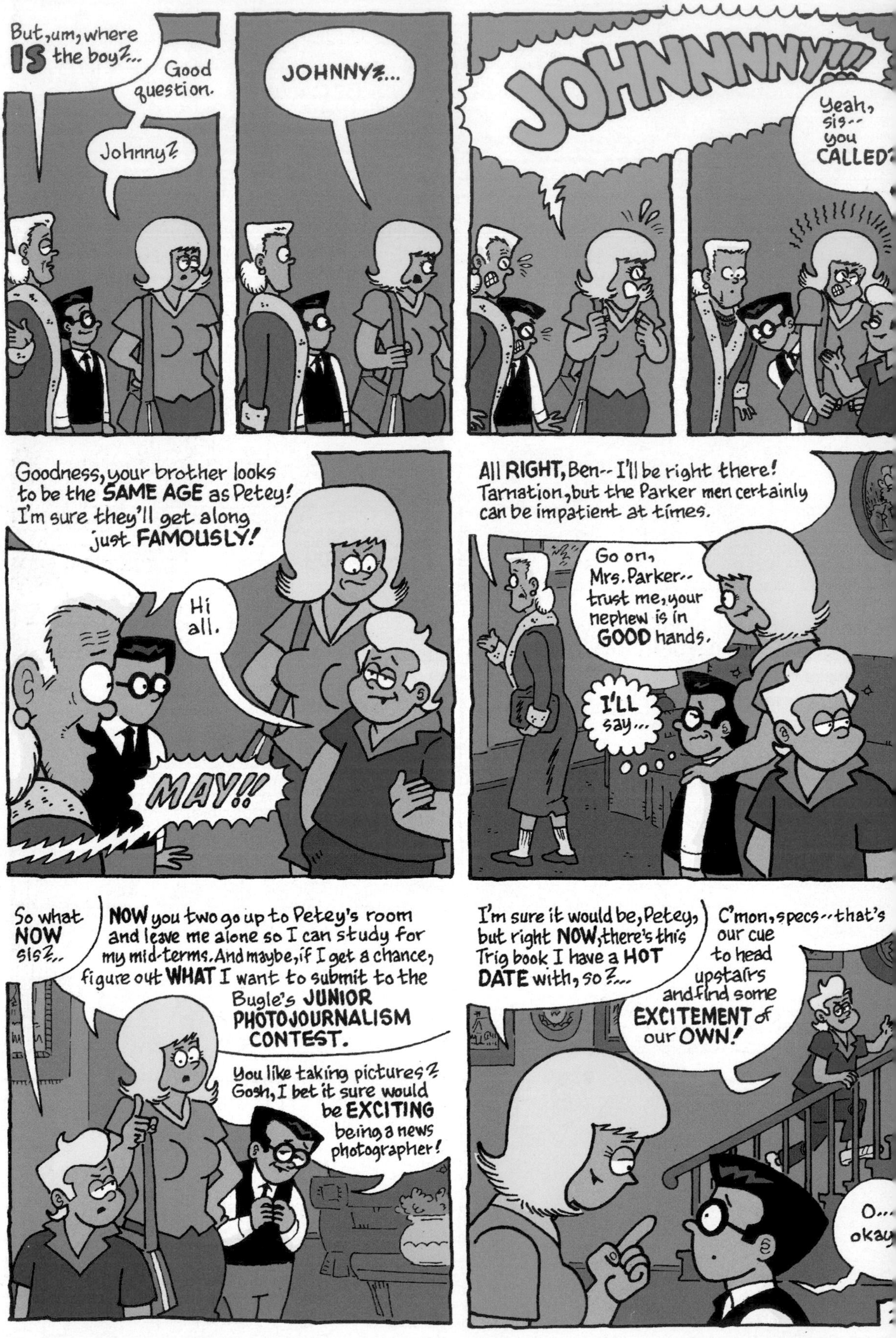
But, um, where IS the boy?..
Good question.
Johnny?
JOHNNY?...
JOHNNNNY!!!
Yeah, sis-- you CALLED?
Goodness, your brother looks to be the SAME AGE as Petey! I'm sure they'll get along just FAMOUSLY!
Hi all.
MAY!!
All RIGHT, Ben-- I'll be right there! Tarnation, but the Parker men certainly can be impatient at times.
Go on, Mrs. Parker-- trust me, your nephew is in GOOD hands.
I'LL say...
So what NOW sis?..
NOW you two go up to Petey's room and leave me alone so I can study for my mid-terms. And maybe, if I get a chance, figure out WHAT I want to submit to the Bugle's JUNIOR PHOTOJOURNALISM CONTEST.
You like taking pictures? Gosh, I bet it sure would be EXCITING being a news photographer!
I'm sure it would be, Petey, but right NOW, there's this Trig book I have a HOT DATE with, so?...
C'mon, specs--that's our cue to head upstairs and find some EXCITEMENT of our OWN!
O... okay

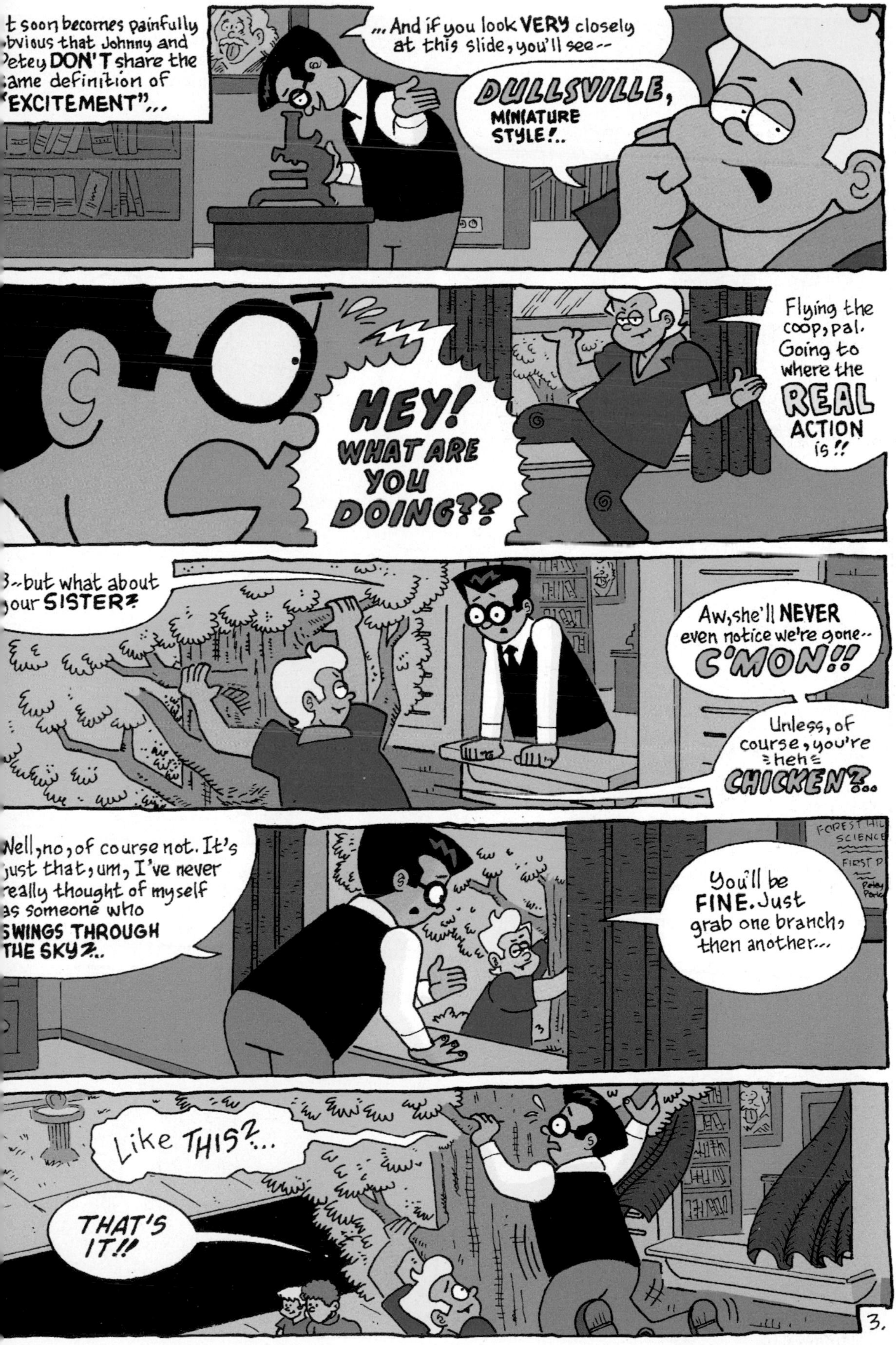
t soon becomes painfully
bvious that Johnny and
etey DON'T share the
ame definition of
"EXCITEMENT"...
...And if you look VERY closely at this slide, you'll see--
DULLSVILLE, MINIATURE STYLE!..
HEY! WHAT ARE YOU DOING??
Flying the coop, pal. Going to where the REAL ACTION is!!
B--but what about our SISTER?
Aw, she'll NEVER even notice we're gone-- C'MON!!
Unless, of course, you're heh CHICKEN?...
Well, no, of course not. It's just that, um, I've never really thought of myself as someone who SWINGS THROUGH THE SKY?..
FOREST HIL
SCIENCE
FIRST P
You'll be FINE. Just grab one branch, then another...
Like THIS?...
THAT'S IT!!

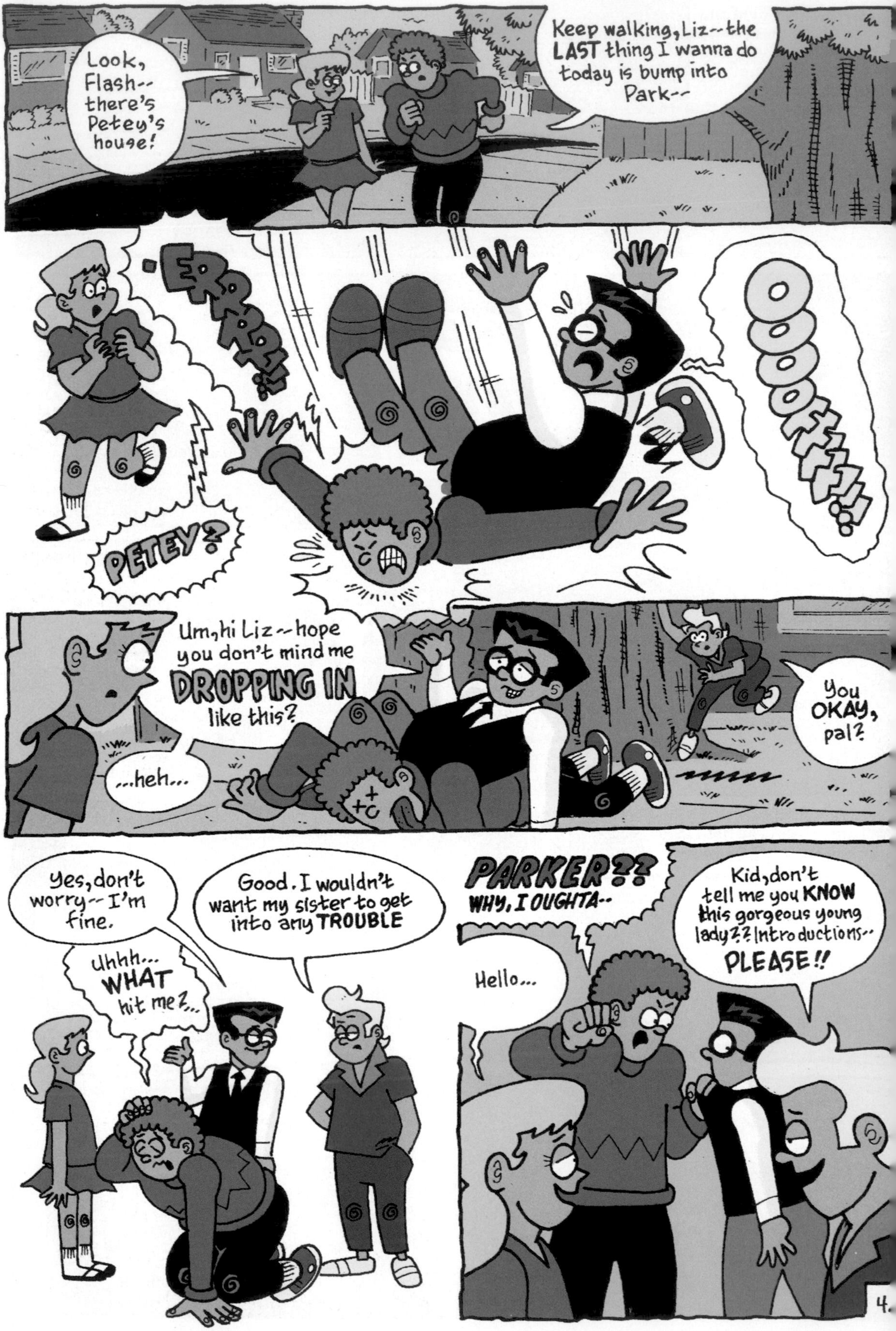
Look, Flash-- there's Petey's house!
Keep walking, Liz-- the LAST thing I wanna do today is bump into Park--
ERRRP!
OOOOOFFF!!
PETEY?
Um, hi Liz--hope you don't mind me DROPPING IN like this?
...heh...
You OKAY, pal?
Yes, don't worry-- I'm fine.
uhhh... WHAT hit me?...
Good. I wouldn't want my sister to get into any TROUBLE
PARKER?? WHY, I OUGHTA--
Hello...
Kid, don't tell me you KNOW this gorgeous young lady?? Introductions-- PLEASE!!

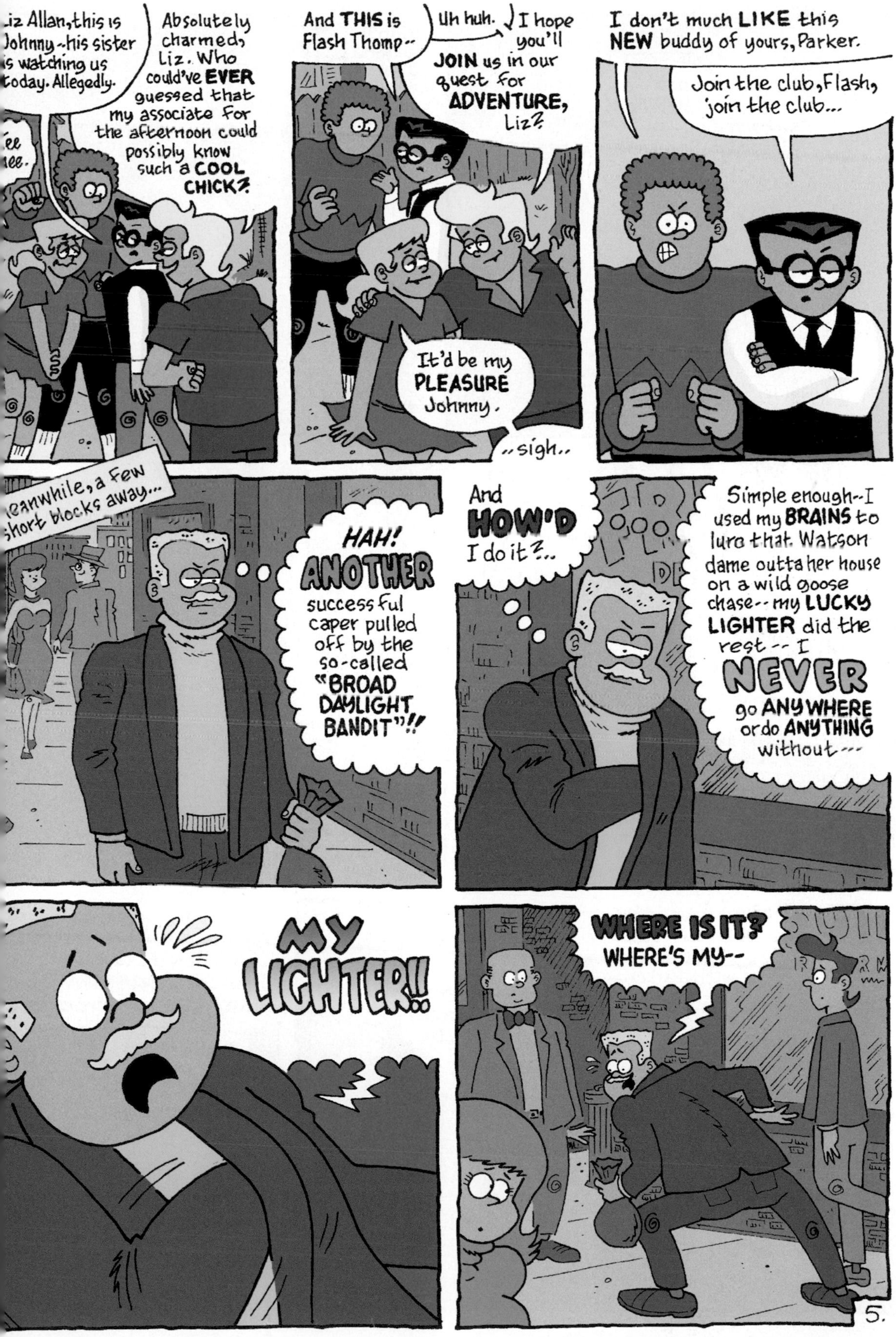
Liz Allan, this is Johnny -- his sister is watching us today. Allegedly.
Absolutely charmed, Liz. Who could've EVER guessed that my associate for the afternoon could possibly know such a COOL CHICK?
And THIS is Flash Thomp--
Uh huh.
I hope you'll JOIN us in our quest for ADVENTURE, Liz?
It'd be my PLEASURE Johnny.
..sigh..
I don't much LIKE this NEW buddy of yours, Parker.
Join the club, Flash, join the club...
Meanwhile, a few short blocks away...
HAH! ANOTHER successful caper pulled off by the so-called "BROAD DAYLIGHT BANDIT"!!
And HOW'D I do it?..
Simple enough -- I used my BRAINS to lure that Watson dame outta her house on a wild goose chase -- my LUCKY LIGHTER did the rest -- I NEVER go ANYWHERE or do ANYTHING without---
MY LIGHTER!!
WHERE IS IT? WHERE'S MY--

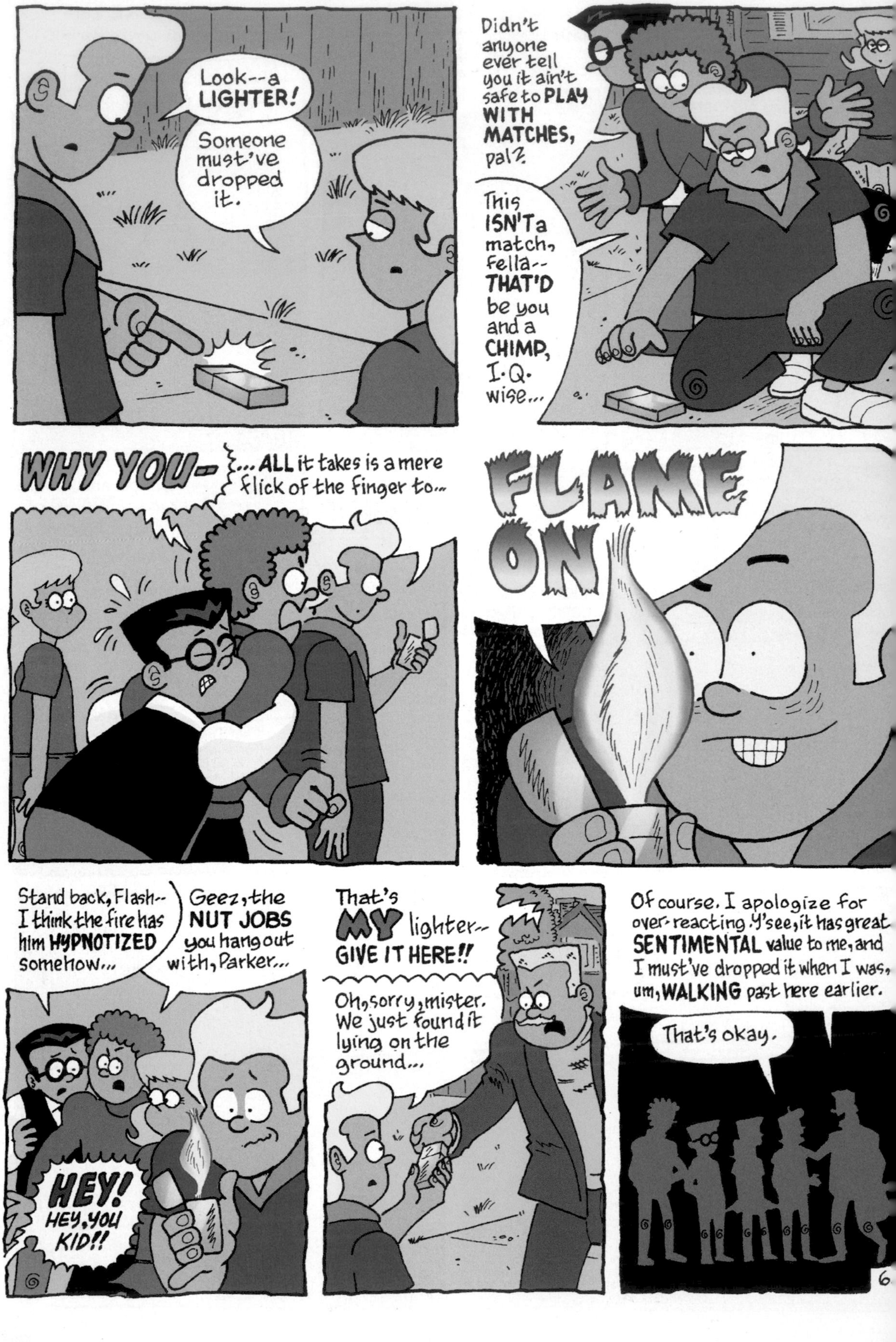

Look--a LIGHTER!
Someone must've dropped it.
Didn't anyone ever tell you it ain't safe to PLAY WITH MATCHES, pal?
This ISN'T a match, fella-- THAT'D be you and a CHIMP, I.Q. wise...
WHY YOU-
...ALL it takes is a mere flick of the finger to...
FLAME ON
Stand back, Flash-- I think the fire has him HYPNOTIZED somehow...
Geez, the NUT JOBS you hang out with, Parker...
HEY! HEY, YOU KID!!
That's MY lighter-- GIVE IT HERE!!
Oh, sorry, mister. We just found it lying on the ground...
Of course. I apologize for over-reacting. Y'see, it has great SENTIMENTAL value to me, and I must've dropped it when I was, um, WALKING past here earlier.
That's okay.

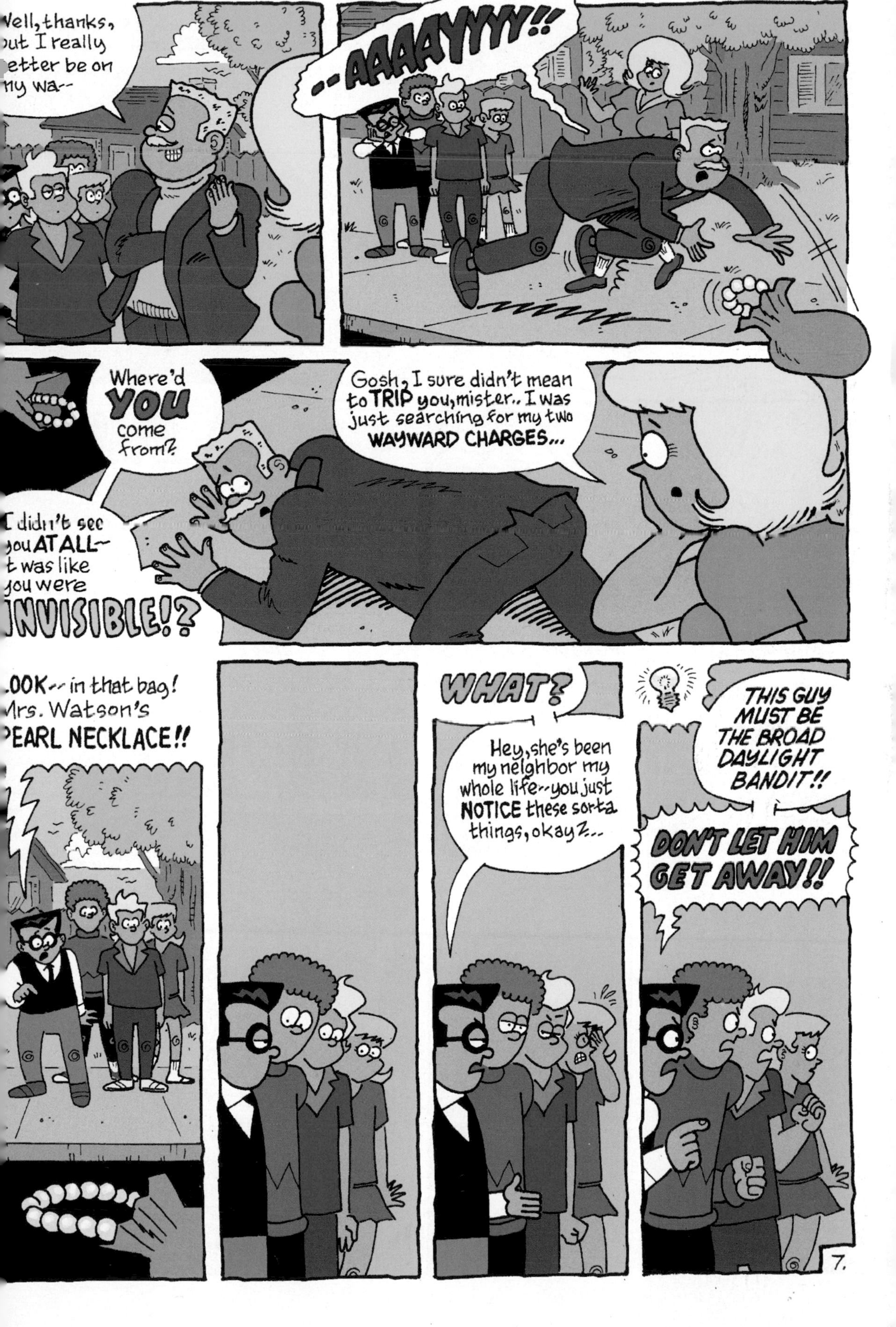

Vell, thanks, out I really etter be on my wa--
--AAAAYYYY!!
Where'd YOU come from?
I didn't see you AT ALL-- t was like you were NVISIBLE!?
Gosh, I sure didn't mean to TRIP you, mister.. I was just searching for my two WAYWARD CHARGES...
.OOK-- in that bag! Mrs. Watson's PEARL NECKLACE!!
WHAT?
Hey, she's been my neighbor my whole life--you just NOTICE these sorta things, okay?..
THIS GUY MUST BE THE BROAD DAYLIGHT BANDIT!!
DON'T LET HIM GET AWAY!!

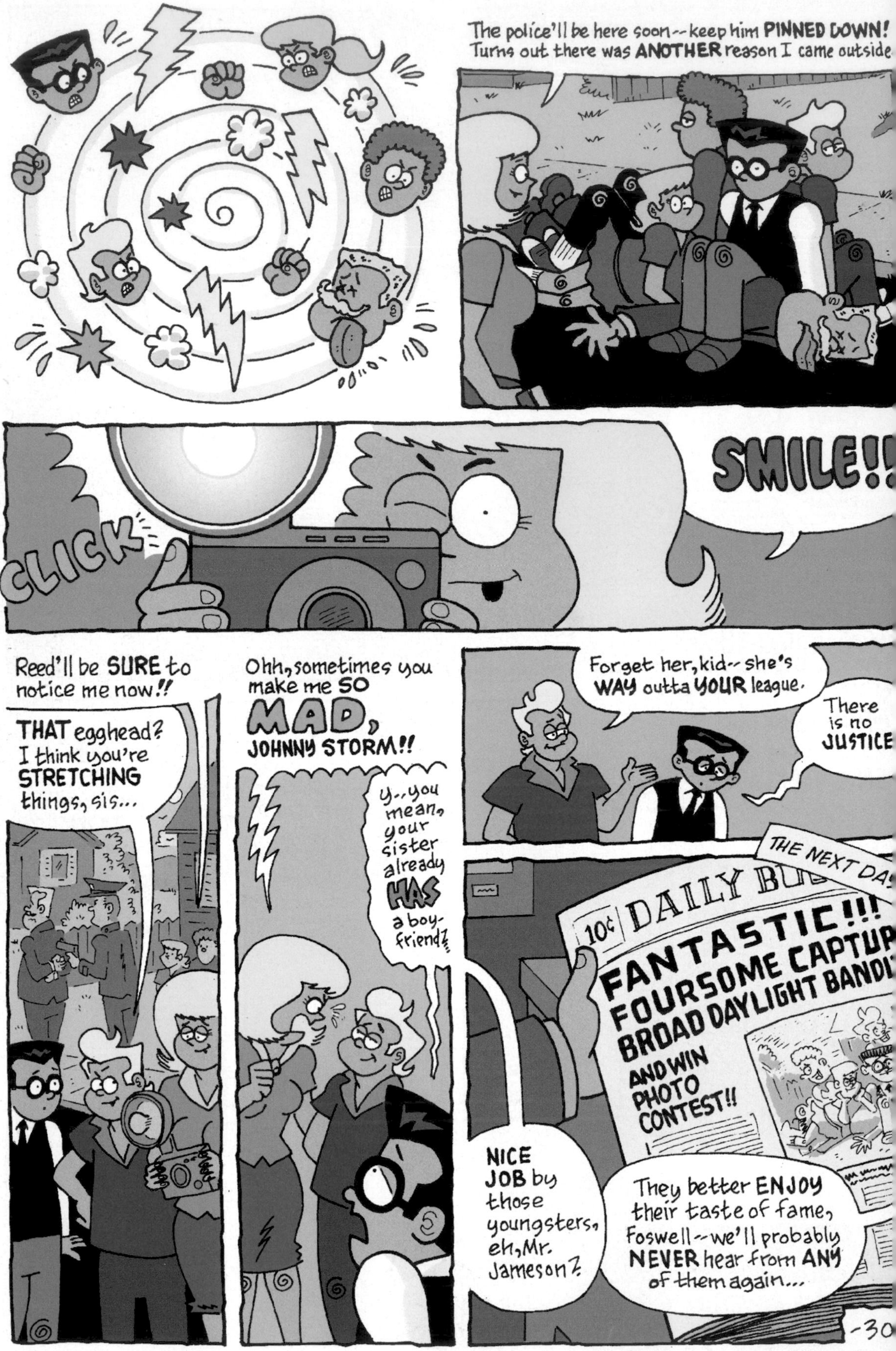
The police'll be here soon-- keep him PINNED DOWN! Turns out there was ANOTHER reason I came outside
CLICK
SMILE!!
Reed'll be SURE to notice me now!!
THAT egghead? I think you're STRETCHING things, sis...
Ohh, sometimes you make me SO MAD, JOHNNY STORM!!
y-- you mean, your sister already HAS a boy-friend?
Forget her, kid-- she's WAY outta YOUR league.
There is no JUSTICE
THE NEXT DA
10¢ DAILY BU
FANTASTIC!!! FOURSOME CAPTUR BROAD DAYLIGHT BANDI
AND WIN PHOTO CONTEST!!
NICE JOB by those youngsters, eh, Mr. Jameson?
They better ENJOY their taste of fame, Foswell-- we'll probably NEVER hear from ANY of them again...

Howdy, folks! Tom Brennan, the Spidey-Office's resident foot massager here. I'm taking a quick break from the "fun" to show you guys a little behind-the-scenes peek at the comic you just read.

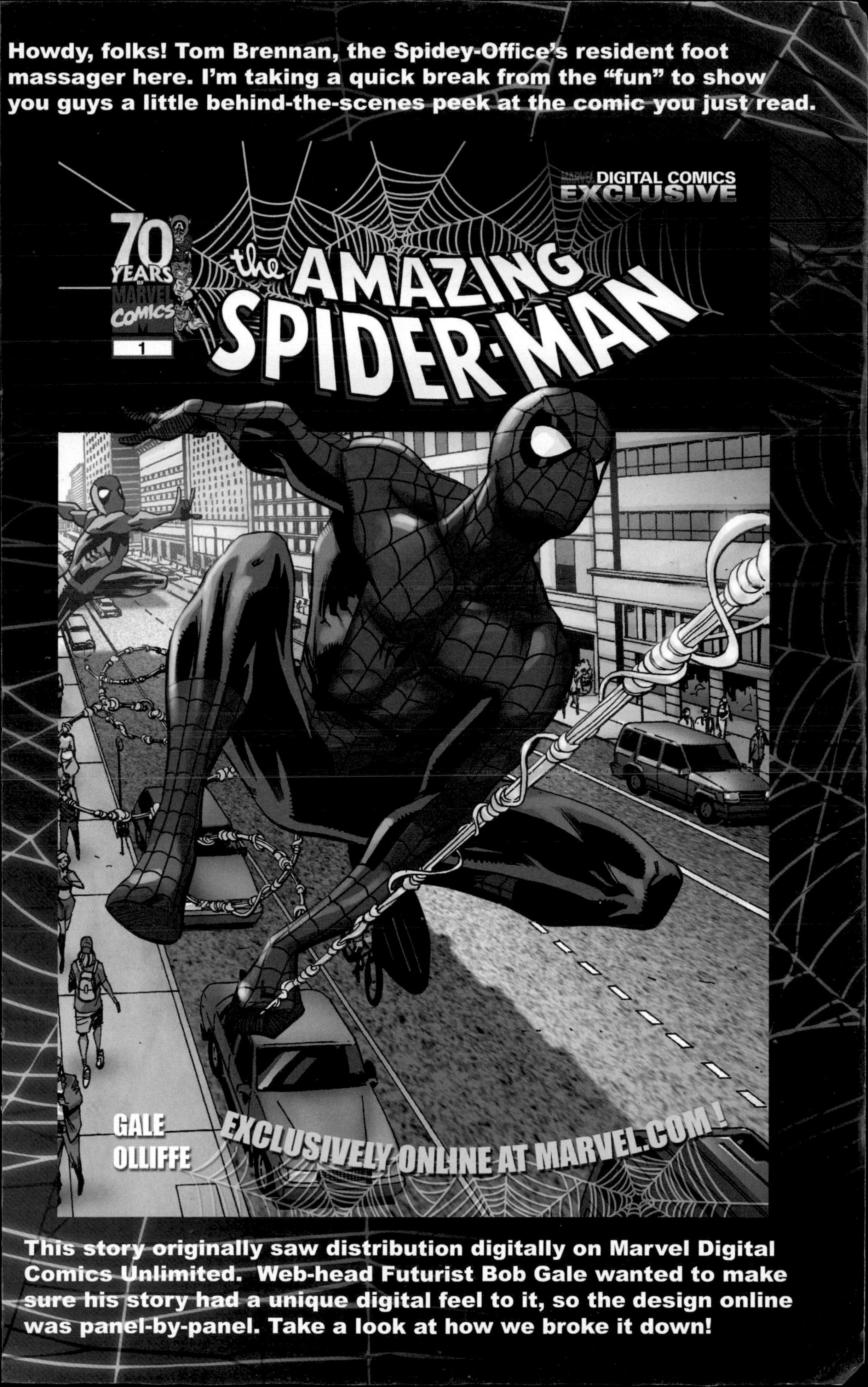

MARVEL DIGITAL COMICS
EXCLUSIVE
70 YEARS OF MARVEL COMICS
1
the AMAZING SPIDER-MAN
GALE
OLLIFFE
EXCLUSIVELY ONLINE AT MARVEL.COM!

This story originally saw distribution digitally on Marvel Digital Comics Unlimited. Web-head Futurist Bob Gale wanted to make sure his story had a unique digital feel to it, so the design online was panel-by-panel. Take a look at how we broke it down!

First, Pat Olliffe laid out thumbnails for us to review. Given the meticulous nature of the presentation, he wanted to keep us in the loop page by page from the barest of bare bones. Then, he moved onto pencils...

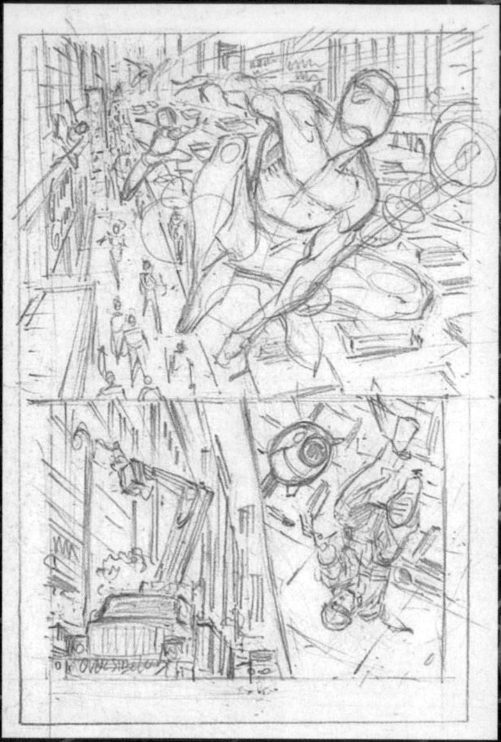

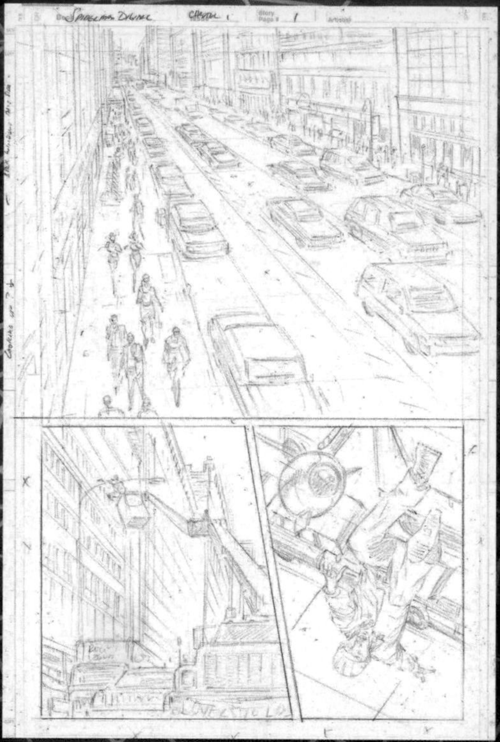

...and full inks, too! In some cases, such as this page, he provided overlays to help give the panel its own animated feel online.

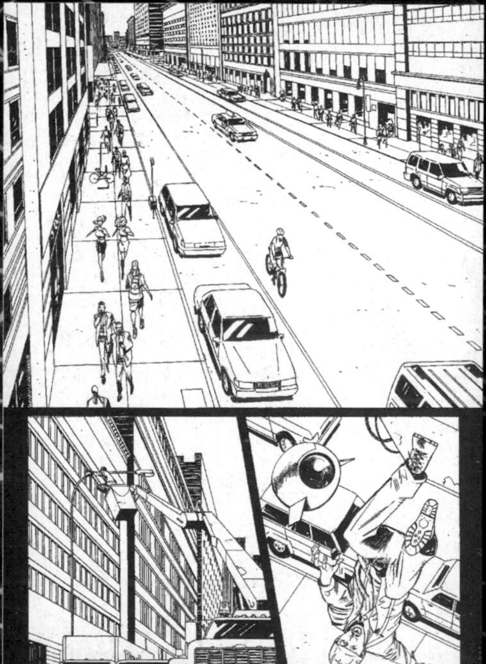

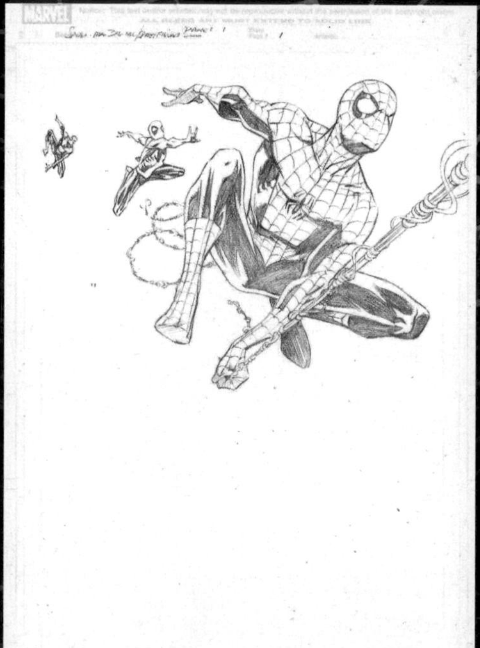

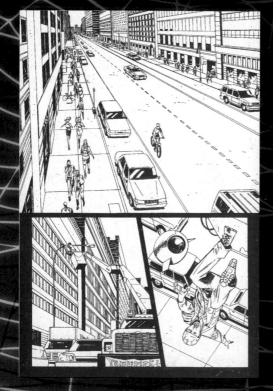

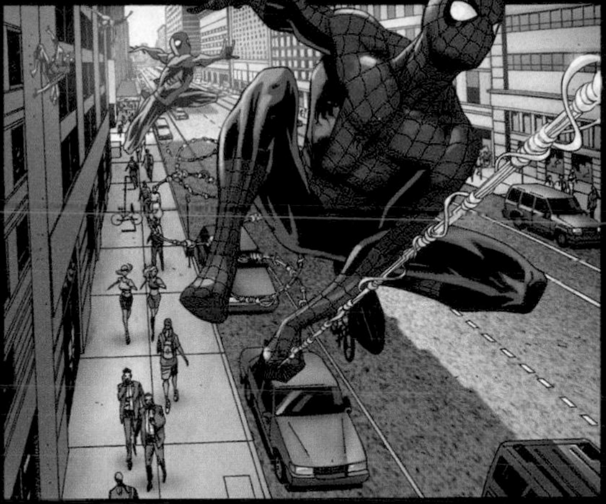

These files were sent to Antonio Fabela, one of the colorists who helped us kick off Thrice Monthly Spidey way back in 2008. Antonio made sure to keep the overlays separate so we could have room to play with on the digital presentation.

From there our digital production team, led by the eminent Tim Smith 3, broke down the pages panel-by-panel so that with each click of the mouse, the action moved with your eyes!

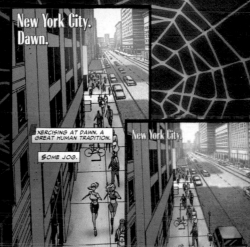

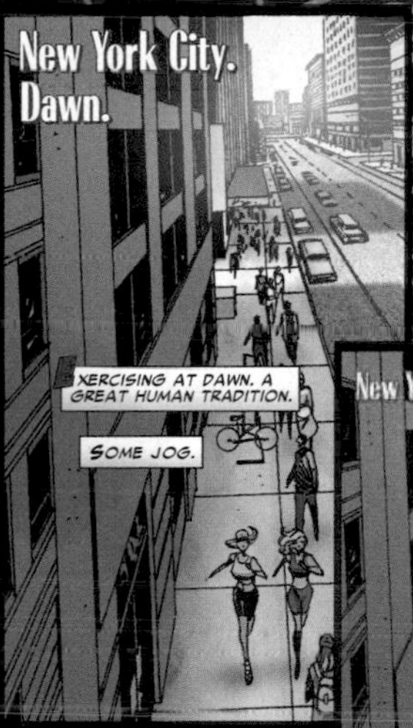
New York City.
Dawn.
XERCISING AT DAWN. A GREAT HUMAN TRADITION.
SOME JOG.

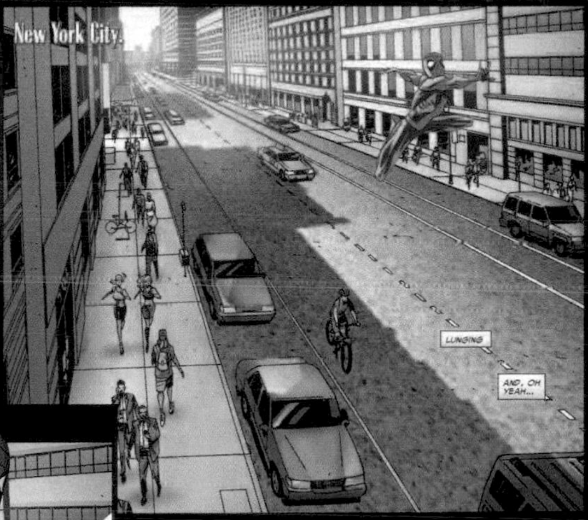
New York City.
LUNGING
AND, OH YEAH...

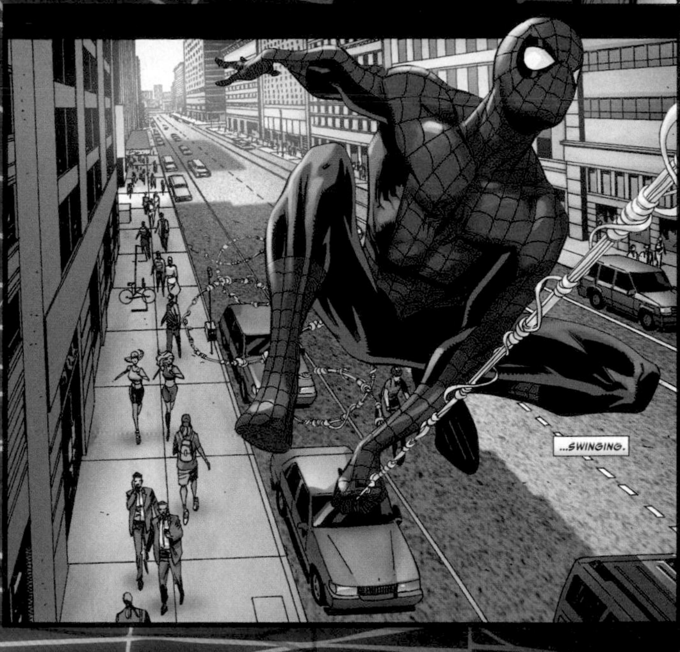
...SWINGING.

And there you have it, a unique reading experience only possible in the Marvel (Digital) Age of comics! Check it out at Marvel.com.

We also had the honor of a living legend of comics, Mr. Fred Hembeck, with another Li'l Petey adventure. Fred does almost all of the comic-ing himself, handling script, pencils, inks and letters (he letters right on the art board, an oft-mentioned lost art of comics). Mr. Javier Rodriguez finished the job on colors, really popping those pages.

WHY YOU--
FLAME ON!!
HEY! HEY, YOU KID!!
That's okay.
6

Look--a LIGHTER!
Someone must've dropped it.
Didn't anyone ever tell you it ain't safe to PLAY WITH MATCHES, pal?
This ISN'T a match, fella-- THAT'D be you and a CHIMP, I.Q.-wise...
WHY YOU--
...ALL it takes is a mere flick of the finger to--
FLAME ON
Stand back, Flash-- I think the fire has him HYPNOTIZED somehow...
Geez, the NUT JOBS you hang out with, Parker...
That's MY lighter-- GIVE IT HERE!!
Oh, sorry, mister. We just found it lying on the ground...
Of course. I apologize for over-reacting. Y'see, it has great SENTIMENTAL value to me, and I must've dropped it when I was, um, WALKING past here earlier.
That's okay.
HEY! HEY, YOU KID!!
6.

Look--a LIGHTER!
Someone must've dropped it.
Didn't anyone ever tell you it ain't safe to PLAY WITH MATCHES, pal?
This ISN'T a match, fella-- THAT'D be you and a CHIMP, I.Q.-wise...
WHY YOU--
...ALL it takes is a mere flick of the finger to--
FLAME ON
Stand back, Flash-- I think the fire has him HYPNOTIZED somehow...
Geez, the NUT JOBS you hang out with, Parker...
HEY! HEY, YOU KID!!
That's MY lighter-- GIVE IT HERE!!
Oh, sorry, mister. We just found it lying on the ground...
Of course. I apologize for over-reacting. Y'see, it has great SENTIMENTAL value to me, and I must've dropped it when I was, um, WALKING past here earlier.
That's okay.
6.

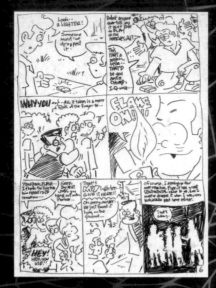

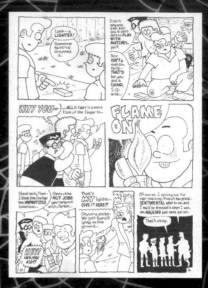

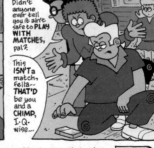

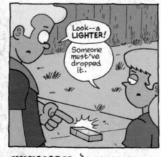

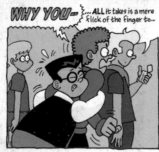

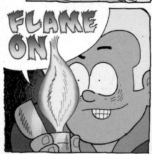

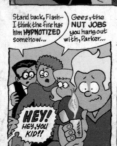

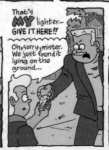

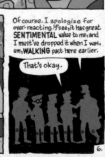

And that's how we did it! Hope you liked this backstage look. Back to the foot massaging!